HISTORIC PHOTOS OF
PUGET SOUND

TEXT AND CAPTIONS BY DAVID WILMA

TURNER

PUBLISHING COMPANY

Peter Kirk, a steel mill owner from Workington, England, picked this spot on the eastern shore of Lake Washington for his new mill. In 1888, he and local investors founded the Moss Bay Iron and Steel Works, and he predicted the area would become a "Pittsburgh of the West." Kirk platted the town of Kirkland with English street names. In this 1889 view, the Bank Building housing Kirk's company stands at the corner of Market and Waverly streets.

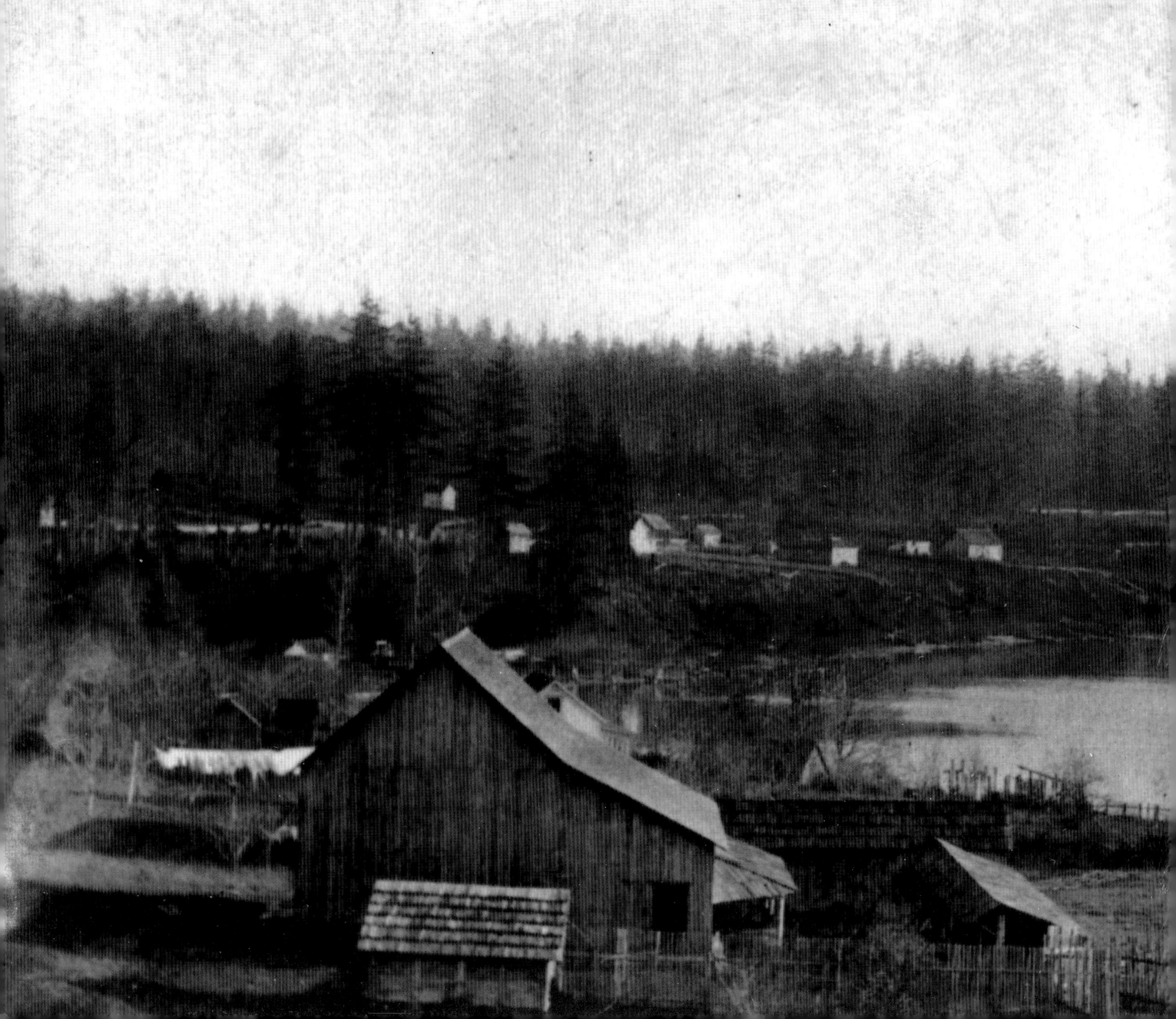

HISTORIC PHOTOS OF
PUGET SOUND

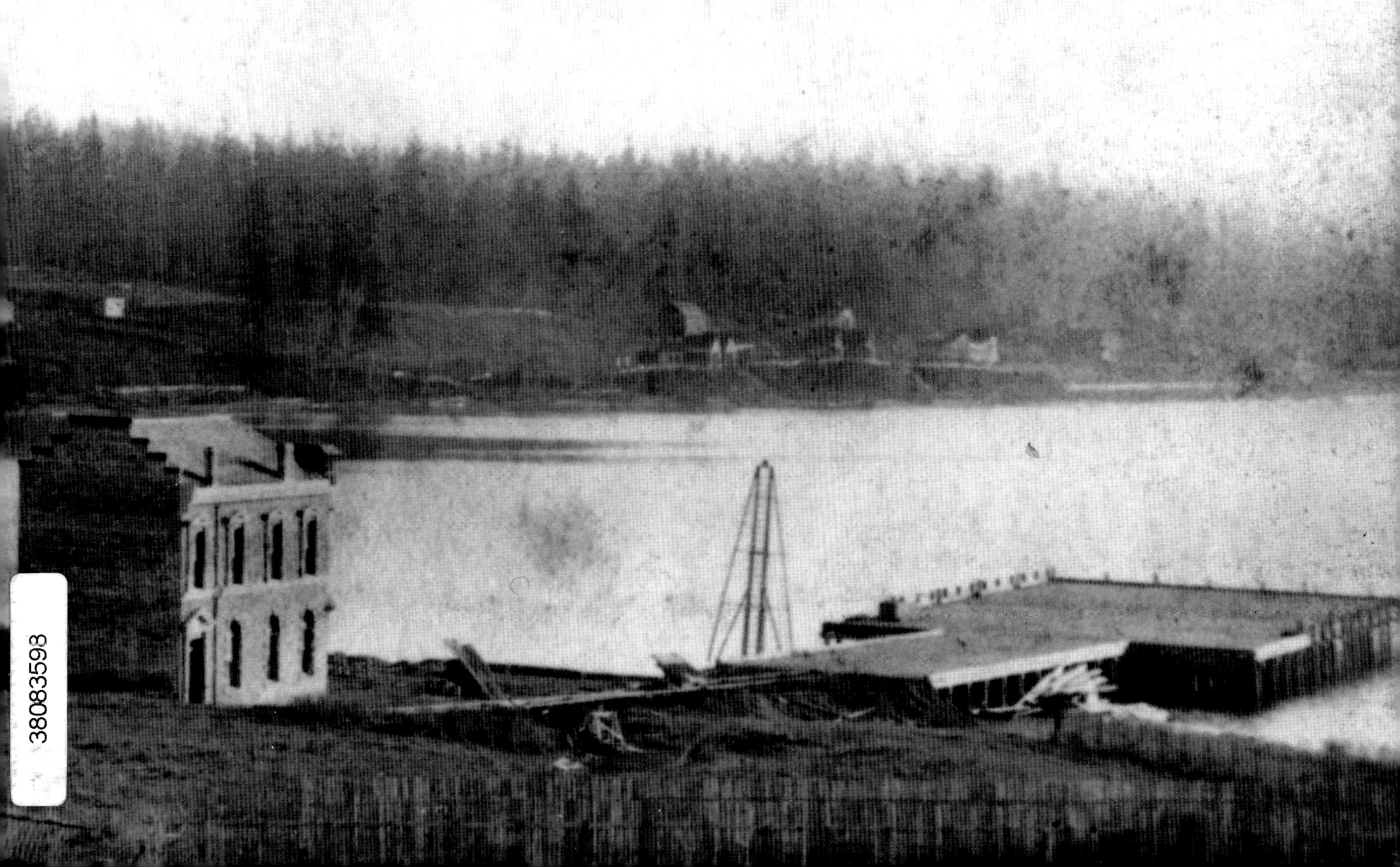

Turner Publishing Company
200 4th Avenue North • Suite 950
Nashville, Tennessee 37219
(615) 255-2665

www.turnerpublishing.com

Historic Photos of Puget Sound

Library of Congress Control Number: 2009922630

ISBN: 978-1-59652-544-3

Printed in China

09 10 11 12 13 14 15 16—0 9 8 7 6 5 4 3 2 1

Contents

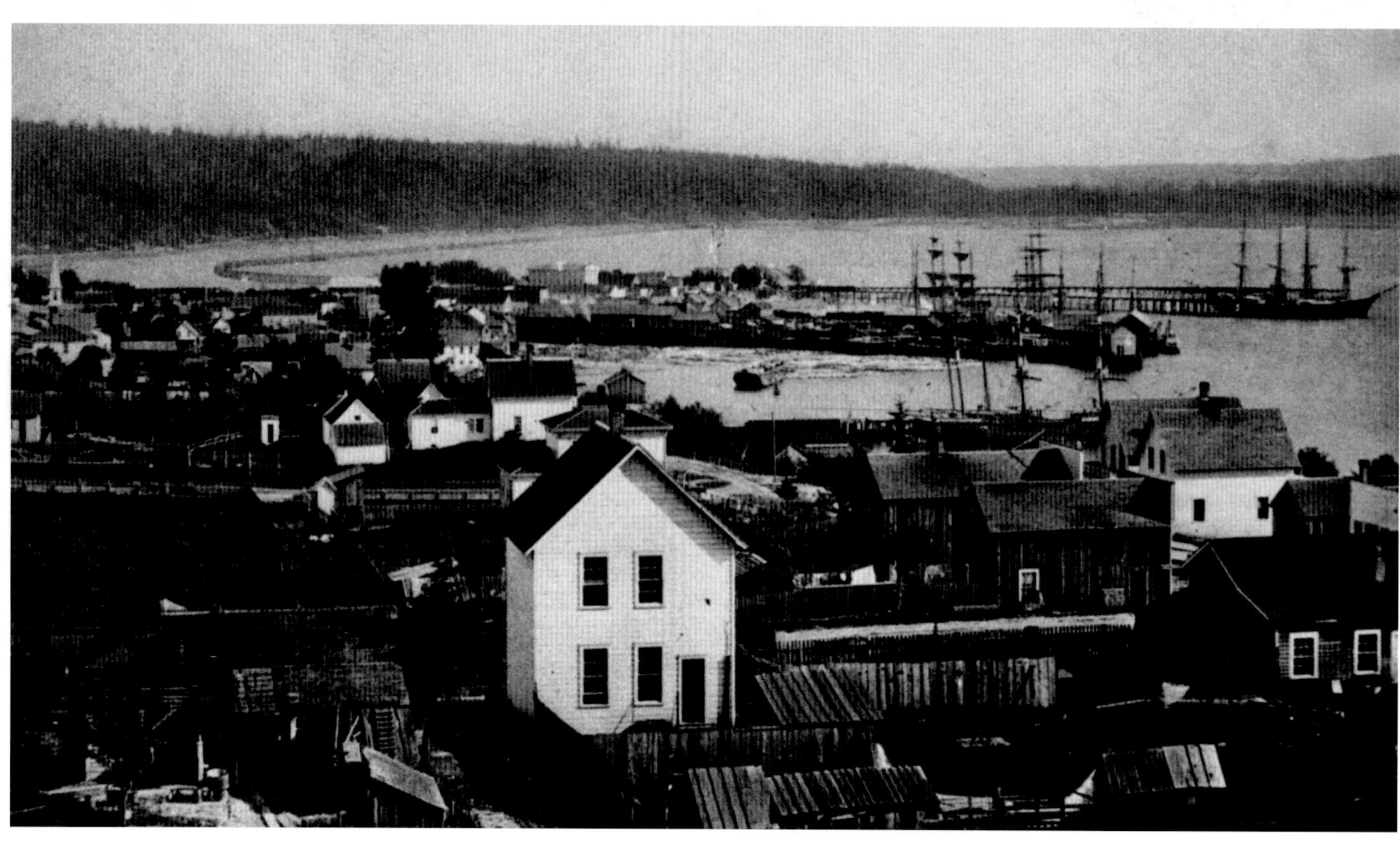

Seattle in the 1880s looks south from Pike Street and Second Avenue. At right several ships wait at Yesler's Wharf, while two are docked at the Columbia and Puget Sound Railway coal wharf at the foot of Jackson Street. The railroad trestle curves in from the south across the tide flats.

Acknowledgments

This volume, *Historic Photos of Puget Sound,* is the result of the cooperation and efforts of many individuals, organizations, and corporations. It is with great thanks that we acknowledge the valuable contribution of the following for their generous support:

Everett Public Library
Olympia Historical Society
Seattle Municipal Archives
South Whidbey Historical Society
University of Washington Libraries
www.HistoryLink.org

We would also like to thank Lorraine Howell for her valuable contributions and assistance in making this work possible.

With the exception of touching up imperfections that have accrued with the passage of time and cropping where necessary, no changes have been made. The focus and clarity of many images is limited by the technology and the ability of the photographer at the time they were taken.

PREFACE

Whether stepping off a jetliner or setting foot ashore from a schooner, newcomers to Puget Sound invariably marvel at the scenic wonder of land and mountains crowding around blue water. The legendary rain—actually less than New York City receives—scrubs the air and feeds clear, swift rivers. The mountains—the Olympics to the west, the Cascades to the east, Mount Rainier to the south, and Mount Baker to the north—frame a seemingly endless system of bays and inlets.

More than 15,000 years ago, advancing and retreating glaciers two-thirds of a mile thick left deep gashes in the earth. Rising sea levels filled these channels with salt water, and snowmelt and rain carved river systems.

As the vast glaciers melted for the last time, people and animals moved in. The Native Americans who made homes along the shore called the water *Wulch,* or *Whulge*, meaning salt. Salt provided them with nutritious lives in the form of abundant runs of salmon and basketsful of oysters. The bays, inlets, and river mouths allowed free communication by canoe between the hundreds of permanent settlements. Peoples from the Nisqually in the south to the Skagit and the Lummi in the north spoke a common language. They frequently intermarried, contributing to peace among those who lived beside the Salt. Only canoe raiders from the north and enemies from across the mountains to the east threatened them.

In April 1792, George Vancouver, on behalf of the King of England, explored the coast of North America aboard HMS *Discovery.* Vancouver named the waters off the Strait of Juan de Fuca after Lieutenant Peter Puget, a member of his expedition. Fur traders from the Hudson's Bay Company established a settlement at the mouth of the Nisqually River in 1833. Fifteen years later, settlers from the United States staked claims to Olympia, and settlement grew in the 1850s around lumber mills. Some of these communities were orderly company towns like Port Blakely or less organized responses like Seattle.

In the 1850s, the first photographers began capturing scenes of life on Puget Sound. They positioned their heavy cameras with glass plate negatives on whatever stable platform they could find, frequently a wharf or pier. The images celebrated the pride of Puget Sound, its ships, homes, businesses, and industries. Since social, commercial, and political activity depended on the water, many early shots include Puget Sound's canoes, launches, fishing boats, steamers, sailing ships, and massive warships.

Just as it did for the Native Americans, Puget Sound provided the highway that linked the region's communities with each other and with the world. At first, Indian canoes and New England schooners moved people and goods up and down the Sound until steamers of the Mosquito Fleet took over. All attention and activity focused on wharves from Olympia to Bellingham, where side-wheelers and stern-wheelers called regularly to deliver news, mail, and travelers. Residents of remote mill towns and farming communities visited big cities for both business and fun in the company of friends and neighbors. City dwellers found restful resorts and quiet picnics as close as a stroll up a Mosquito Fleet gangplank.

Even at the beginning of the twenty-first century, when some have proposed that Puget Sound be expanded into British Columbia and called the Salish Sea, the Sound is the center of attention—not for how it can be used, but how it can be protected. As the once-abundant salmon runs have dwindled from a commercial mainstay to a tourist attraction, residents realized that they need to change the role of the Sound in order to keep it. All that remains of canneries are broken rows of pilings. The fishing fleets no longer pull their bounty within sight of home, but have to sail a thousand miles to Alaska to stay in business. The Mosquito Fleet has been replaced by highways, bridges, and a ferry system that caters to the automobile. However, the natural scenery remains appealing today to residents, visitors, and admirers alike.

The following images in *Historic Photos of Puget Sound* preserve Puget Sound as its residents once knew it.

—*David Wilma*

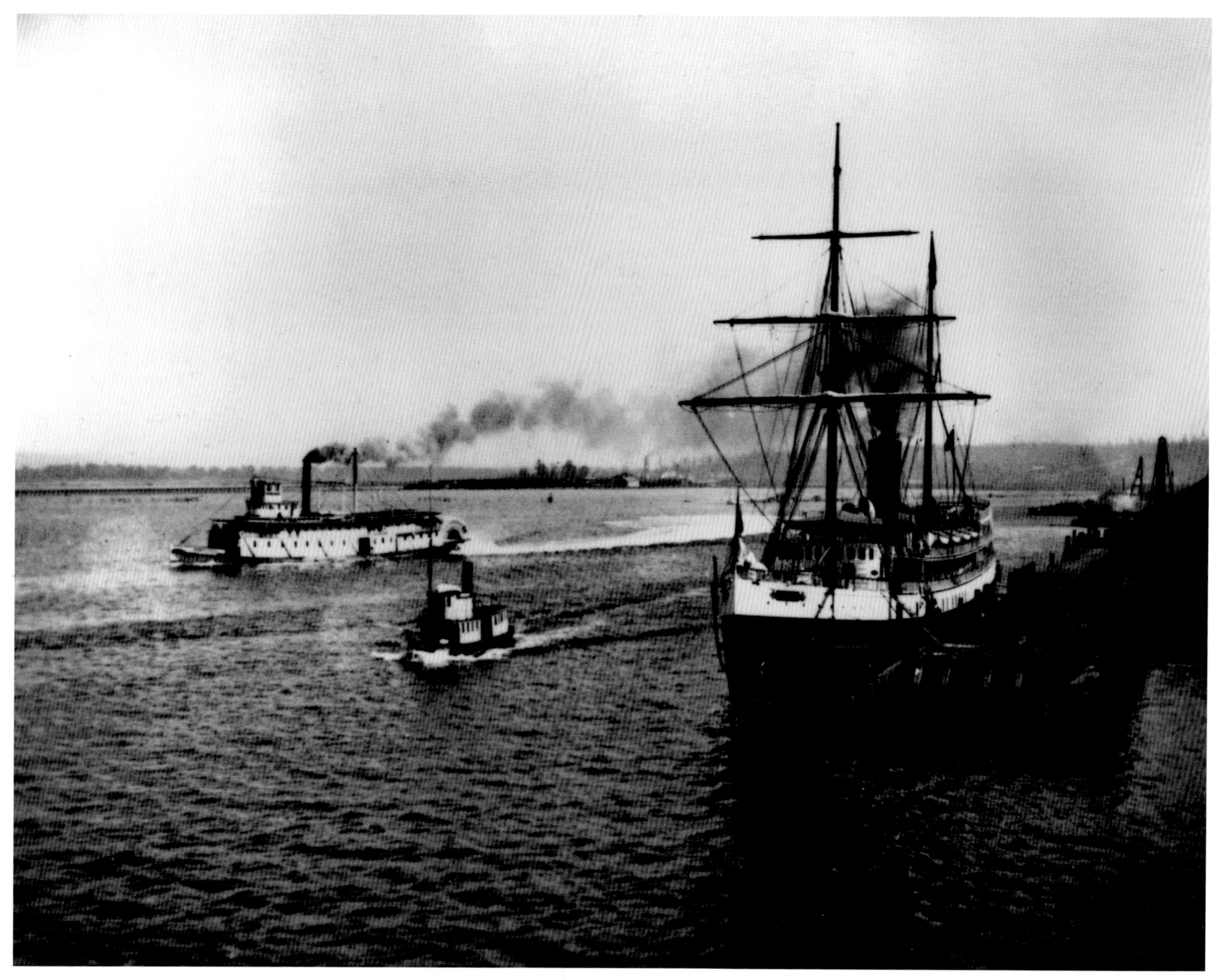

While *State of Washington* gets up steam at a Tacoma dock, the stern-wheeler *Queen* cruises by. A smaller local steamer heads out, too, probably for Olympia or Steilacoom up the Sound. Even though the *State of Washington* was equipped with steam engines, her designers did not intend to waste the wind. Thus, they equipped her with a mast and sails to save on fuel.

FOUNDATIONS

(1850–1885)

In the middle of the nineteenth century, the dense forests of Puget Sound country stood as obstacles to the agriculture that composed much of the U.S. economy. Hemlock, spruce, and cedar grew to the water's edge and ultimately peaked at 200 feet high and 300 years old. Light rarely reached the fern-covered forest floor. The first settlers quickly learned that they could earn cash by felling the giants and shipping them to California, where San Francisco and its frequent fires presented a steady market. When prospectors found coal in the region, entrepreneurs built the first railroads and shipped fuel to heat and power the West Coast and even the Hawaiian Islands.

Like the Native Americans, the settlers followed the shores of the Sound and its rivers to establish their farms, mills, trading posts, and communities. Ox teams skidded the massive logs out of the forests and rolled them into the water to transport to mills.

The early industrialists built lumber mills, which anchored the first villages and towns. Workers loaded immense square-cut timbers into three- and four-masted barks and barkentines. The plentiful and high-quality spruce and hemlock spawned a ship-building industry that exceeded San Francisco's in production. Mill towns such as Port Blakely, Port Gamble, Utsalady, and Port Ludlow grew into self-contained communities.

The loggers left behind "stump ranches" where families built a few farms. Without any meaningful system of roads, Puget Sound residents remained tied to the rest of the region by water. The first settlers reached "town" by Indian canoe and later by schooner and steamer.

The area's Native Americans who ceded their lands to the United States could find little employment on their small reservations, so they took work in logging camps and in mills. The soil and climate of the region proved ideal for hops, and whole families earned wages as seasonal agricultural workers. They followed the crops by canoe and camped all summer, much as they did before Europeans arrived in the 1700s and 1800s. Many tribal members continued to catch salmon in the rivers and gather shellfish along the largely unoccupied shorelines.

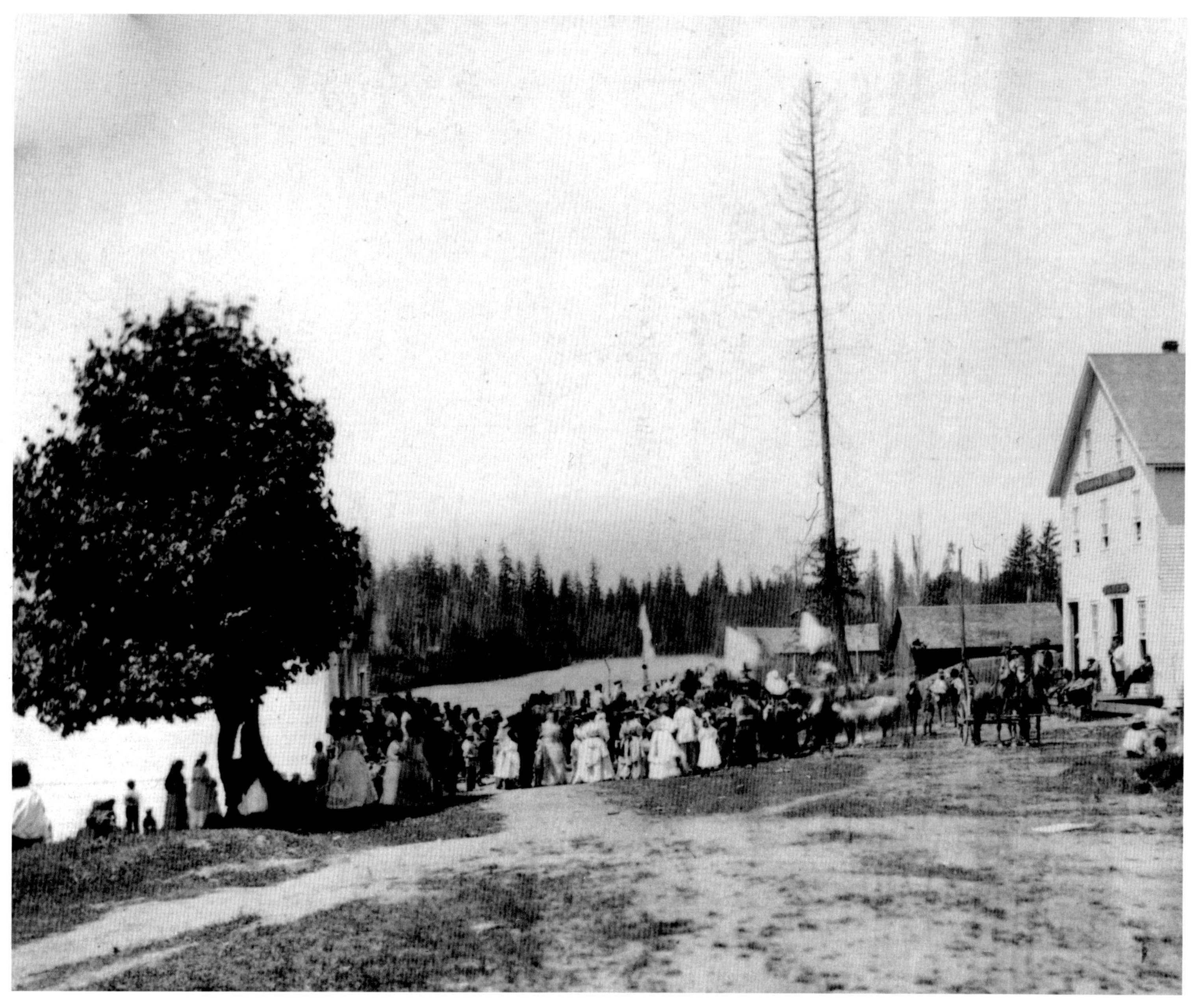

Originally called Cadyville, Snohomish began in the 1850s as a busy river port 12 miles up the Snohomish River from Port Gardiner Bay. From 1861, it served as the seat of Snohomish County until upstart Everett took the honor 36 years later. In this photo dated around 1874, citizens gather at the Snohomish Exchange Hotel to celebrate the Fourth of July.

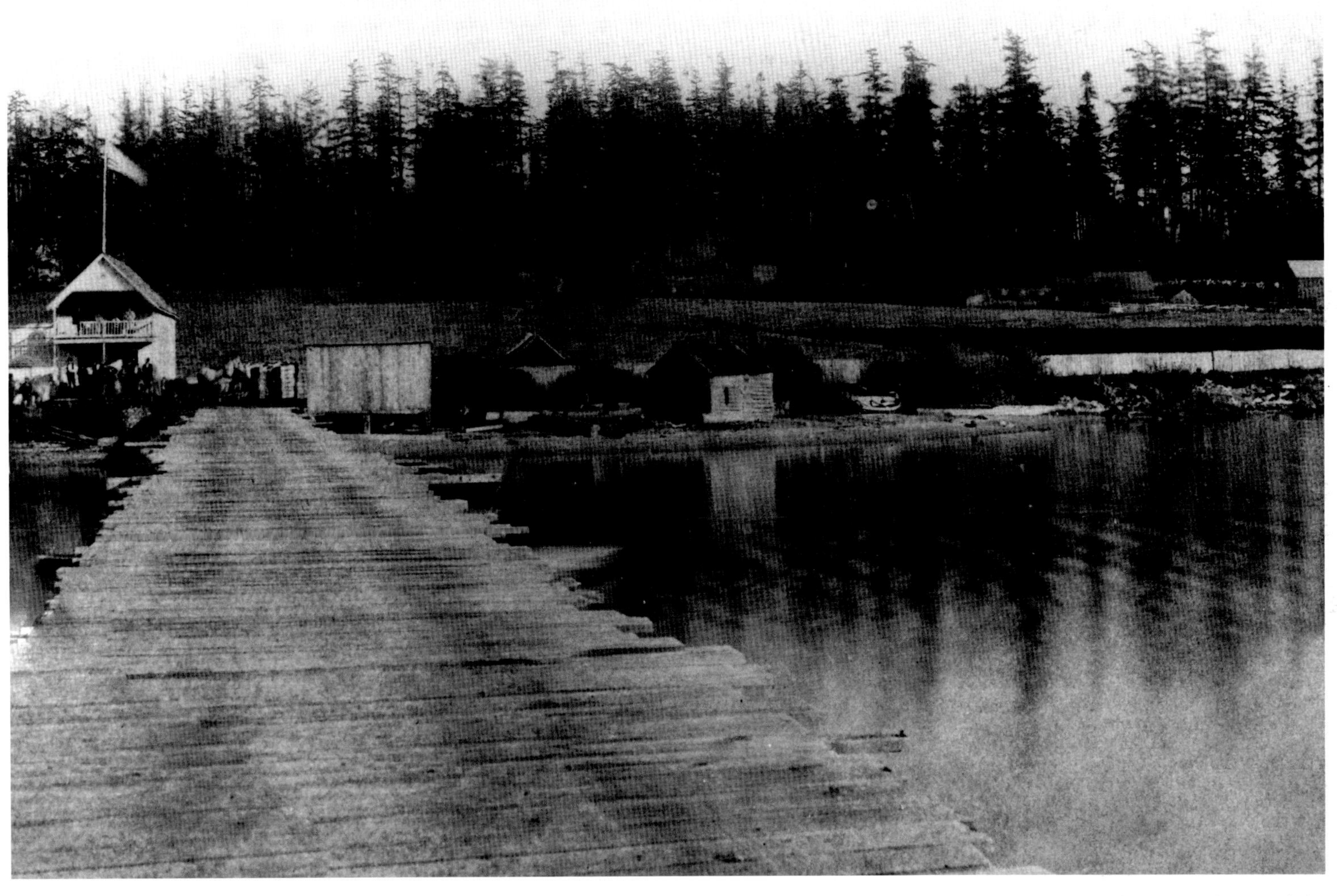

In the mid-1850s, the early settlers of Fidalgo fled the Indian troubles of north Puget Sound. In 1860, William Munks joined the few returnees and staked a claim. In 1870, he opened this store at his wharf on Fidalgo. Munks became postmaster as well as a real estate investor and a prosperous breeder of Percheron horses.

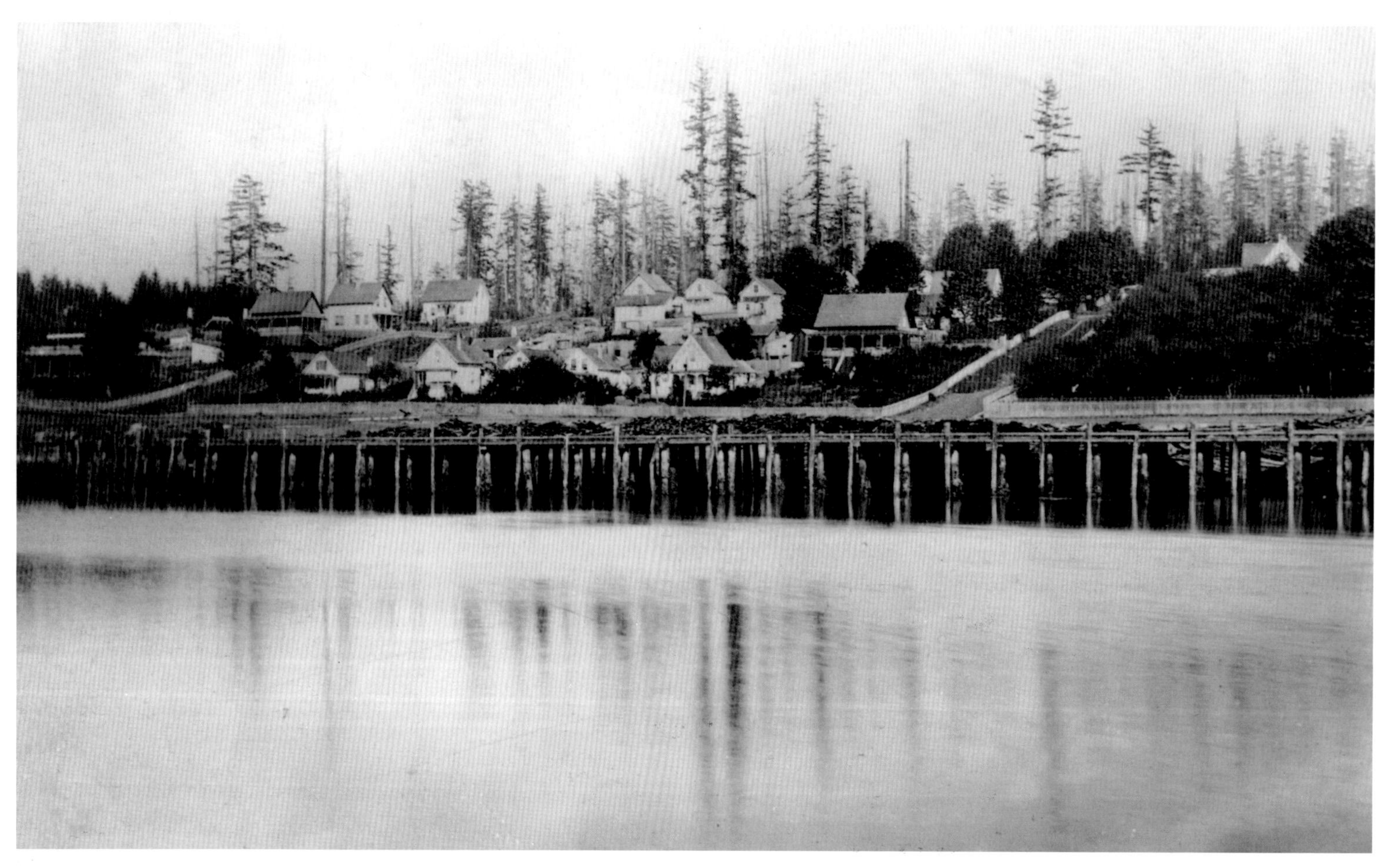

In 1880, Port Madison residences in Kitsap County look down on the ferry dock. At left is the Philip Wist Hotel.

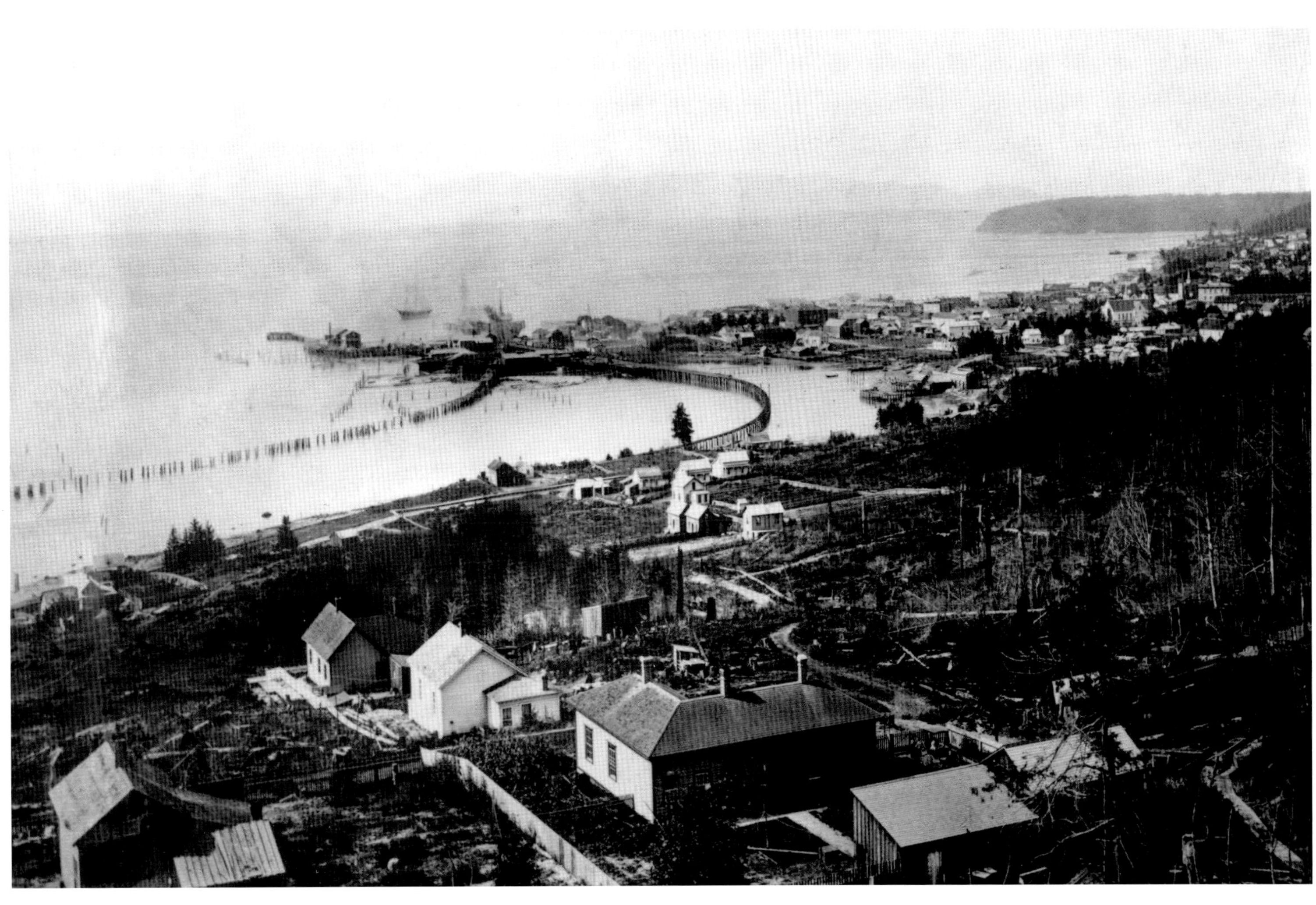

In this shot of Seattle taken in the early 1880s, probably by Carleton Watkins from Beacon Hill, the trestle of the Columbia and Puget Sound Railway curves across tide flats to a coal dock on Elliott Bay. Lumber mills crowd the piers at the end of the peninsula, which the Denny party chose as the site for their city.

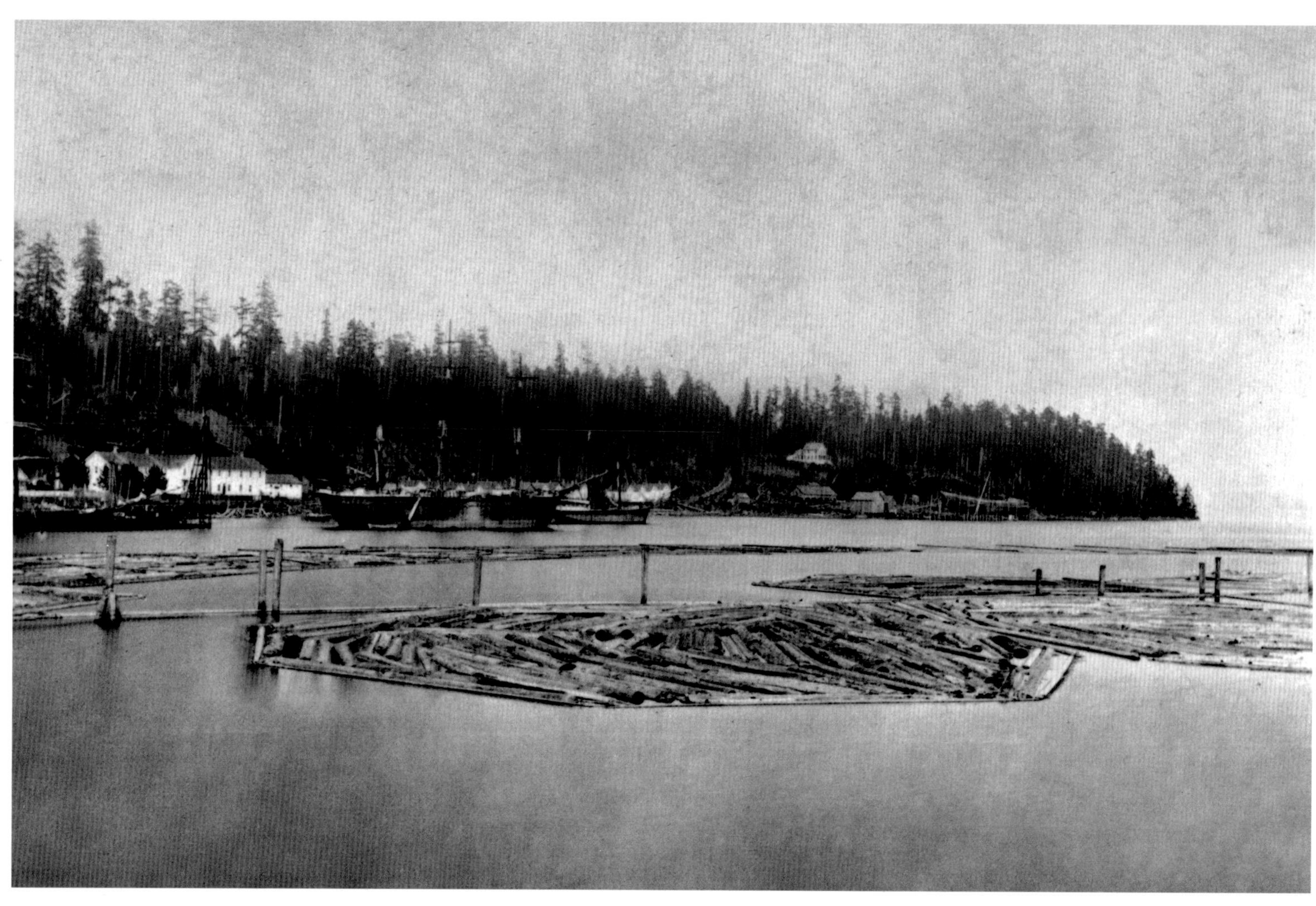

Vast quantities of high-quality wood made Puget Sound a center of shipbuilding on the West Coast. In the 1870s, Henry, Isaac, and Winslow Hall founded the Hall Brothers Marine Railway and Shipbuilding Company at Port Ludlow. The following decade, they moved to Port Blakely on Bainbridge Island. The brothers relied upon the Blakely Mill Company as a source for cut lumber. In 1902, Hall Brothers moved to Madrone (later Winslow) on Eagle Harbor and operated there until 1959.

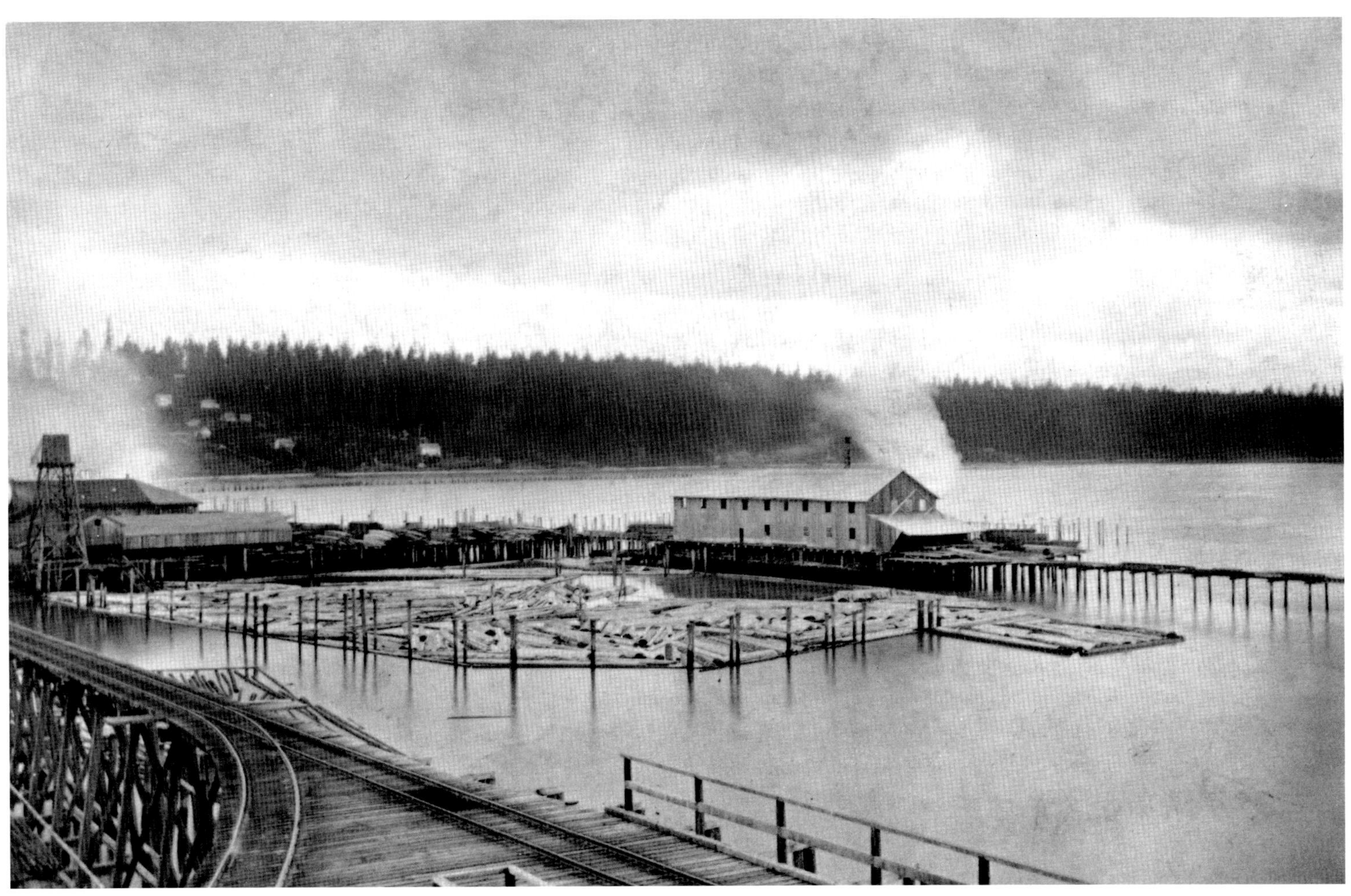

This view of the Stetson and Post Company sash and door factory on the Seattle waterfront dates from before 1885, the year the mill burned. In the foreground the Columbia and Puget Sound Railway Company tracks curve onto the coal dock at the foot of Jackson Street. Mines at Renton, Newcastle, and Squak (later Issaquah) shipped their coal to San Francisco and Hawaii. Coal gas lit Seattle streets, homes, and businesses.

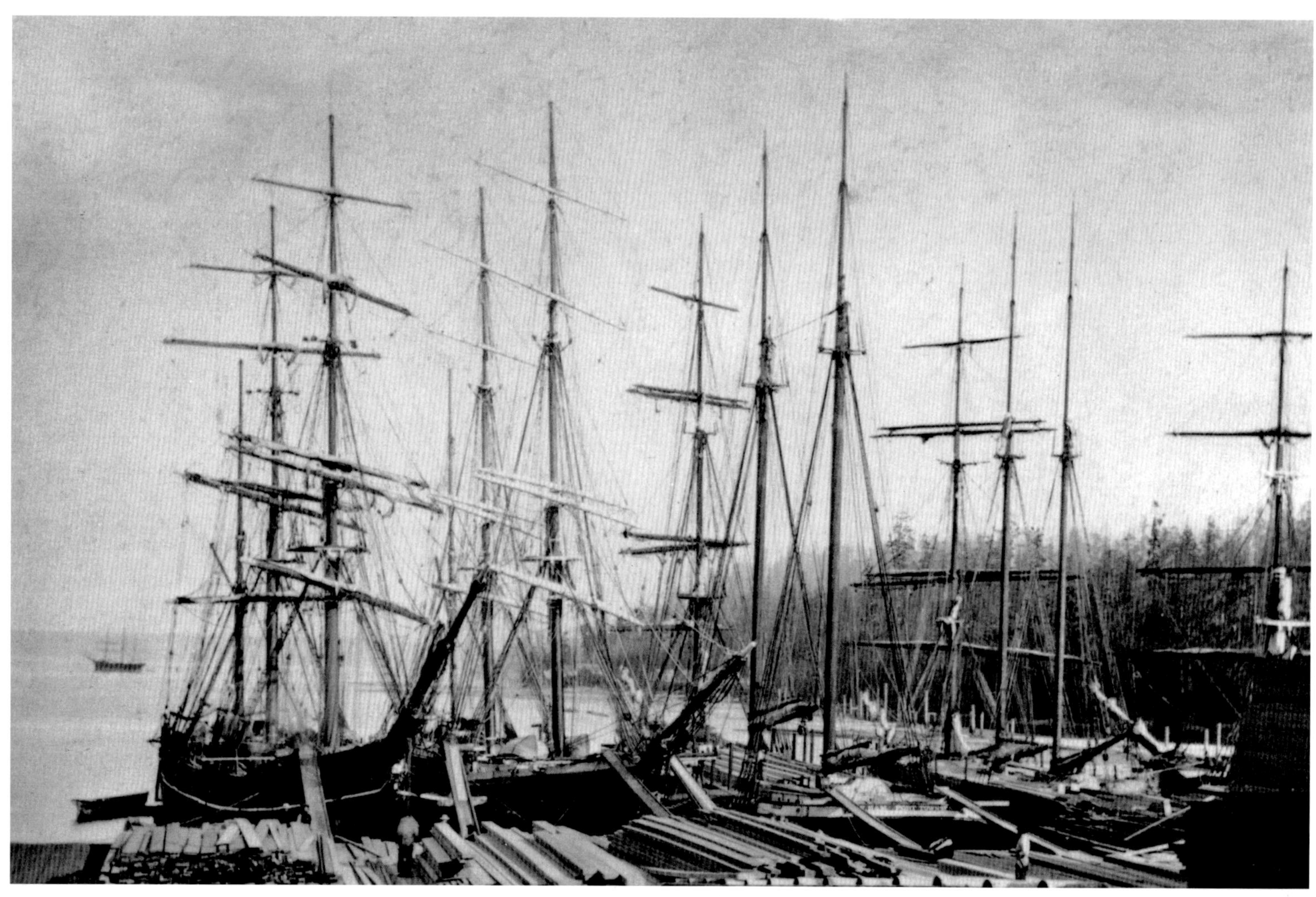

Port Blakely on Bainbridge Island drew its name from a member of the 1844 U.S. Exploring Expedition headed by Commander Charles Wilkes. In 1864, Captain William Renton moved his Port Blakely Mill Company there, and the bay soon became a busy center for lumbering and shipbuilding. Here five sailing ships jam the wharf where the cut lumber is being loaded.

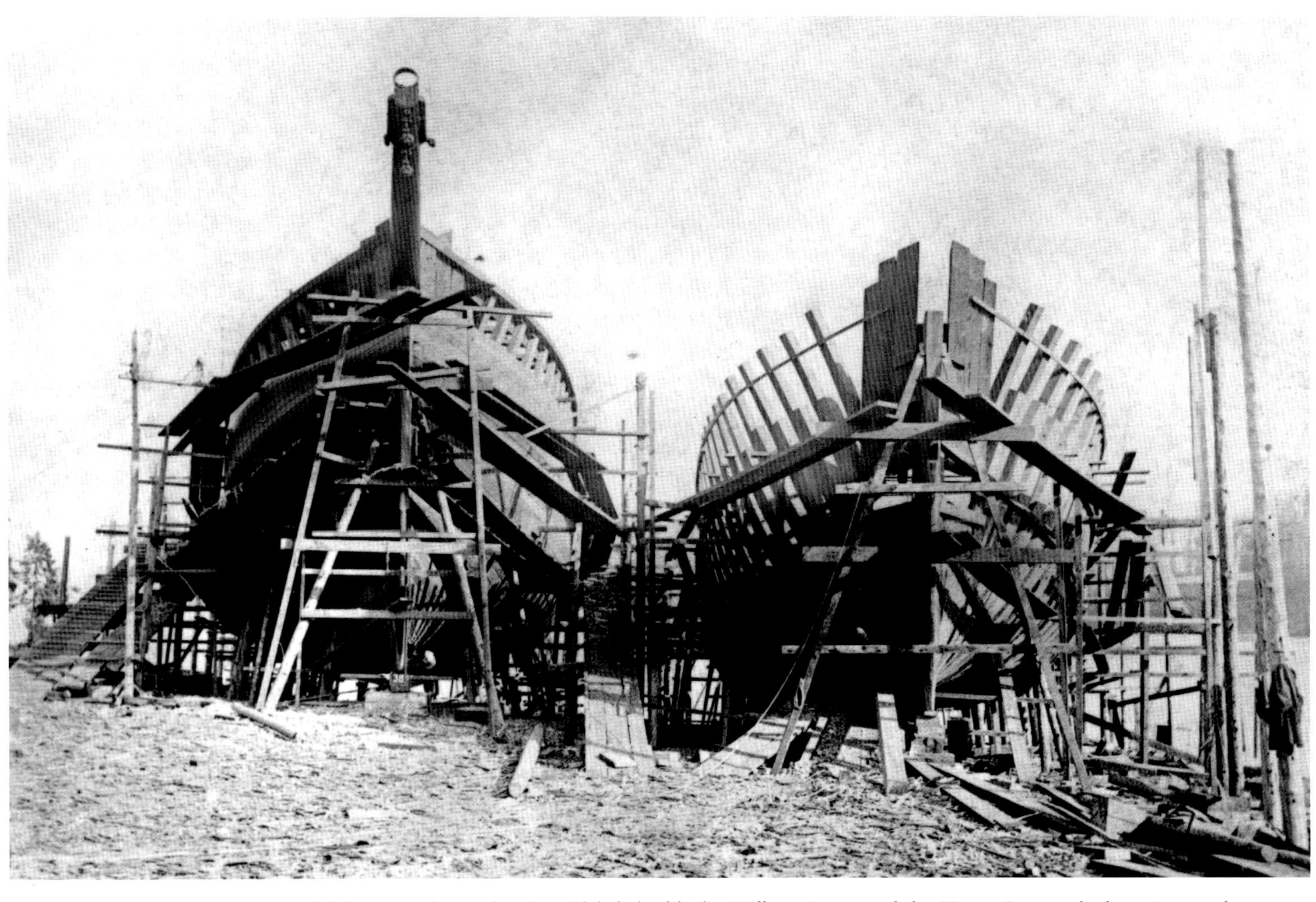

In 1882, the Hall Brothers shipyard at Port Blakely builds the *William Renton* and the *Hesper*. During the late nineteenth century, Puget Sound built more ships than the entire San Francisco Bay Area.

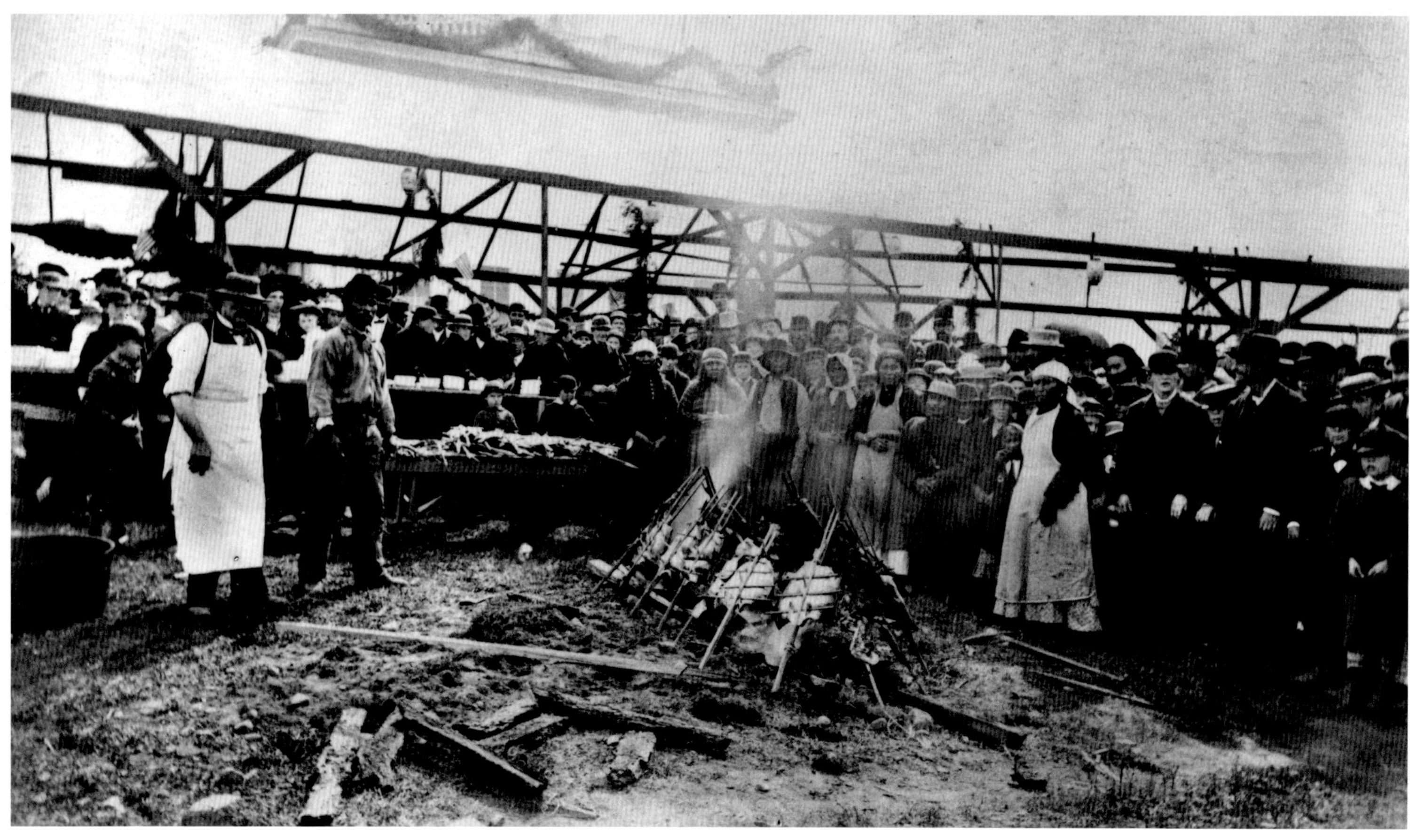

In 1884, at the Railroad Jubilee on the grounds of the University of Washington in Seattle, celebrants gather to mark the completion of the Northern Pacific Railroad from Tacoma. White folks barbecue beef, and the Indians roast salmon and clams in their traditional way. The euphoria will soon pass as they discover the railroad provides poor service. People would eventually call the line the Orphan Road.

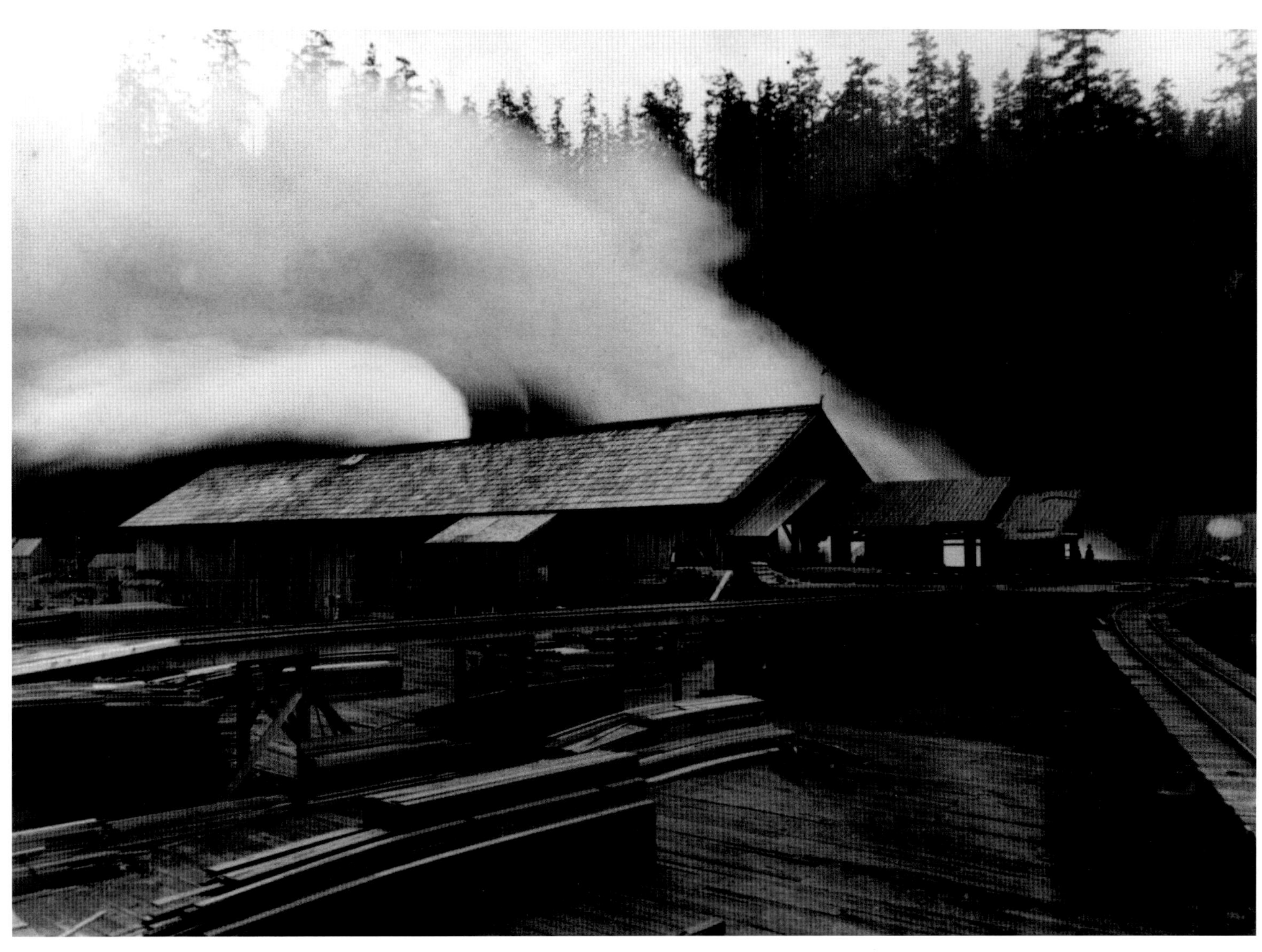

The Puget Mill Company, later Pope and Talbot, opened its first mill at Port Gamble Bay in 1853. The company expanded operations to include Port Ludlow on the Olympic Peninsula and this mill at Utsalady on Camano Island. George A. Pope took this photo of the Utsalady mill on June 10, 1884.

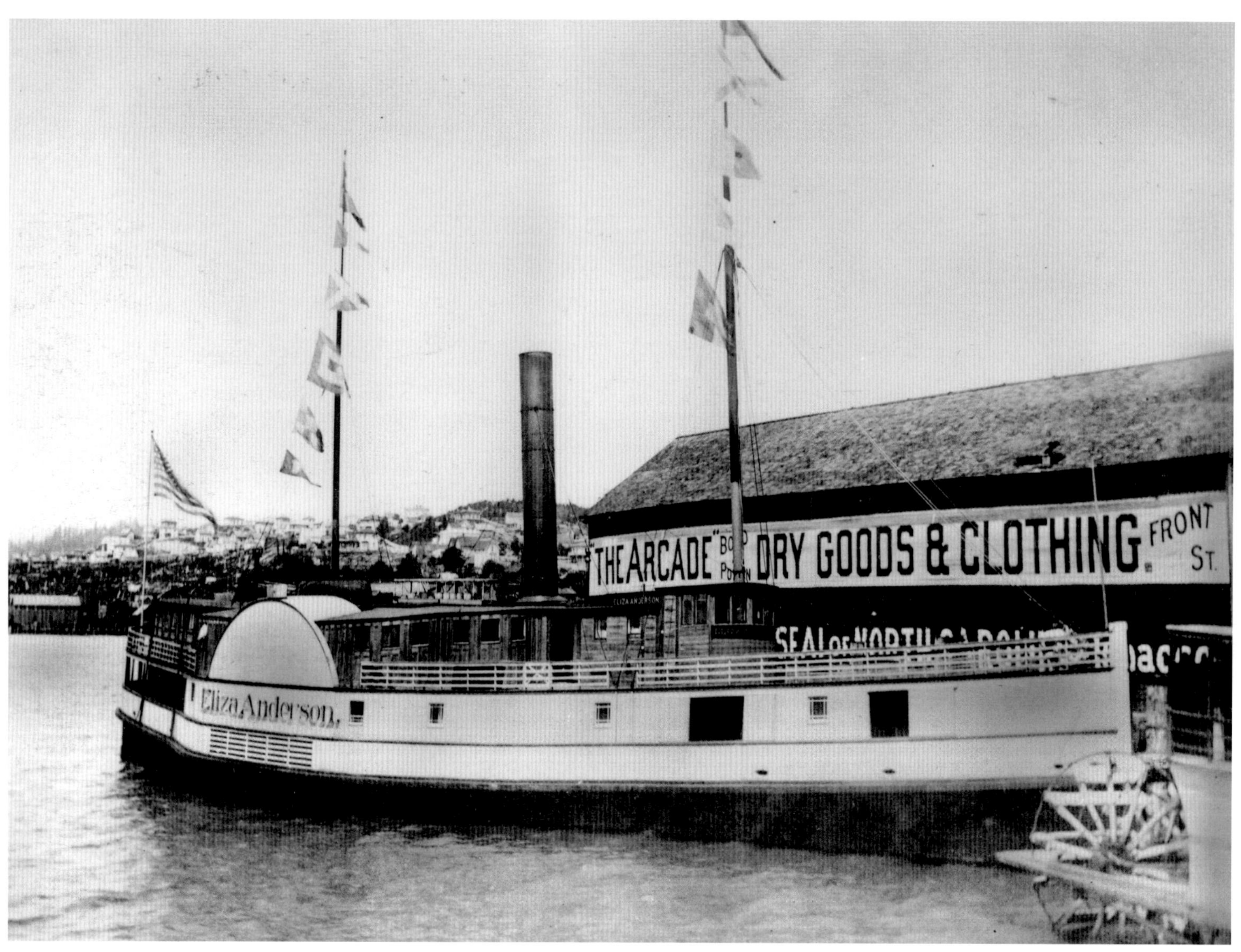

The dense stands of timber that covered the land meant that water provided early travel around Puget Sound. The Indians and early settlers used canoes, but as immigration increased, sailing ships and then steamships served ports from Olympia to Bellingham. Locals called the steamers the Mosquito Fleet because, compared against the vast size of the Sound, they looked like insects on a pond. Here the side-wheeler *Eliza Anderson* waits aft of a stern-wheeler around 1884 at Yesler's Wharf, later called the Colman Ferry Dock.

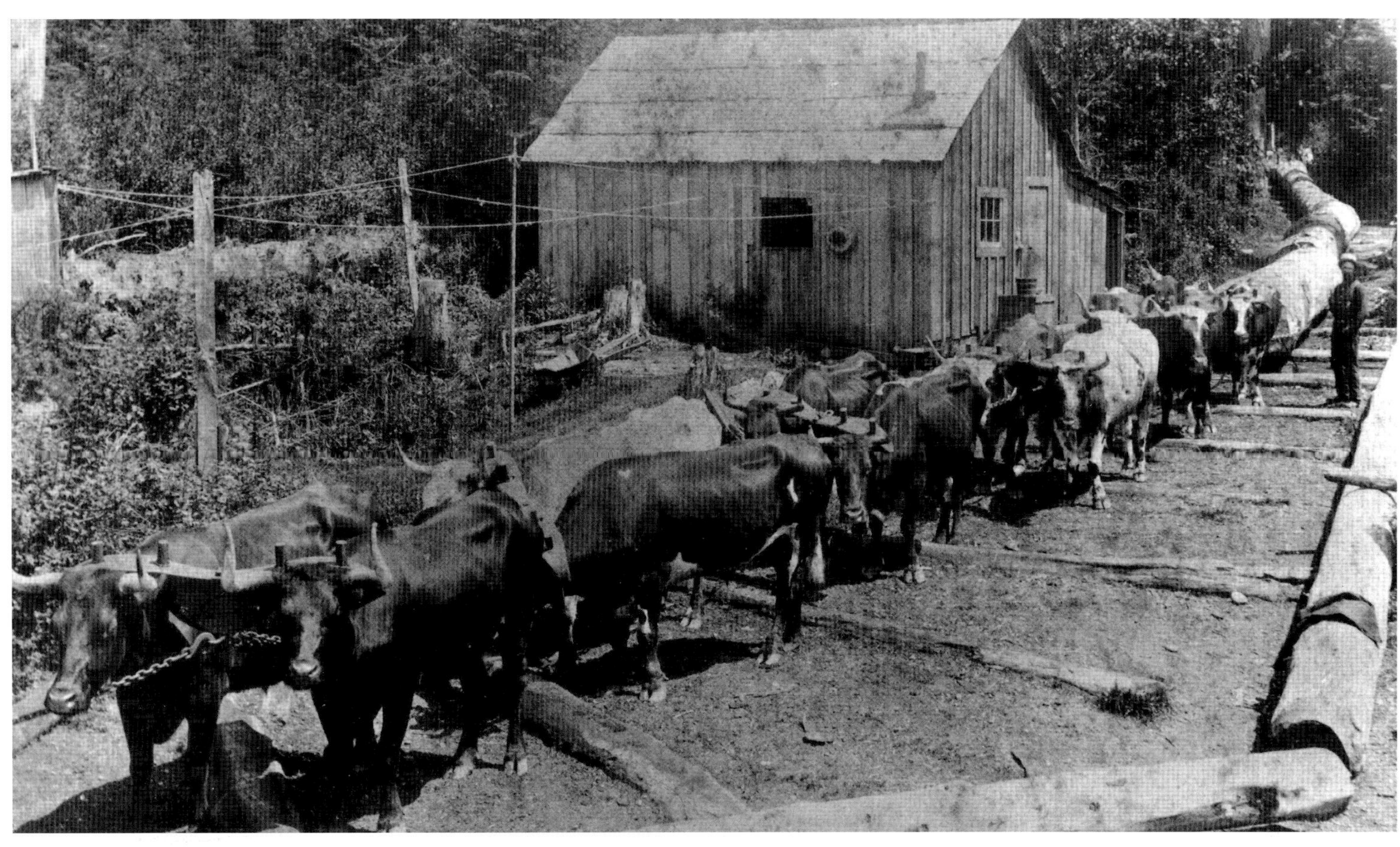

The immense, 300-year-old trees that drew loggers to Puget Sound presented serious challenges before they were brought to market. After felling the trees, loggers bucked them into manageable lengths, lashed them to teams of oxen, and skidded the forest's bounty across greased wood ties. In this view from around 1885, one of Peter D. Jorup's crews hauls logs down to his mill at Utsalady on Camano Island.

In the 1880s, the donkey engine's steam-driven capstans and cable drums replaced ox teams to haul great logs from forest to rail cars and waterfront. This engine revolutionized logging. To move the donkey, the crew secured a cable to a tree, wrapped the other end around the capstan, engaged the capstan, and the donkey dragged itself to a new location—in this case, a flatcar bound for its next job.

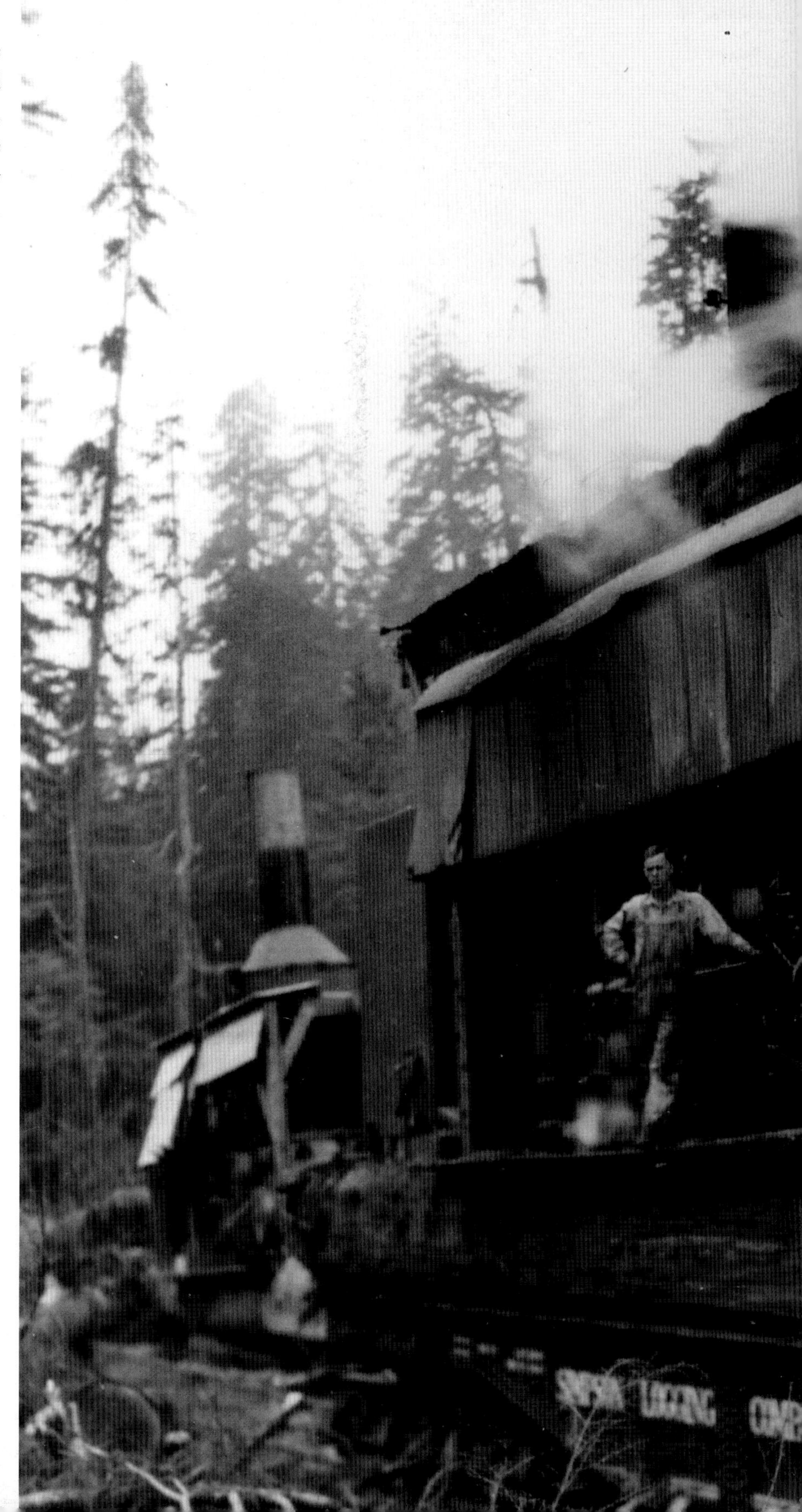

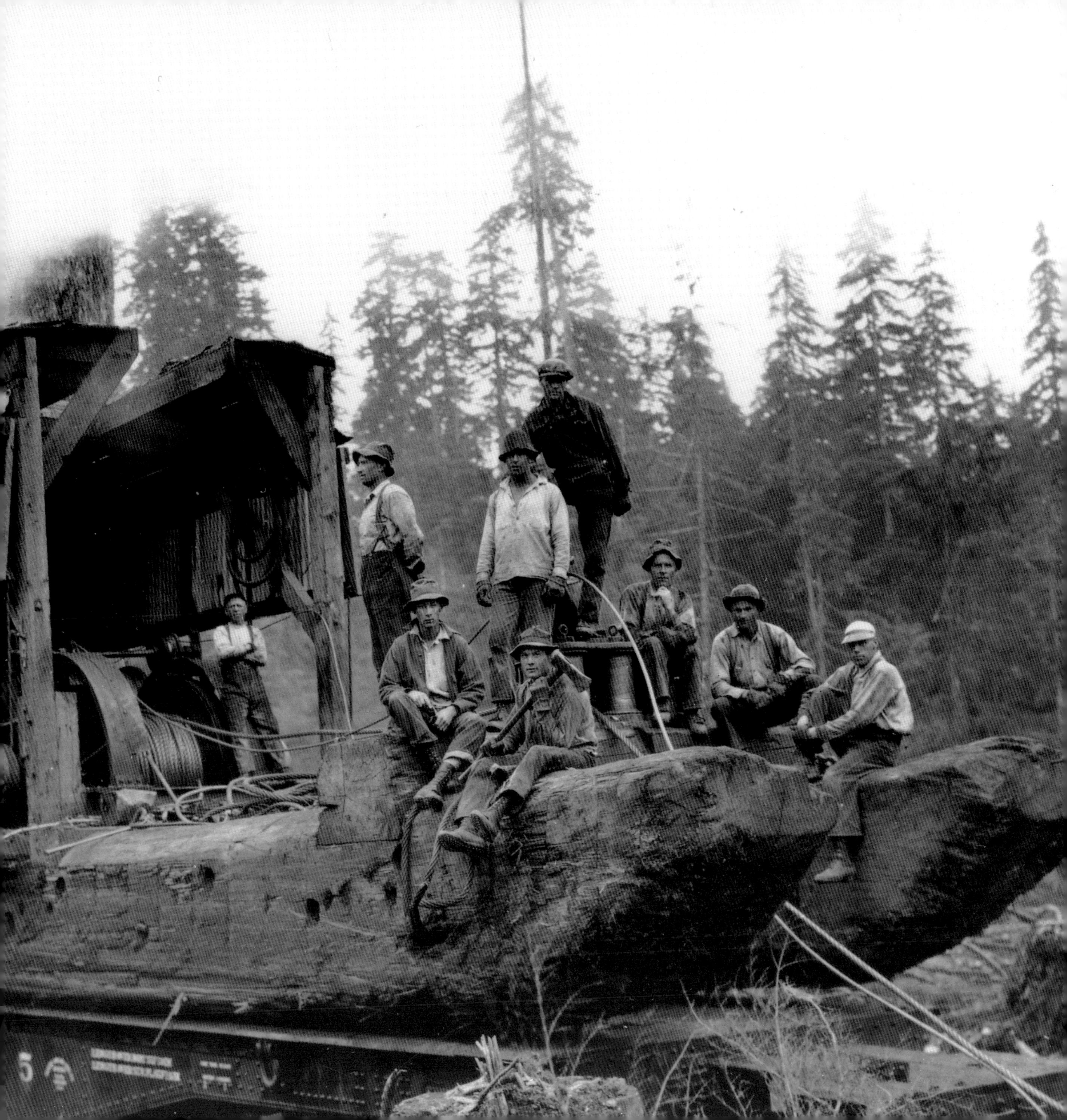

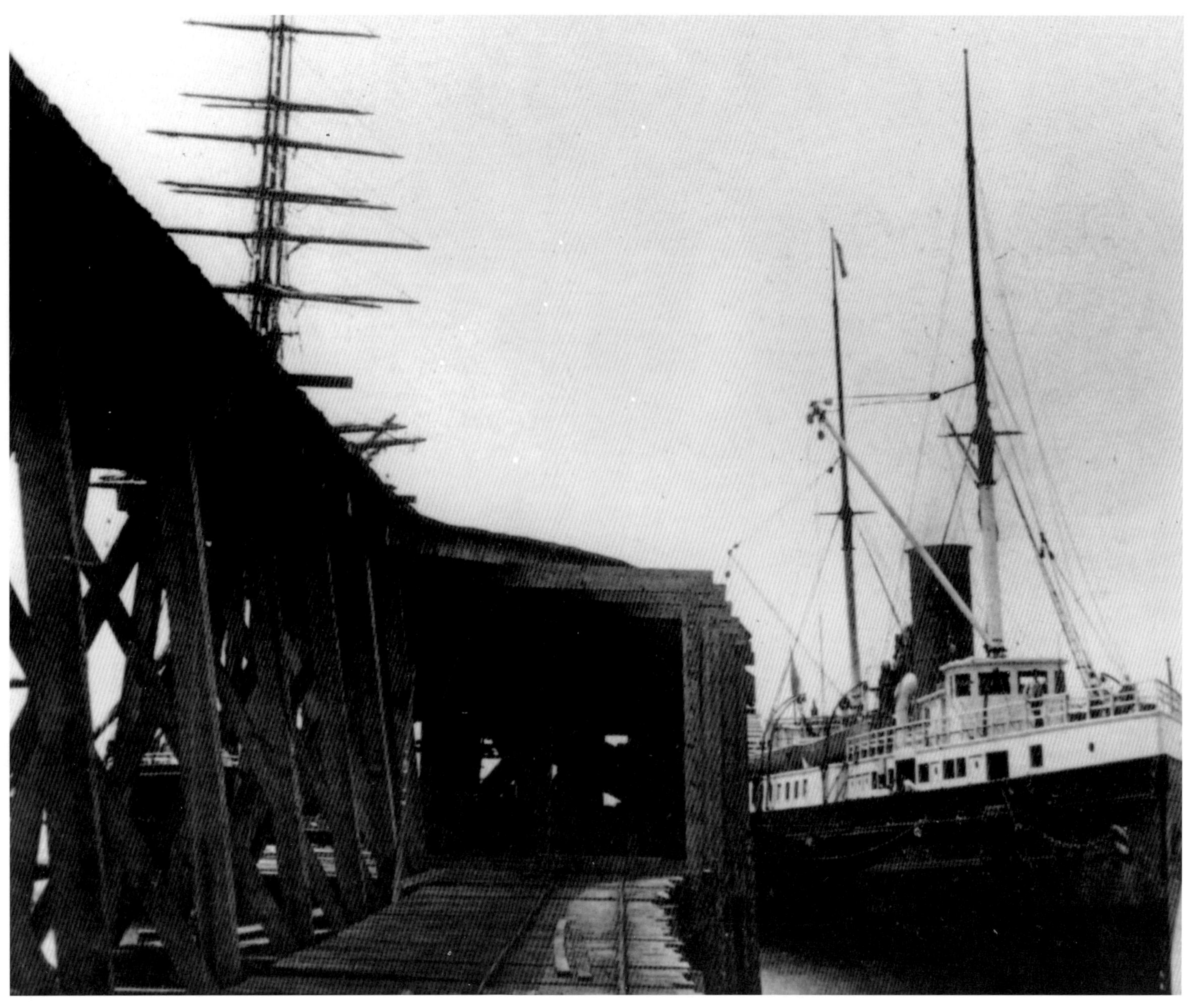

Around 1885, the steamer *Idaho* fills its bunkers with coal at the Columbia and Puget Sound Railway coal dock, located at the foot of Jackson Street in Seattle. On the opposite side, a sailing ship fills its holds with coal for either San Francisco or Hawaii. At this time, coal was as important an export from Puget Sound as lumber.

Puget Sound and the World

(1886–1910)

In addition to Puget Sound's economic potential for its wealth in lumber, coal, and fish, its place on the map caught the eyes of capitalists seeking to link these resources with markets of Asia and the rest of the United States. Steamers, known as the "Mosquito Fleet," served the Sound, as did the railroad. Four transcontinental railroads laid tracks to Commencement Bay, Elliott Bay, and Port Gardiner, where goods and passengers flowed across wharves. Originally, the railroads were intended to link the East Coast of the U.S. with Asia. The Northern Pacific reached Washington Territory and Puget Sound in the mid-1880s, and almost instantly, other industries became more viable. Lumbermen, miners, and salmon canners could ship their products east in weeks rather than months by sea.

With the railroads came thousands of new residents. Capitalists saw investment opportunities in towns quickly growing into cities. Homesteaders looked to build farms on logged-over "stump ranches." European and Asian immigrants just wanted work. King County grew from 7,000 to 42,000 in the 1880s, a sixfold increase in ten years. Dozens of communities sprouted along the shores of the Sound to process logs, fish, coal, and harvests from the region.

In the late 1800s, European powers built navies to carve empires out of the rest of the world. U.S. Navy strategists looked at their maps and realized that Puget Sound might hide an invading fleet. They took steps to garrison the Sound and selected Port Orchard and Sinclair Inlet for a base to repair and supply the battleships protecting the West Coast. The Puget Sound Naval Shipyard docked its first battleship in 1897, and the city of Bremerton sprang up around the yard. With the sailors came the Coast Artillerymen of the U.S. Army, who built forts to protect the shipyard and critical ports of the Sound.

Logging and milling took off in the late 1880s when the steam donkey engine and geared steam locomotive were introduced. These allowed loggers to overcome grade and distance and reach back into the hills for their logs. In the 1890s, as the rest of the nation languished in economic depression, Puget Sound ports cashed in on gold seekers en route to Alaska and the Yukon. Businessmen stayed open late to sell supplies, mining tools, and steamer tickets north. The gold craze really took off in 1897, when the steamer *Portland* landed in Seattle with "a ton of solid gold." Not only did Klondike gold rejuvenate the Puget Sound economy, it helped the rest of the U.S. recover from the Panic of 1893.

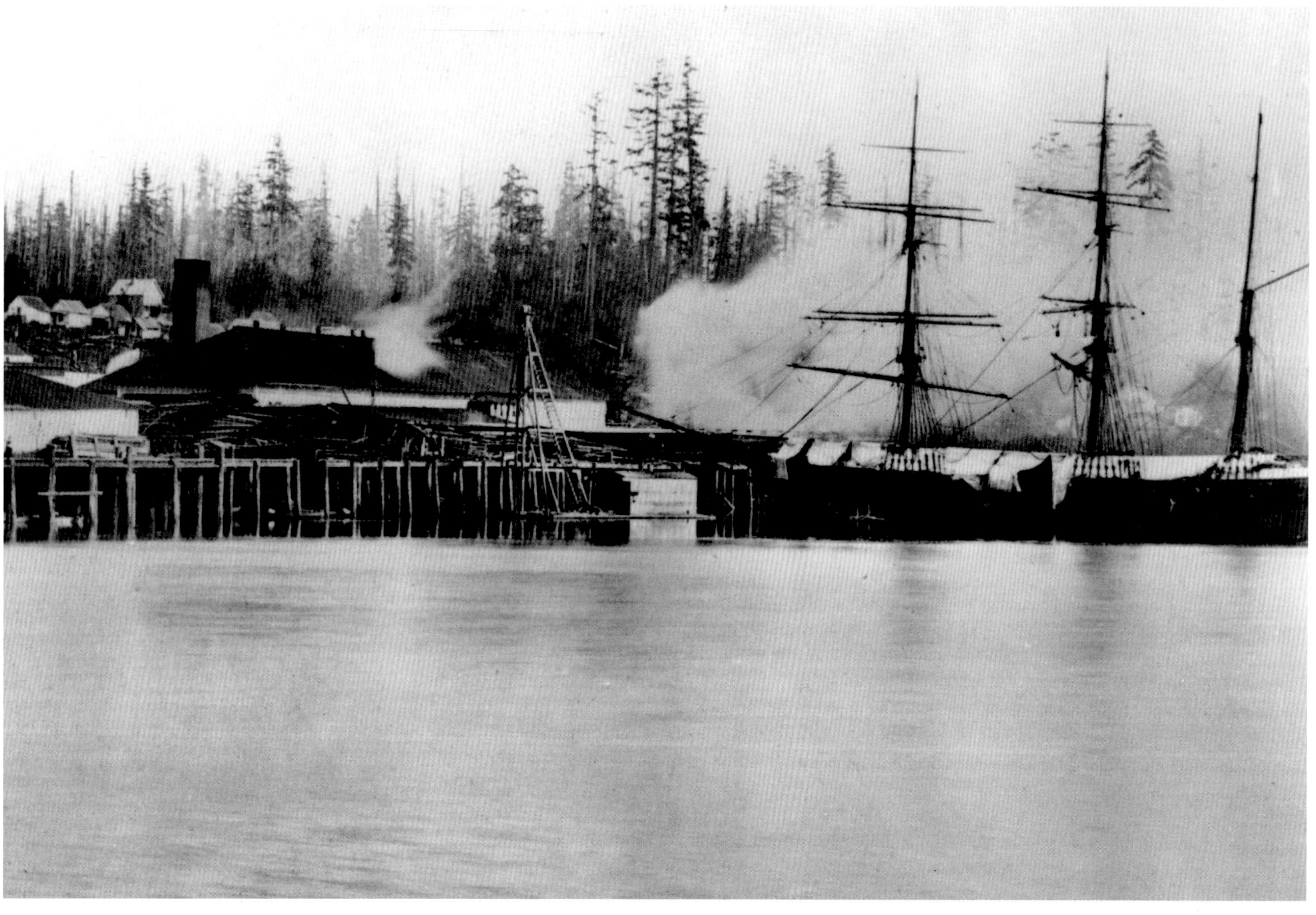

Dozens of sawmills dotted Puget Sound in the late nineteenth century. This winter shot shows a typical mill, its wharf, a waiting lumber vessel, worker homes, and company buildings. Most mills provided modest houses for the employees and paid them in scrip redeemable only at the company store or for cash at the company headquarters in Seattle. Owners and managers enjoyed the largest homes.

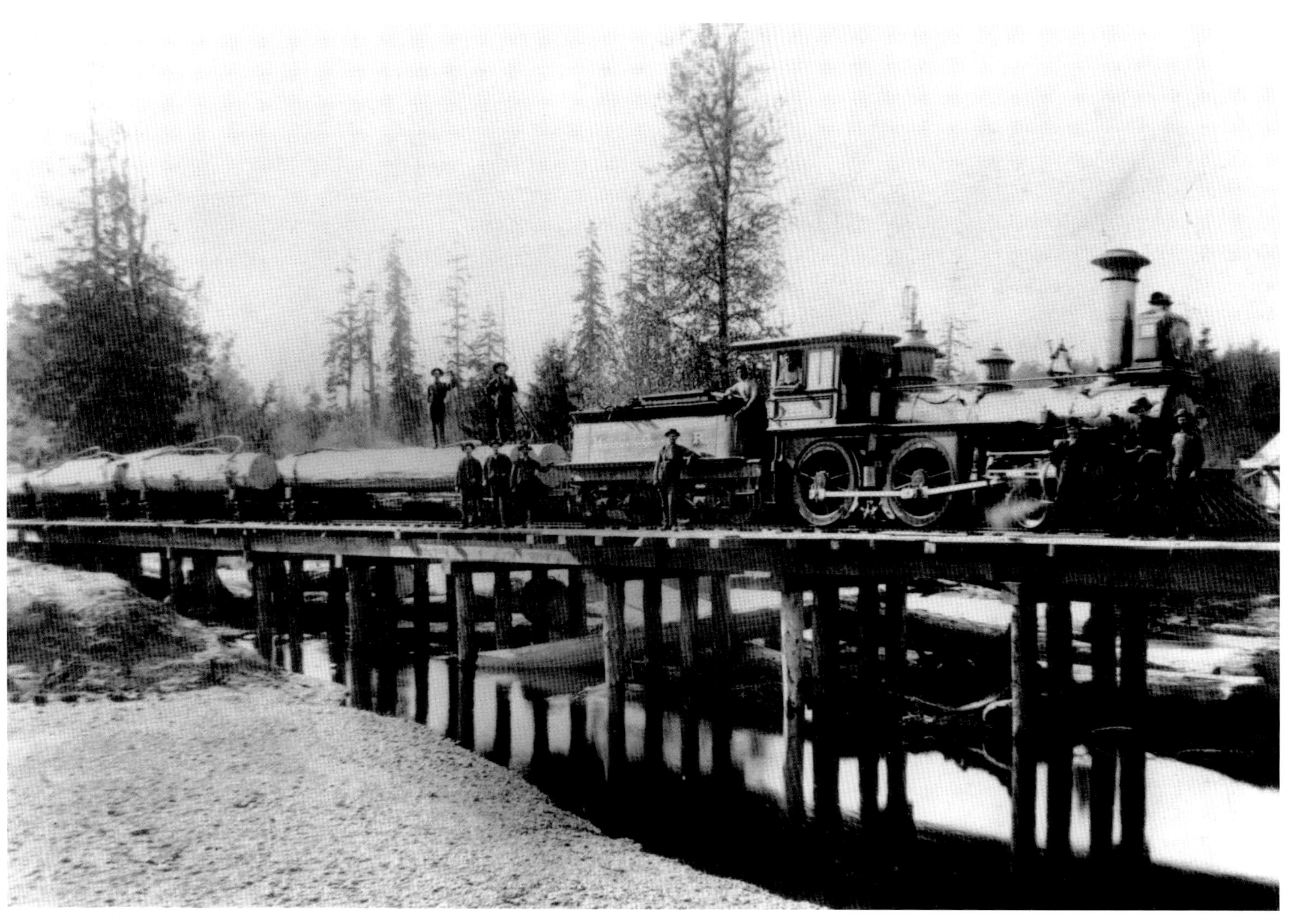

In 1886, loggers and the crew of a Mason County Central Railroad Baldwin locomotive pose on a trestle with their load of logs. By replacing ox teams, steam railroads helped revolutionize logging because they could move logs to mills more efficiently. The large logs here are fitted to sets of wheels called bunks, eliminating the need for flatcars. In the late 1880s, geared locomotives capable of mastering steep grades replaced conventional locomotives such as this one.

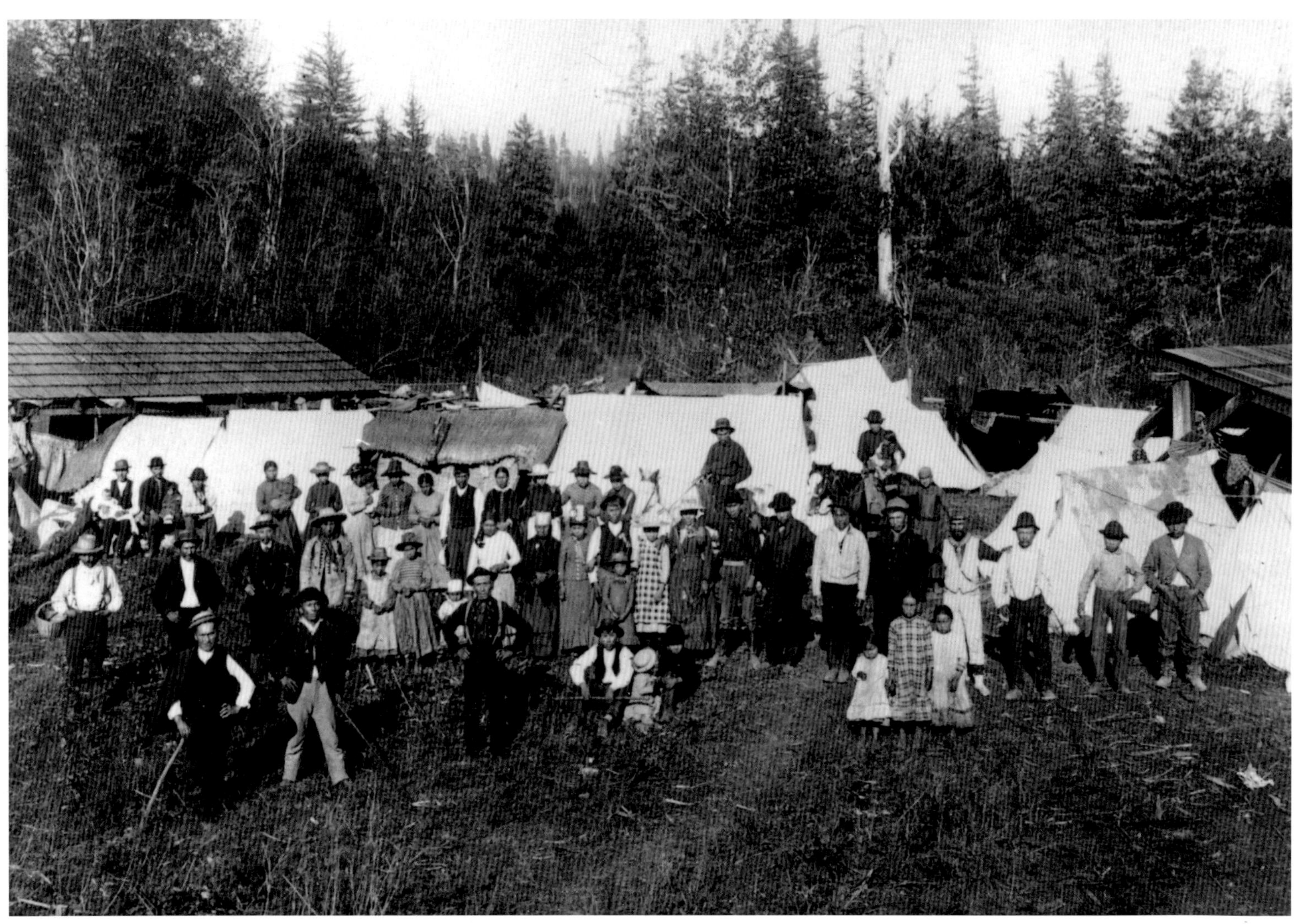

Most of the Indians of Puget Sound who spoke the South Coast Salish language adopted American dress as more practical than traditional clothing woven from cedar bark and as a way to assimilate into American society. Few surviving photographs show the native peoples in their traditional dress. This group of migrant farm workers poses in front of their tents around the year 1889.

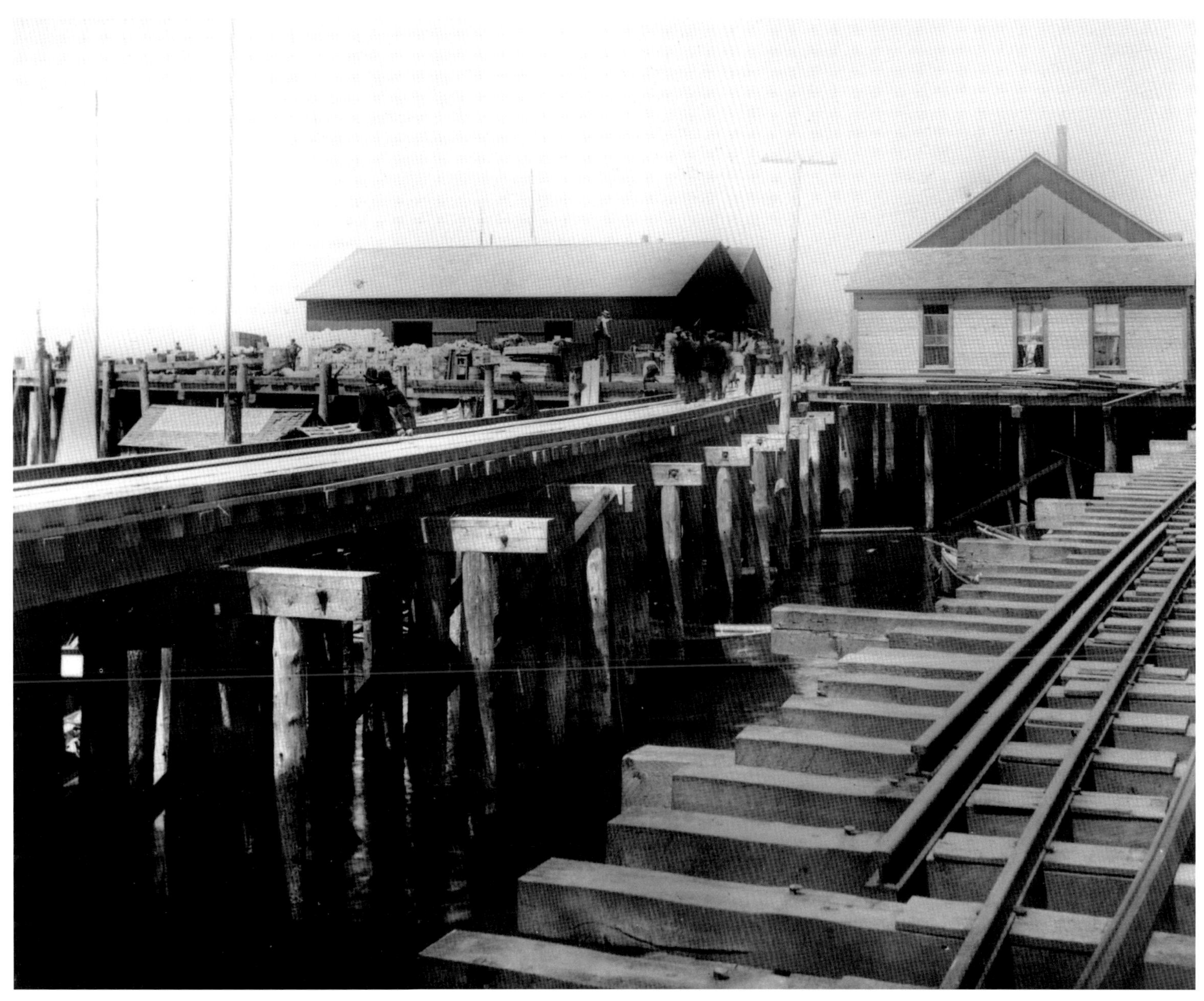

After Seattle's Great Fire on June 6, 1889, only one dock, that of the Oregon Improvement Company, a subsidiary of the Northern Pacific Railroad, survived the flames. At the far dock, a small schooner has just offloaded goods. At the near dock, new steel rails wait next to the Puget Sound Machinery Depot to replace those damaged in the fire. The Great Fire began when cabinet maker John Back had been heating a pot of glue over a fire, and the glue boiled over into the flames. By the end of the day, 29 blocks of downtown and the waterfront had become a smoking ruin.

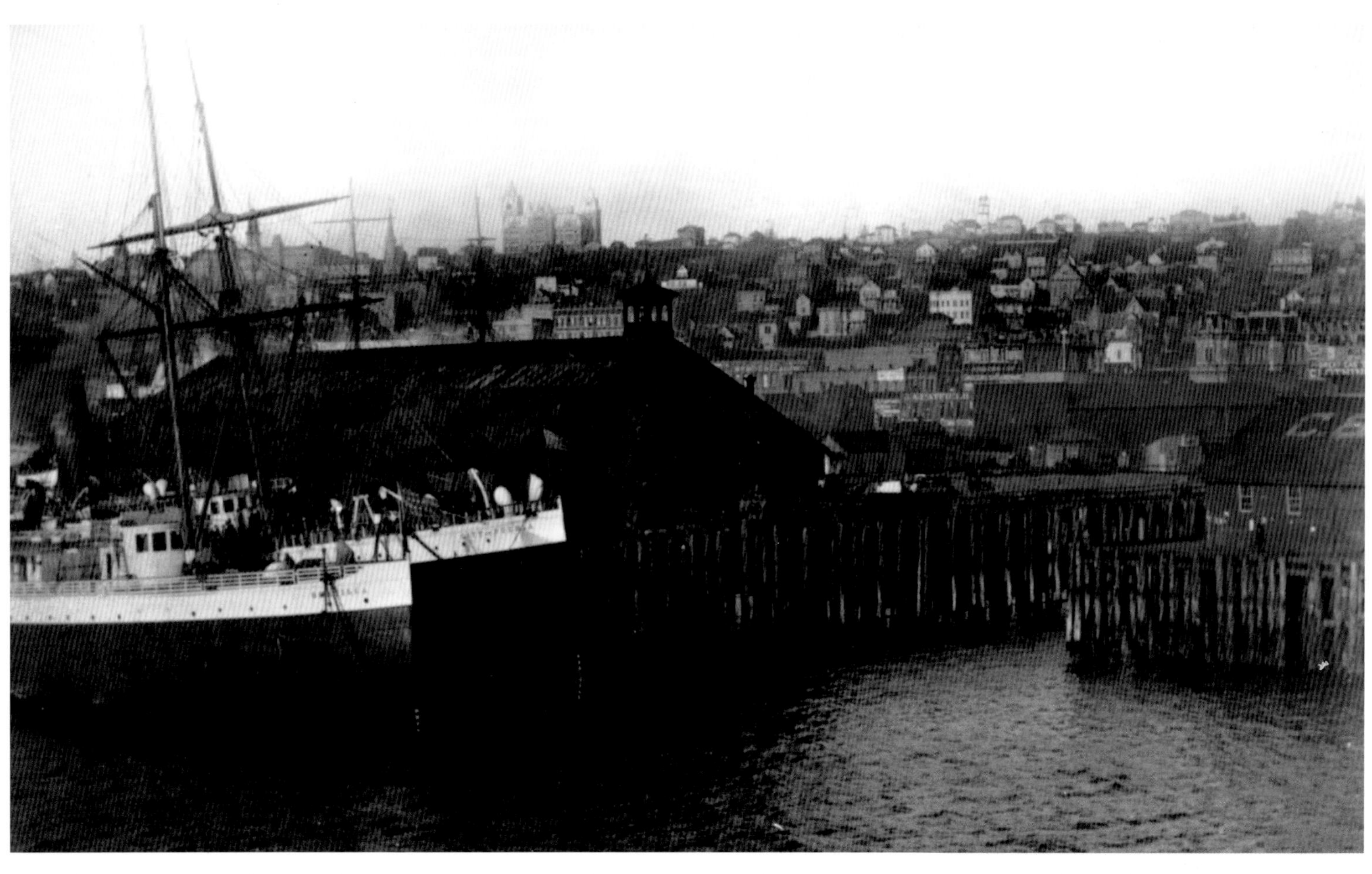

Just before the Great Seattle Fire of June 6, 1889, the steamers *Umatilla* and *City of Puebla* wait at a pier north of Yesler's Wharf. To the right is the dock of the Columbia and Puget Sound Railway Company, which hauled coal from Renton, Newcastle, and Olney (later Issaquah).

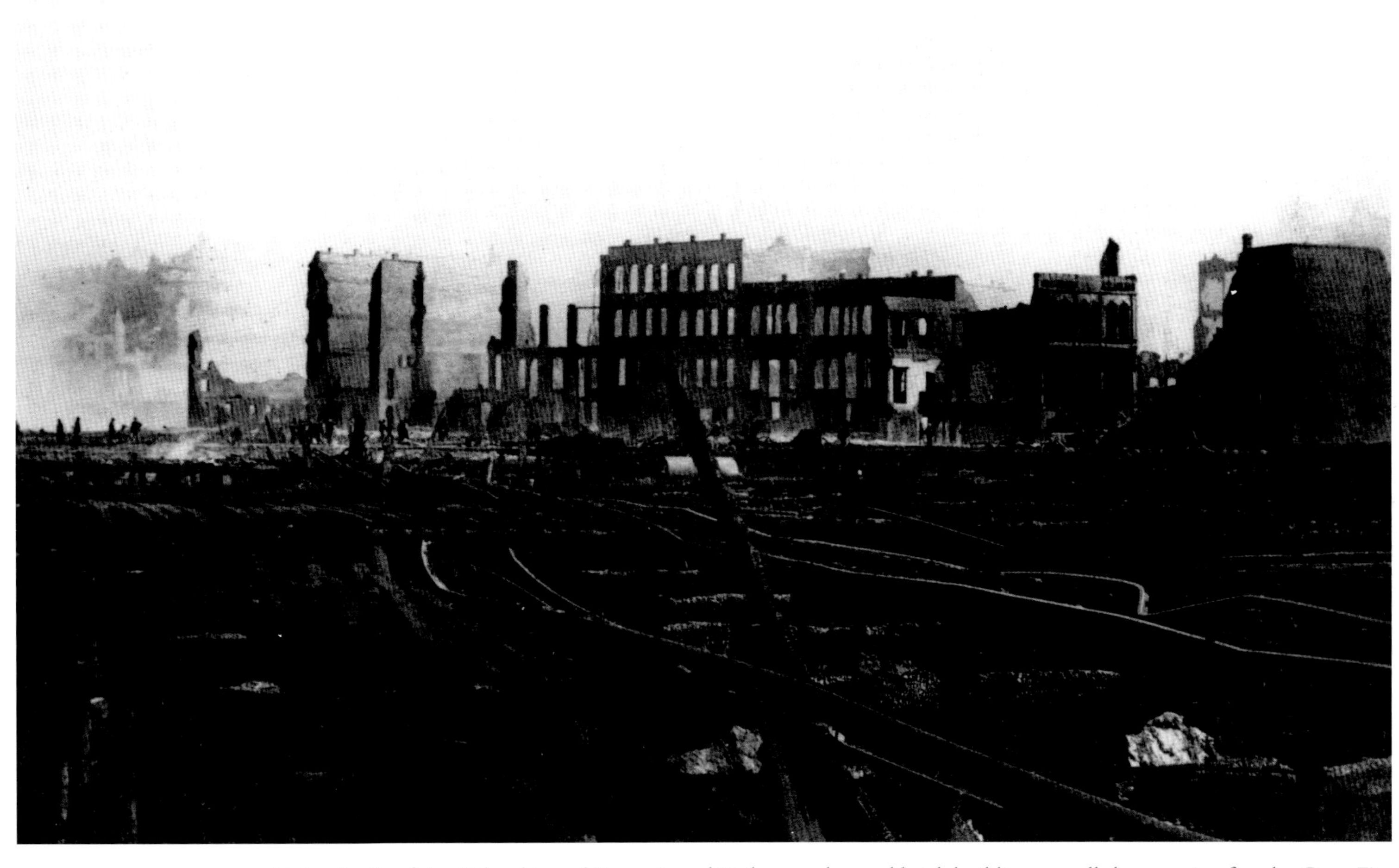

Twisted rails of the Columbia and Puget Sound Railway and gutted brick buildings are all that remain after the Great Fire consumed Seattle on June 6, 1889. From left to right the businesses are—or were—Frye's Opera House, Toklas and Singerman Company, the Union Block, Merchants National Bank, and the Seattle Post-Intelligencer. The disaster allowed Seattle to rebuild with brick and marked a rebirth of the city.

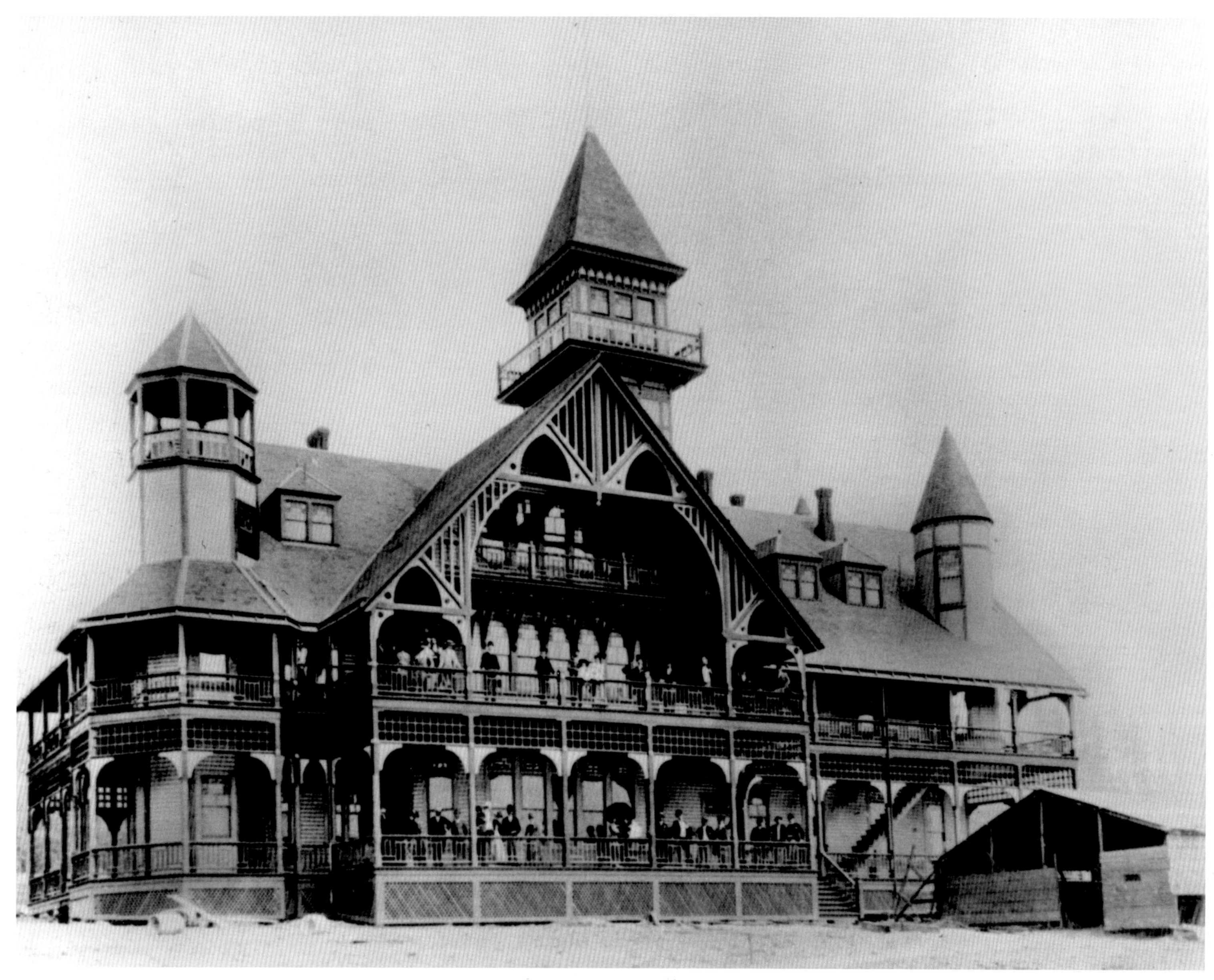

In the late 1880s, Mercer Island was a quiet refuge for Seattleites seeking to escape the stress of their growing city. C. C. Calkins built the lavish, storybook Calkins Hotel on the island's northern shore in a community then called East Seattle. The guests posing here in 1890 have traveled by ferry from Leschi, at the foot of Yesler Way in Seattle.

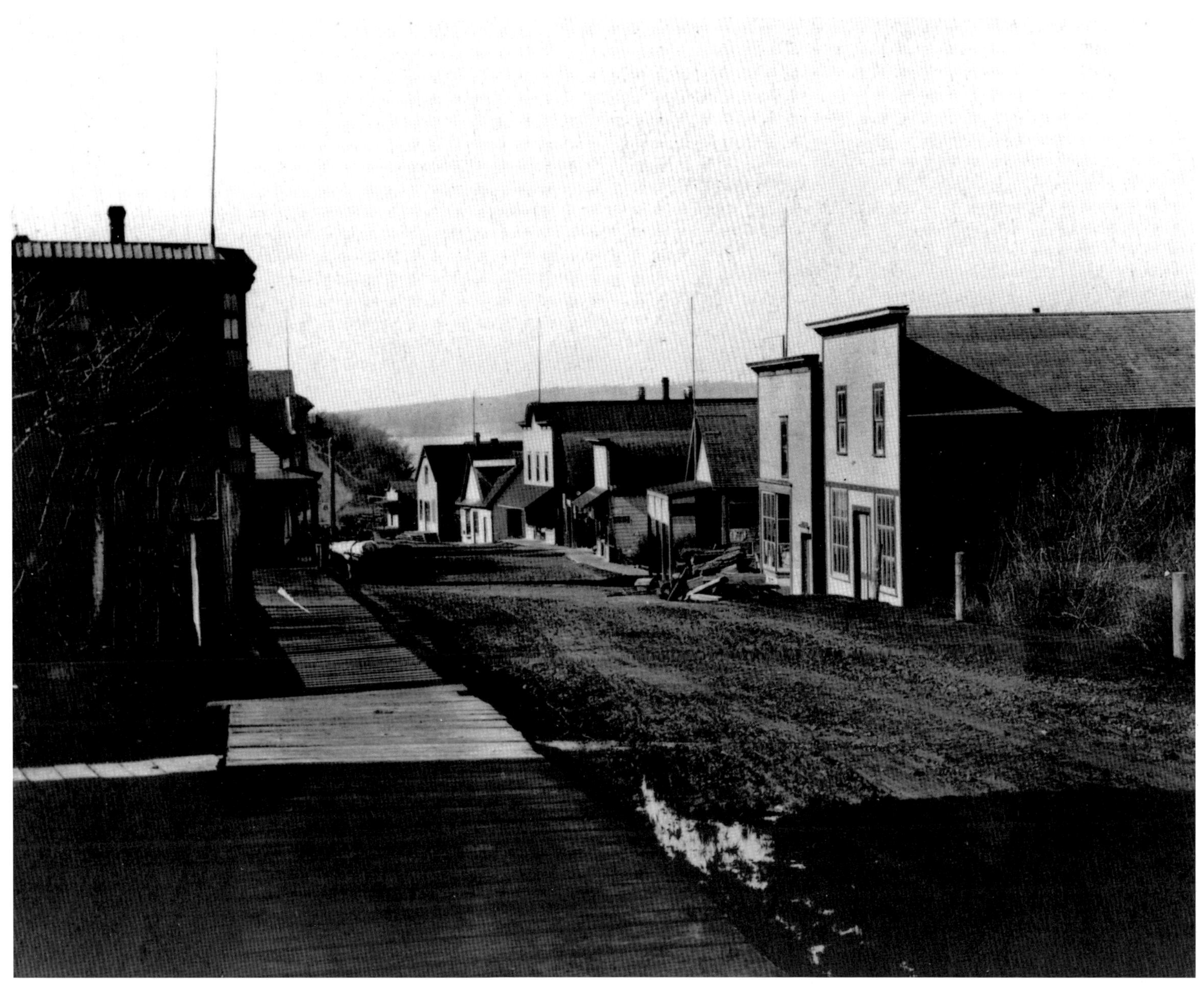

In the 1850s, sea captain Thomas Coupe filed a Donation Land Claim on Penn Cove on Whidbey Island. He then established Coupeville, and other retired seamen joined him to form a community. Coupeville replaced Coveland as the county seat in 1881. Oliver S. Van Olinda snapped this image of the town's wooden sidewalks and mud streets in the 1890s.

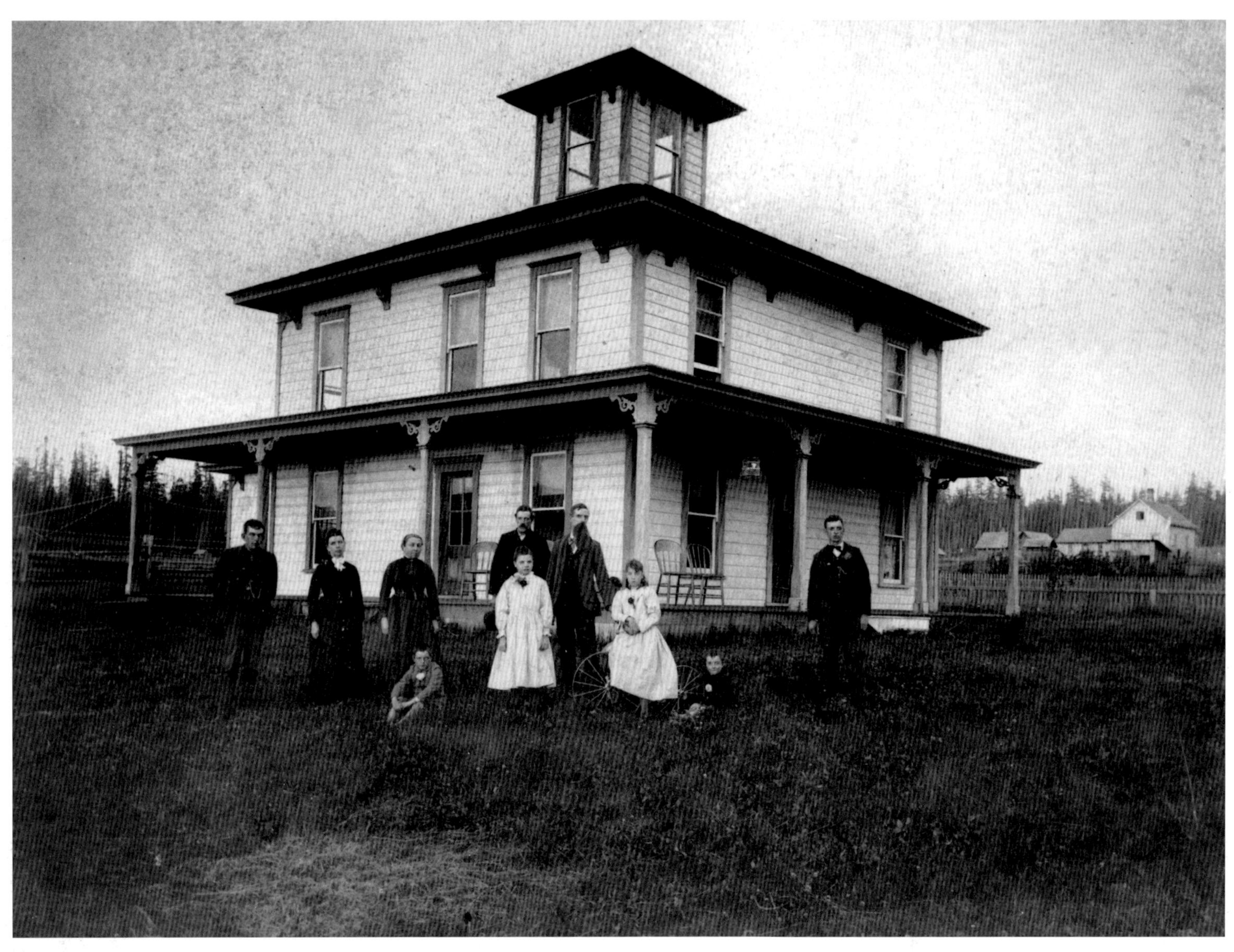

Canadian George Brackett first saw potential for a town at Point Edmonds in Snohomish County while rowing around Puget Sound looking for harvestable timber stands in 1871. In 1876, he bought property and by 1880 had opened a store. A decade later, Edmonds incorporated as a city and boasted residences such as this one belonging to the Hyner family.

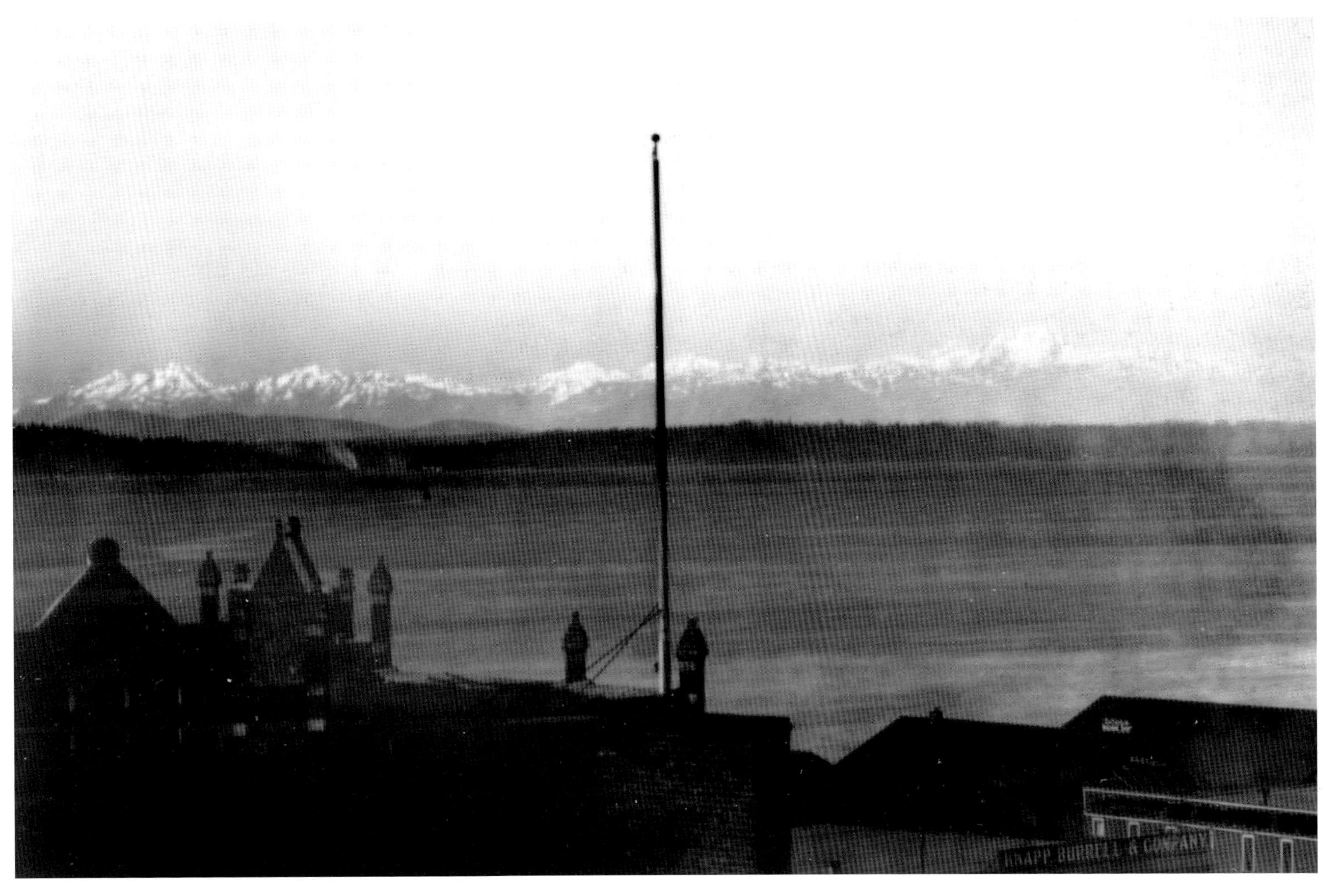

Everyone who lives on and visits Puget Sound marvels at the stunning scenery. Photographer Frank La Roche was no exception when he captured this panorama of the Olympics from Seattle on February 23, 1891.

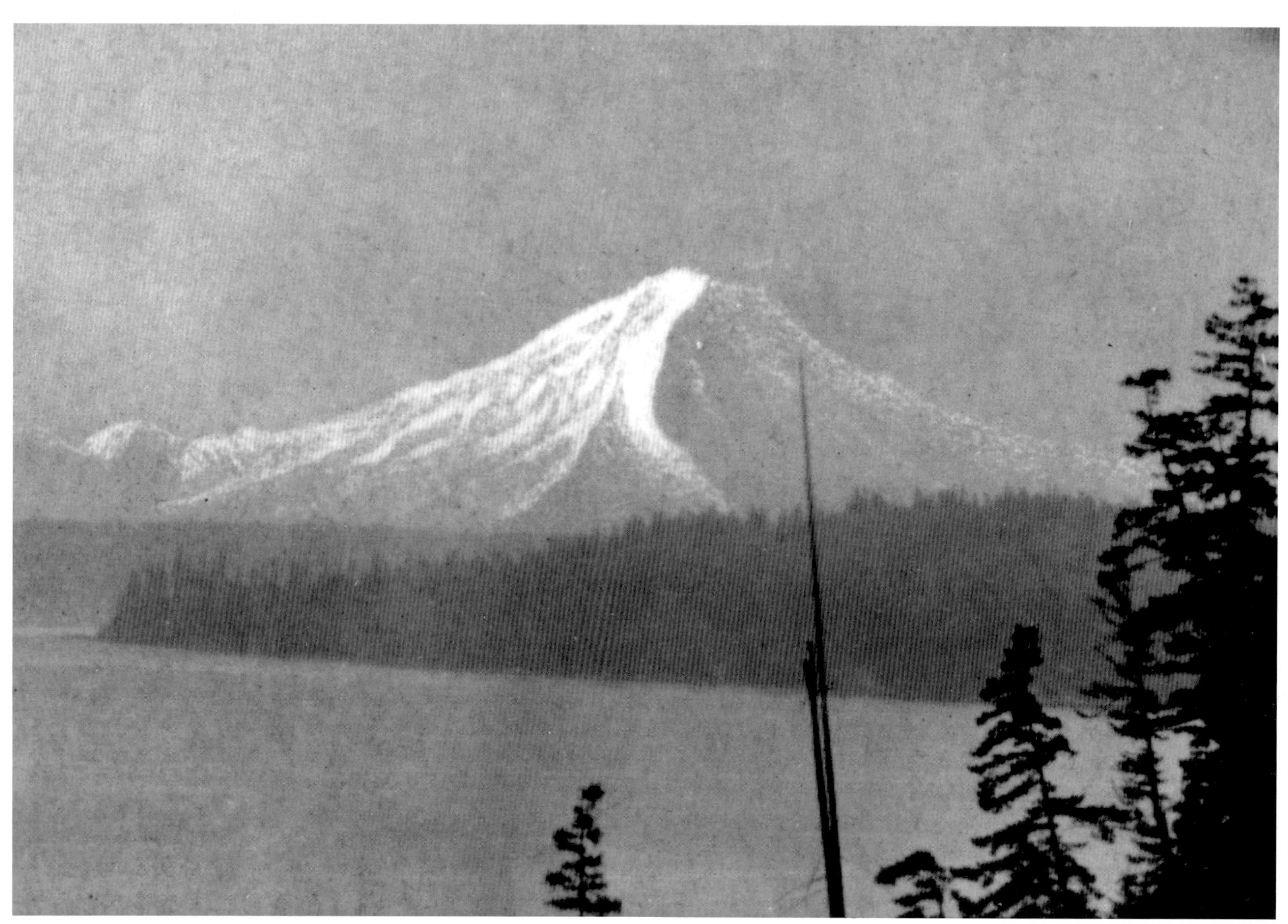

The Indians of Puget Sound called the dormant volcano Tahoma, but Royal Navy Captain George Vancouver named it after his friend, Rear Admiral Peter Rainier, in 1792. The 14,411-foot peak last erupted in 1894, and five years later, Congress established Mount Rainier as a National Park. On clear days in Puget Sound, locals comment that "the mountain is out."

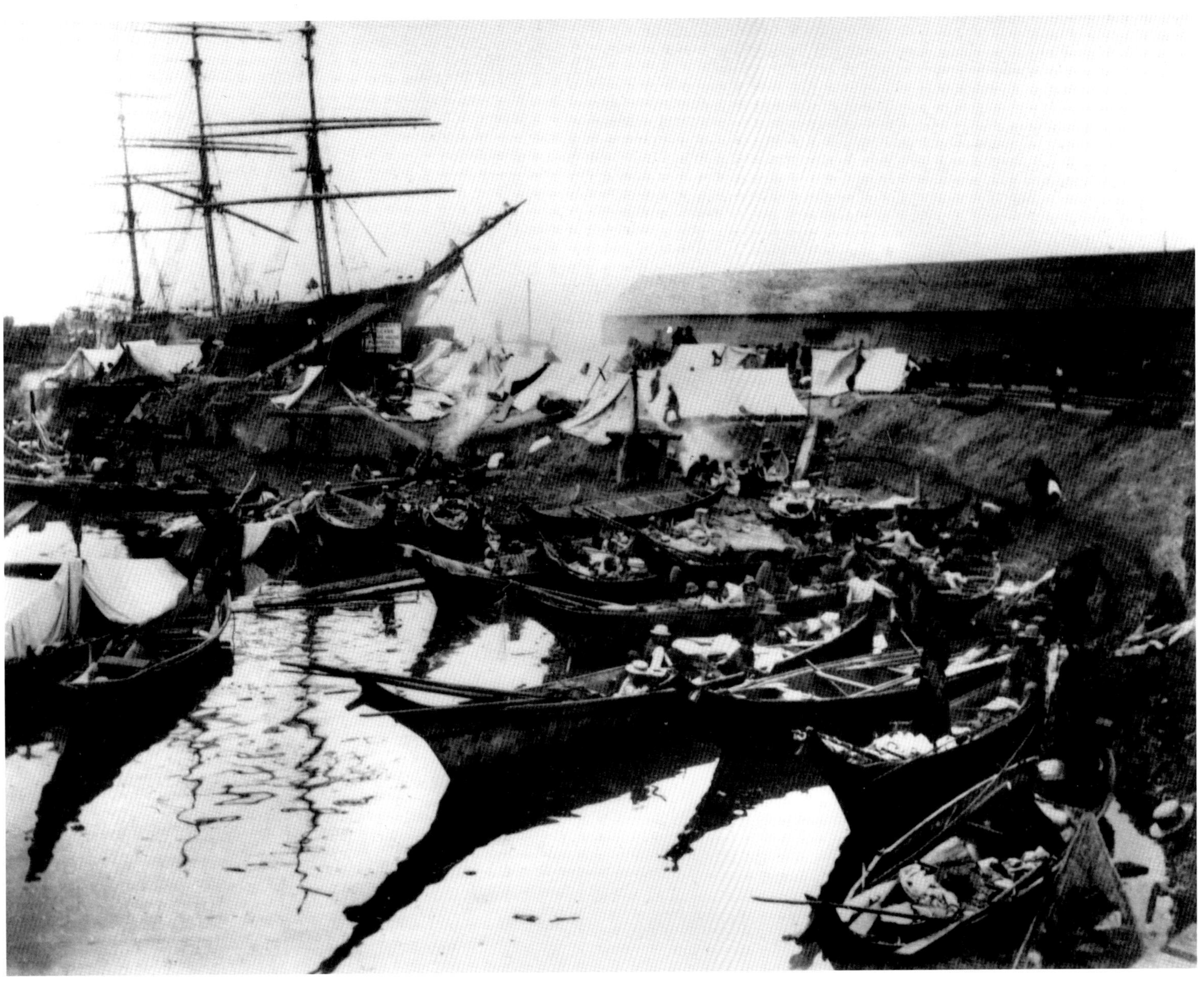

In the nineteenth century, sailing ships often arrived empty in Seattle except for rocks in their holds (in ballast) to maintain stability at sea. To make room for coal and lumber, captains dumped the rocks overboard. Years of this practice resulted in Ballast Island at the foot of Washington Street. In their journeys up and down Puget Sound, Native Americans would camp here overnight, as seen in this 1891 photograph. A city ordinance prohibited Indians within the city limits after dark.

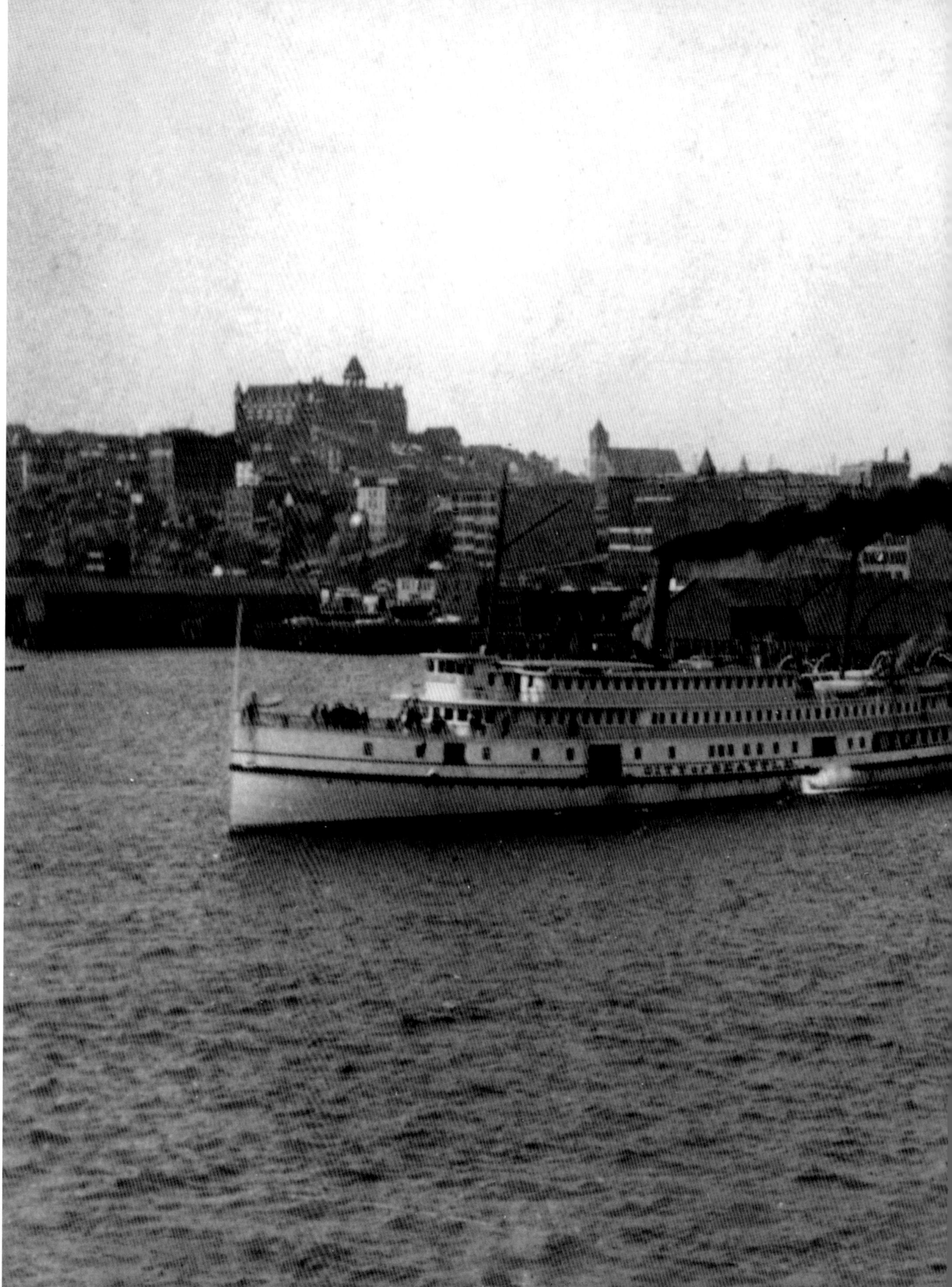

At the foot of Washington Street in Seattle, a photographer from Warner and Randolph has set up his camera to catch this 1891 scene of the steamer *City of Seattle* as she leaves the Oregon Improvement Company dock. The *Umatilla* awaits passengers at right.

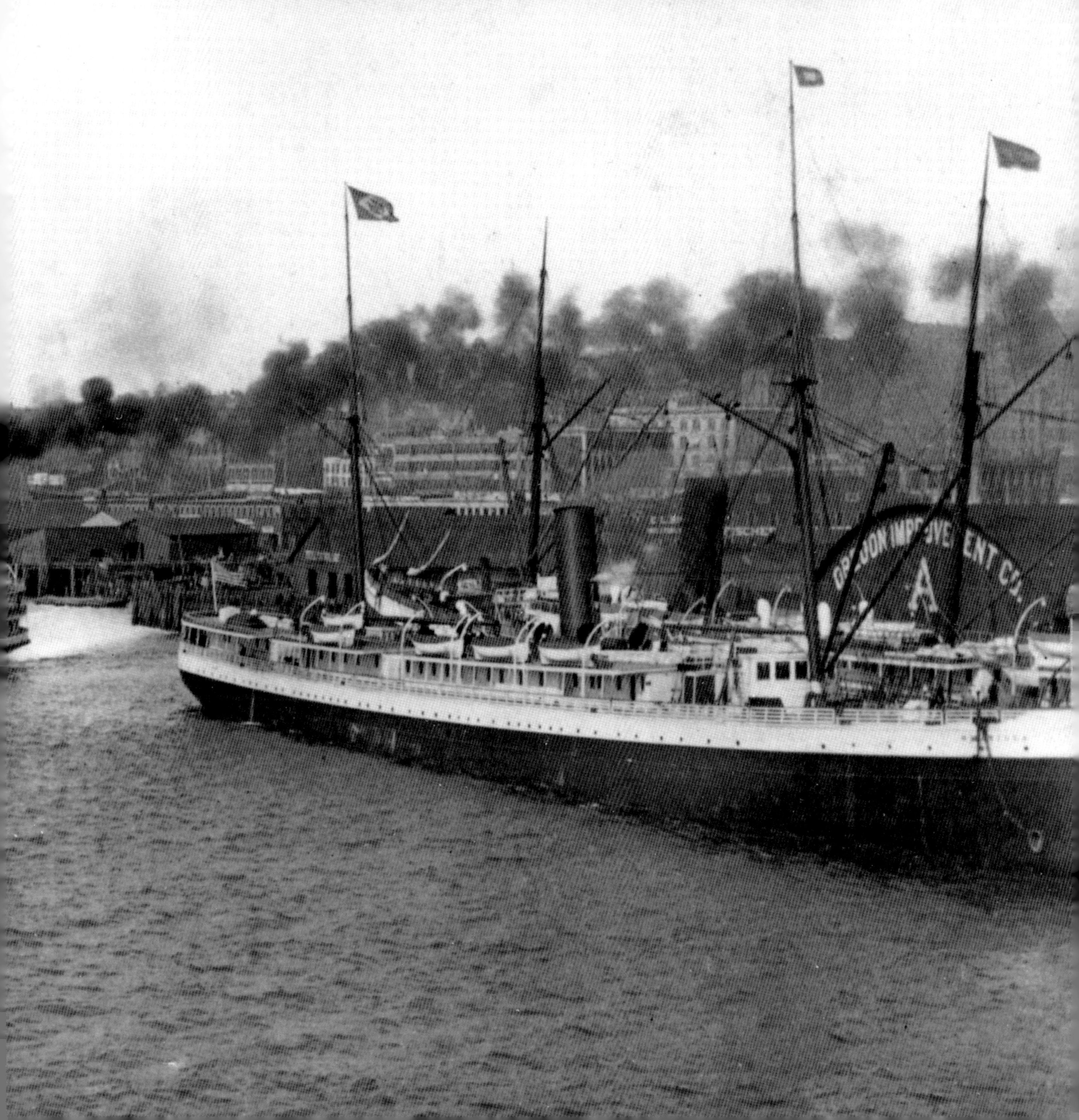

OREGON IMPROVEMENT CO.

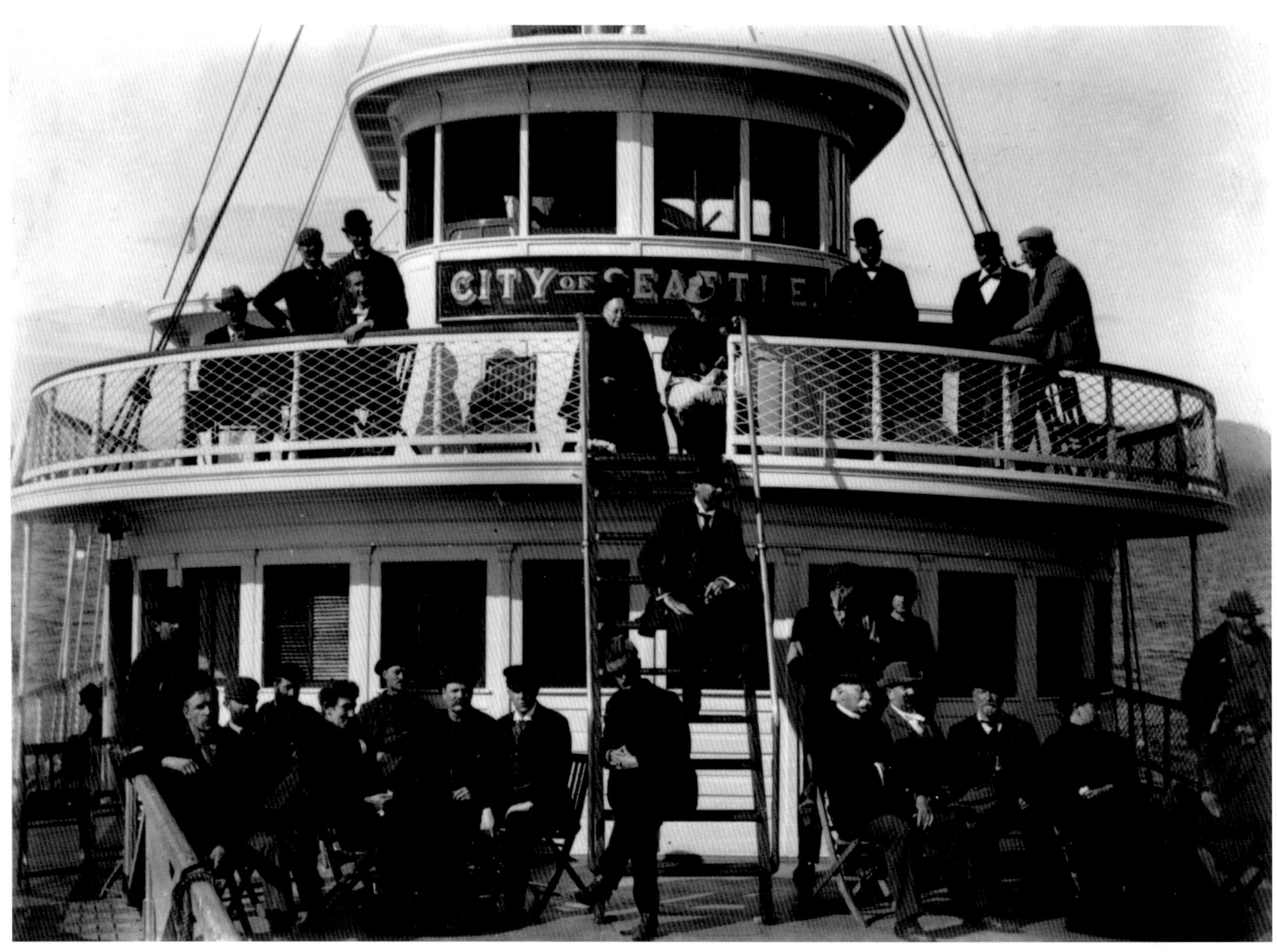

Passengers pose on the deck of the *City of Seattle,* watching Arthur Churchill Warner snap their picture as they cross Puget Sound in the 1890s. The *City of Seattle* flew the flag of the Puget Sound and Alaska Steamship Company and would later become the first double-ended vehicle ferry to operate on the Sound. The ship finished her career in San Francisco Bay.

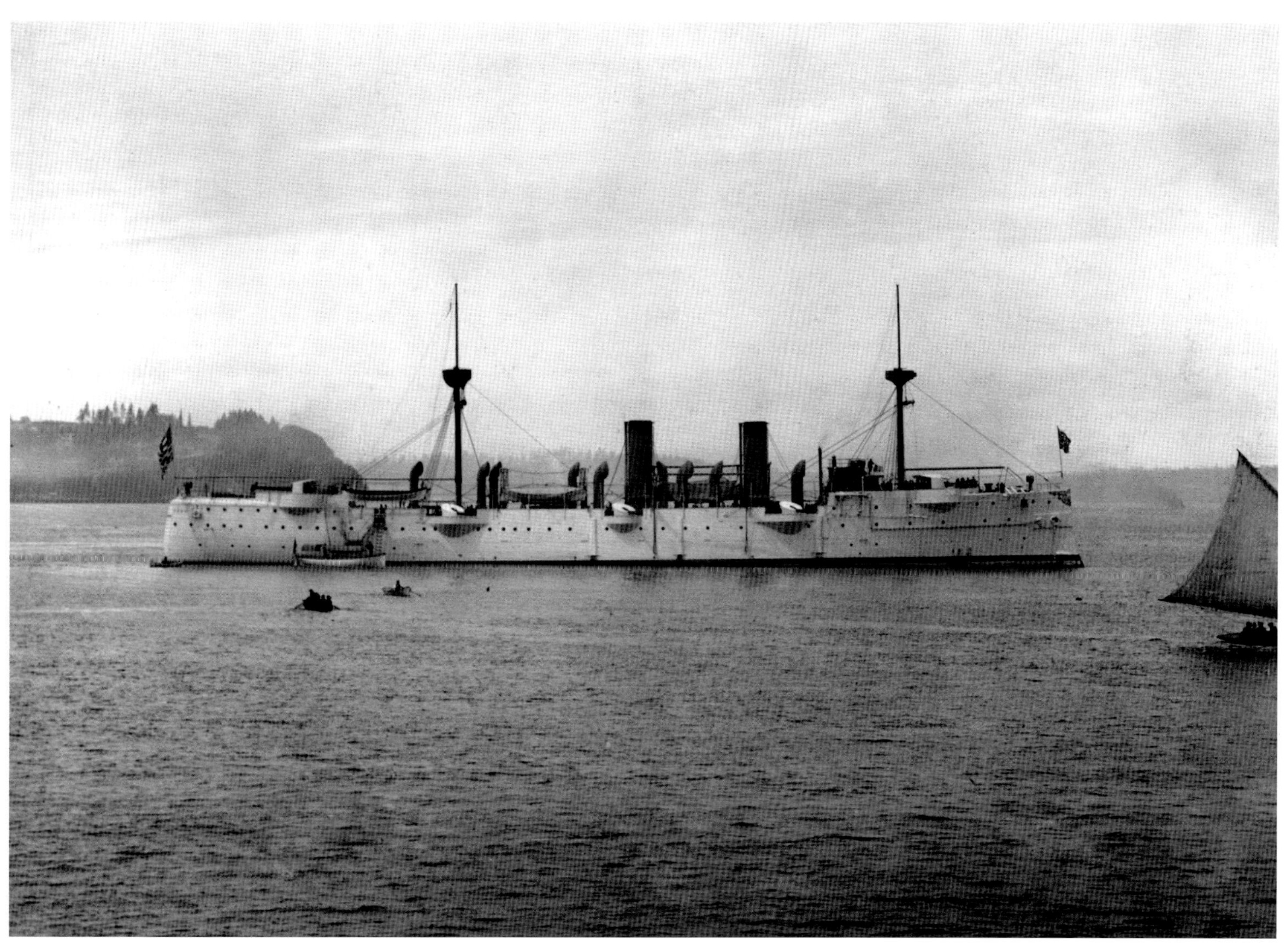

Classified as a protected cruiser, the USS *Baltimore* served in the U.S. Navy's South Pacific Station in 1891 and 1892. The ship visited ports in North and South America, including this stop in Elliott Bay. In the distance is Duwamish Head and West Seattle. The *Baltimore* took part in the Battle of Manila Bay in 1898 and served in World War I. She carried 8-inch, 6-inch, and 3-inch guns.

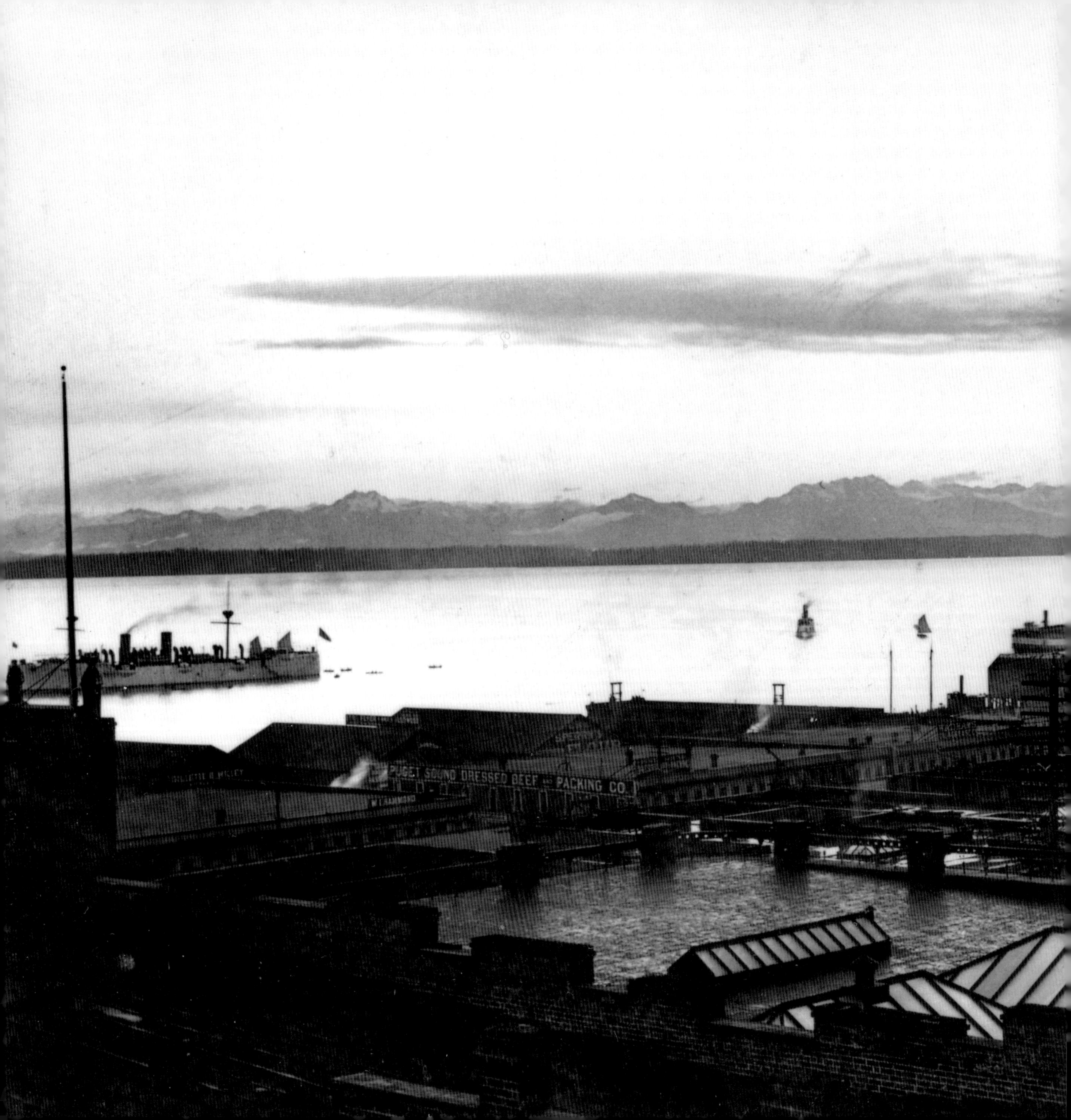
PUGET SOUND DRESSED BEEF AND PACKING CO.
W. T. HAMMOND

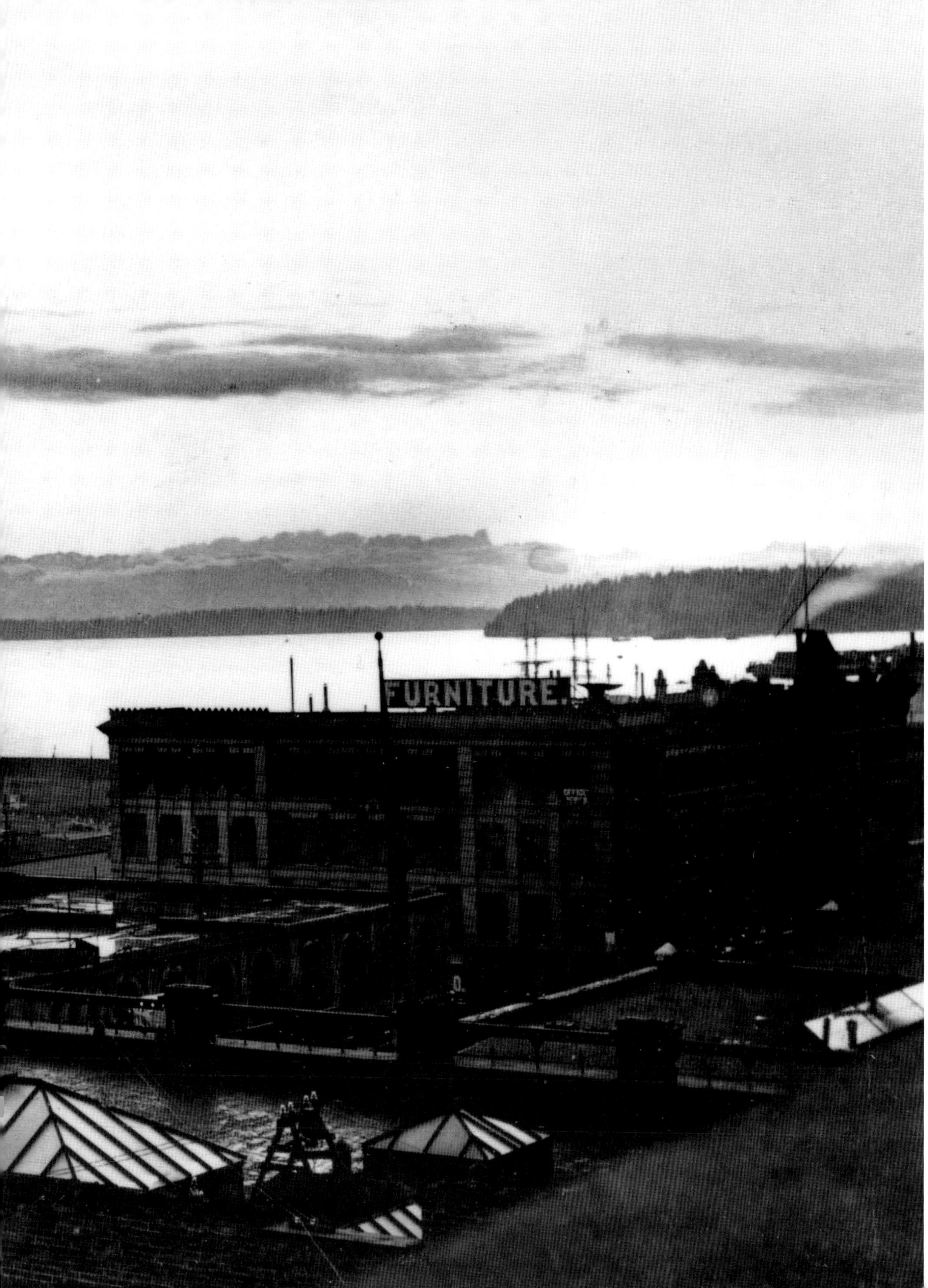

This view of Elliott Bay and the cruiser USS *Baltimore* shows how Seattle built out over the beach with an extensive network of wharves. At high tide the bay washes under piers, warehouses, businesses, and even railroads. This area at First Avenue and Columbia Street would eventually be filled behind a seawall.

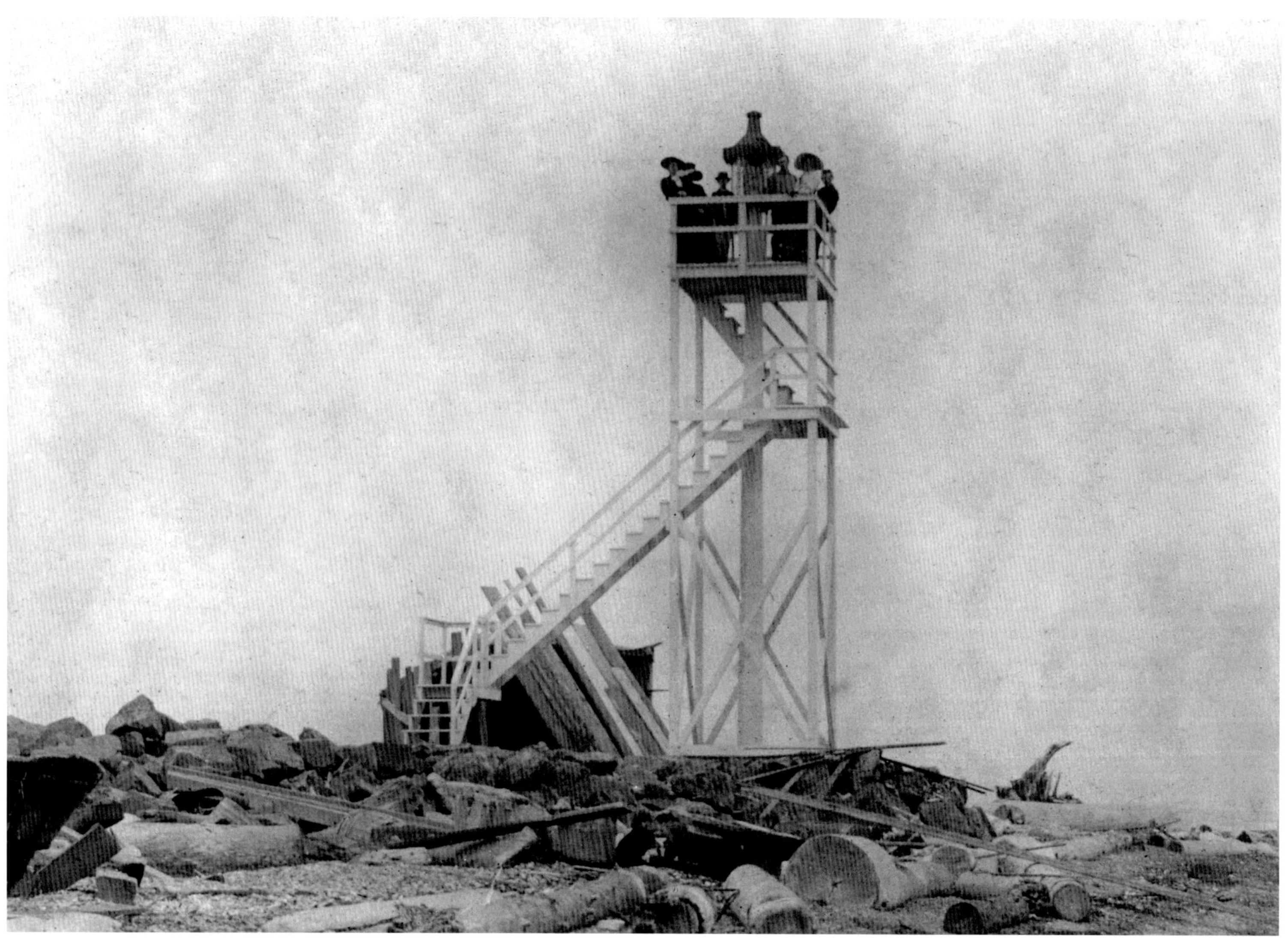

In June 1885, the U.S. Lighthouse Board completed a light station at Point Robinson on Maury Island, just north of Tacoma. The first station consisted of a 12-inch steam whistle to act as a signal during foggy conditions. The Lighthouse Board found this inadequate for the anticipated traffic to Tacoma and improved the station by installing a 25-foot-tall post lantern with a red lens. The kerosene lamp contained enough fuel to burn for eight days.

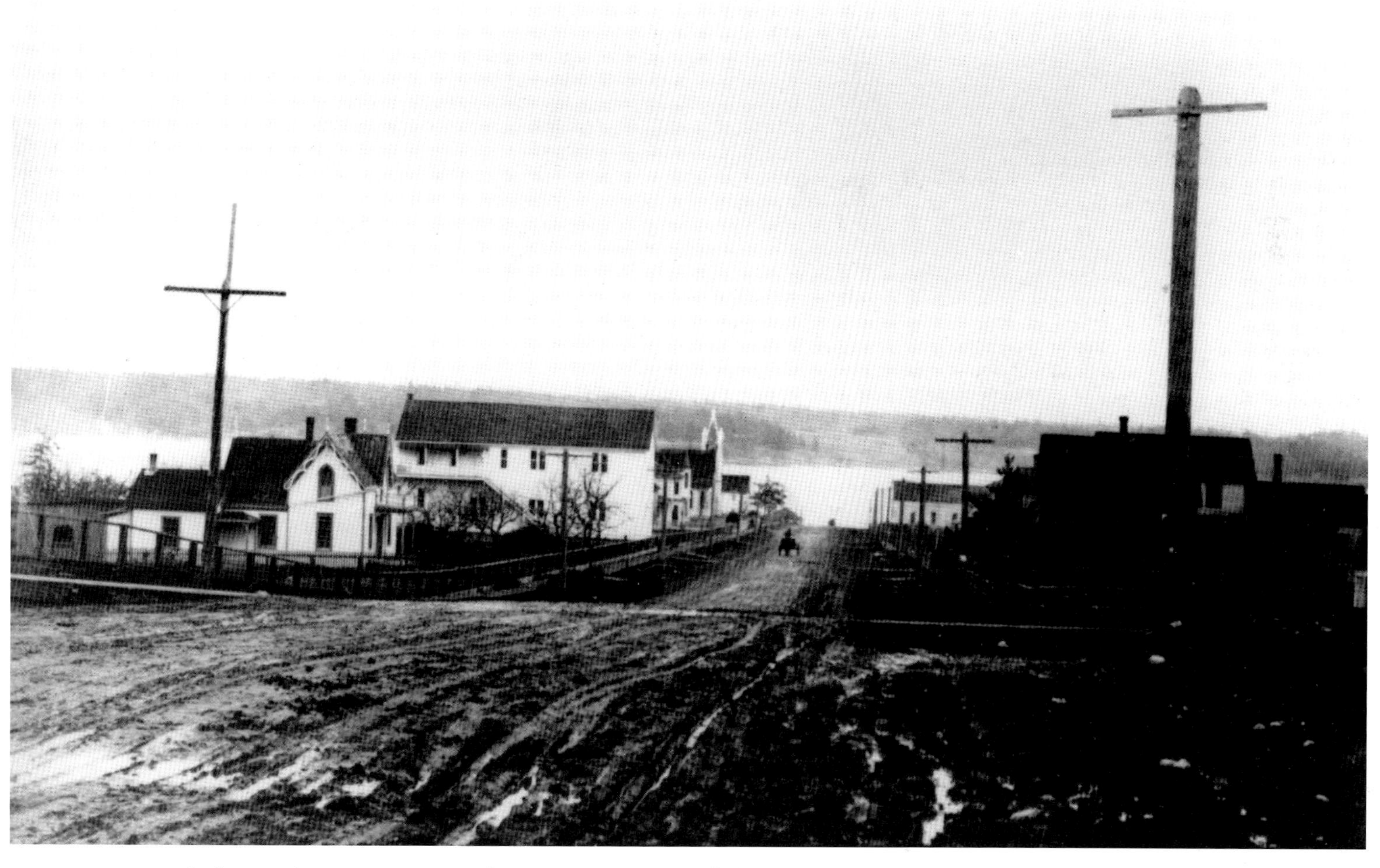

At first a retirement community for sea captains, Coupeville became the Island County seat in 1881 and incorporated as a town in 1910. In this view facing north, the camera captures mud streets and Penn Cove.

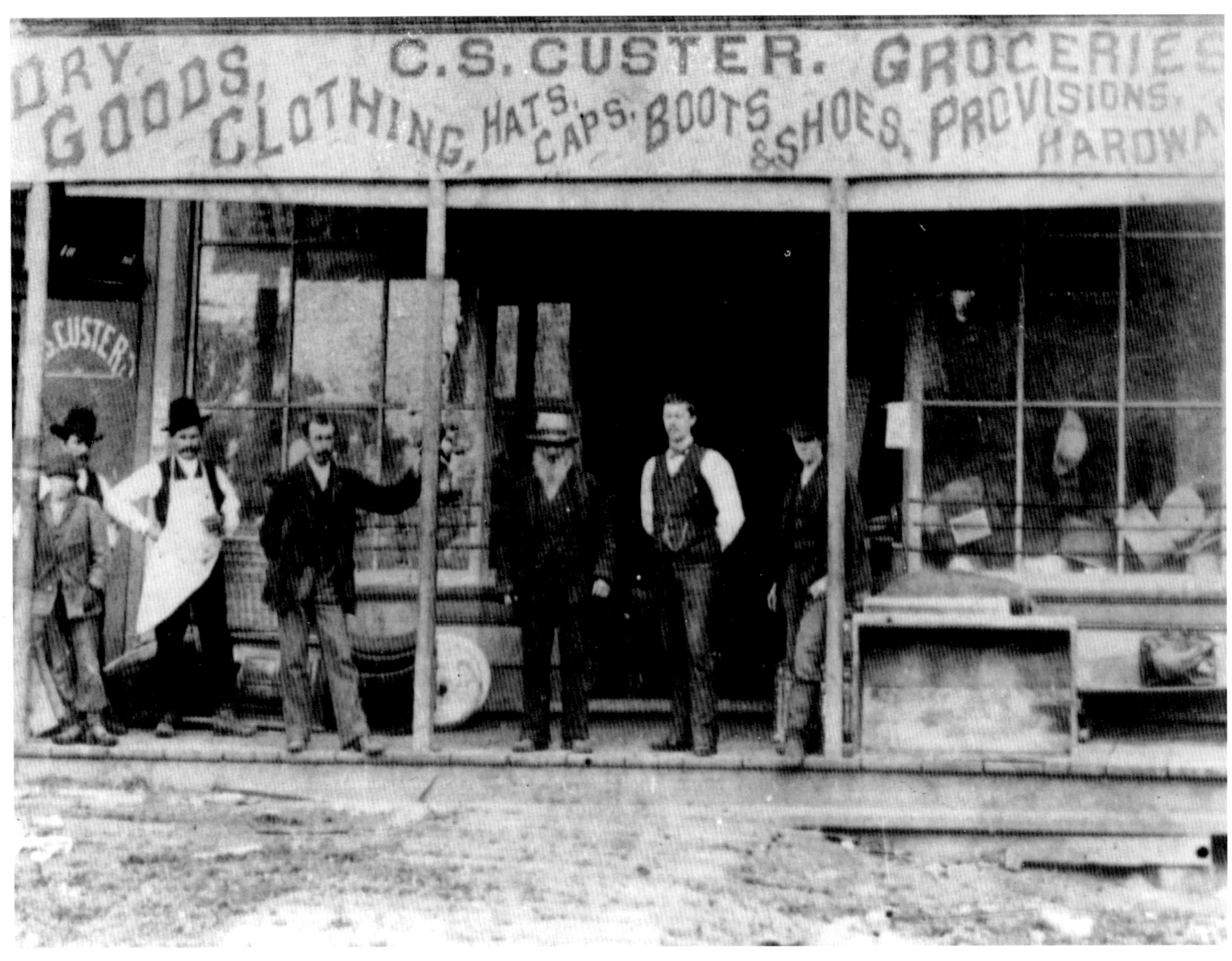

Discovery of coal in 1873 near Lake Washington's south end spurred the development of Renton. Within two years, coal shipments out of Seattle exceeded that of lumber. In this 1892 view, C. S. Custer poses in front of his general store, one of the first stores in Renton.

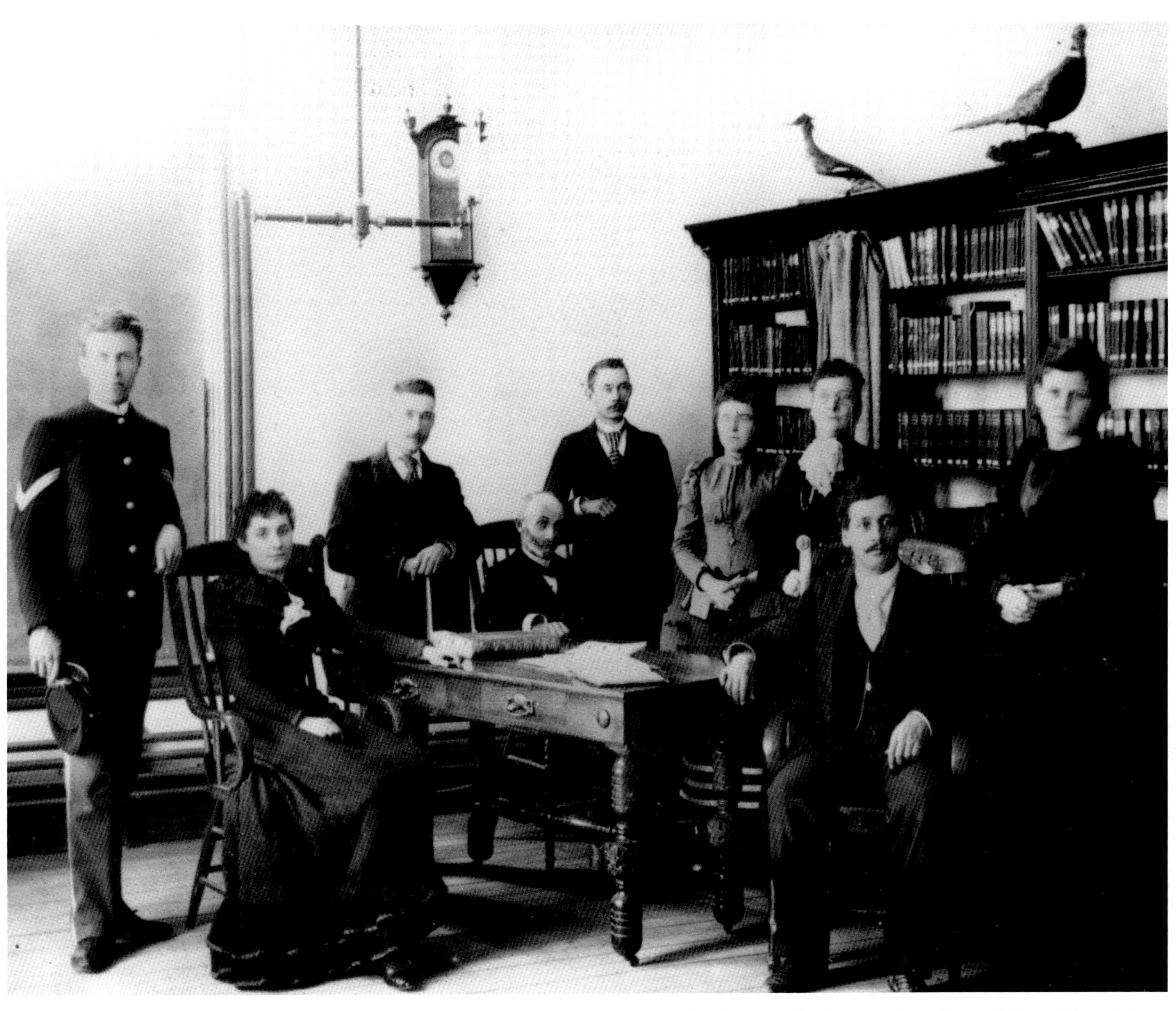

In 1892, Vashon College opened on Vashon Island near Burton. The first-term faculty poses here. Pictured from right to left are Mrs. A. C. Jones, elocution; President A. C. Jones; Mrs. Anna Farrow, matron; Nora A. Gilmour, librarian; O. S. Van Olinda, stenographer; L. P. Venen, languages and higher math; D. E. Crandall, commercial; Cora Teatt, music; and W. H. P. Redinger, military tactics.

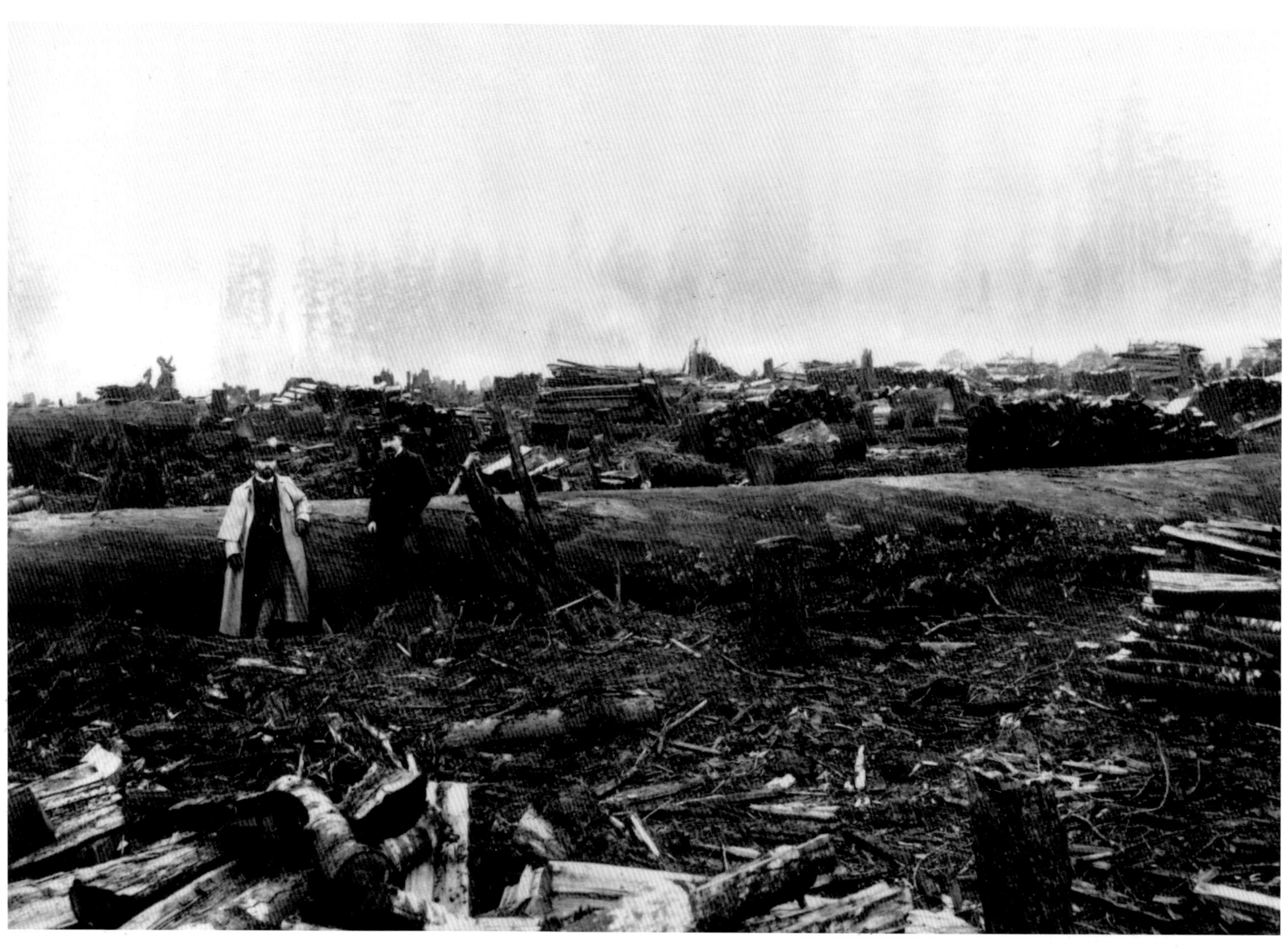

In 1890, the Great Northern Railway announced that its transcontinental line would touch Puget Sound at the peninsula between the mouth of the Snohomish River and Port Gardiner Bay. Speculators arrived with plans to build a great industrial center. Within a year a nail factory, barge works, smelter, and paper mill rose, and the town became Everett. In this 1892 view on Pine Street, cleared lots remain jammed with logging slash.

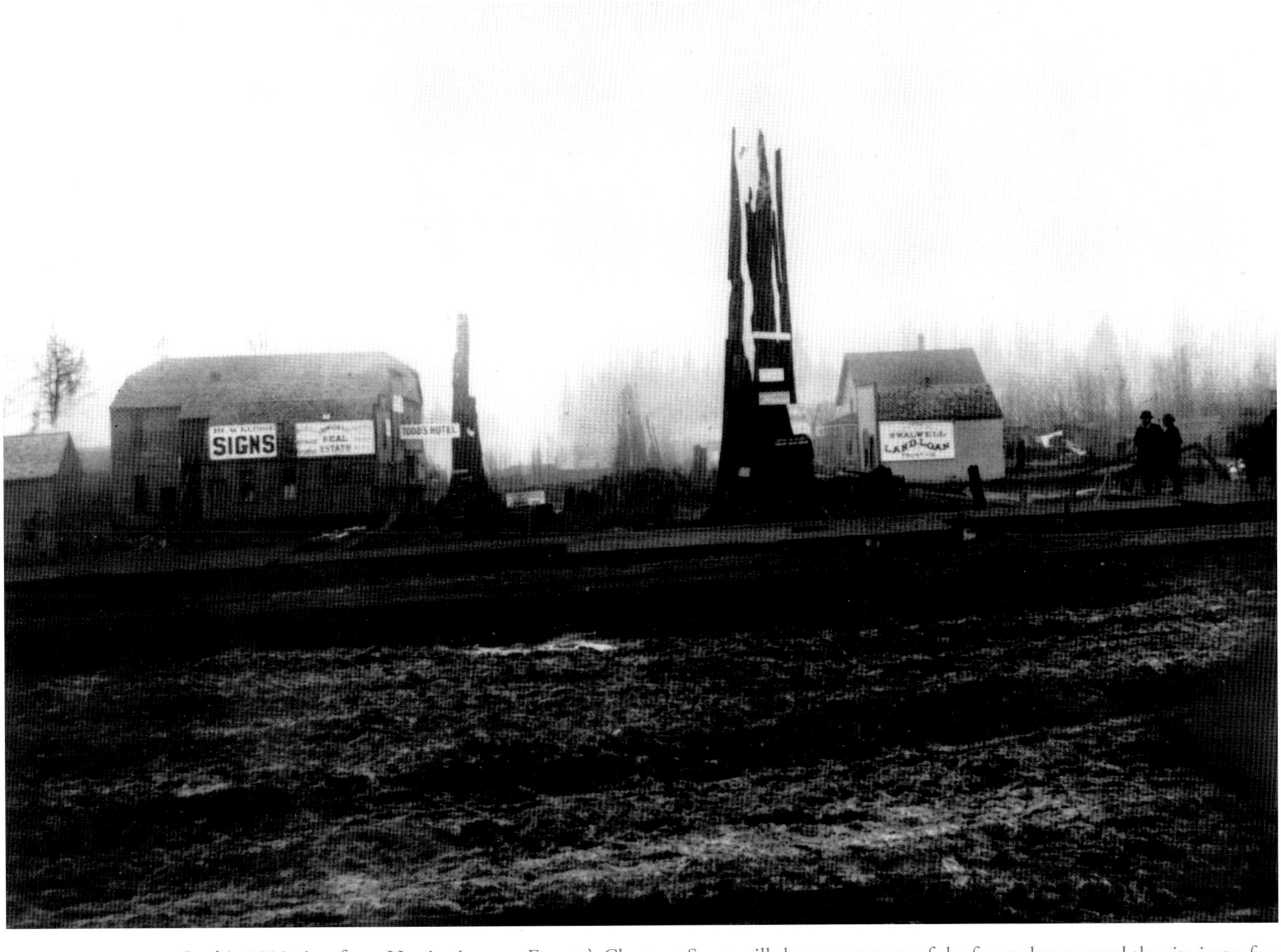

In this 1892 view from Hewitt Avenue, Everett's Chestnut Street still shows remnants of the forest that covered the site just a few years before. Impatient developers cleared enough land to allow them to build, and they allowed buyers to attend to stumps later. The size of the stump next to a building shows the scale of trees that once grew there.

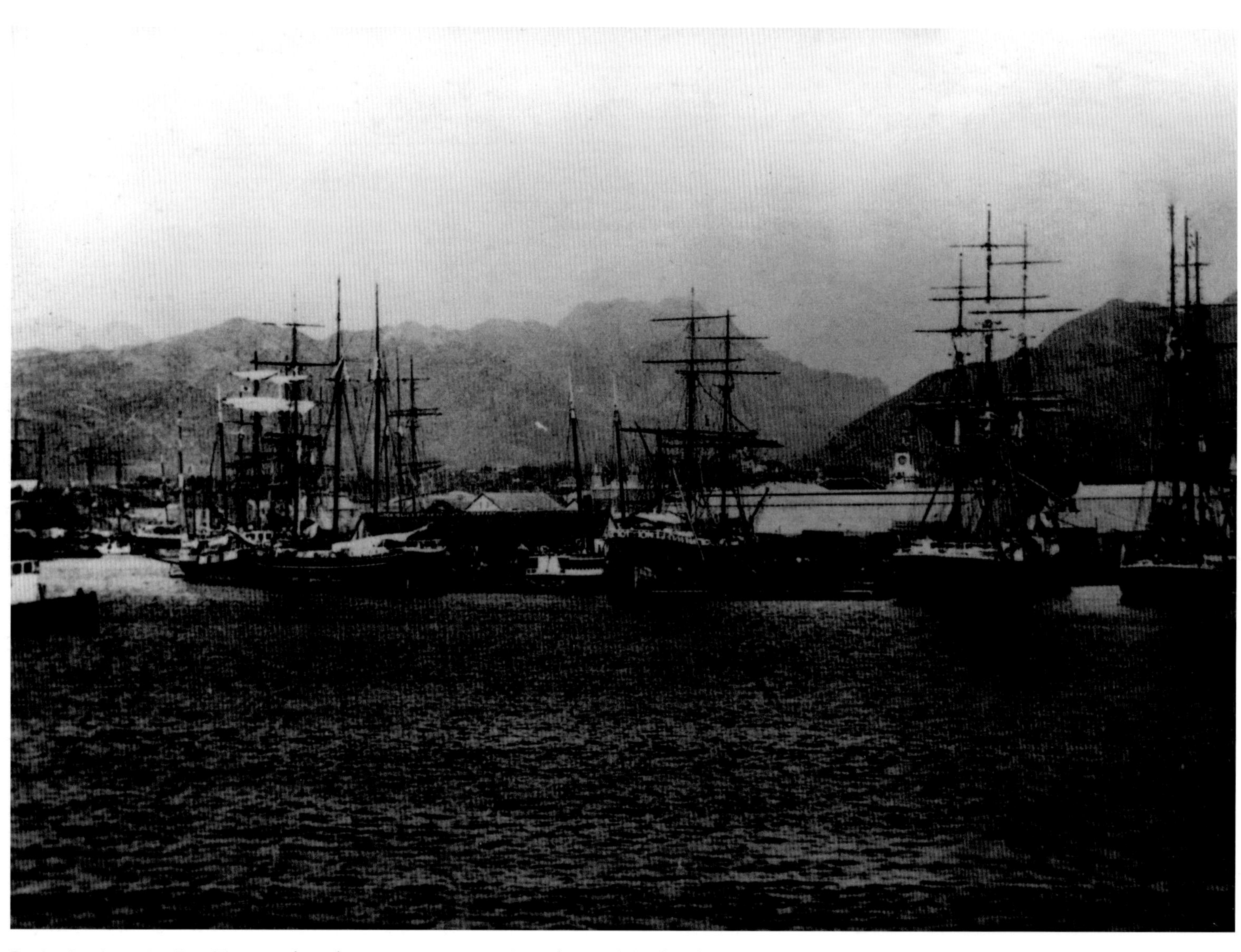

Beginning in 1853, Port Townsend, at the entrance to Puget Sound, served (with a three-year break in the 1860s) as the U.S. Customs Port of Entry where arriving vessels paid duty on imported goods. Here sailing ships, including the schooner *S. N. Castle* at far right, visit the port in 1893.

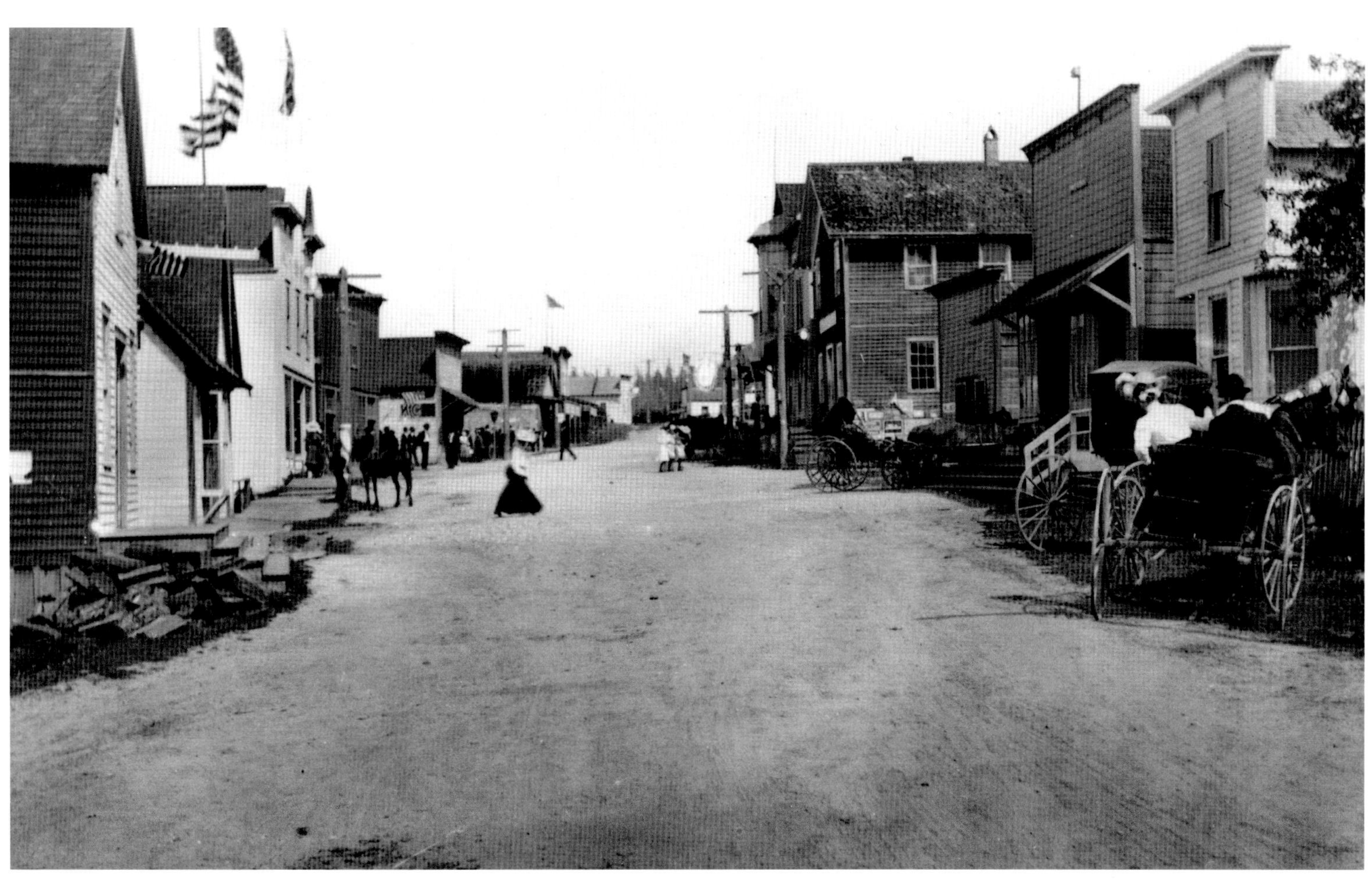

Before automobiles, Vashon Islander Oliver S. Van Olinda snapped this shot of Coupeville looking east during the summer (ca. 1890s). In addition to being the county seat, Coupeville served as a port on Penn Cove that provided access by Mosquito Fleet steamer for farm goods, supplies, and passengers to the rest of Puget Sound.

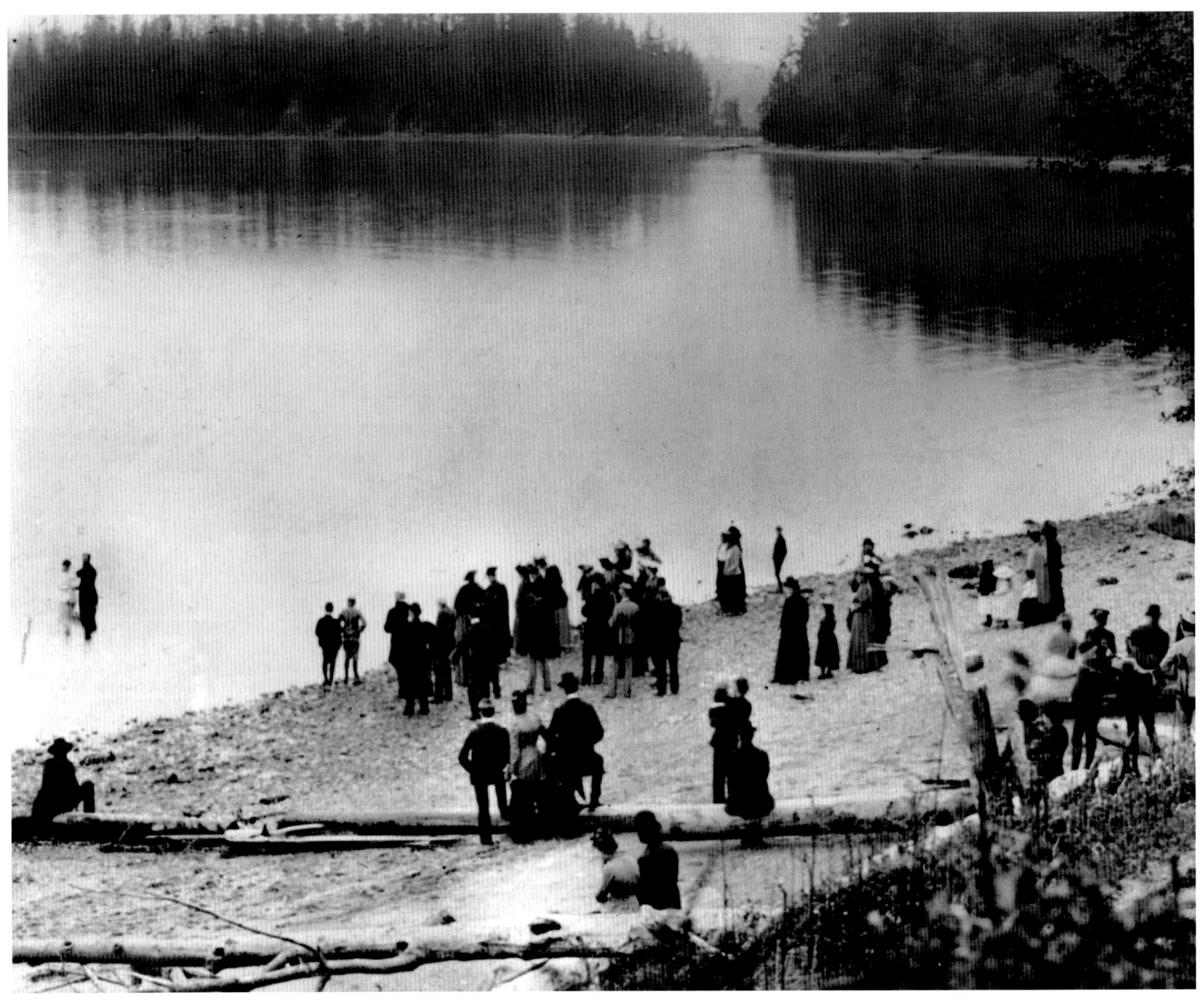

In 1888, the Puget Sound Chautauqua brought the Chautauqua movement—presentations of lectures, discussions, and cultural activities spread over several days—to Tramp Harbor on Vashon Island, where guests arrived by steamer from Seattle. The site grew to 600 acres and included a 1200-seat pavilion. Theodore Roosevelt called Chautauqua "the most American thing in America." Here a church group uses the Chautauqua site to baptize Ella Miner.

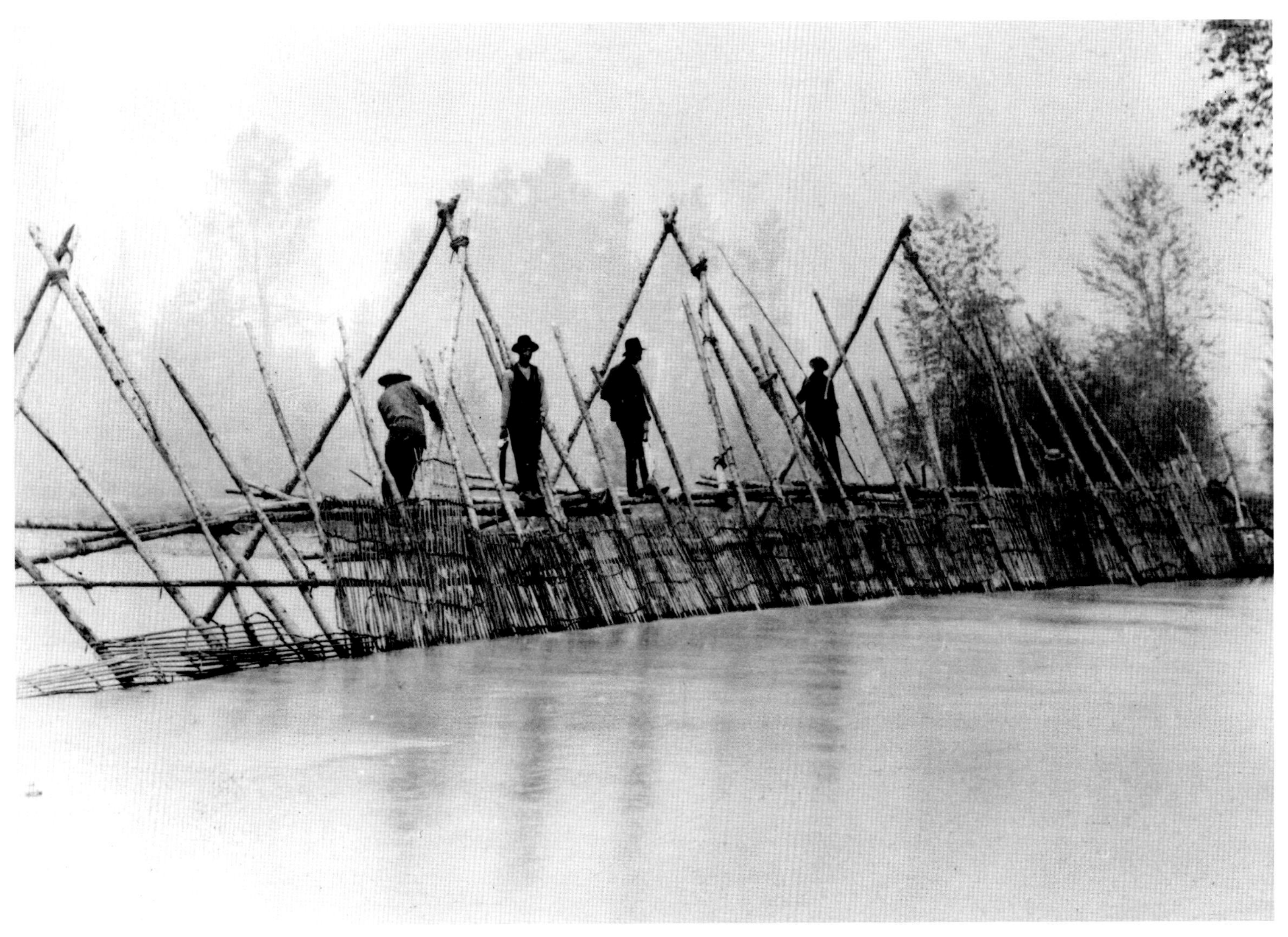

Native Americans of Puget Sound built fishing weirs such as this to catch the salmon that sustained them throughout most of the year. The woven latticework funneled fish to where they could be netted or speared. These men, probably Puyallups in Pierce County, prepare to haul in their catch around 1893. The fish will go to canneries and the Puyallups' own tables.

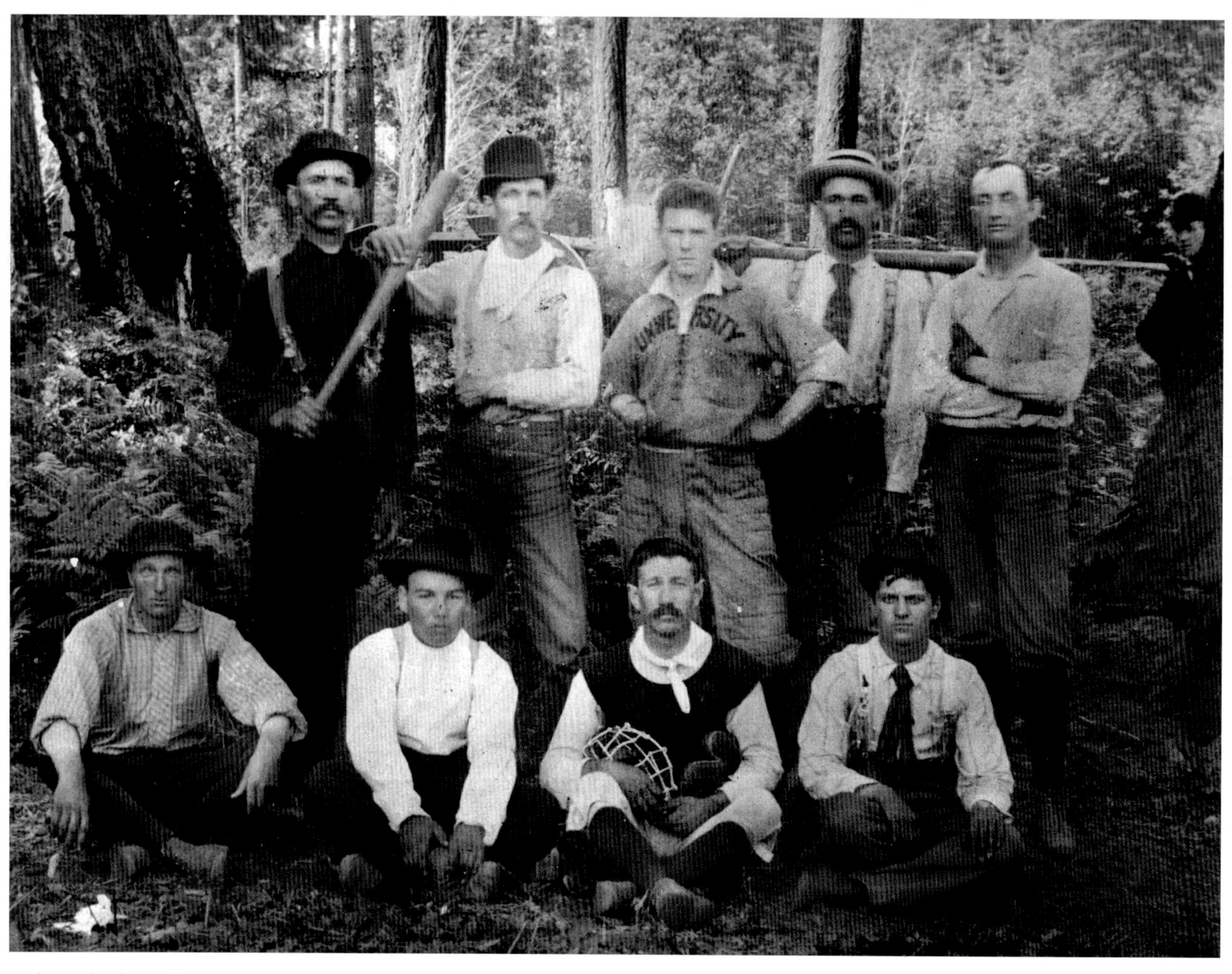

Vashon Islanders celebrated the Fourth of July in 1894 with a picnic and a baseball game. These players include a veteran of the University team.

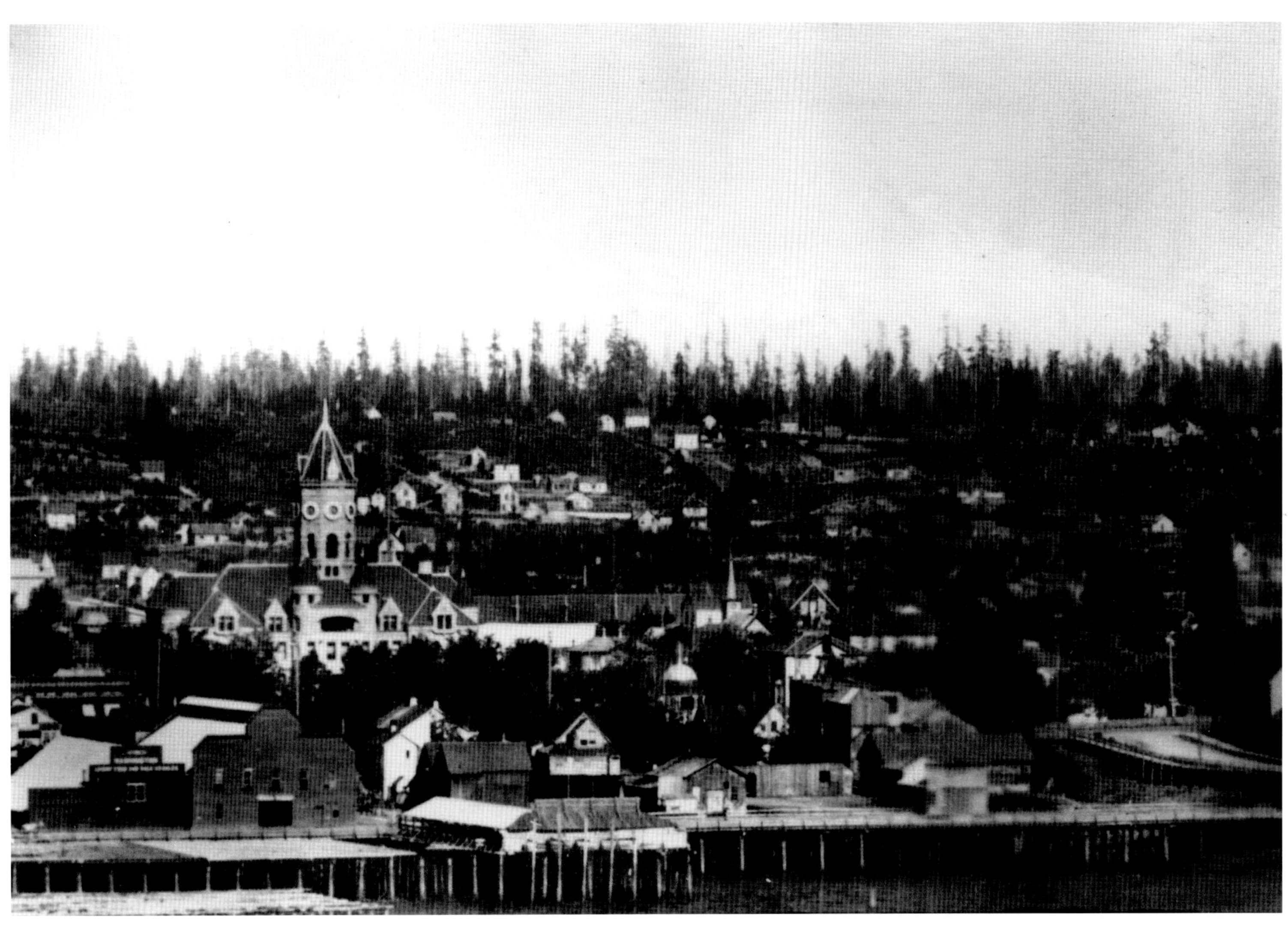

In 1850, settlers dedicated their town on Budd Inlet as Olympia. It first became the territorial capital in 1853 and then the state capital in 1889. In this 1894 view looking east, the old Thurston County Courthouse, later the State Capitol, stands left of center.

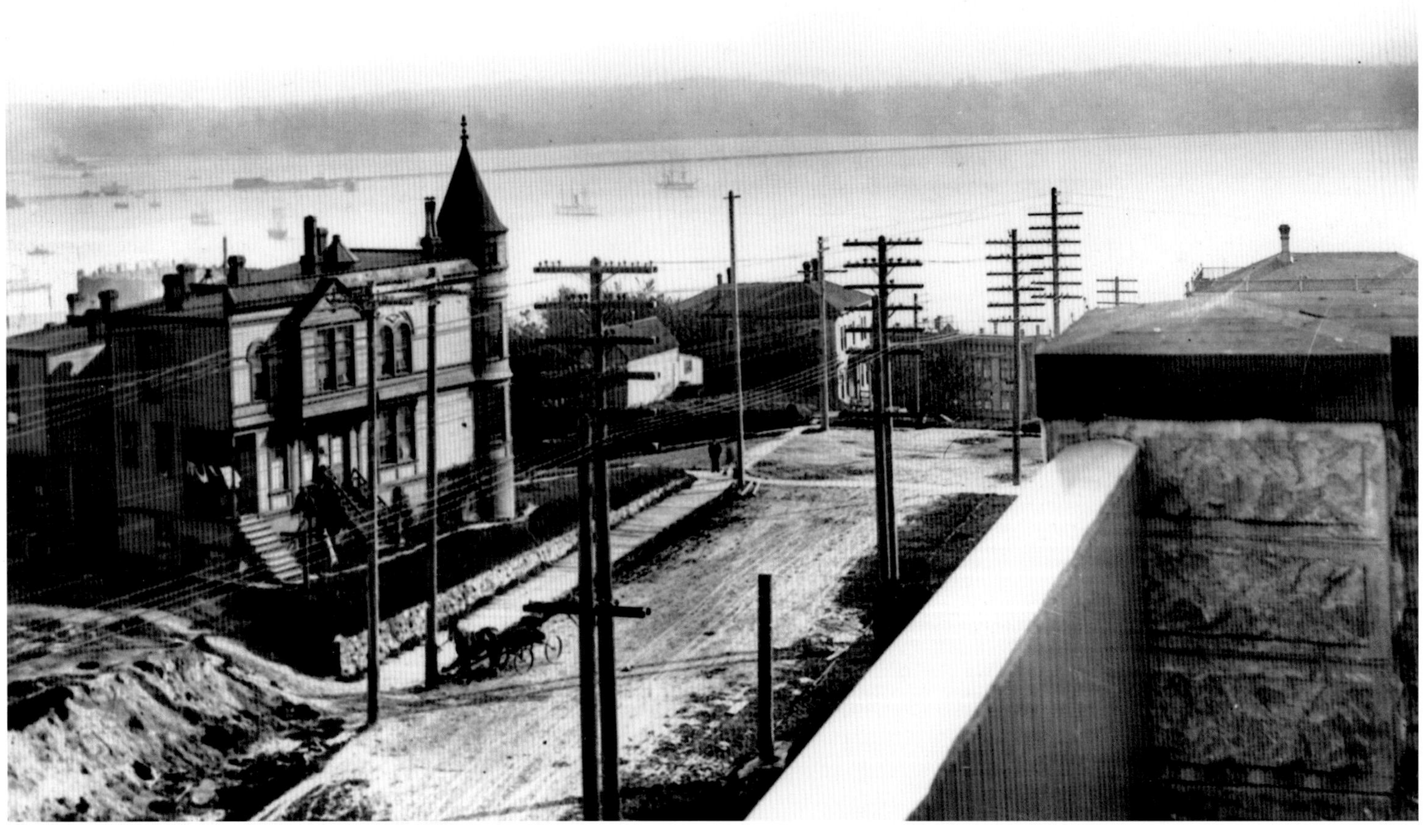

In the mid-1890s, Denny Hill, north of downtown Seattle, rose several hundred feet above Elliott Bay. West Seattle and the community of Youngstown lie across the bay. A railroad trestle stretches across the tide flats that will someday become Harbor Island. Engineers regraded Denny Hill in the early twentieth century, and it became the Belltown neighborhood.

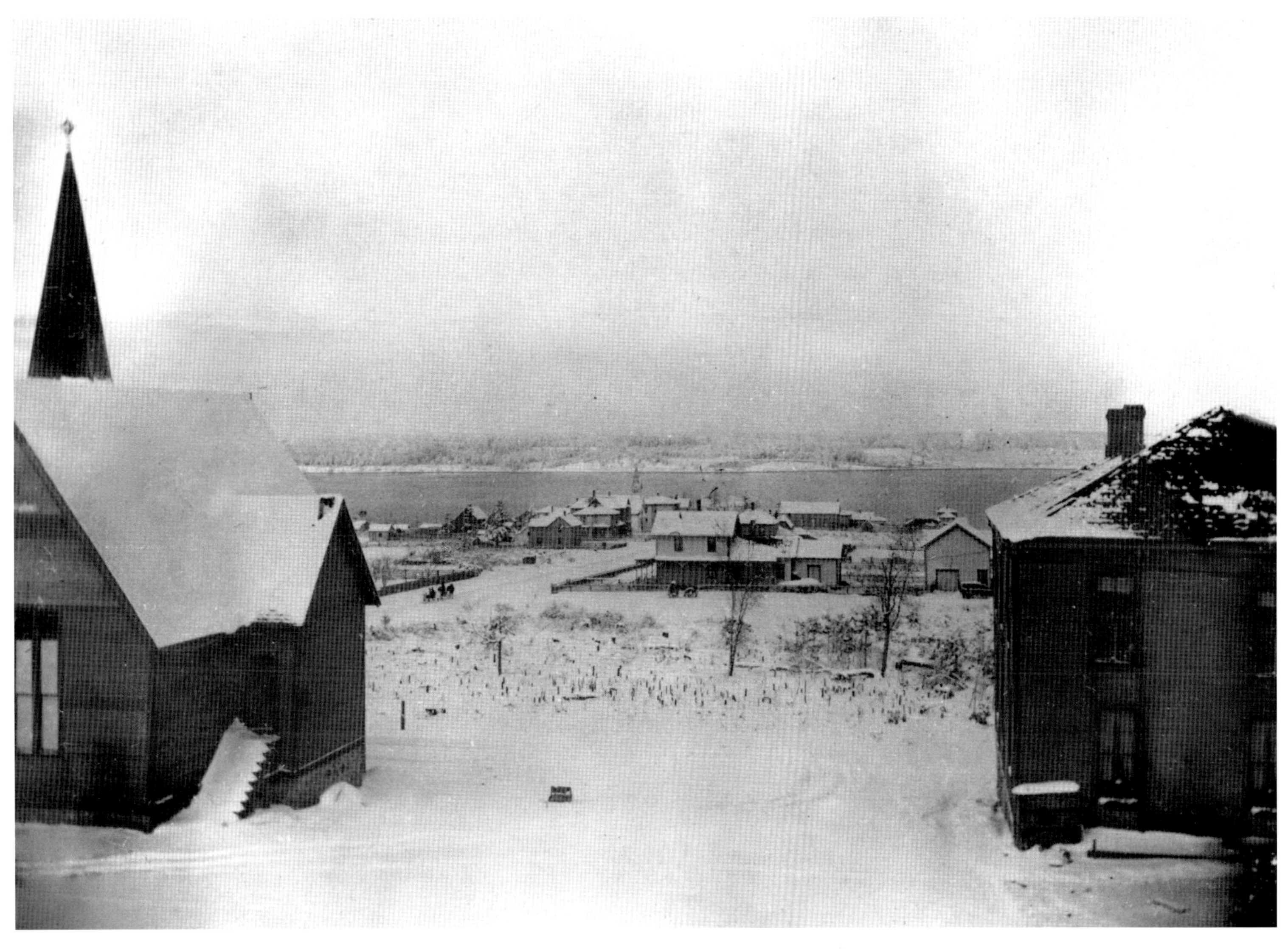

Few residents of Coupeville venture onto Main Street on this winter day around 1895. The snow on the roof and the stairs of the church at left suggest that this is not a Sunday.

Following Spread: Olympia's Fifth Avenue bustles with business in 1895—so much so that at least one pedestrian and horse-drawn wagon are but blurs in this image by A. D. Rogers. The utility poles indicate that the state capital already enjoys telephone service and perhaps some electricity.

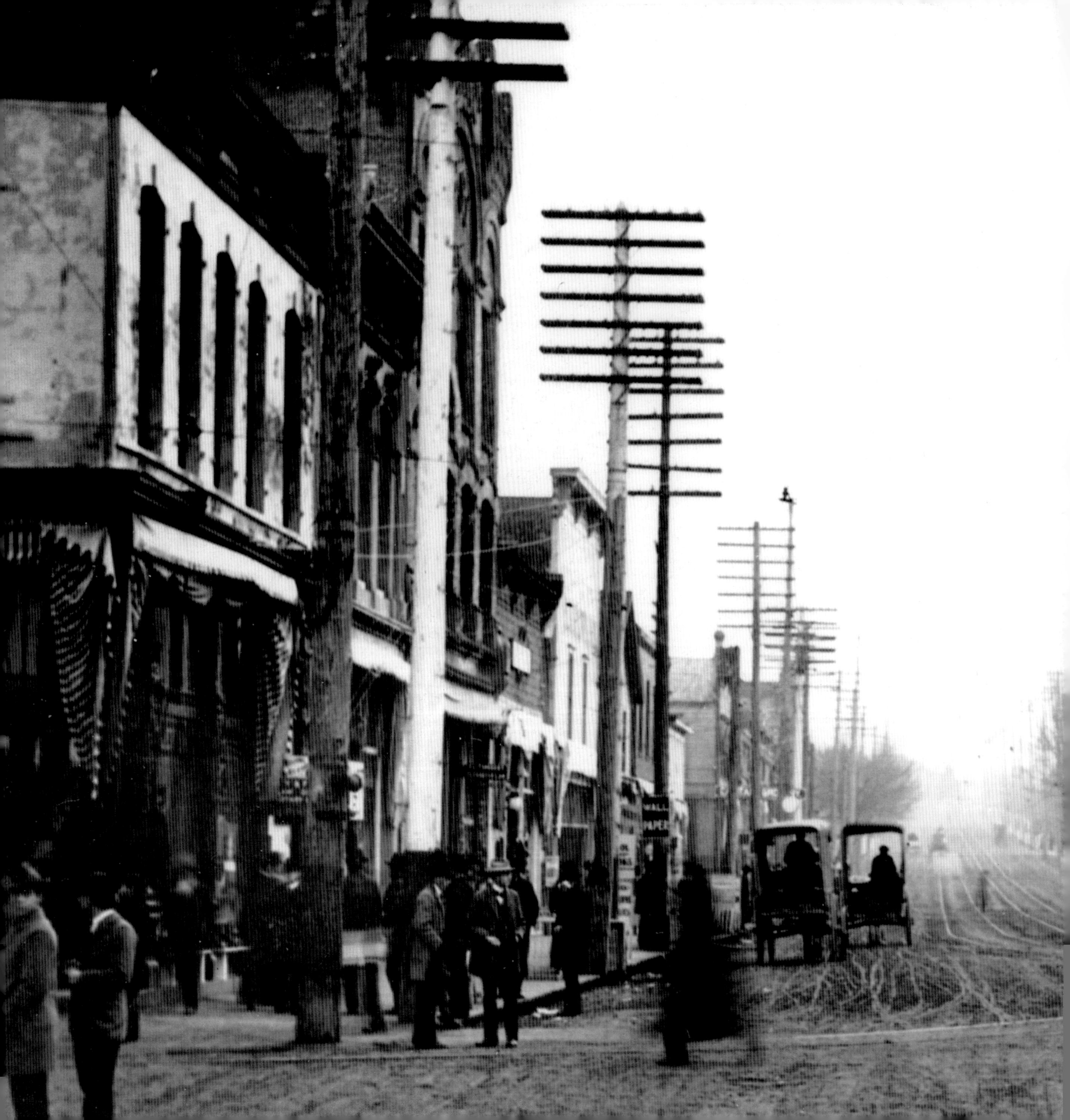

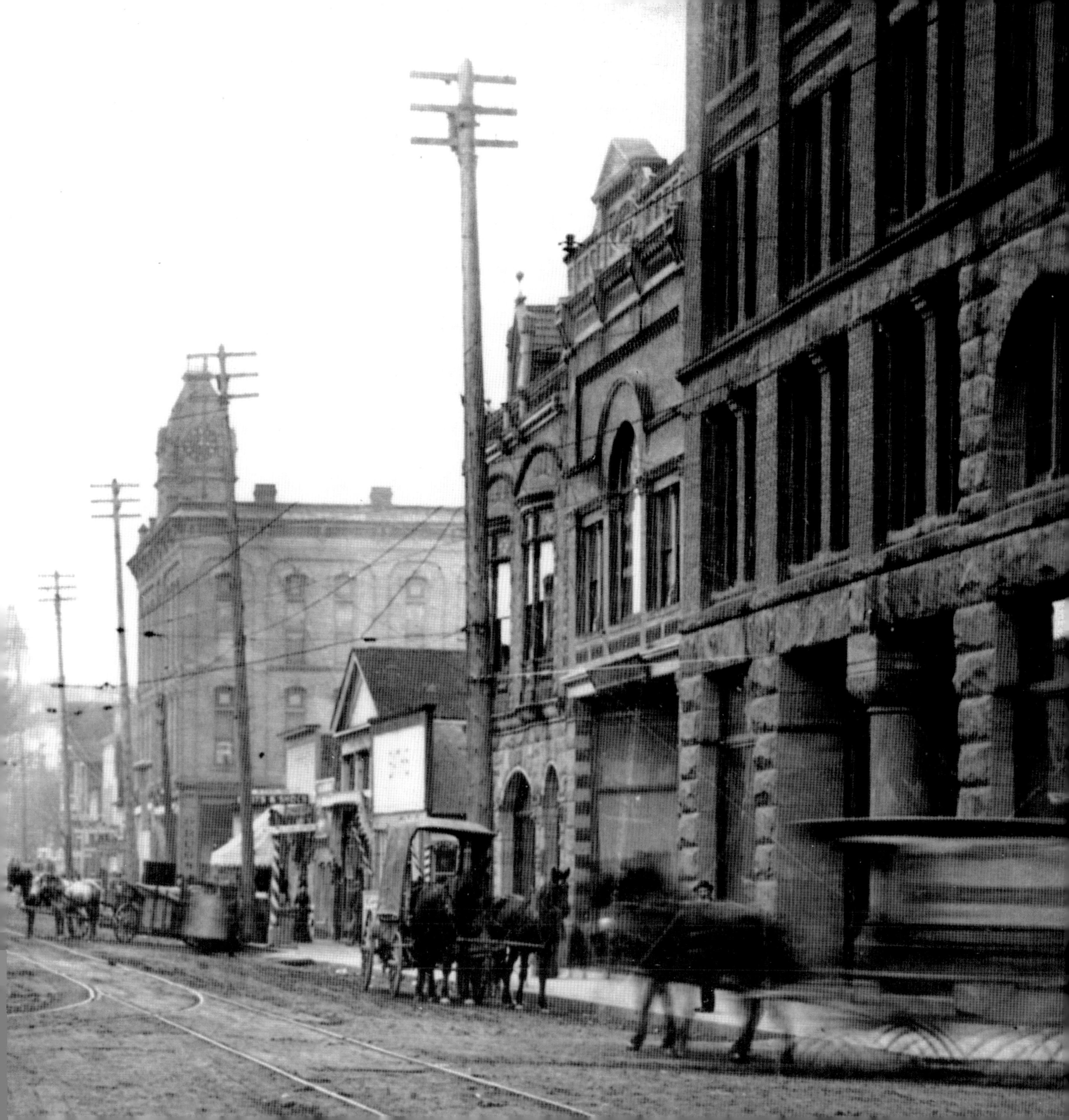

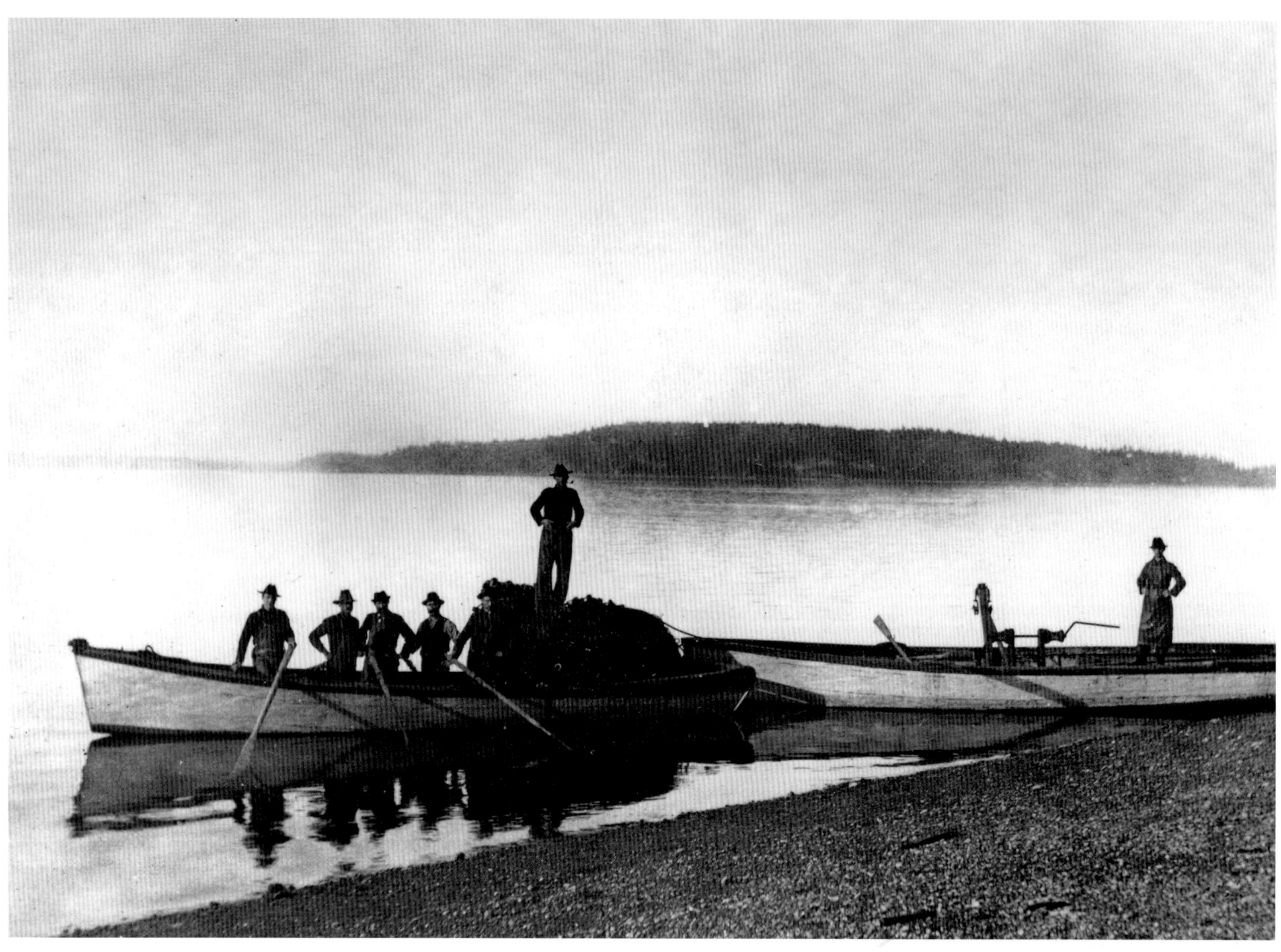

In the late nineteenth century, Norwegian John Salater moved to Lopez Island in the San Juans and became a commercial fisherman. Here he poses with his boats and crews at Iceberg Point on Lopez. In those years, Puget Sound teemed with sea life, and it did not take much in the way of investment for a man to earn a living from the sea.

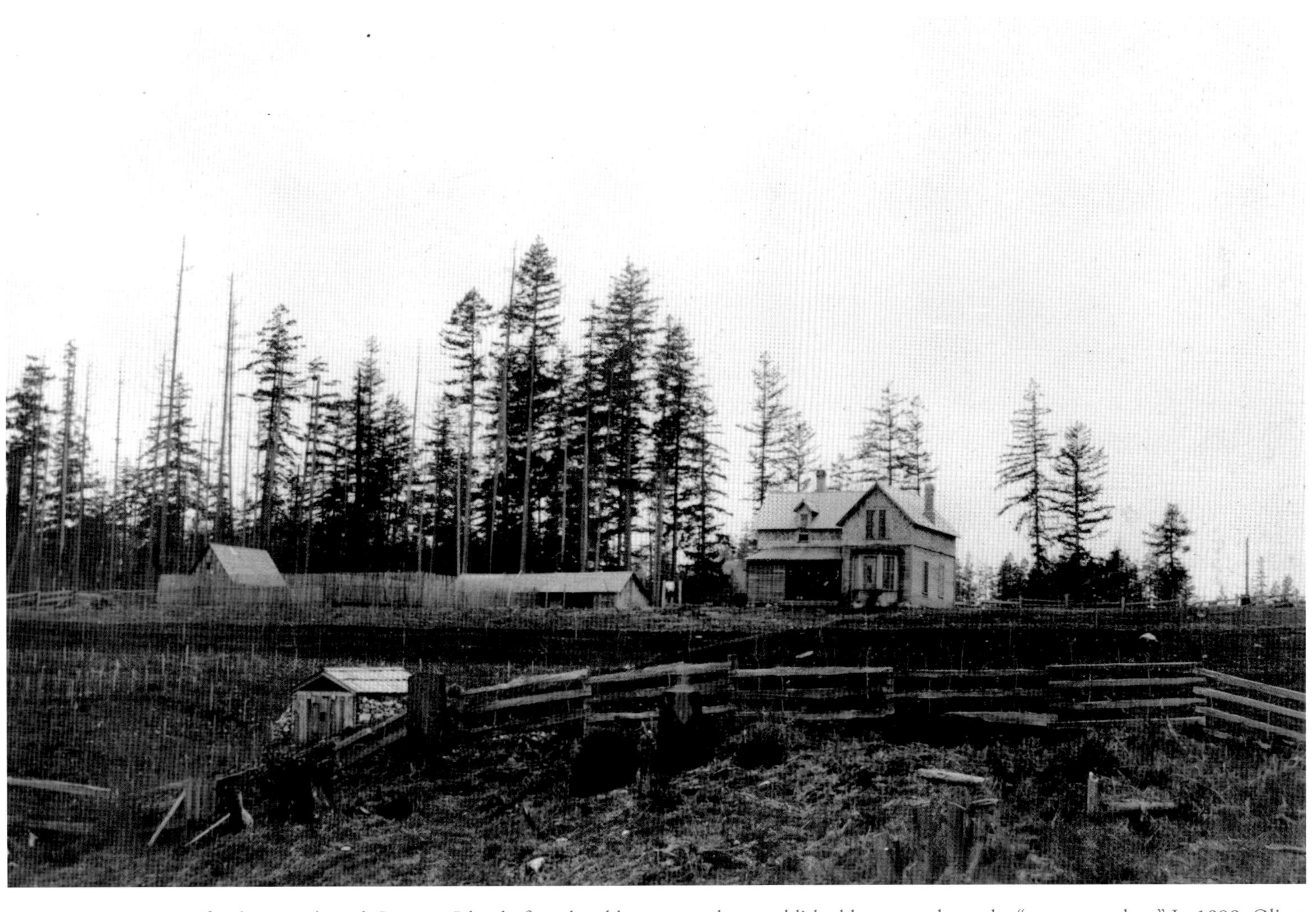

After loggers cleared Camano Island of marketable trees, settlers established homesteads on the "stump ranches." In 1898, Oliver S. Van Olinda visited the area and photographed this prosperous farm with a substantial home and outbuildings.

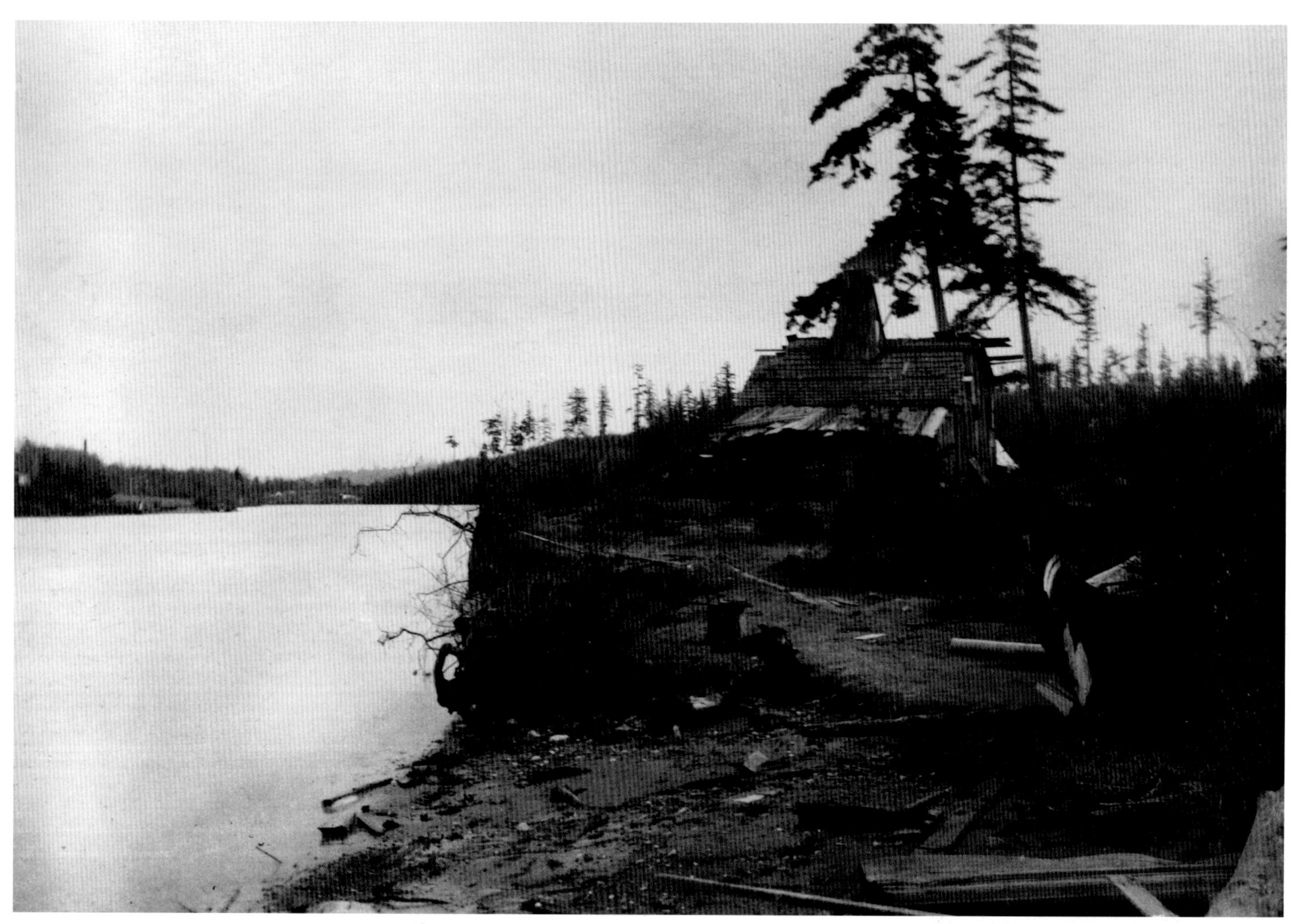

Even though Native Americans were officially removed to reservations following the treaties of 1855, many continued to live on unoccupied stretches of shoreline, where they pulled their livings from the water. Here in 1898, the home of Salmon Bay Charlie of the Duwamish Tribe sits on the Shilshole Bay shore. The high prow of his painted canoe indicates that the craft was designed to deal with the sometimes choppy conditions of the Sound.

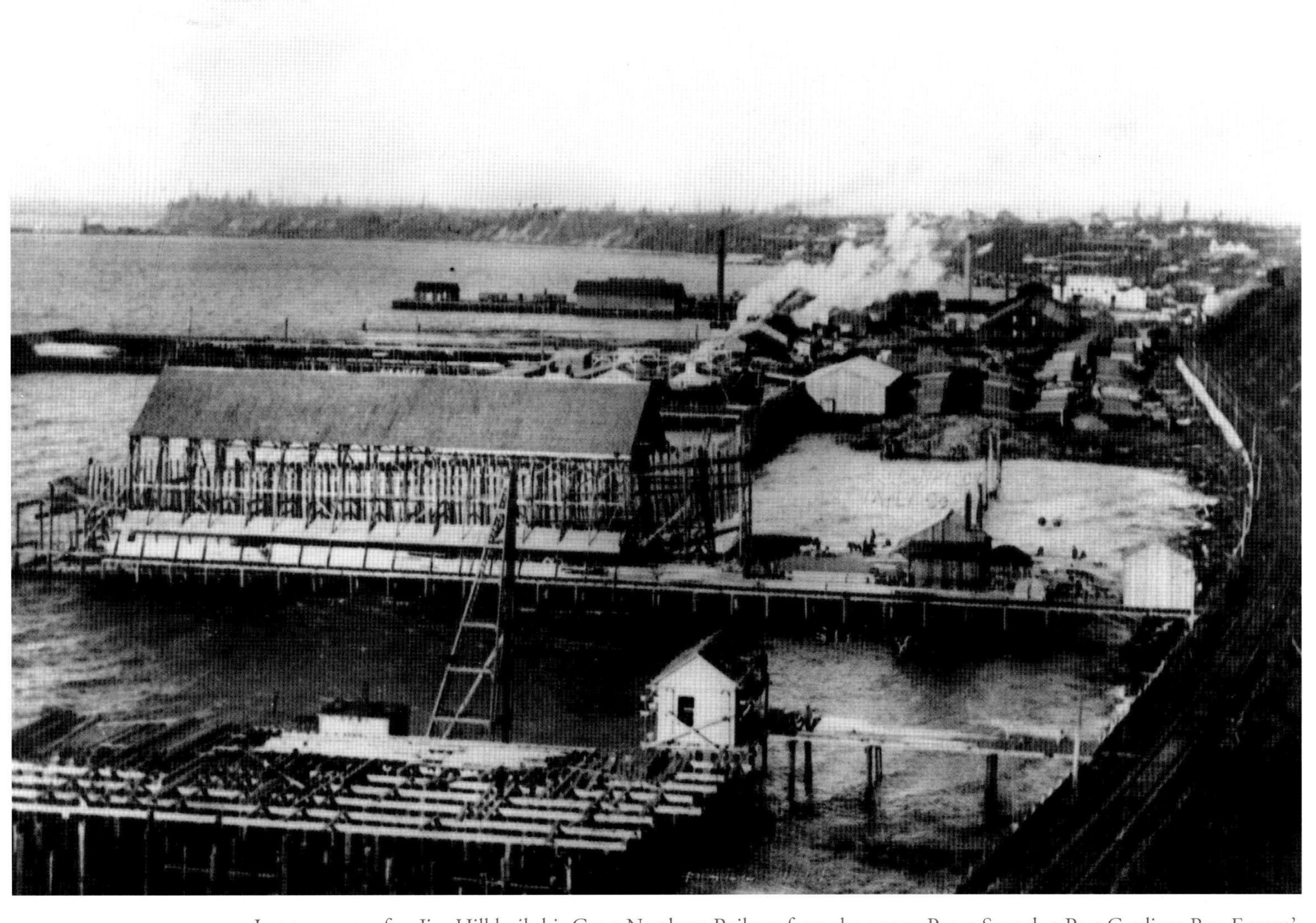

Just ten years after Jim Hill built his Great Northern Railway from the east to Puget Sound at Port Gardiner Bay, Everett's waterfront showed the impact of the intense industrialization of the era. This 1900 view facing north features the Bell-Nelson Mill Company, the Hall Lumber Company, and the tracks of the GN.

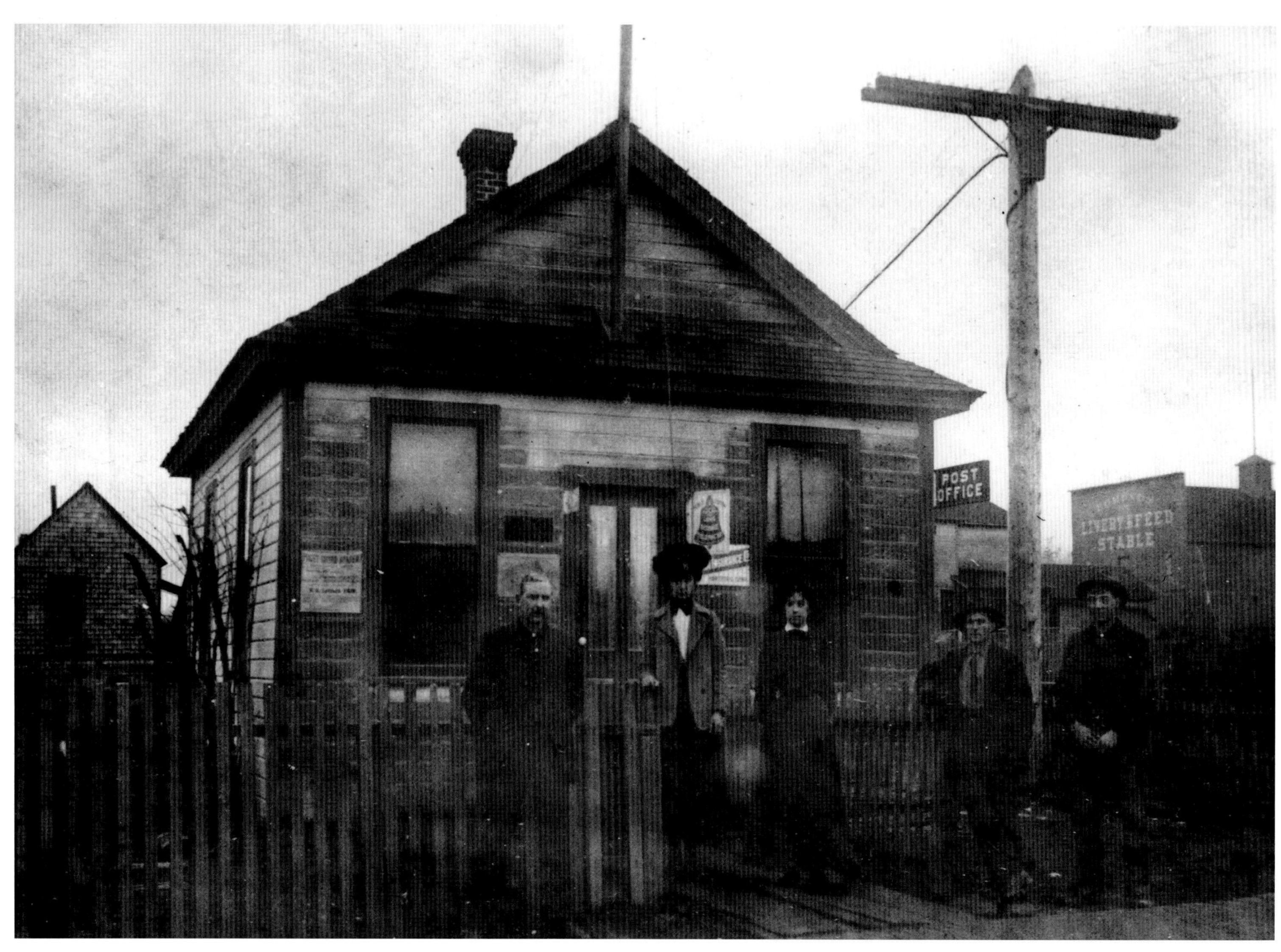

The height of technology came to Edmonds in 1900 in the form of telephone service. The telephone office also served as the post office, and vice versa. Ruth Hyner, the system's first operator, poses here in front of her office with other Edmonds residents.

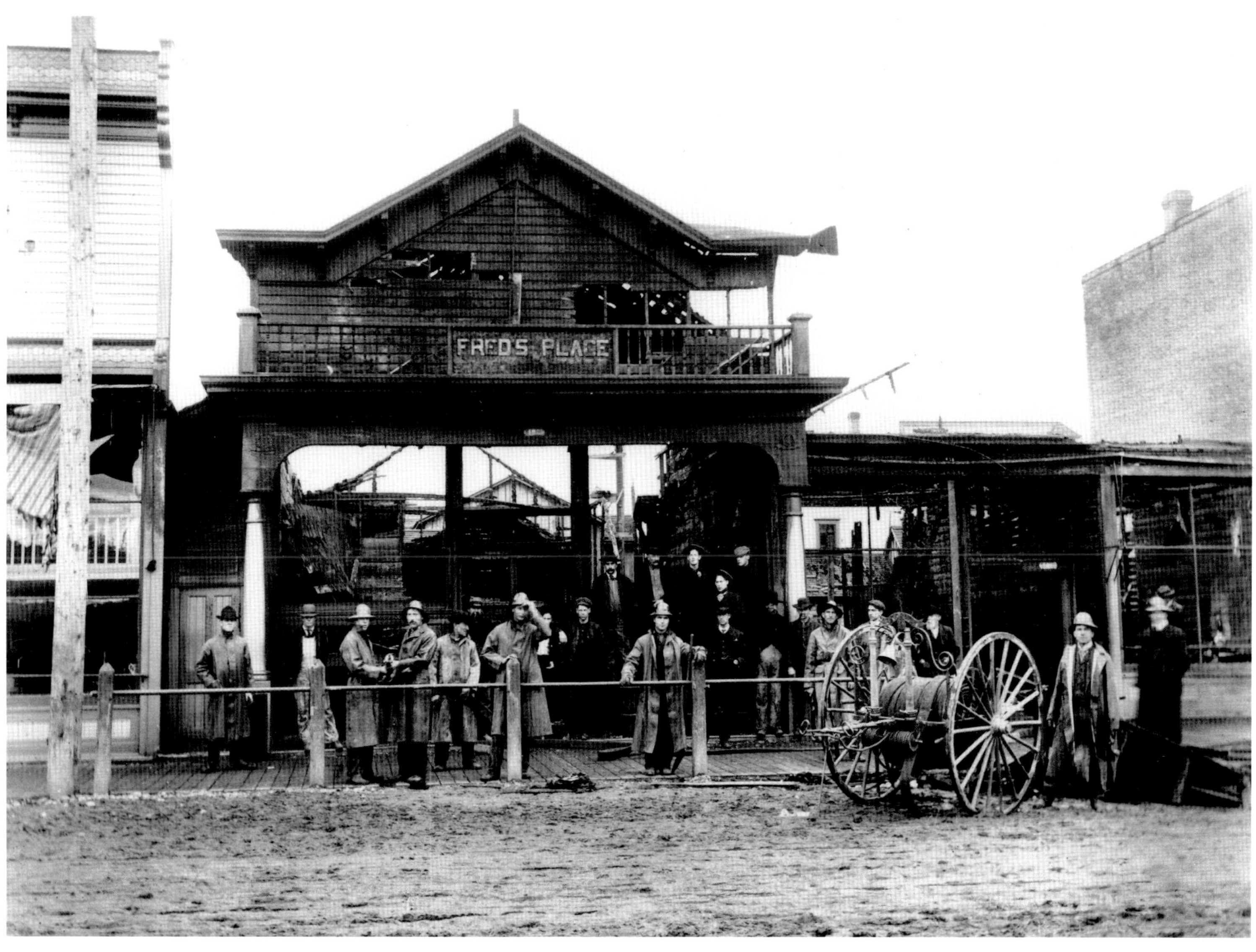

Around 1900, the Kent Fire Department battled a blaze at Fred's Place, a saloon on First Avenue. By the looks of the building, the simple pump and hose cart did not prevent the almost-total destruction of the building. Here the fire fighters pose the next day, one of them casually placing his hand on the railing where patrons tied their horses.

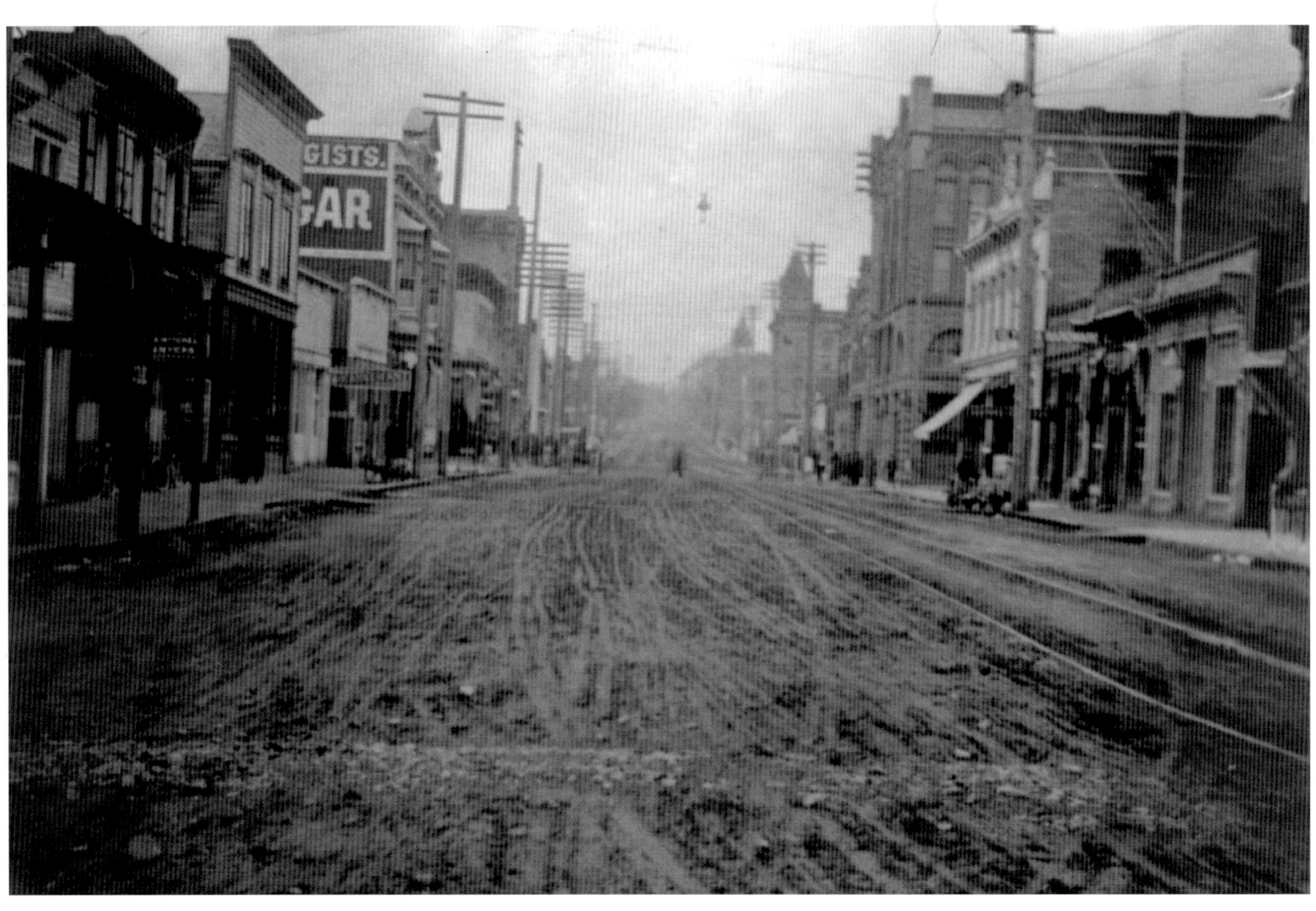

In 1901, a pedestrian walks down an otherwise empty and still unpaved Fifth Avenue in Olympia.

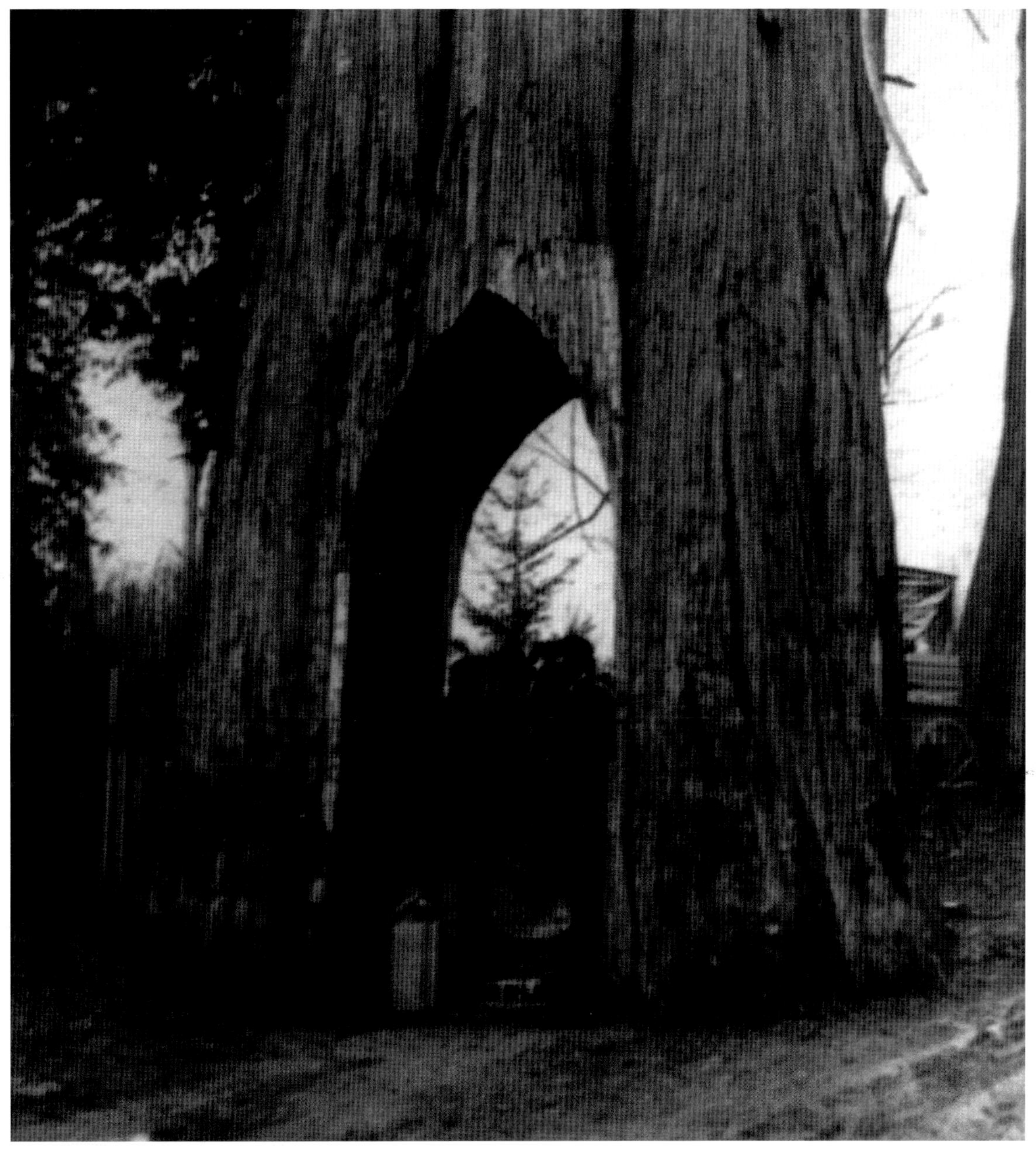

The heavy rains of the Pacific Northwest nurtured the great stands of timber that drew the first industrialists to Puget Sound. Trees grew to such a size that the largest challenged even the most enthusiastic loggers wielding axes and two-man crosscut saws. Instead of felling one great cedar, lumberjacks near Snohomish cut a hole through the trunk large enough for a horse-drawn wagon. This 1901 stereoscopic view amazed viewers in parlors all over the world.

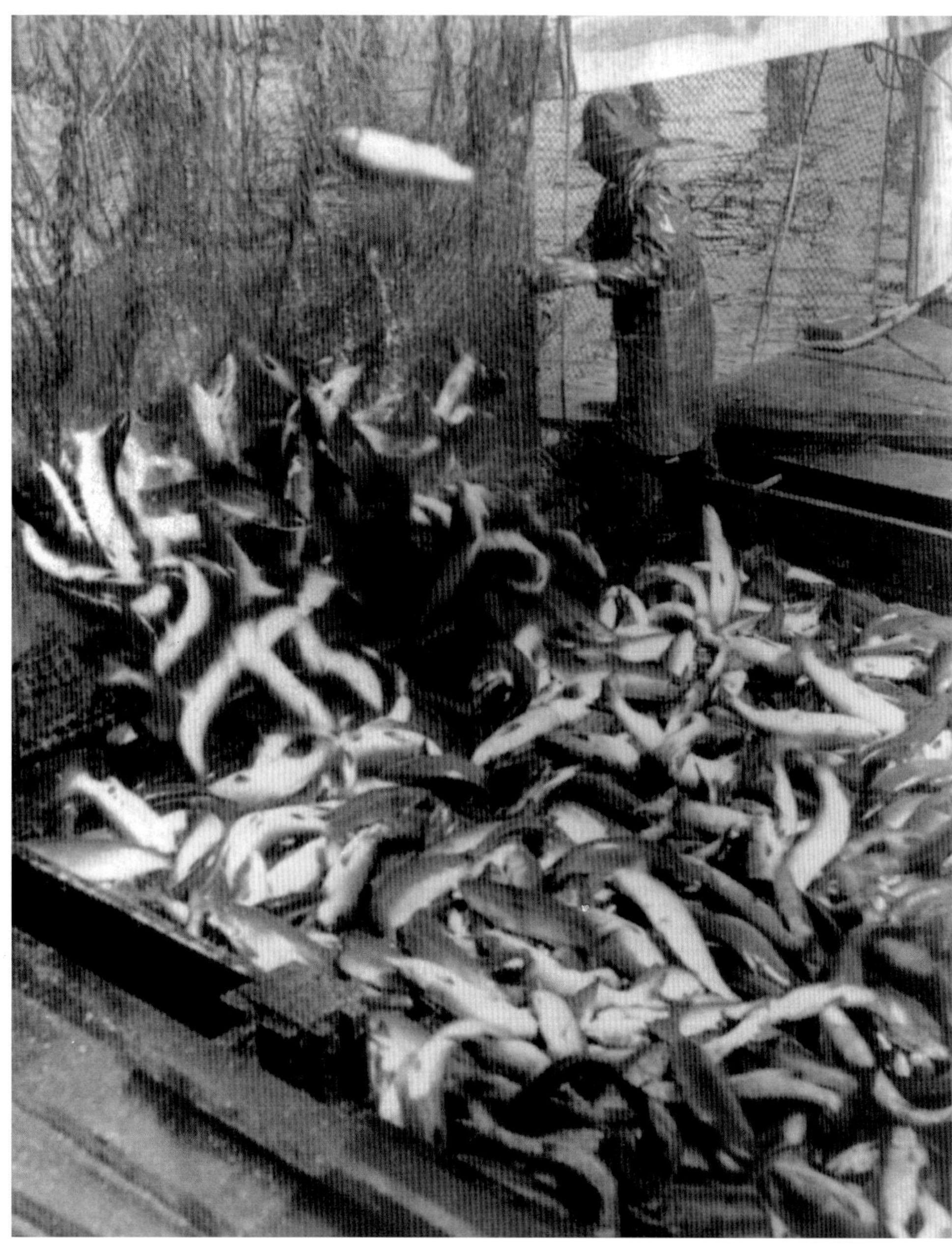

The commercial canning industry discovered the salmon runs of the Pacific Northwest in the 1860s. Canneries sprouted along the shores of Puget Sound, and thousands of fishermen set nets to catch hundreds of millions of fish for dinner plates around the world. The salmon were so plentiful that using a shore-based net such as this one in 1902 could be profitable.

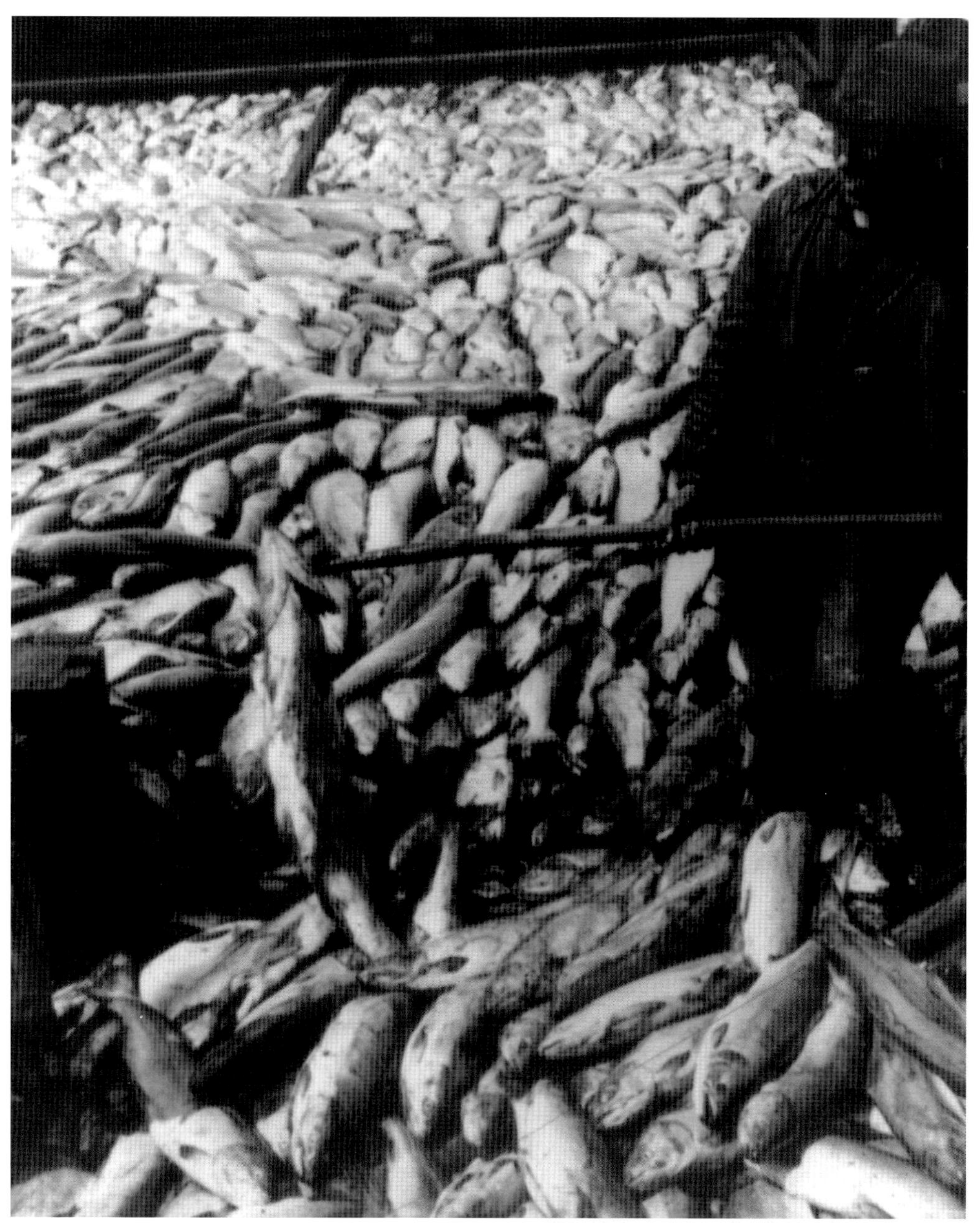

In 1902, a worker uses a pitchfork to load salmon at a Puget Sound cannery.

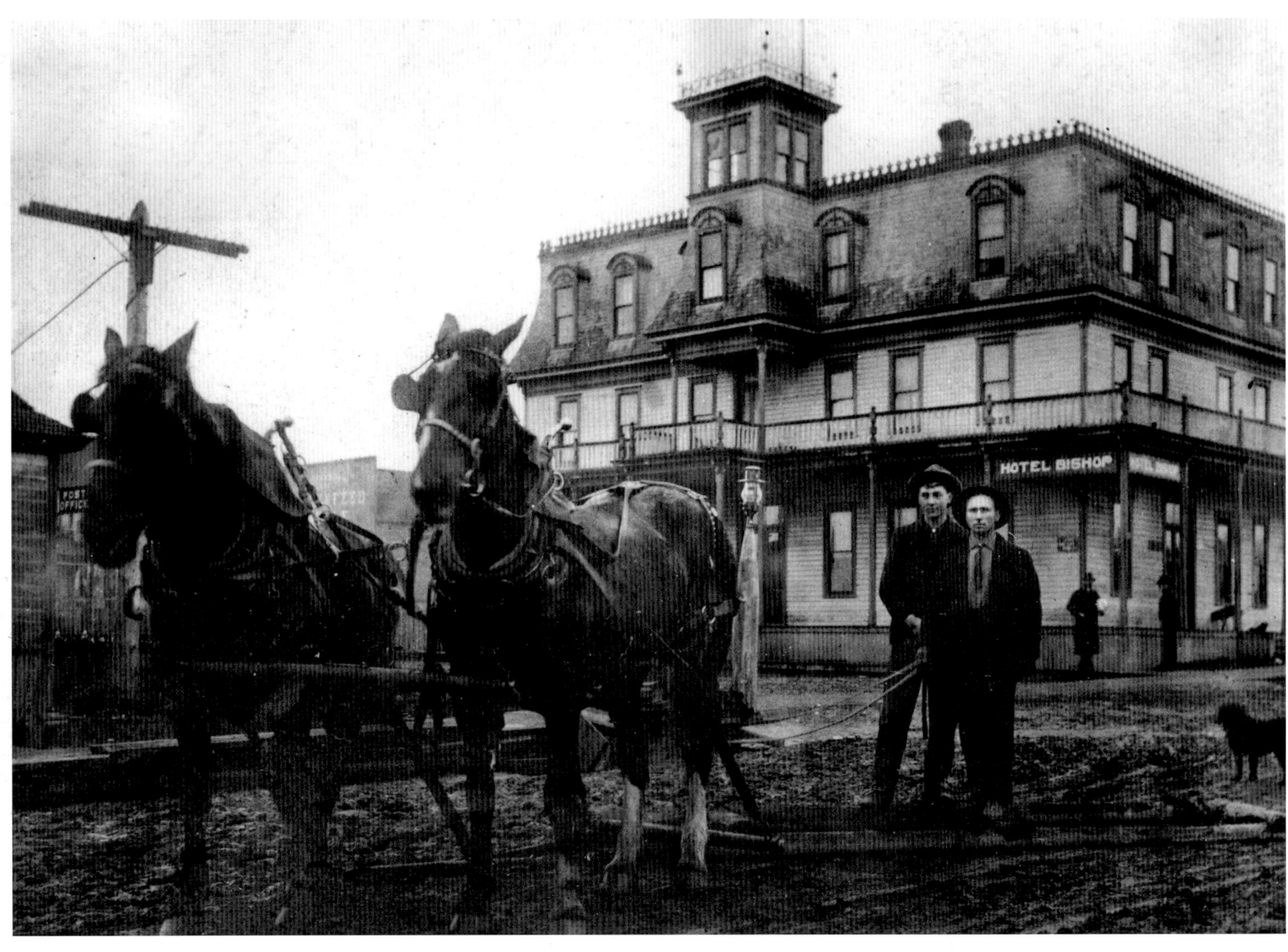

Around 1903, a horse-drawn team grades a street in Edmonds in front of the Hotel Bishop. A neighborhood dog keeps an eye on the job.

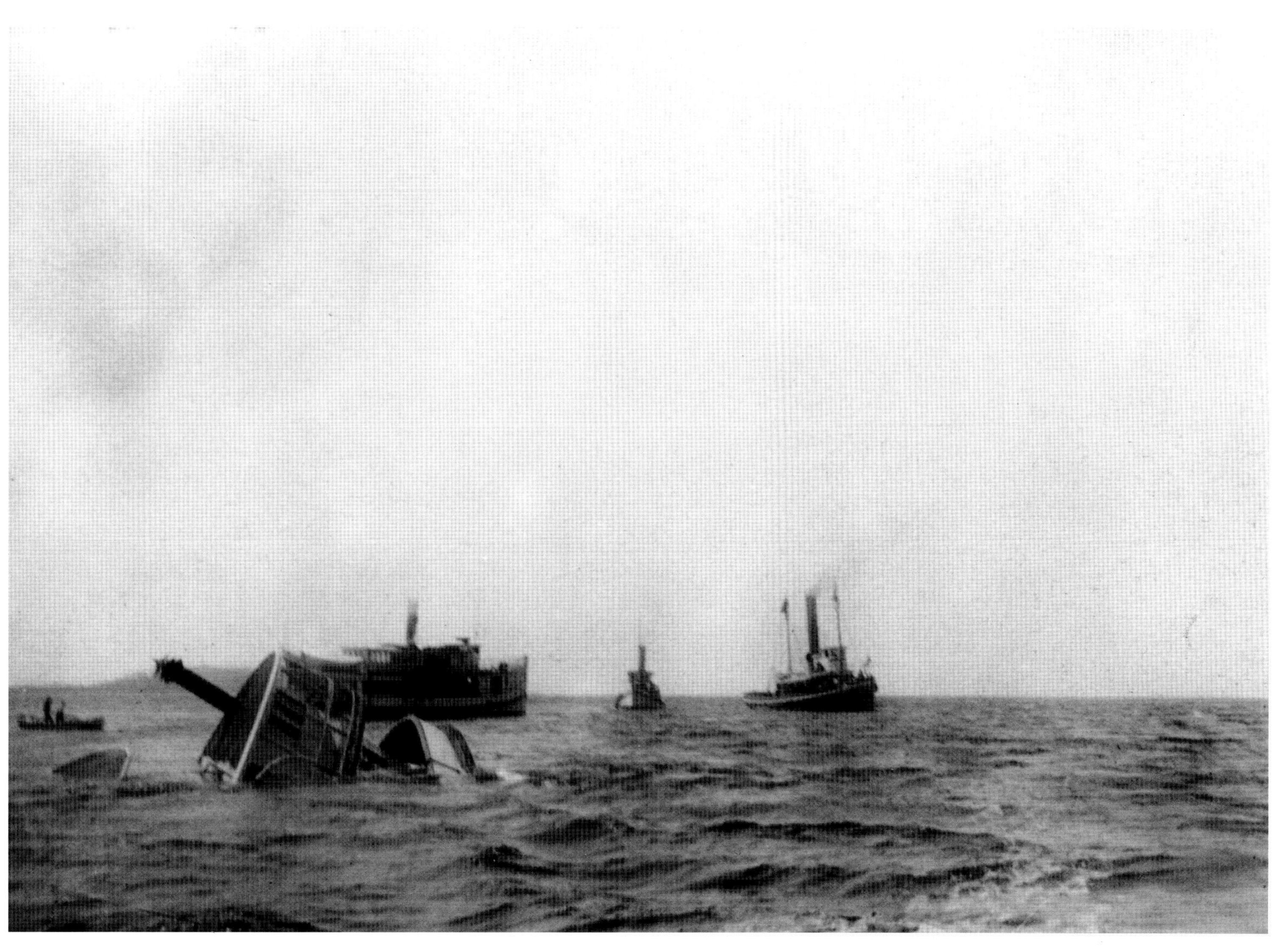

On July 18, 1903, the side-wheel steamer *North Pacific* encountered heavy fog, struck the rocks off Marrowstone Point near Port Townsend, and holed her hull. The *North Pacific* carried passengers between Tacoma and Vancouver, British Columbia. After the tug *C. B. Smith* removed the passengers, the *North Pacific* drifted off the rocks and is seen sinking here in the deep water of Admiralty Inlet.

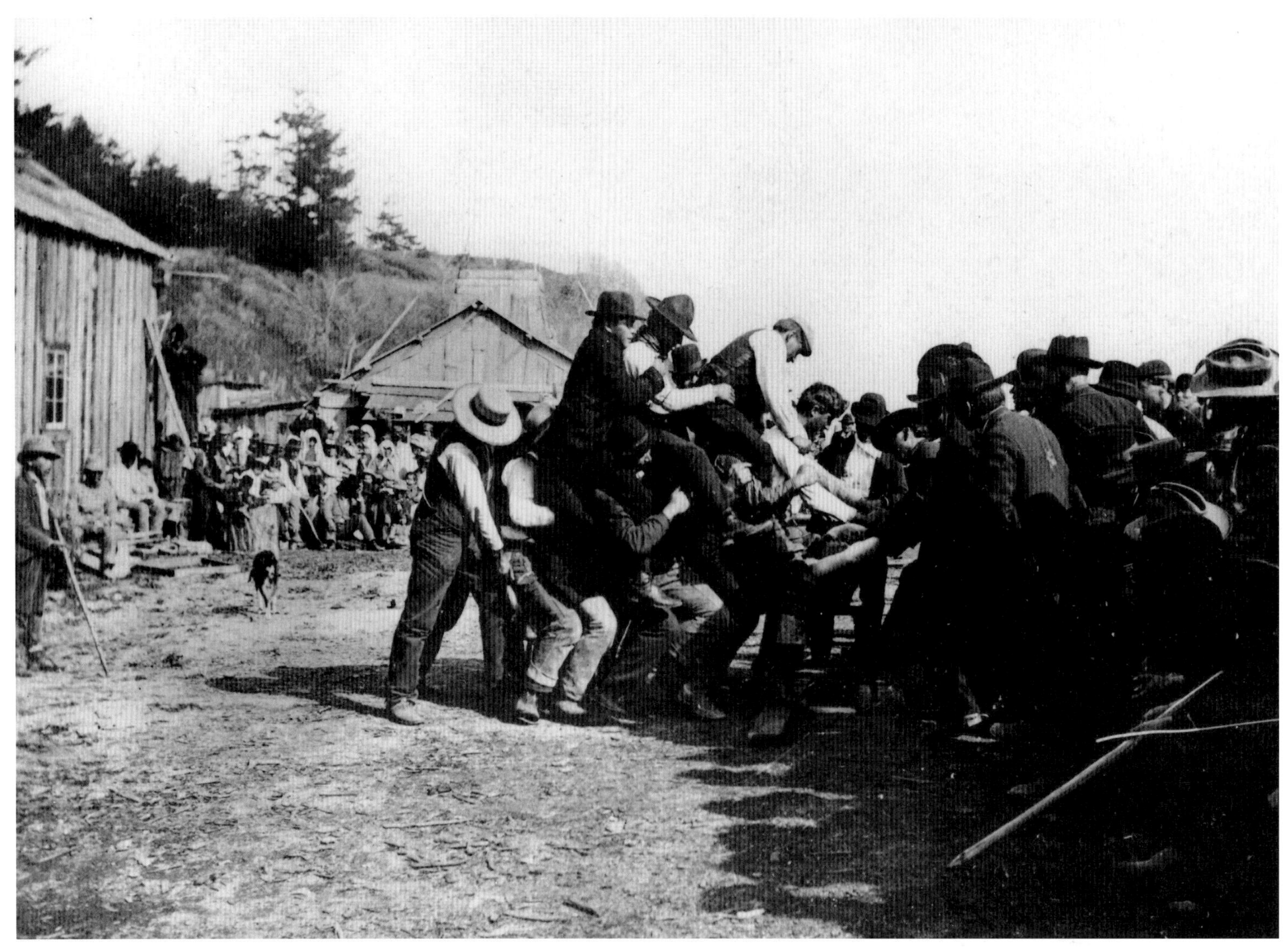

Native Americans of Puget Sound held community celebrations called potlatches. Even after most of the region's first residents had totally adopted American dress, they still enjoyed the traditional games such as this feat of team strength, somewhat the reverse of a tug-of-war. This gathering on April 18, 1904, at Coupeville on Whidbey Island attracted Vashon photographer Oliver S. Van Olinda.

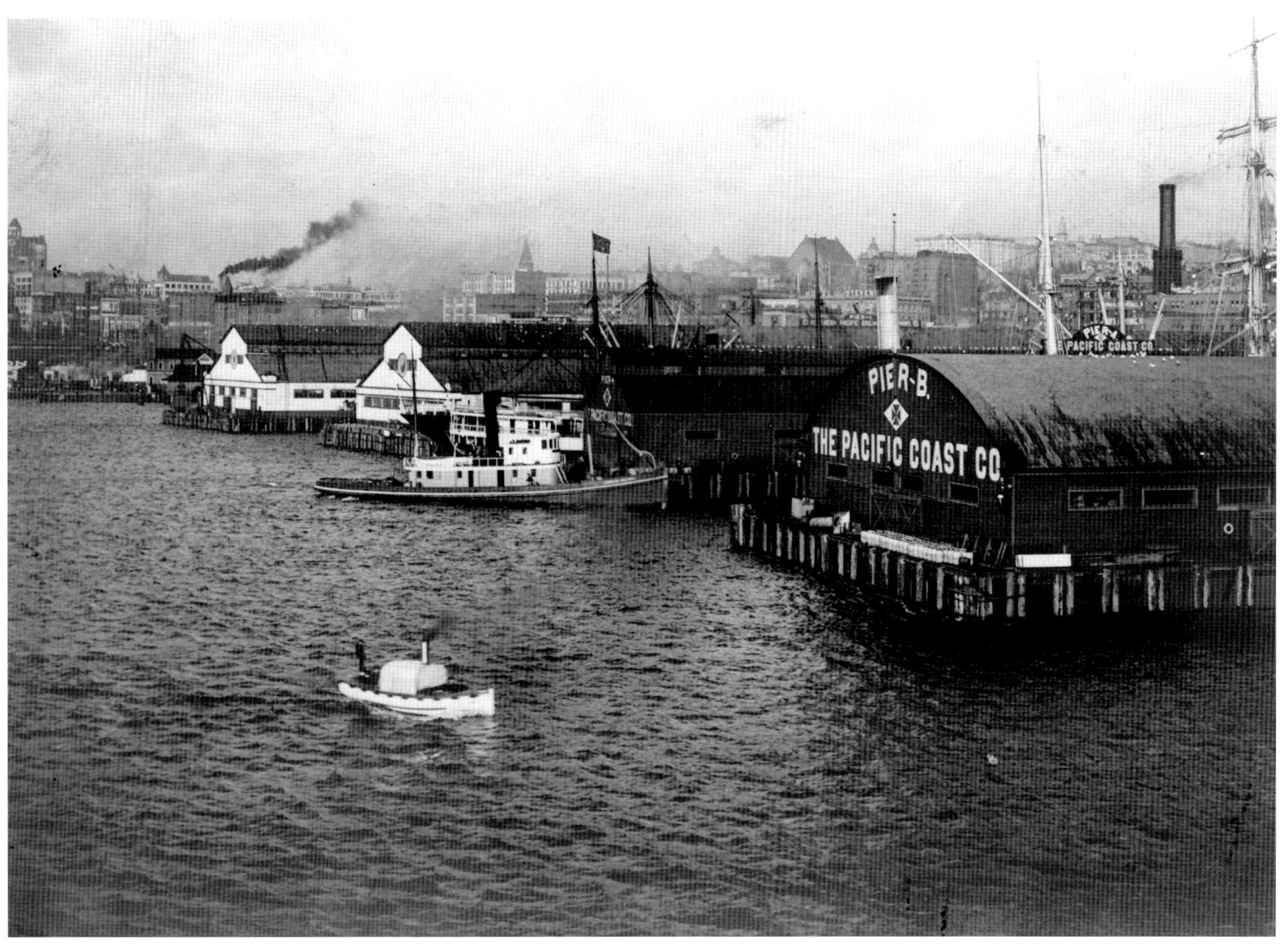

A small steam launch makes its way along the Seattle waterfront off the Pacific Coast Company dock (ca. 1904).

Following Spread: Around 1904, the barkentine *Amaranth* and the steamship *Ivydene* await a cargo of cut lumber at a Puget Sound mill. Lumber mills that loaded their product on ships were called cargo mills. Those with a rail connection were rail mills.

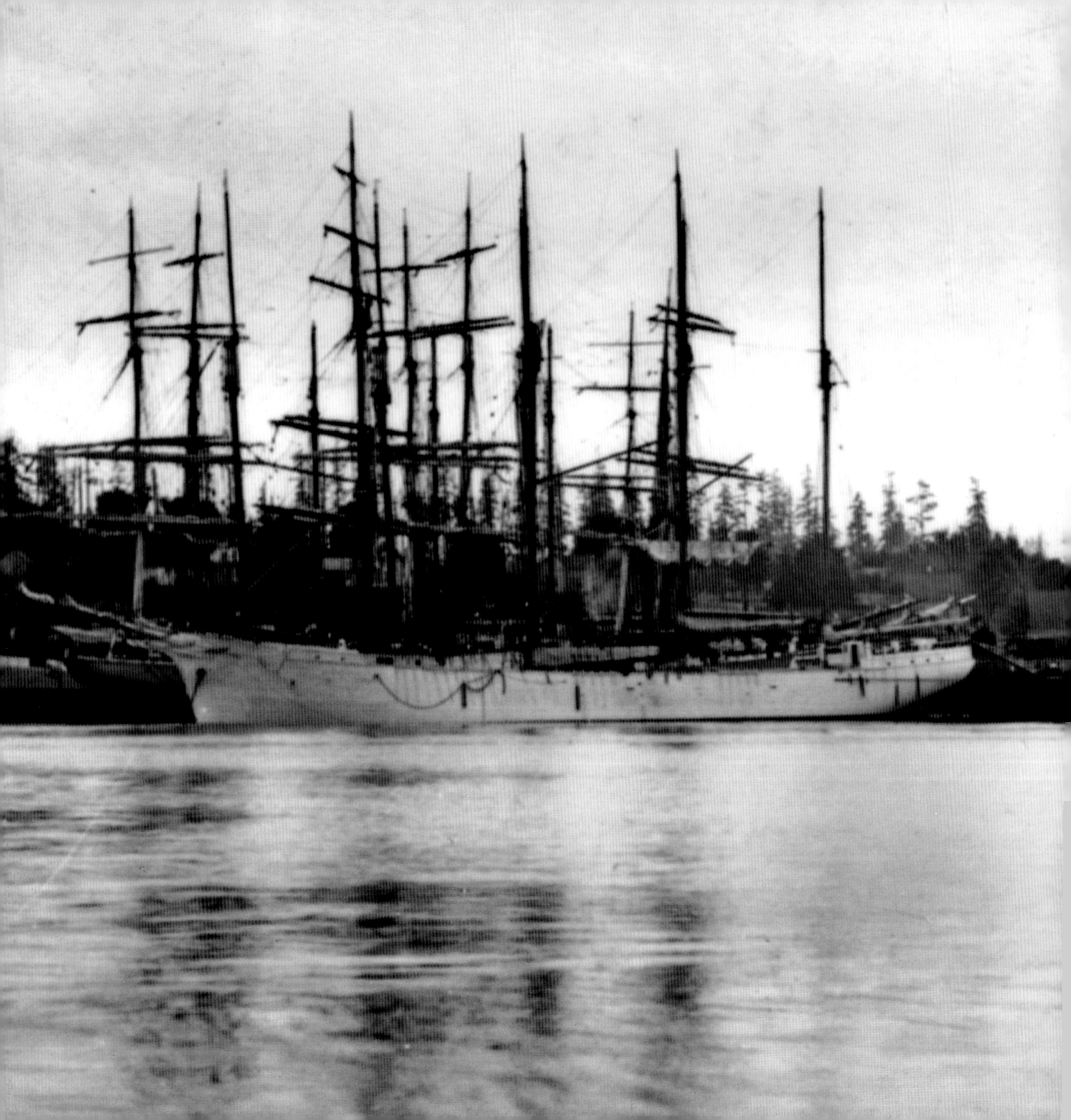

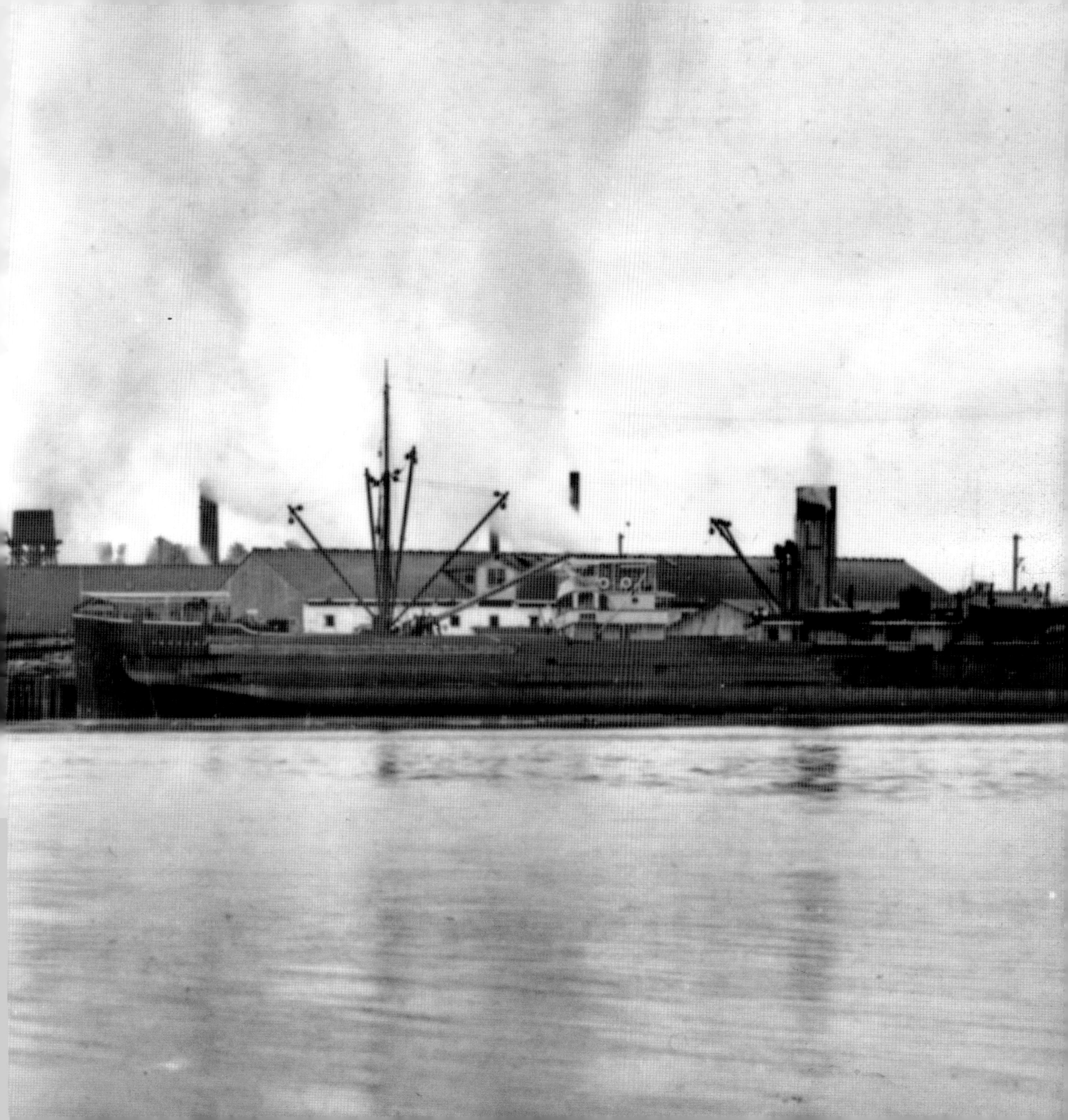

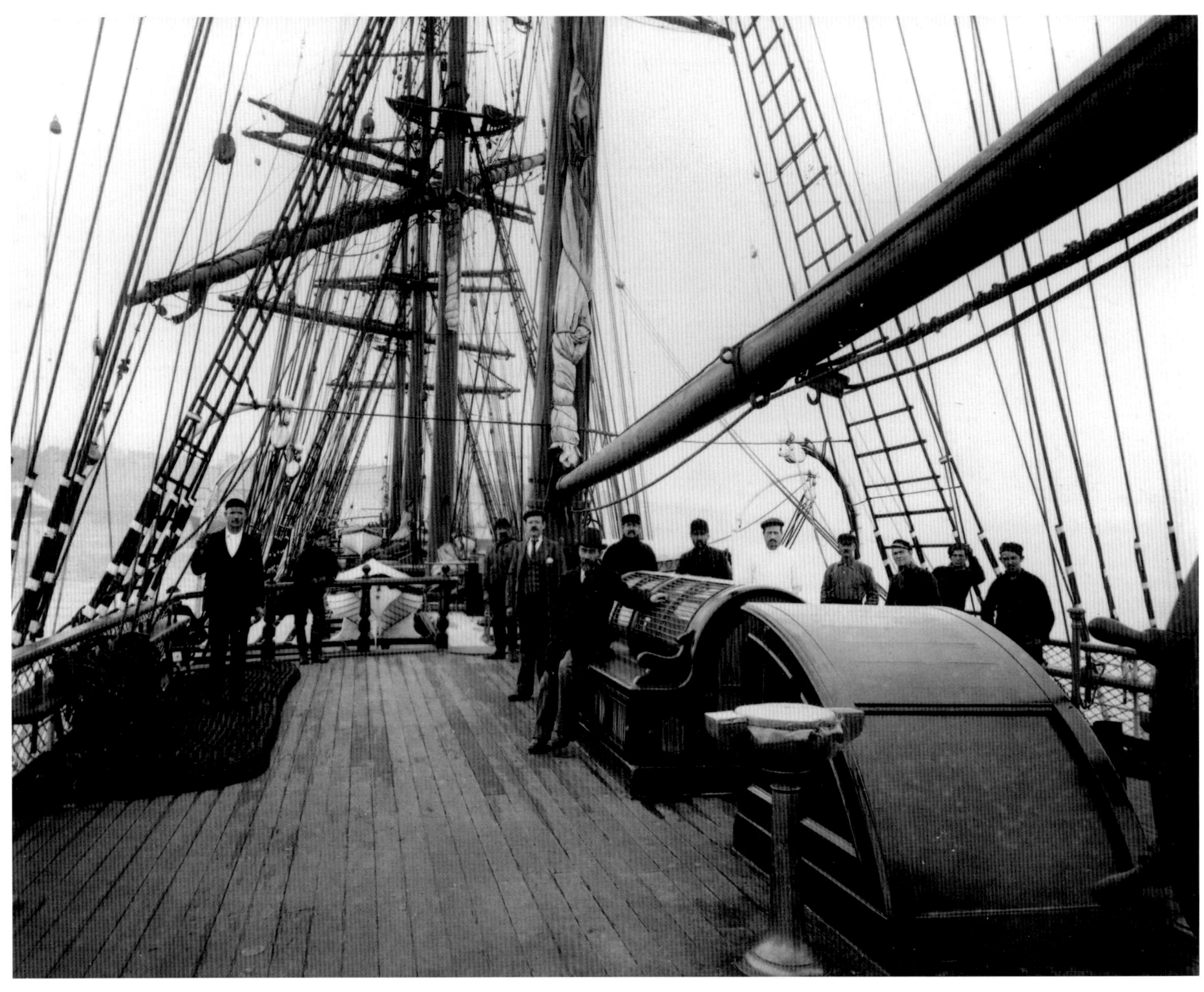

The crew of the four-masted bark *West Lothian* pose on deck somewhere on Puget Sound. Sailing ships carried lumber out of the region well into the twentieth century, while steamers transported more valuable cargoes and passengers.

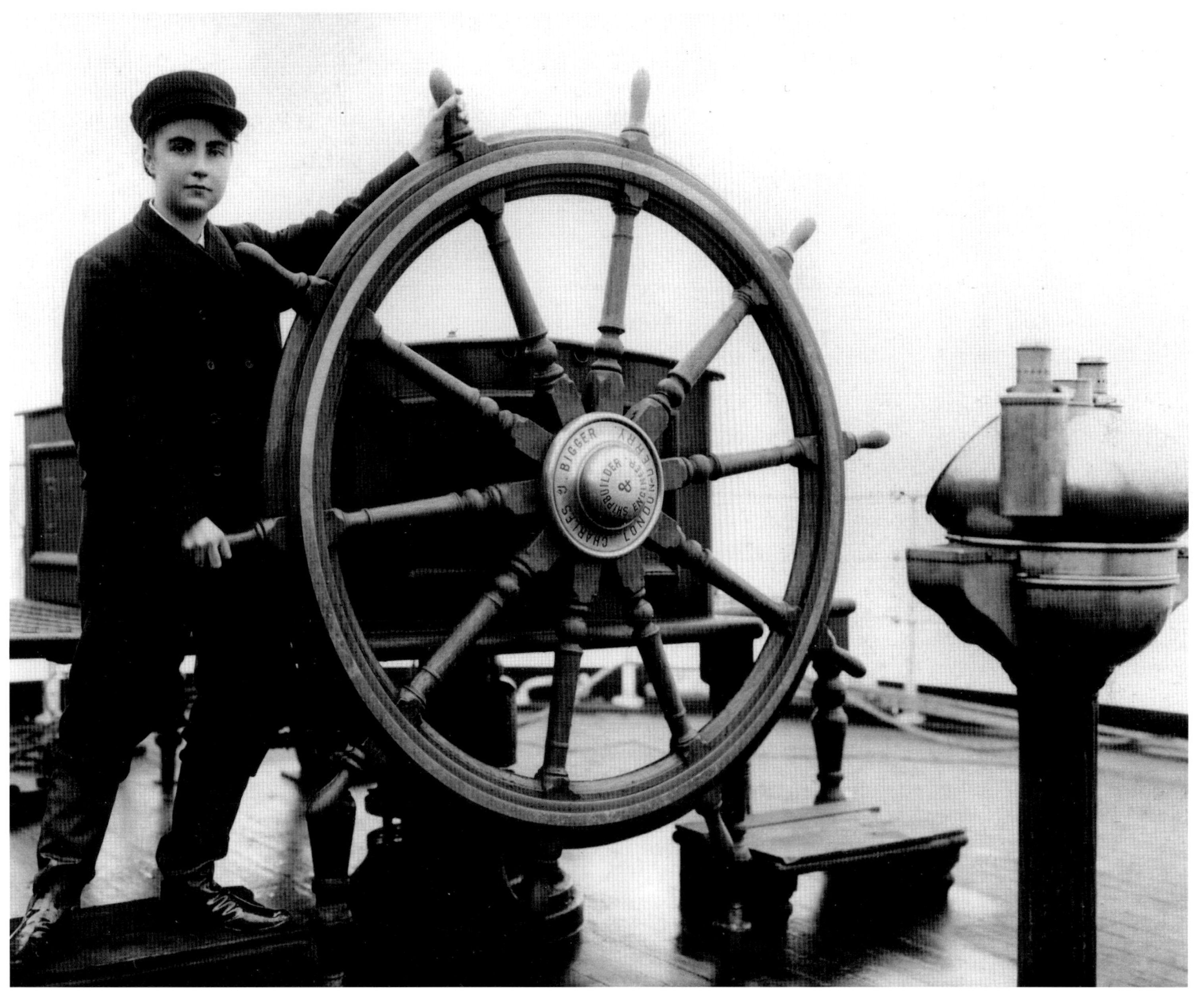

Maritime photographer William Hester posed this young crew member in Sunday best at the helm of the three-masted sailing ship *Dimsdale*. The *Dimsdale*'s crew of 27 included two women on a visit to Puget Sound.

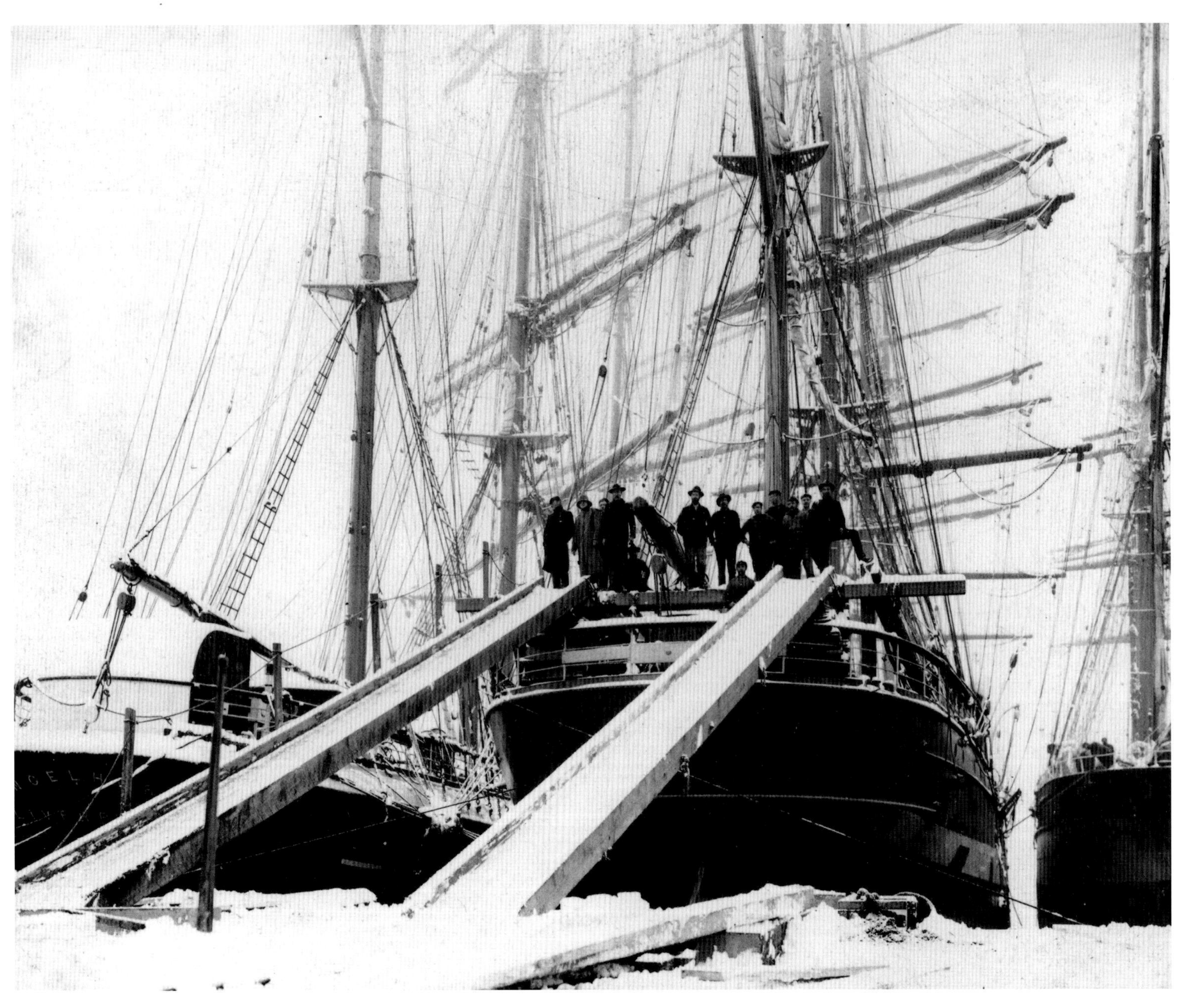

The crew of the Scottish bark *Bracadale* pause while loading lumber one winter day in the early 1900s. A bark featured two or more square-rigged masts forward with a single fore-and-aft, or schooner, sail aft.

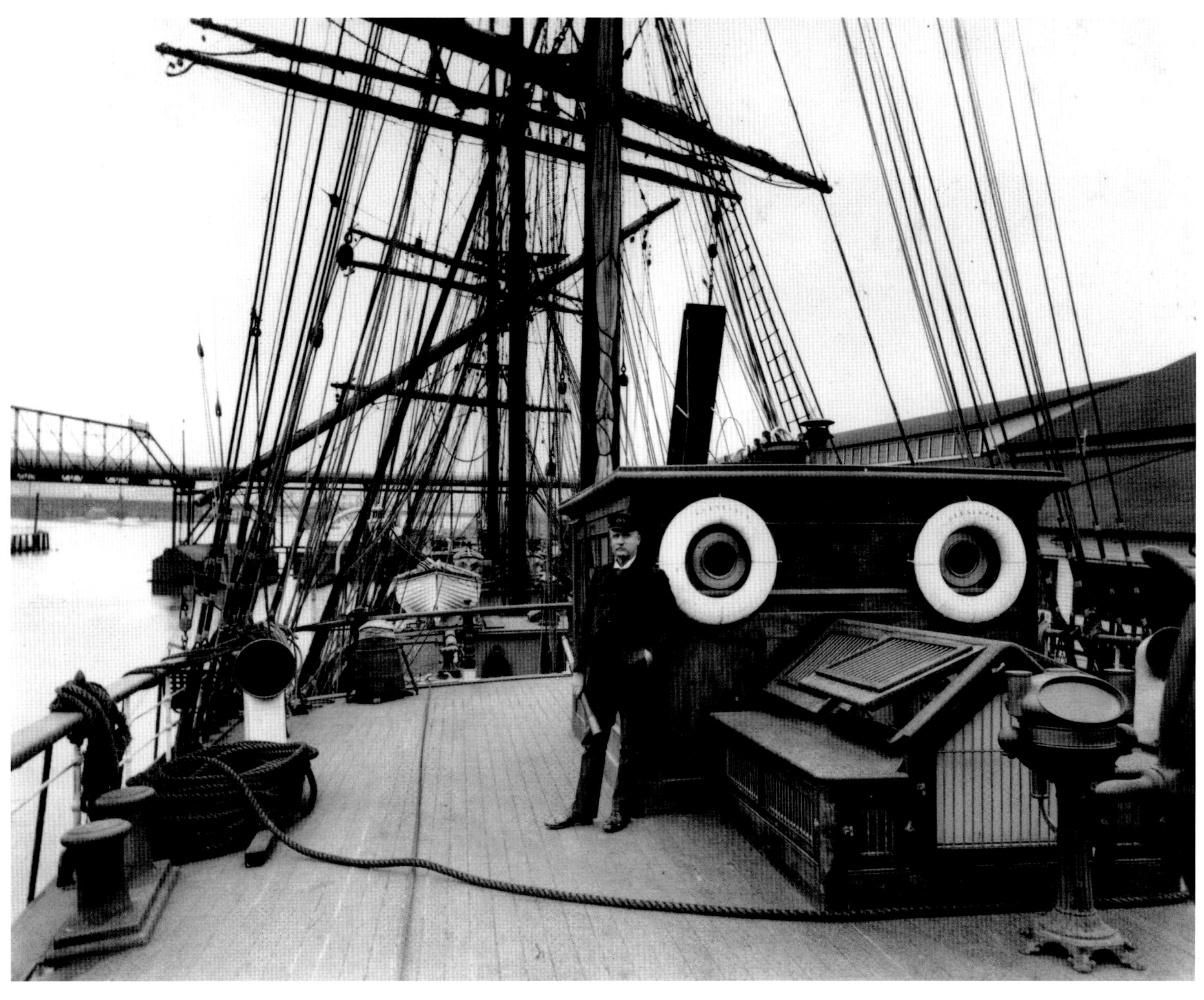

In 1904, Captain E. E. Robbins poses with his telescope on the deck of the three-masted British sailing ship *Glenelvan*. The ship waits at a dock near a Puget Sound river's mouth.

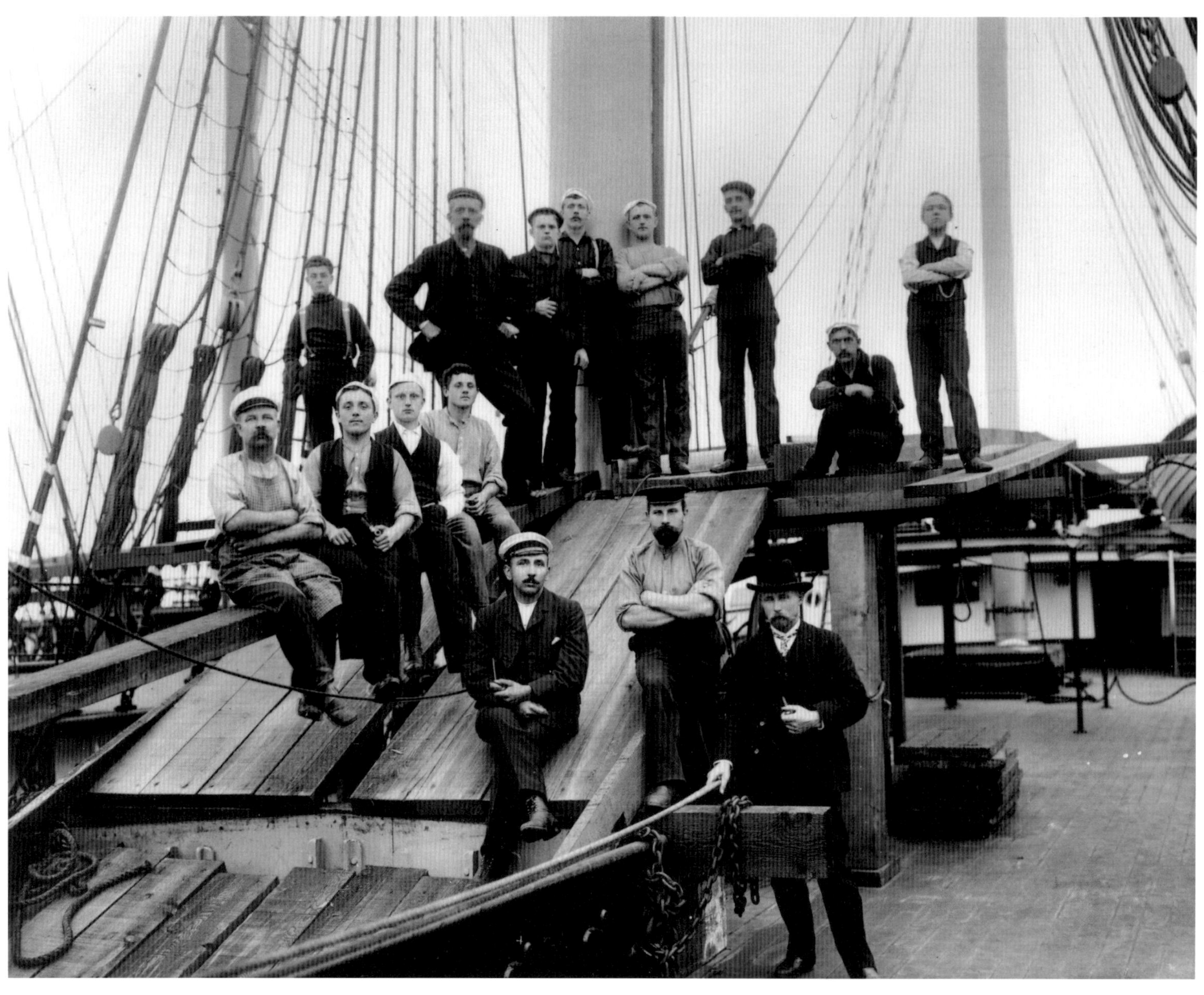

Maritime photographer William Hester called together these crewmen for a portrait on the deck of the three-masted bark *Pera*.

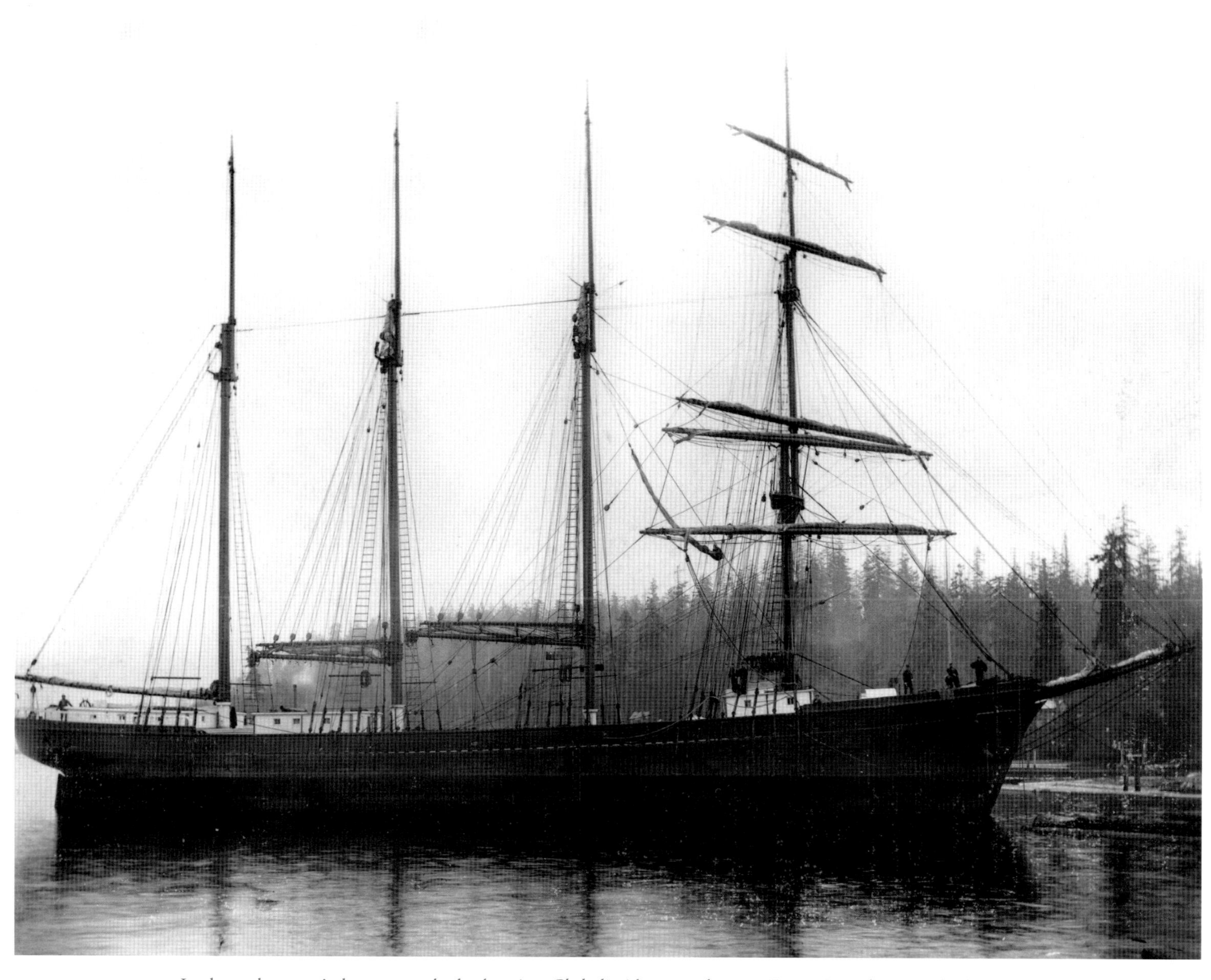

In the early twentieth century, the barkentine *Chehalis* rides at anchor at a Puget Sound port. A barkentine has one square-rigged foremast and three or more schooner-rigged masts. Barkentines required smaller crews than ships fully rigged with square sails.

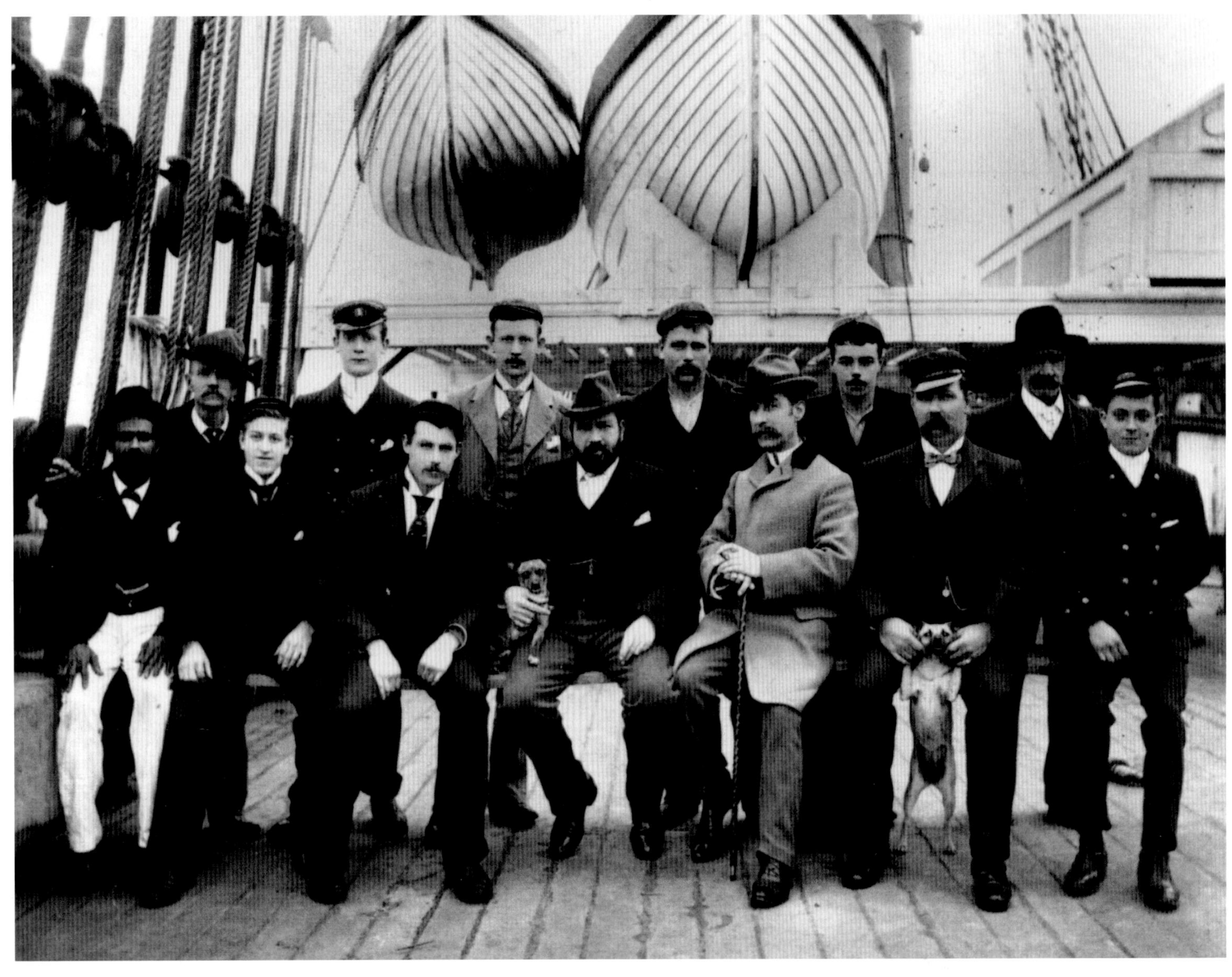

The captain and crew of the three-masted *Stronsa* have donned their best clothing to pose for photographer William Hester (ca. 1904). Included in the portrait are the ship's two dogs.

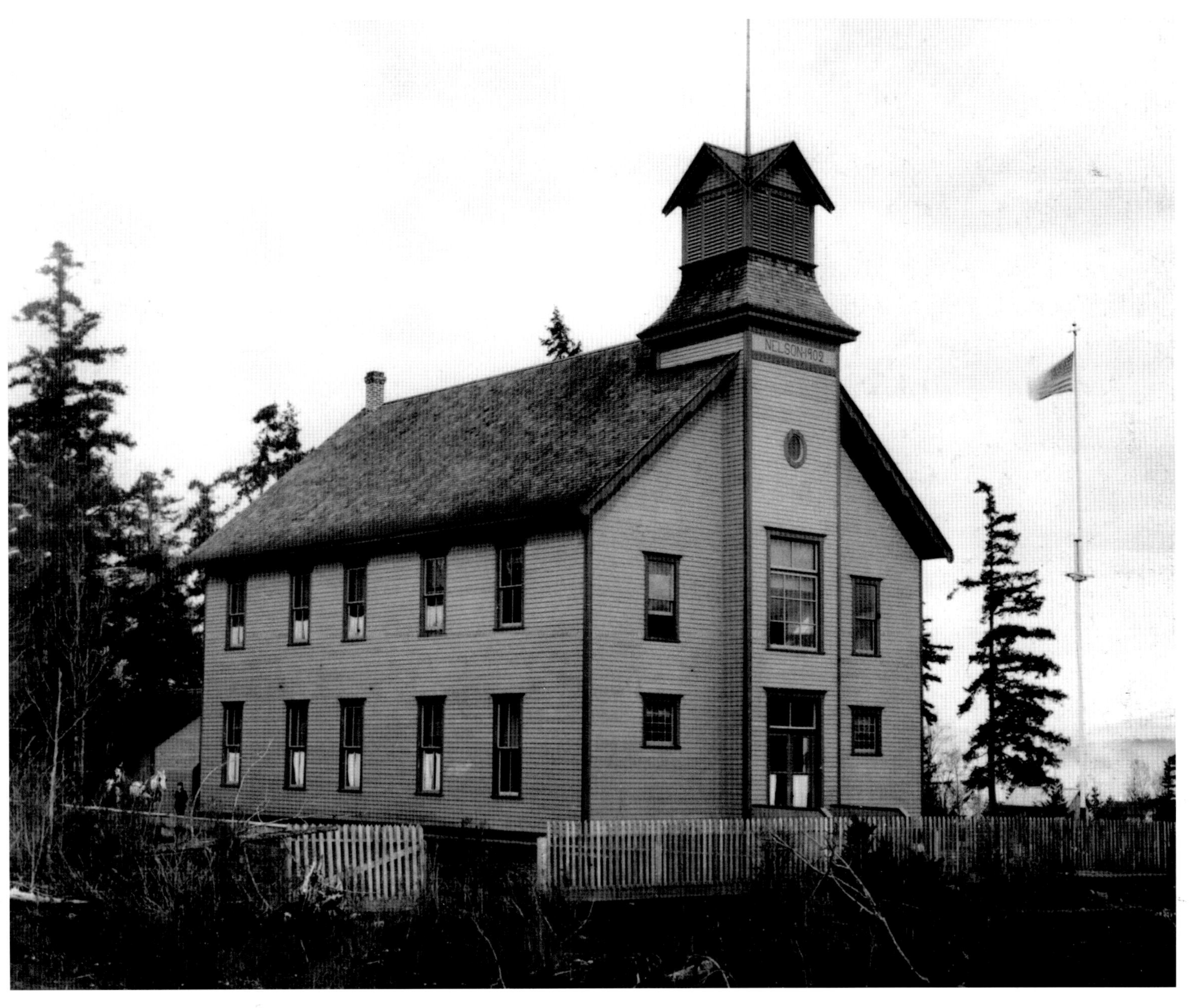

As soon as Puget Sound settlers formed the bare bones of county government and a courts system, they organized school districts and built schools. By 1904, only 25 years after Anacortes was just a general store, the public school boasts several classrooms on two floors.

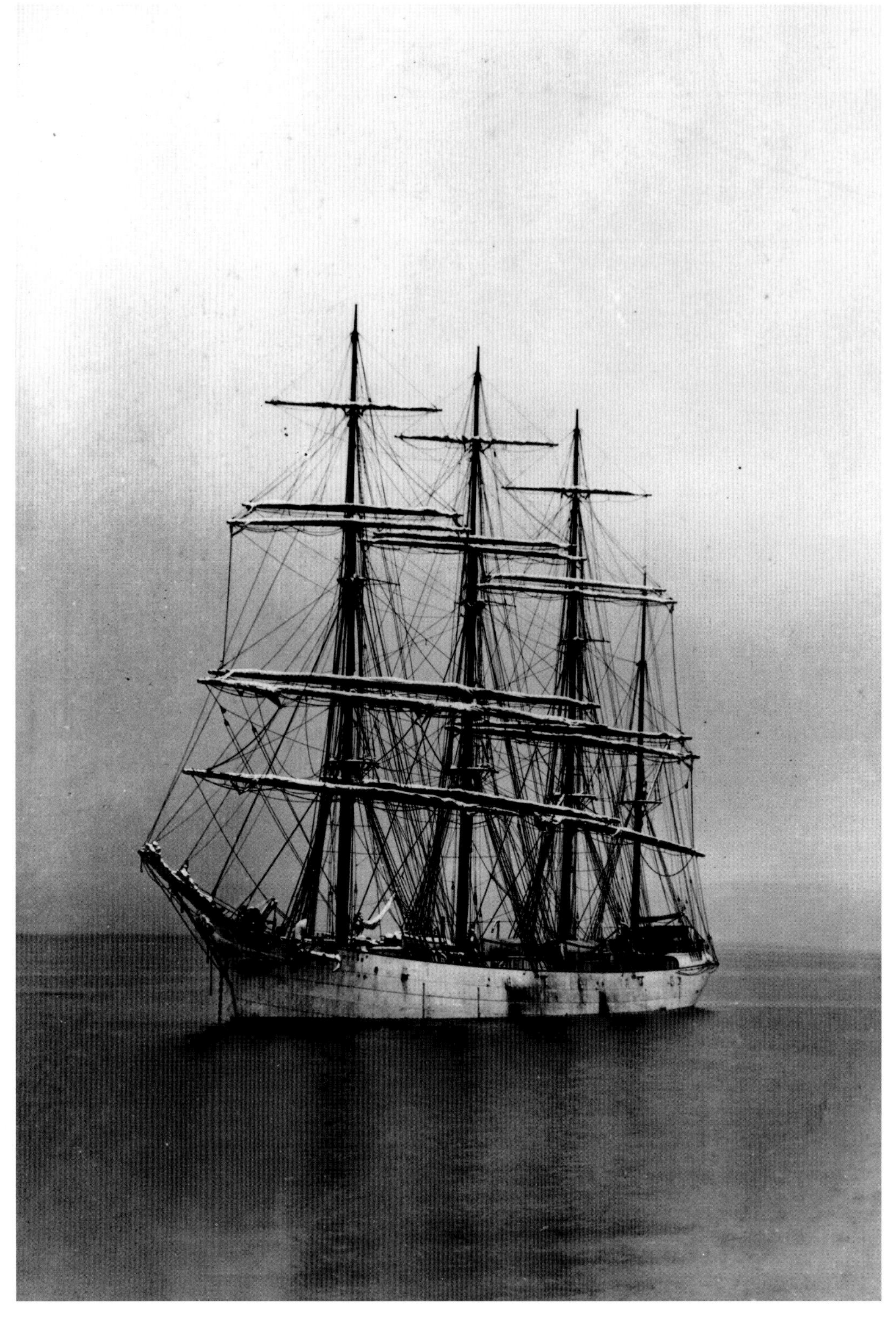

Under a coating of snow in Commencement Bay, the British-flagged four-masted bark *Samaritan* rides at anchor off Tacoma (ca. 1904).

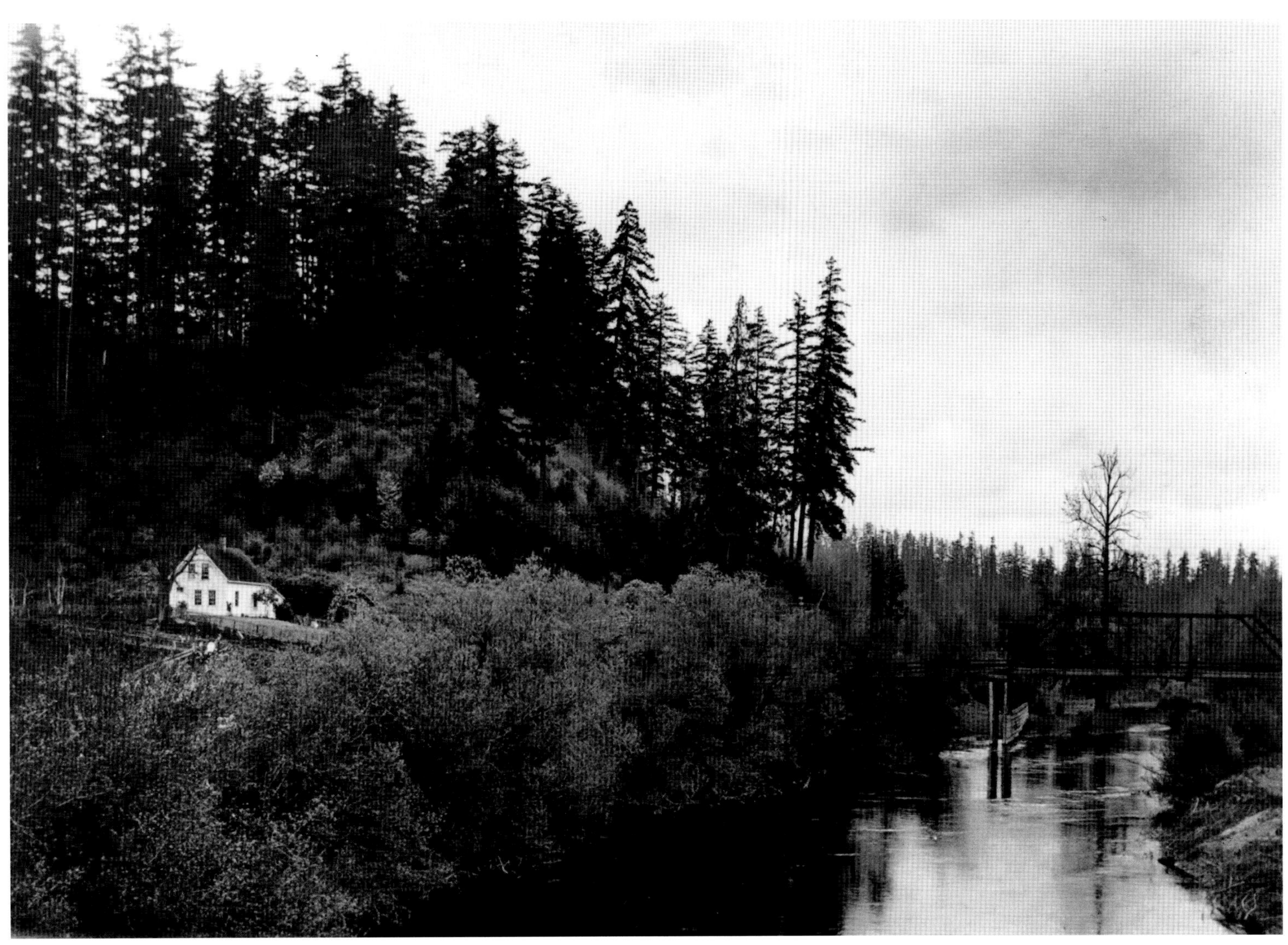

Pictured here in 1905, the Black River flows from Lake Washington's south end, past Renton, to join the Duwamish River south of Seattle. The river disappeared in 1917 when the U.S. Army Corps of Engineers lowered Lake Washington in order to connect the lake with Puget Sound by way of the Lake Washington Ship Canal and Chittenden Locks.

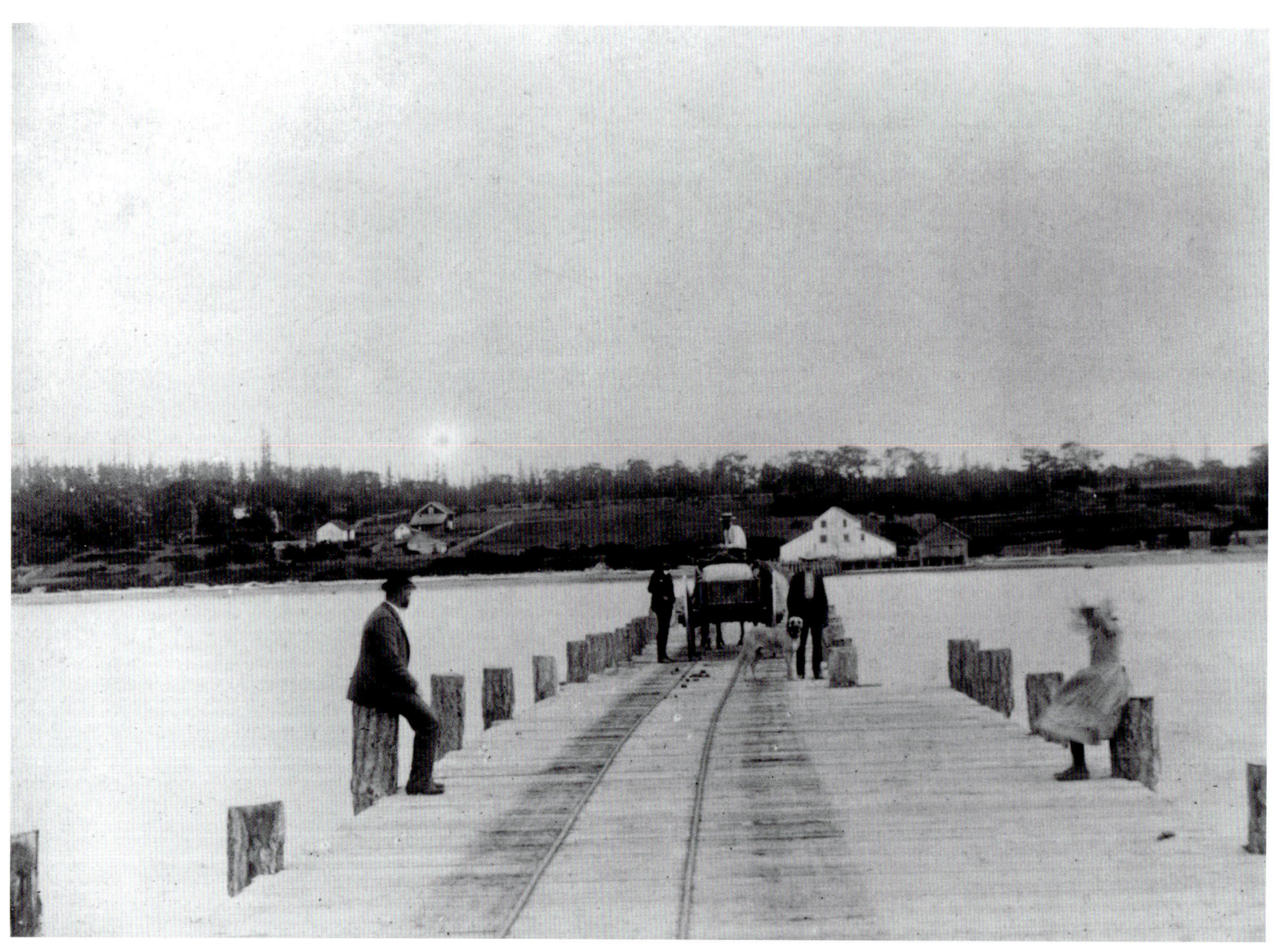

At the beginning of the twentieth century, Oak Harbor's connection from Whidbey Island to the rest of the world was over this dock, where Mosquito Fleet steamers tied up to transfer passengers and goods.

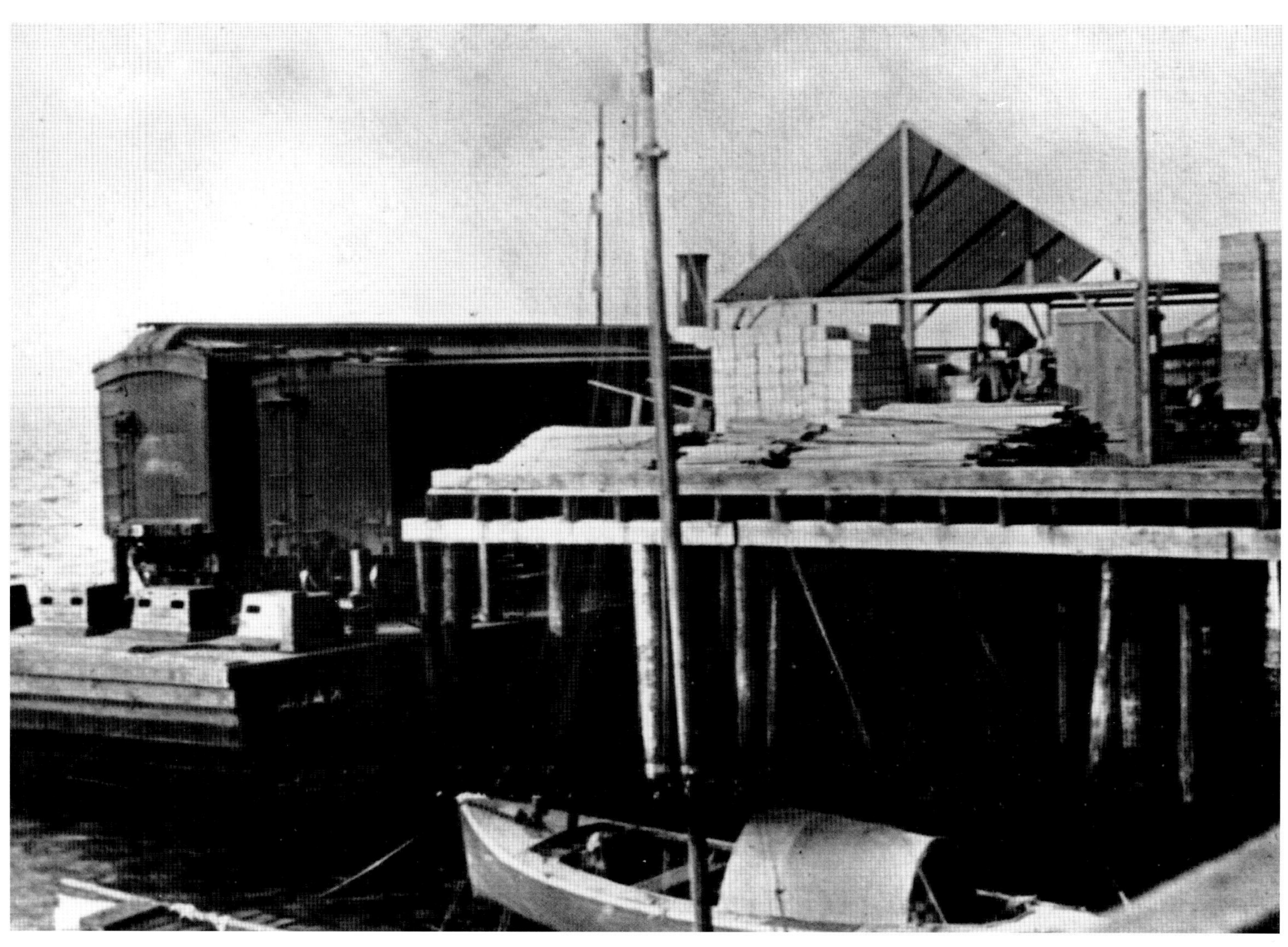

Part of Puget Sound's bounty included both natural huckleberries and berries brought by settlers from the east. To speed the transport of the berry harvest, railroads loaded refrigerated cars on special barges that could be moved to islands and more isolated ports. Here Vashon farmers transfer their crop in crates to the barge and car around 1905.

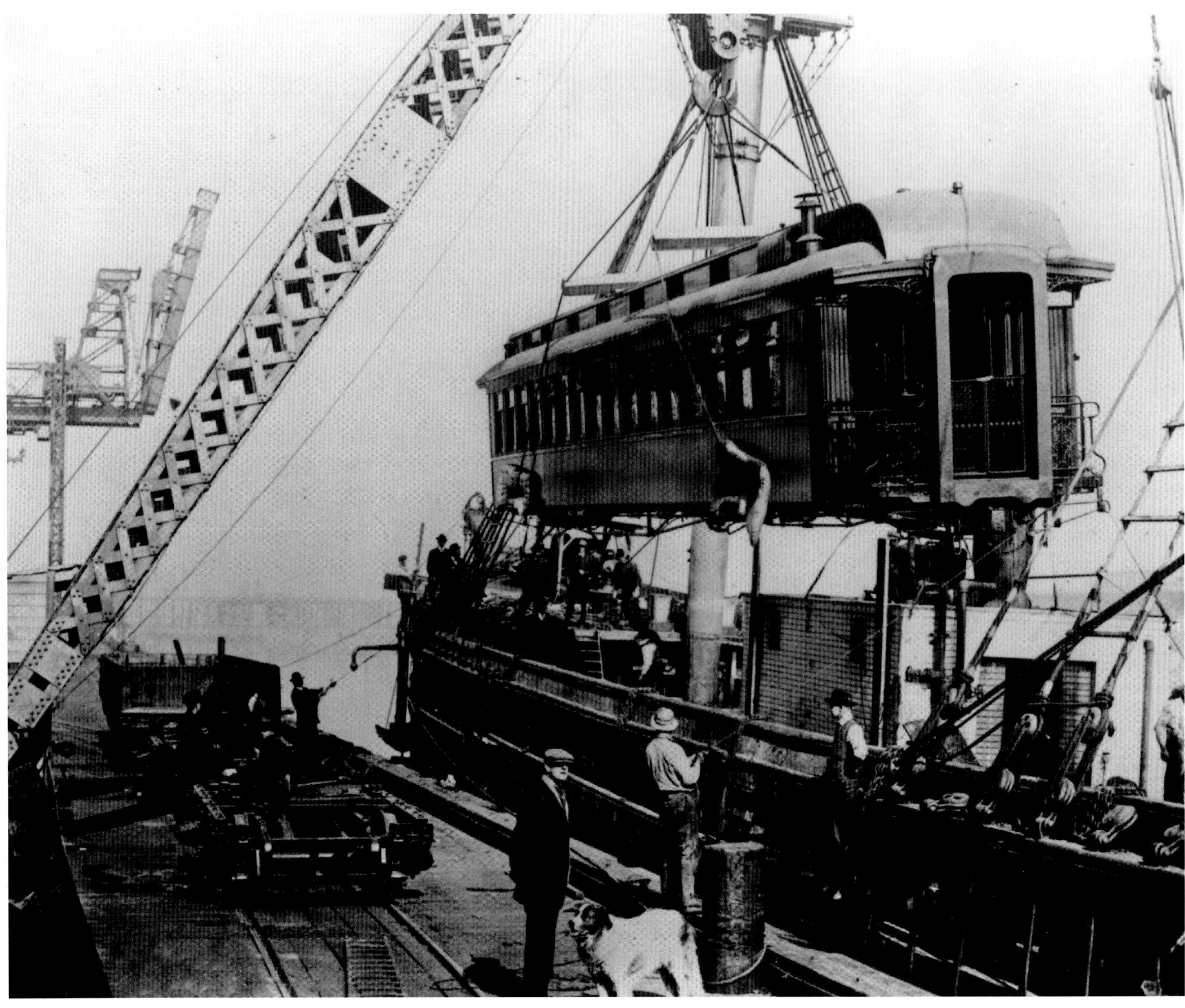

On the heels of thousands seeking fortune during the Klondike Gold Rush, John Ballantine dreamed of building a railroad in Alaska. Beginning in 1902, he and other Seattle businessmen invested $30 million in a 412-mile line starting at Cook Inlet. Here around 1905, a new passenger coach is loaded at Seattle onto a ship bound for Alaska.

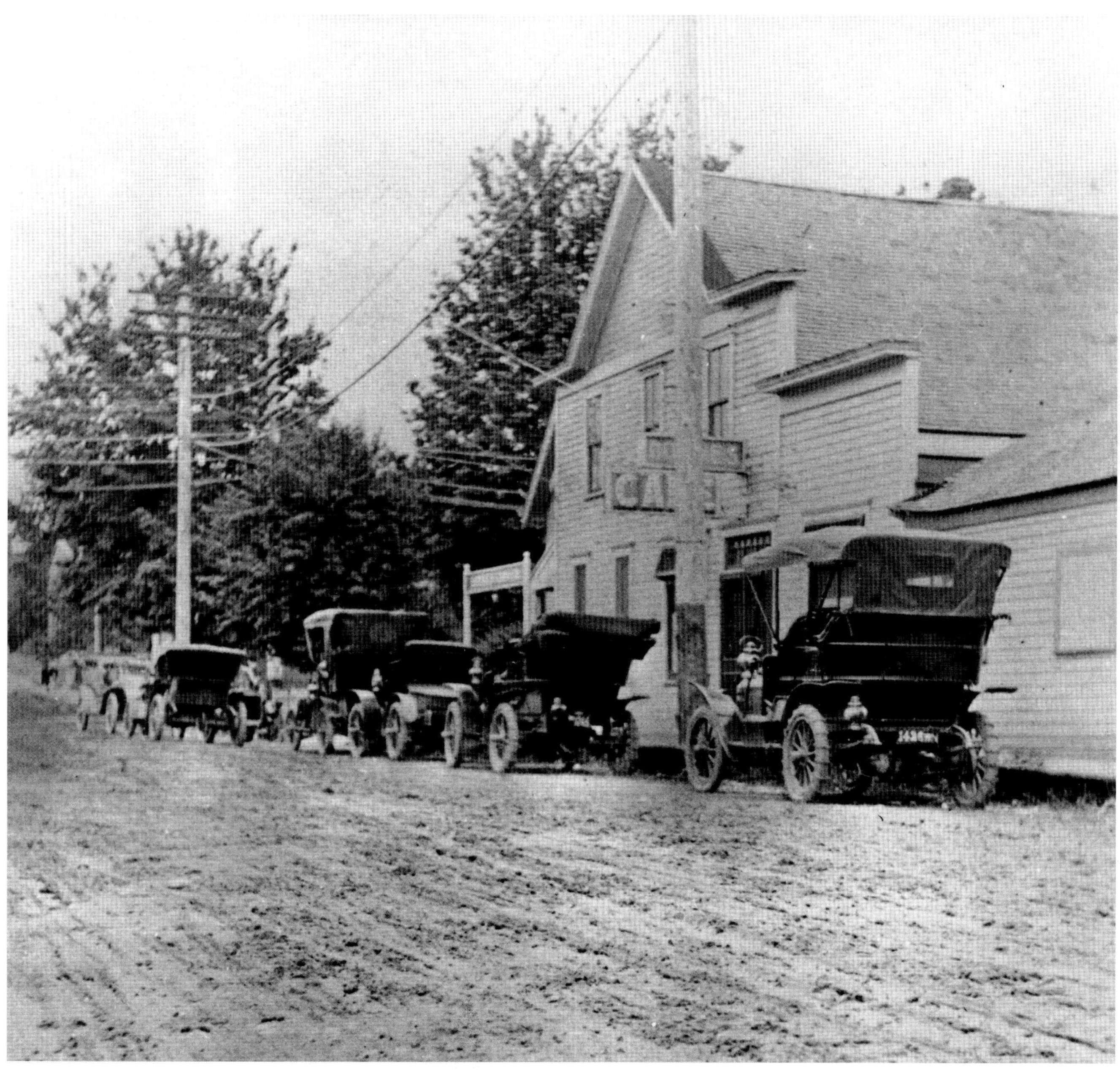

In 1906, owners of businesses such as Doanes Oystery House and Café in Olympia could expect visits for Sunday dinner by motorist parties from as far away as Tacoma. As soon as Puget Sound residents acquired the automobile, they began touring the region, despite the absence of serviceable roads. The muddy tire chains reflect the condition of the roads.

In 1907, photographer Norman Edson catches the
bustle of activity on the Everett waterfront and on
Port Gardiner Bay. Everett is not even 20 years old,
but looks like any long-established
mill town of the era.

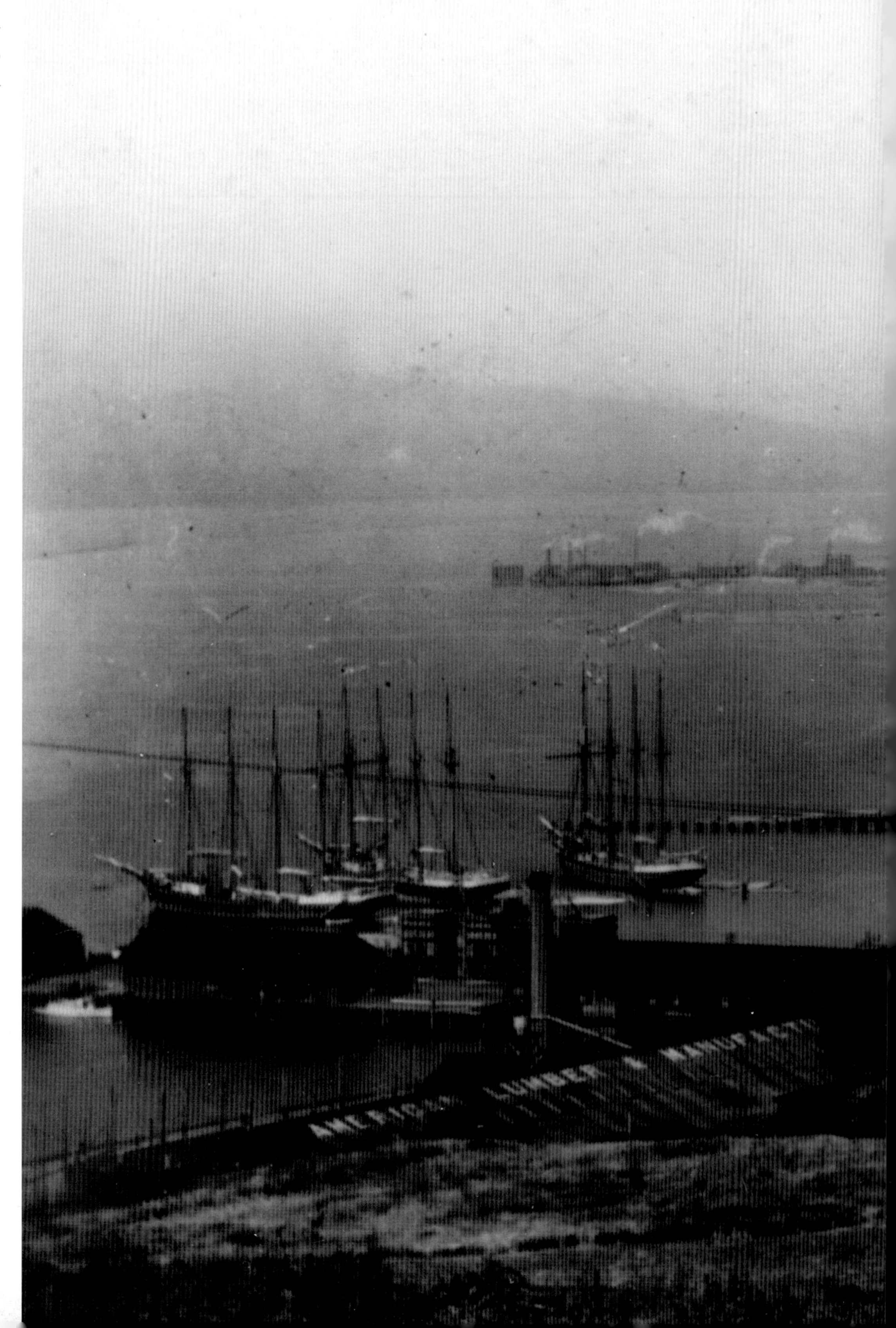

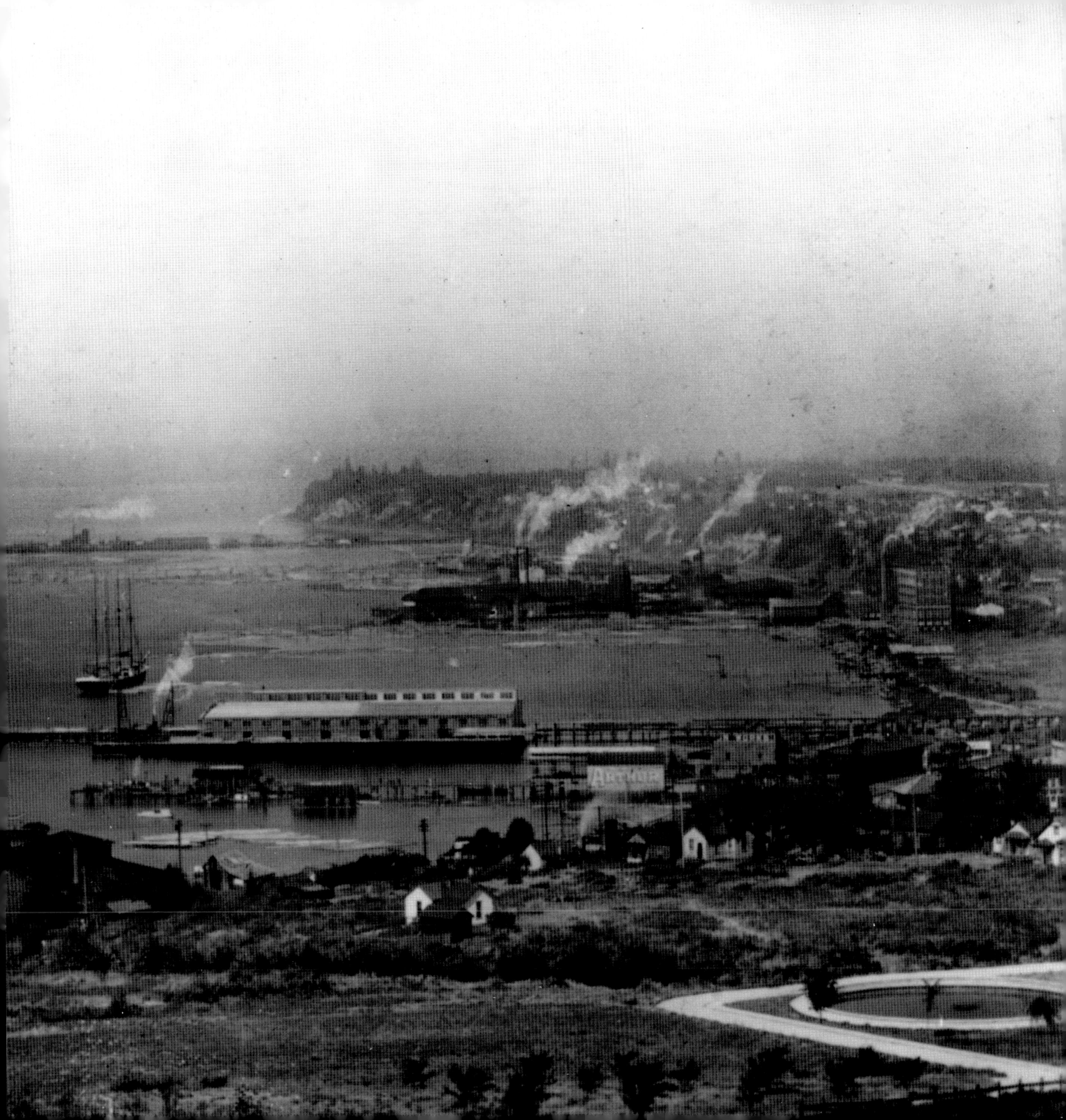

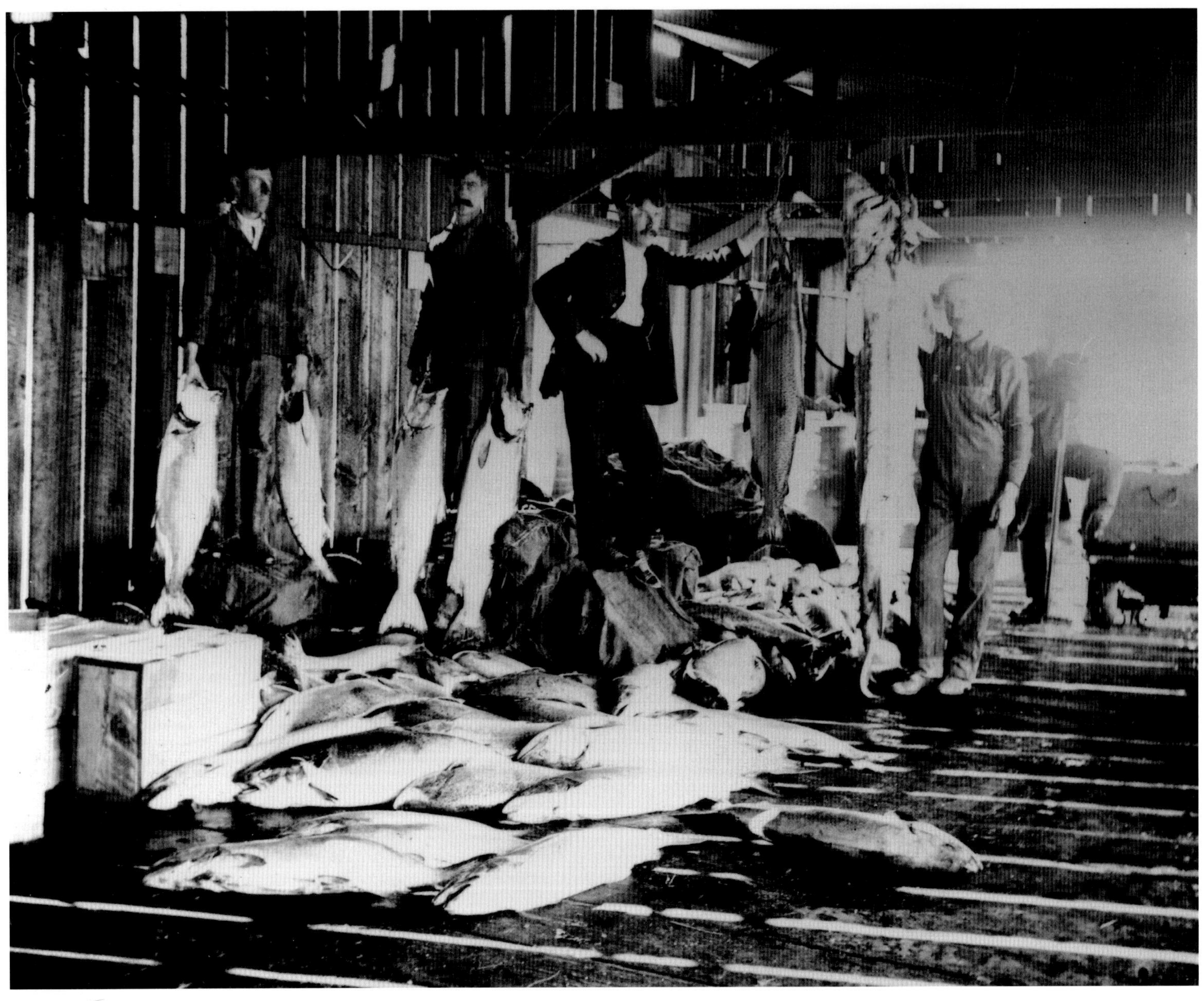

The size of salmon, once routinely caught in Puget Sound waters, is shown in this 1906 photo in a cannery. The workers display an immense wolf eel caught in the salmon net and hung from a crossbeam.

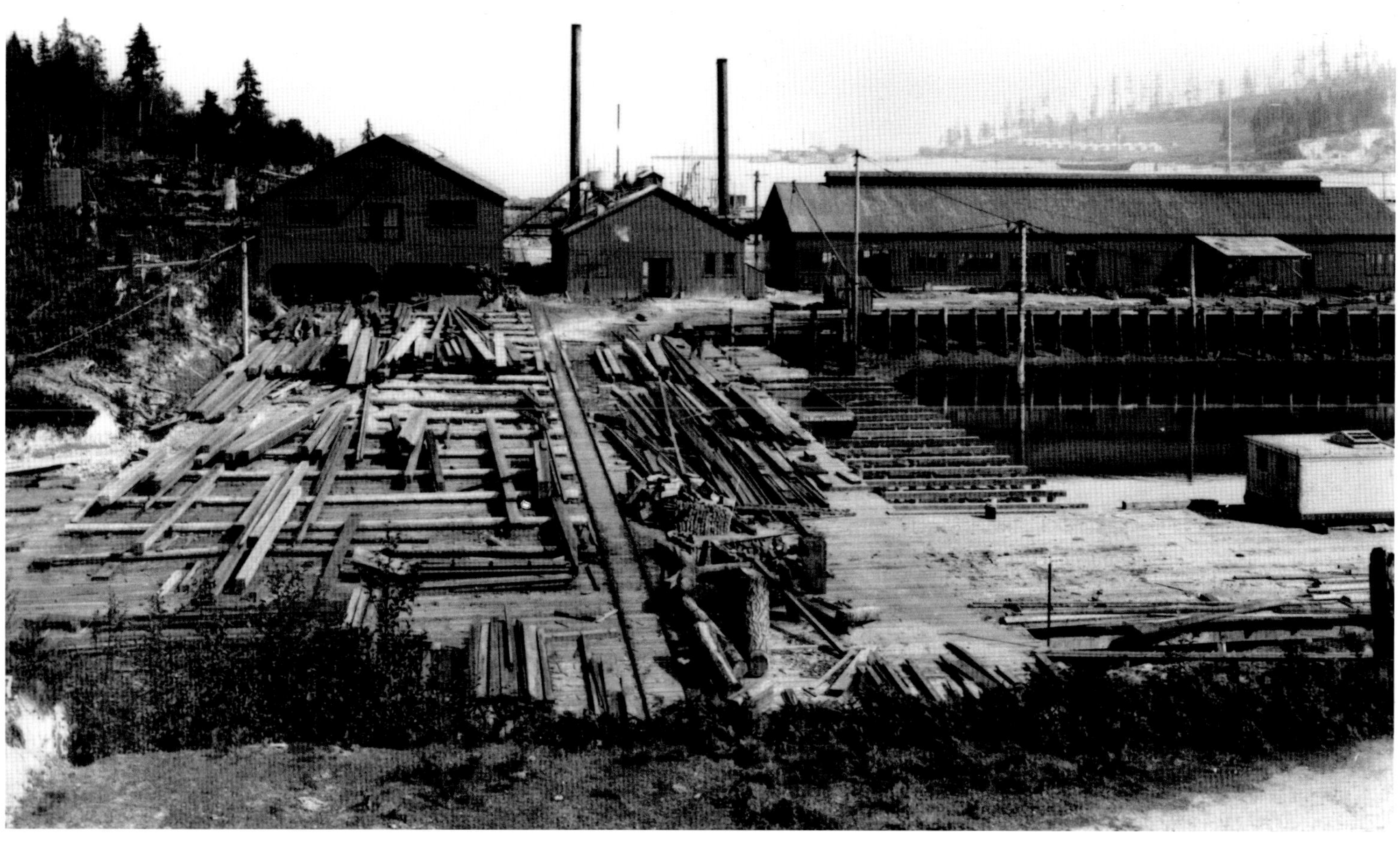

In 1902, the Hall Brothers Marine Railway and Shipbuilding Company moved from Port Blakely to Eagle Harbor on Bainbridge Island, where they found more room for operations. This view by Asahel Curtis shows the main ways and the supporting shops at Winslow, named for one of the founding brothers.

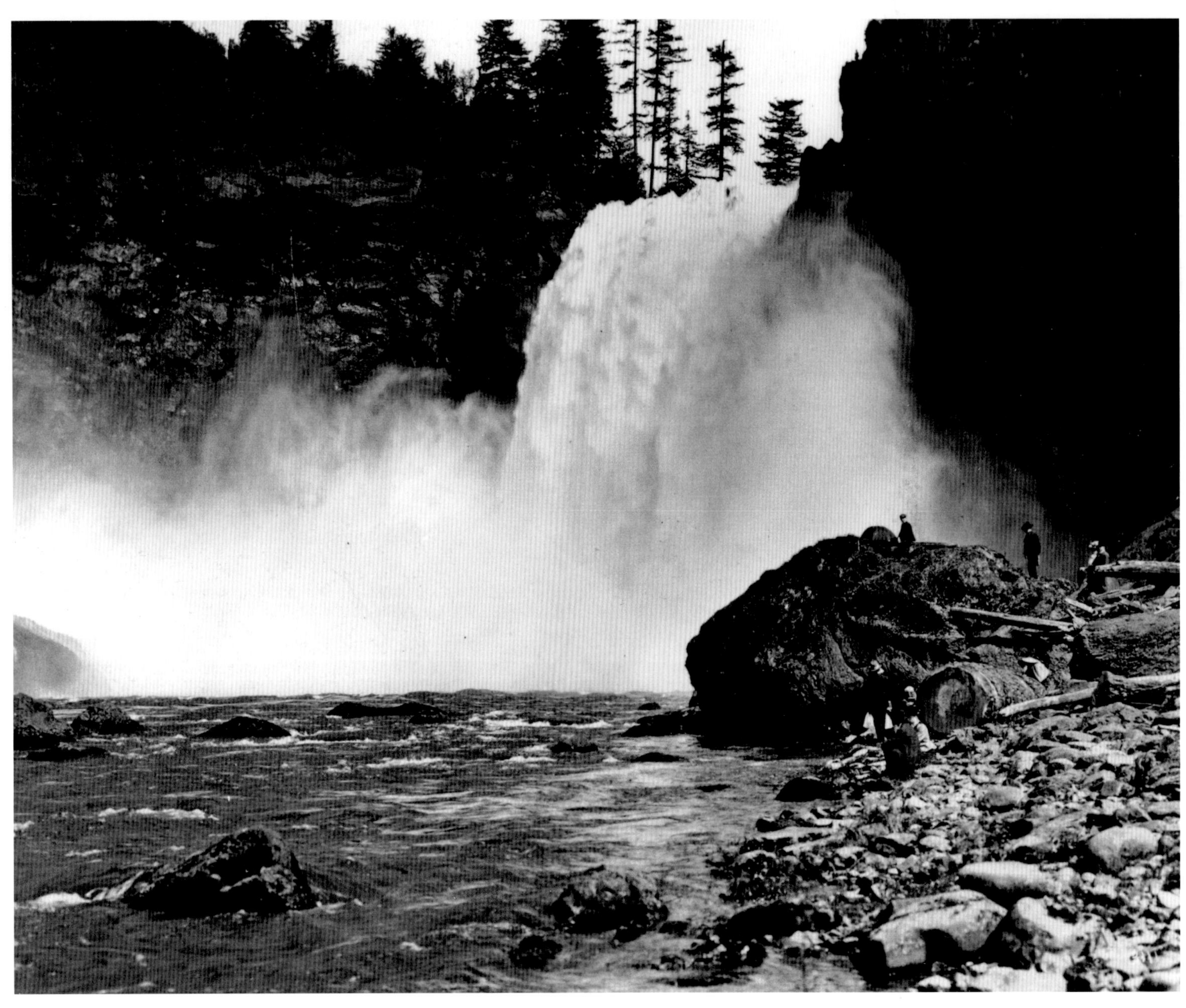

One of the most spectacular natural features of the Puget Sound region is Snoqualmie Falls, dropping 260 feet from the Snoqualmie Plateau. Here in 1906, tourists visit the falls to marvel at their power and grandeur. In 1898, engineer Charles Hinckley Baker built an electricity-generating station 250 feet under the falls by blasting a cavity out of solid rock. That original equipment still generates power for Puget Sound homes.

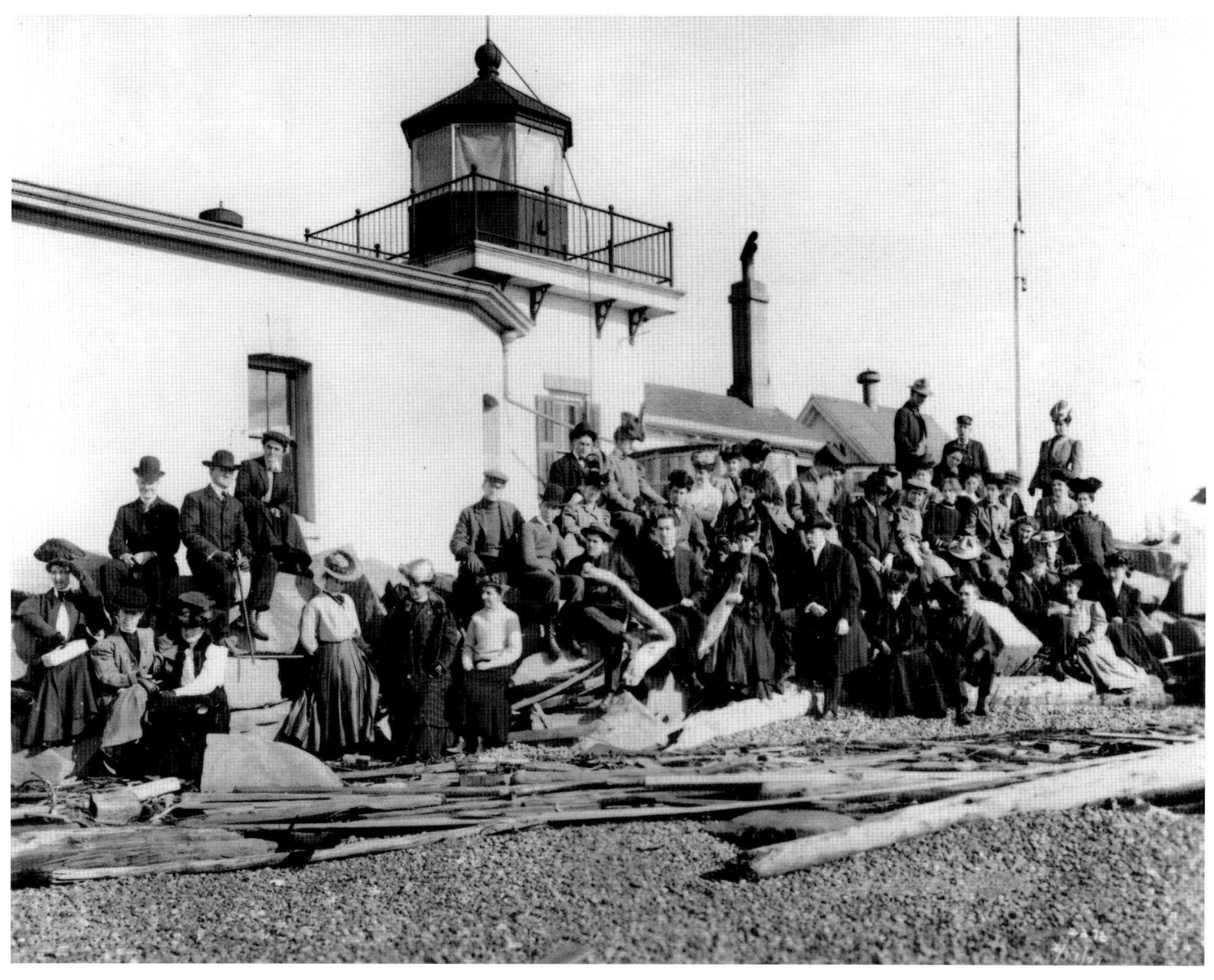

To pose for Asahel Curtis, the newly formed Mountaineers Club hiked from Seattle on February 17, 1907, to the lighthouse at West Point, found at the foot of Magnolia Bluff. West Point marks the entrance to Elliott Bay, and the U.S. Lighthouse Board built a beacon there in 1881. In 2009, the Mountaineers Club was still active with over 10,000 members.

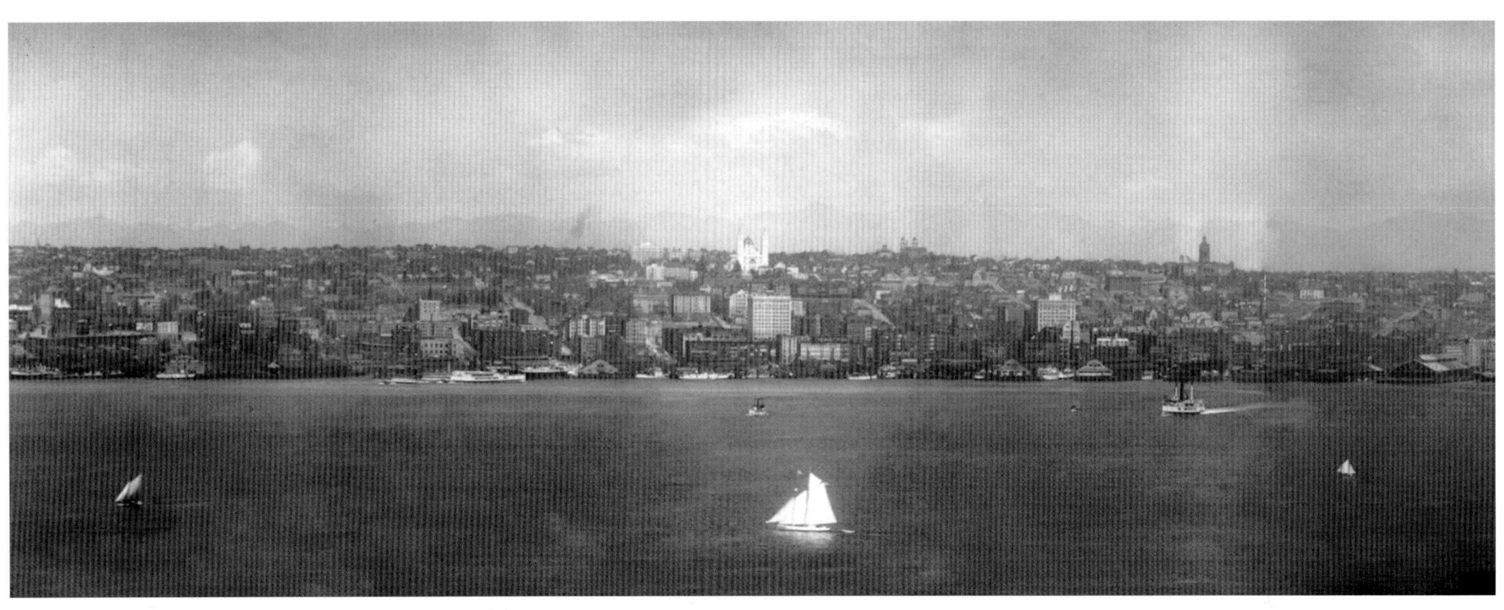

A panorama of Seattle from Elliott Bay captures the waterfront in 1907.

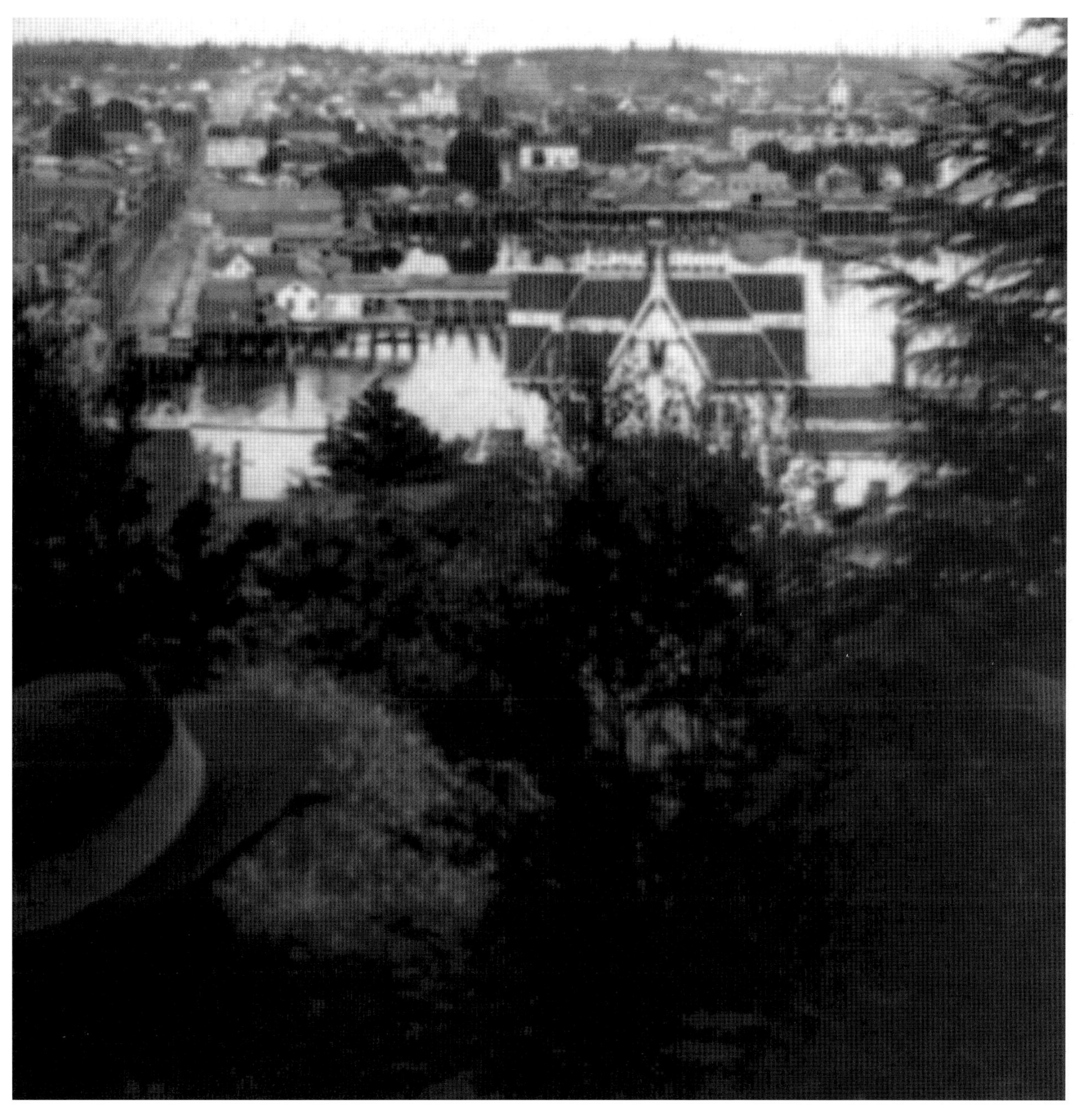

This view over the top of the governor's mansion looks east, taking in Olympia and the State Capitol.

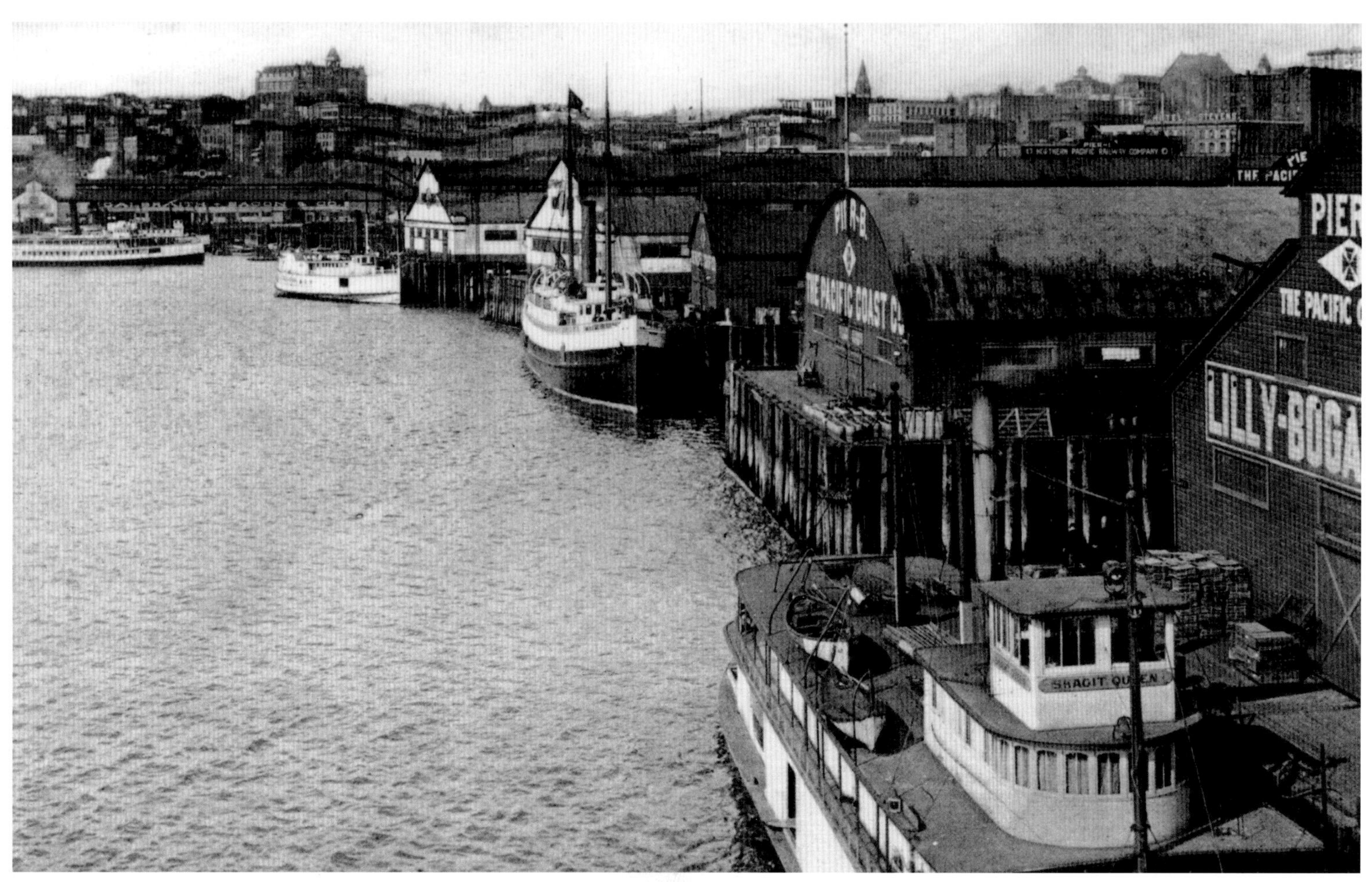

Several Mosquito Fleet steamers wait for passengers along the Seattle waterfront in 1907. The Washington Hotel—"The Scenic Hotel of the West"—sits atop Denny Hill directly above what will become 3rd Avenue and Blanchard Street. Engineers would soon regrade Denny Hill to allow downtown to expand.

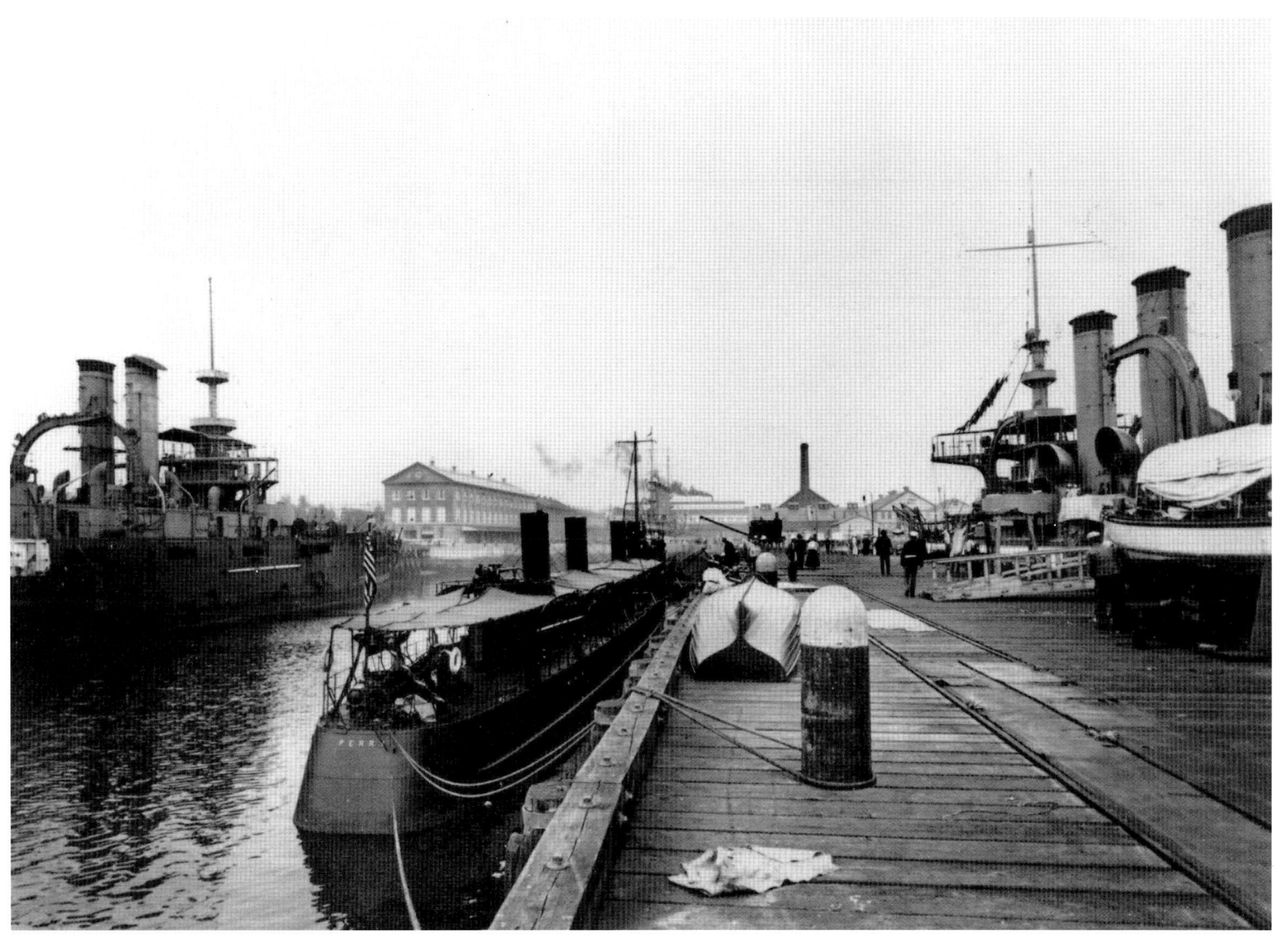

The battleships USS *Wisconsin* and USS *Nebraska* join the revenue cutter *Perry* for maintenance at the Puget Sound Naval Shipyard in Bremerton in 1907. In 1902, 536 Seattle citizens subscribed $100,000 to help pay for *Nebraska*'s construction in the Moran Brothers Shipyard on Elliott Bay.

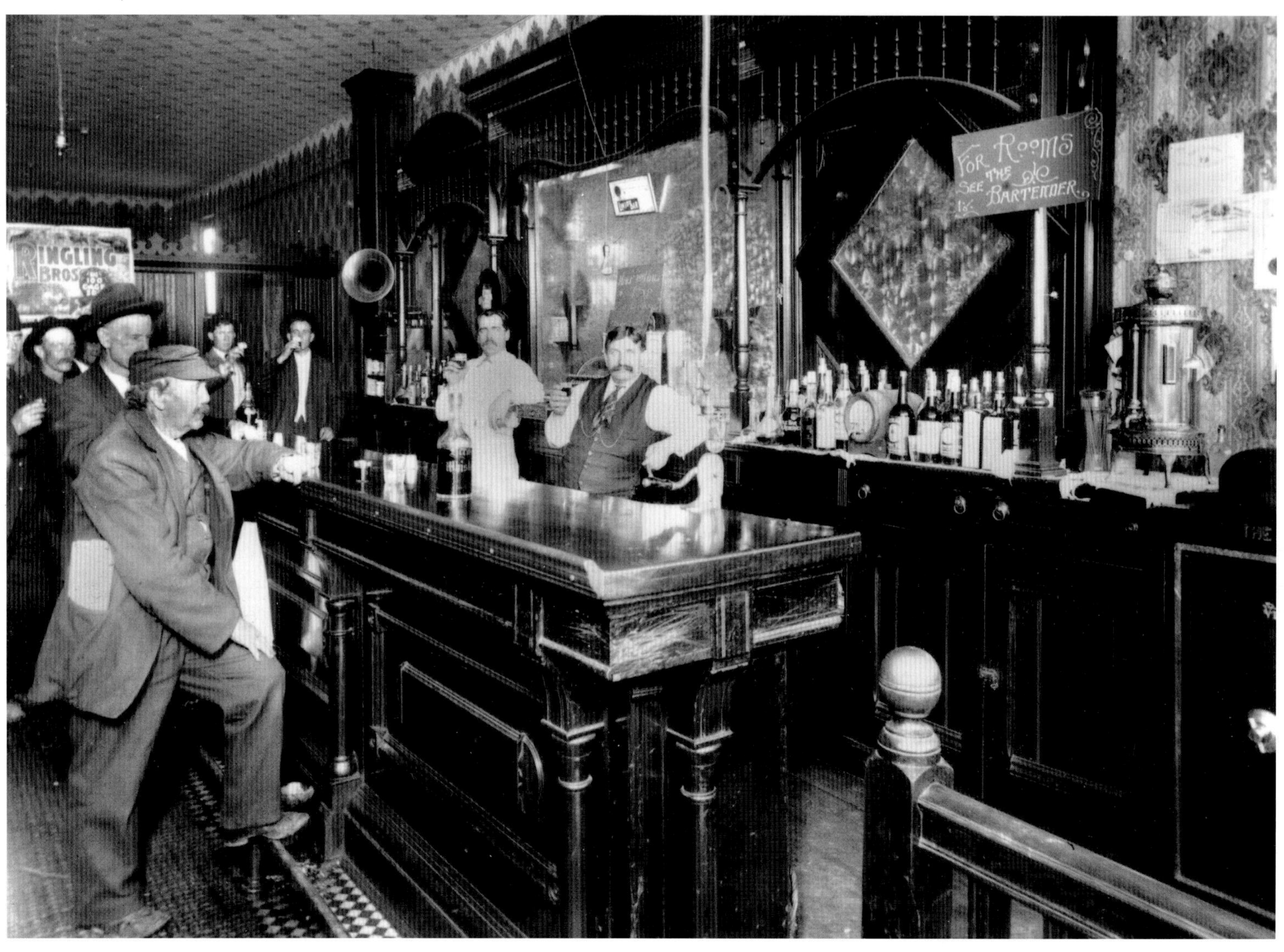

Working men enjoy libation in this Everett saloon in 1907. The bartender also serves as hotel desk clerk as indicated by the sign behind the bar. A poster from the Ringling Brothers Circus provides additional decoration on the back wall.

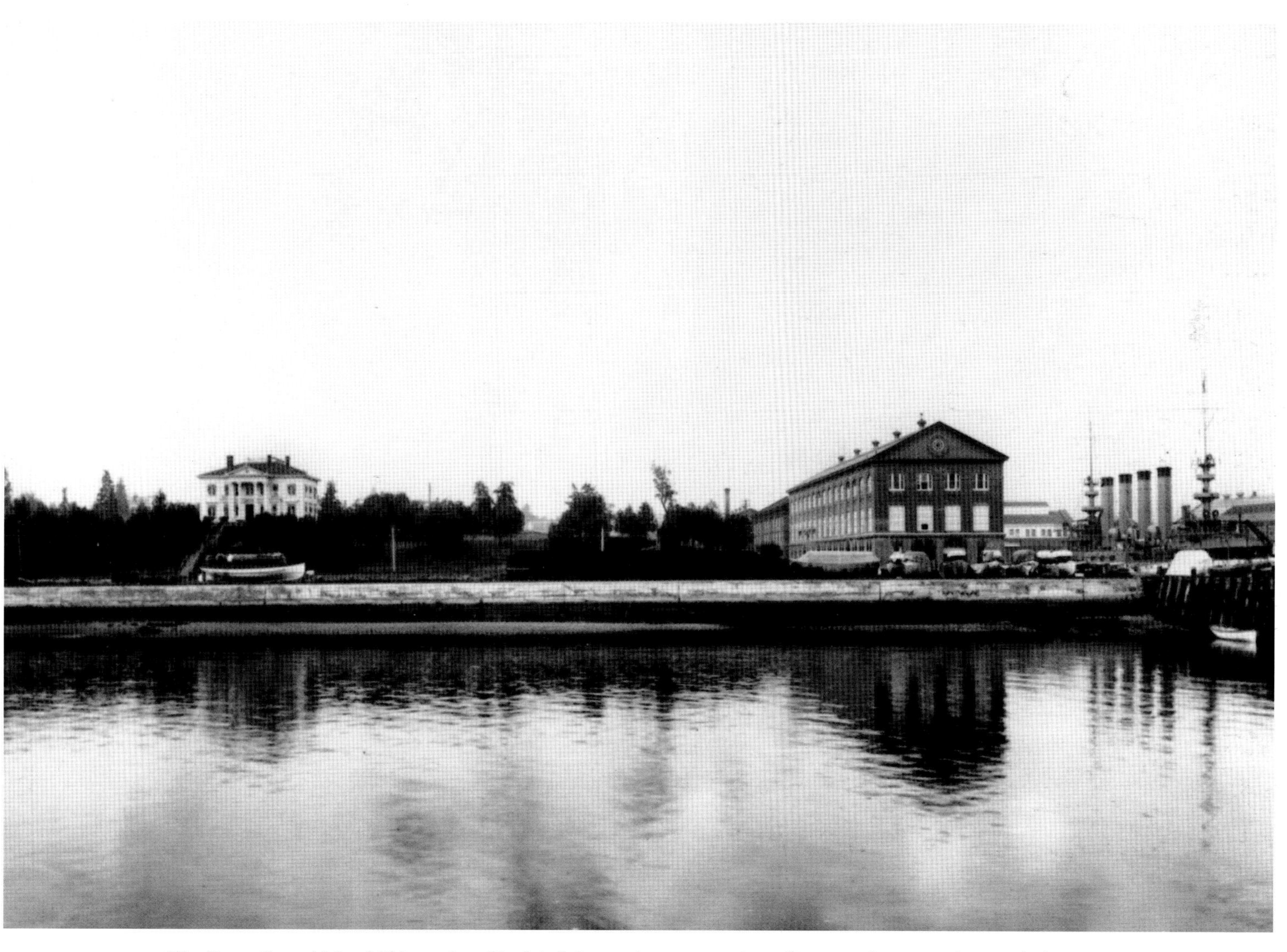

The Puget Sound Naval Shipyard on Sinclair Inlet awaits construction of Dry Dock No. 2 when Asahel Curtis snapped this photo in 1907. The USS *Charleston* sits in the dry dock at right, and one of the officers' homes sits at left. Shipyard expansion would eventually devour the park-like setting around these quarters.

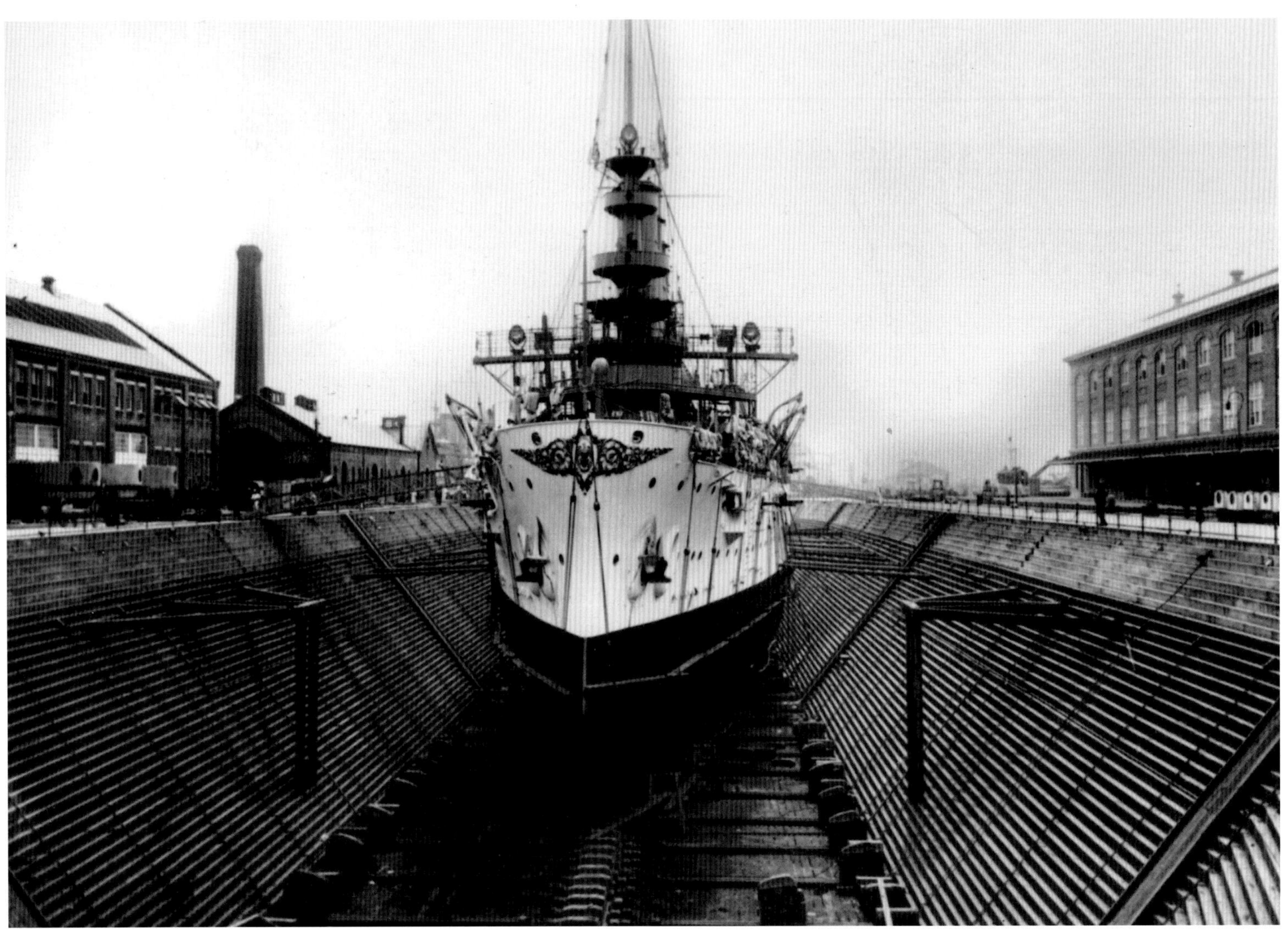

The USS *Charleston* undergoes repairs in Dry Dock No. 1 at the Puget Sound Naval Shipyard prior to being deployed to the Asiatic Station. The *Charleston* was commissioned in 1904 as a protected cruiser and served as flagship of the Pacific Fleet's First Division. She carried fourteen 6-inch guns.

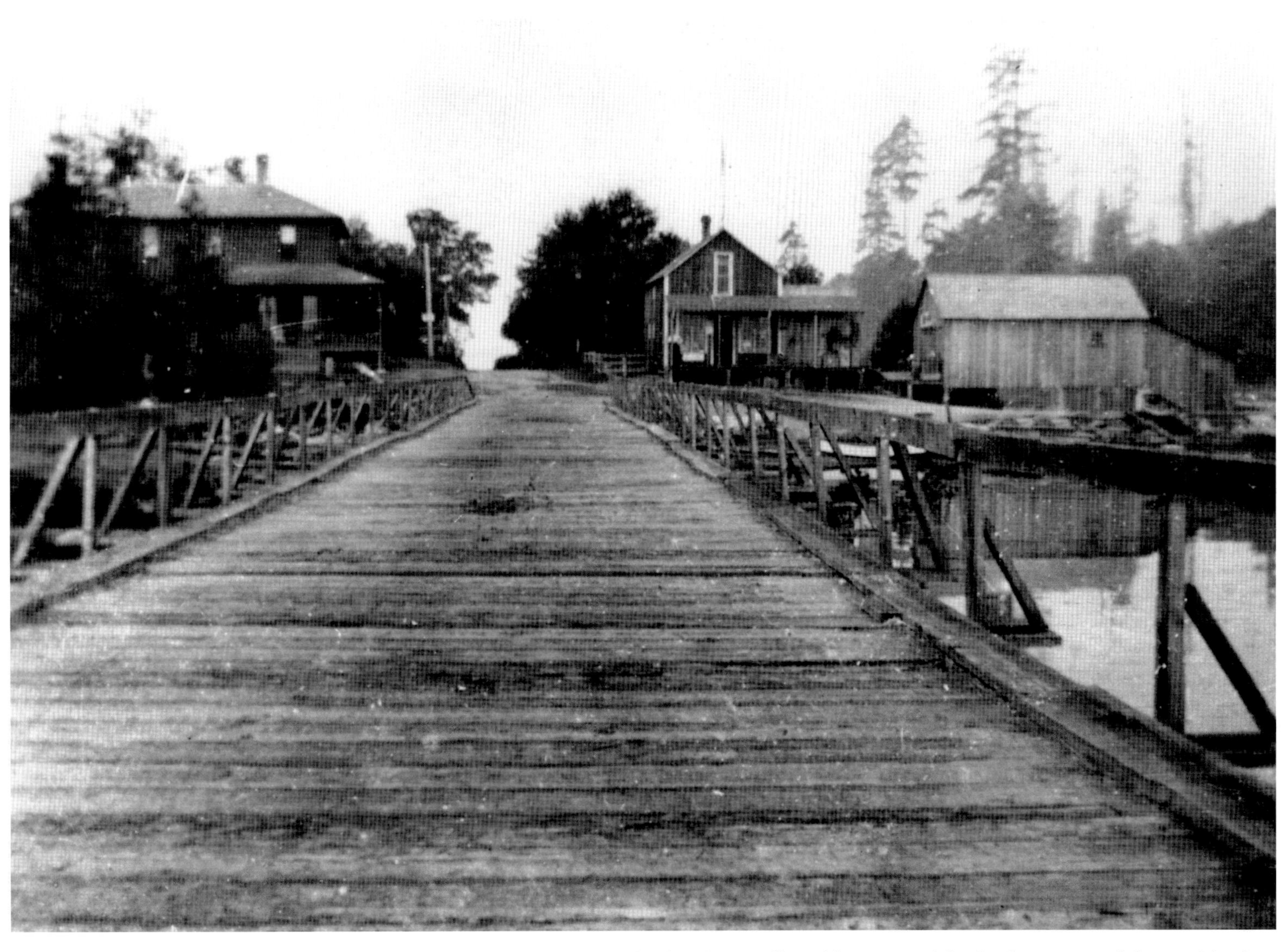

At low tide, a narrow isthmus joined Vashon Island and its small neighbor Maury. This bridge connected the two islands at Portage, where Oliver S. Van Olinda built a store and post office that he photographed in 1908.

In 1896, anarchists of the Mutual Home Association founded Home Colony, situated on Von Geldern Cove (Joe's Bay) on the Key Peninsula. The colonists earned the acrimony of citizens and newspapers in nearby Tacoma over their political beliefs and alleged free love. In 1911, a rift developed in the community over the issue of nude swimming—"nudes" vs. "prudes." The town dissolved in 1920.

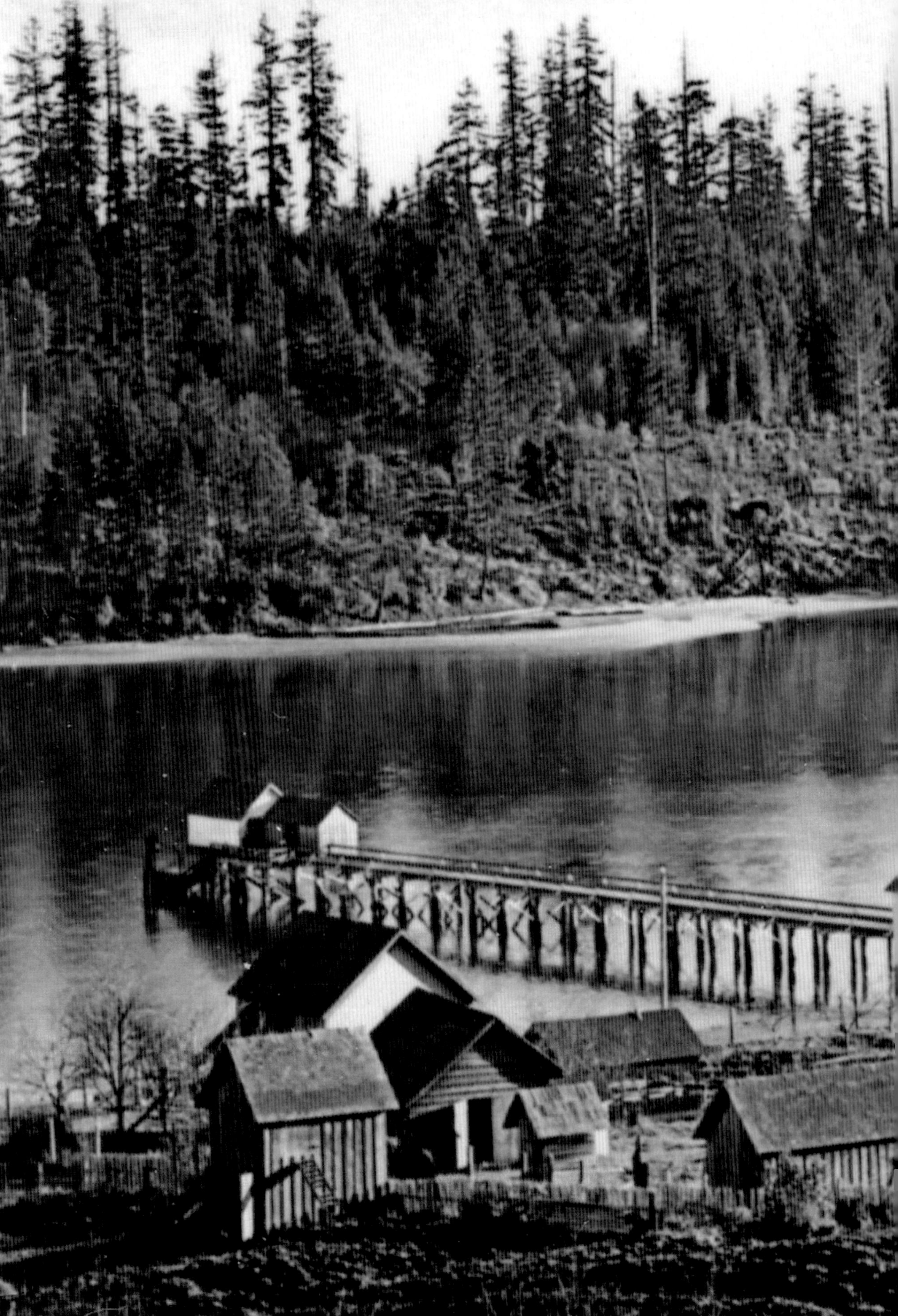

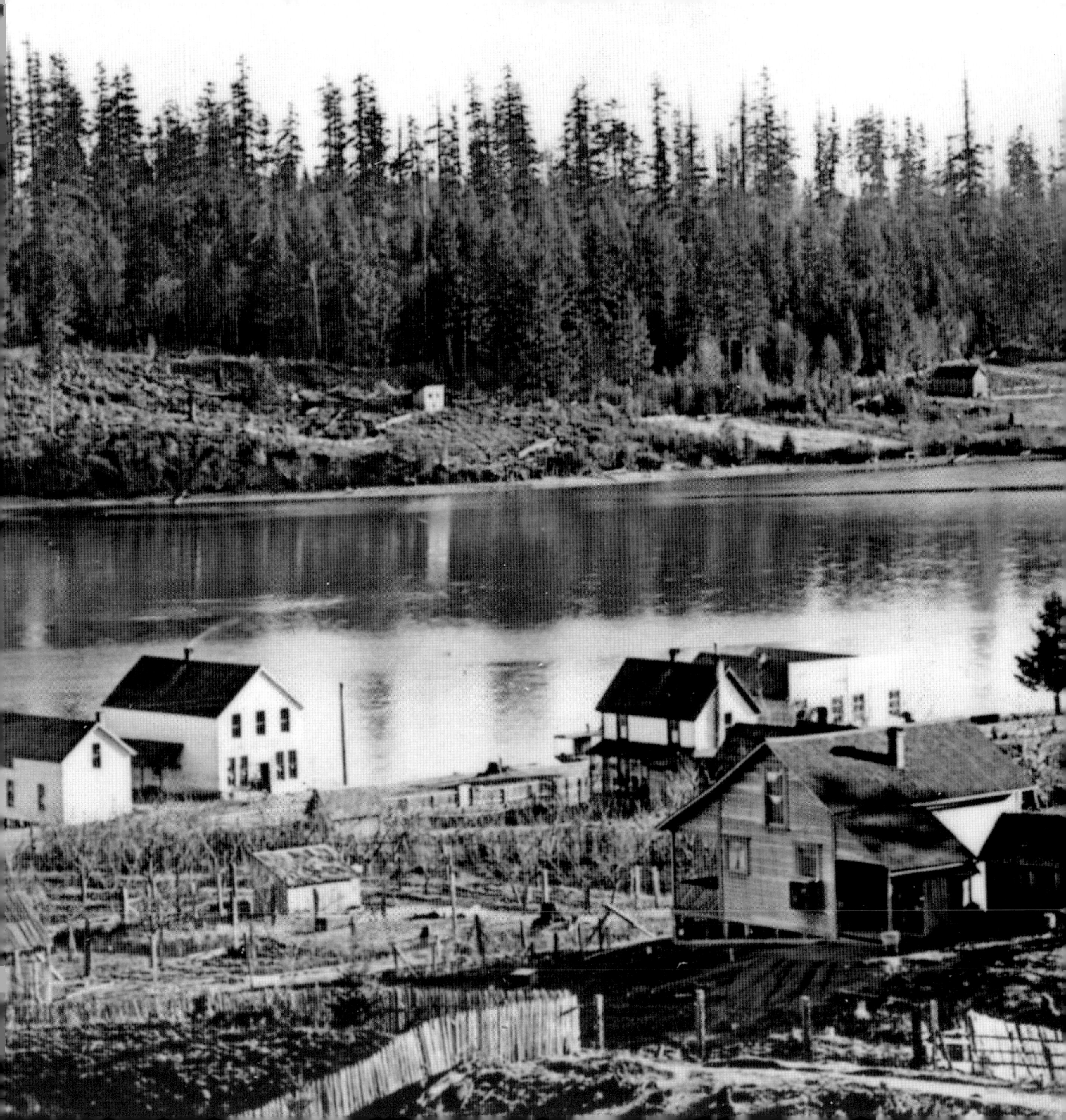

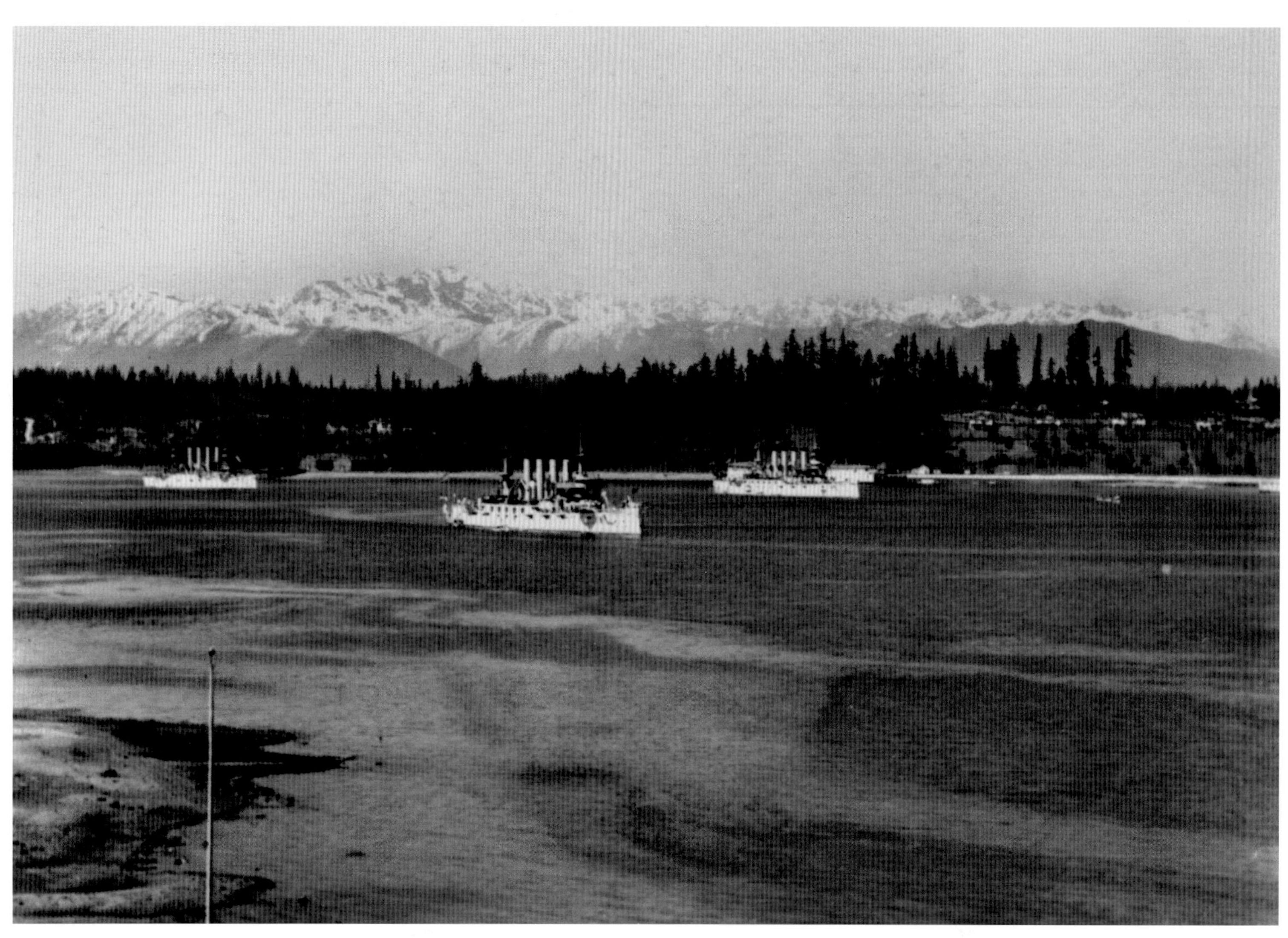

In May 1908, the U.S. Navy's Atlantic Fleet—dubbed the Great White Fleet—swings at anchor in Sinclair Inlet waiting to refit on its voyage around the world. From December 1907 to February 1909, the ships, manned by 14,000 sailors, steamed 43,000 nautical miles and called on six continents.

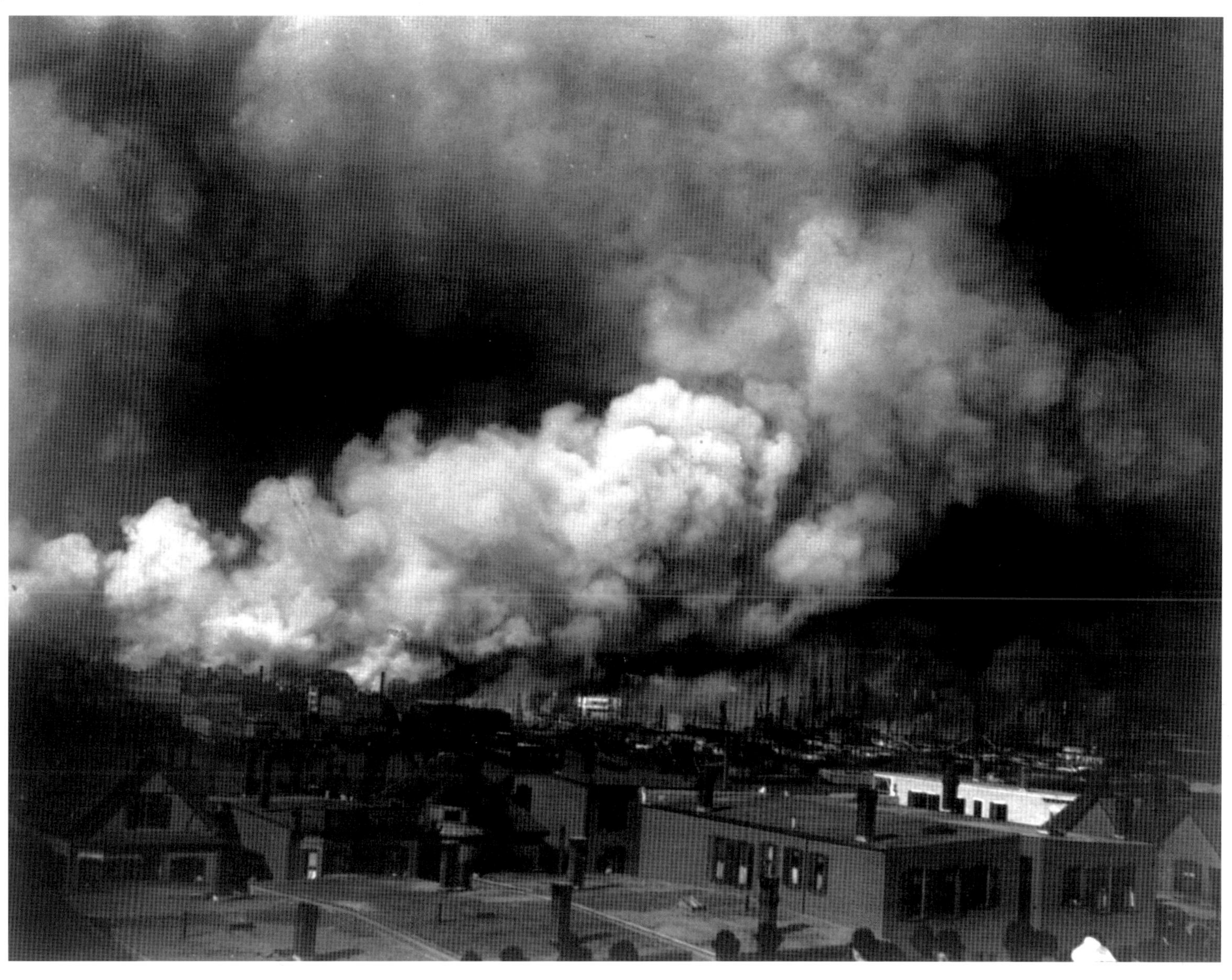

On April 30, 1908, a fire rages in downtown Seattle. The widespread use of coal for heating and coal gas and kerosene for lighting meant that open flames threatened to ignite anything combustible nearby. Fires spread quickly in the dense wood construction.

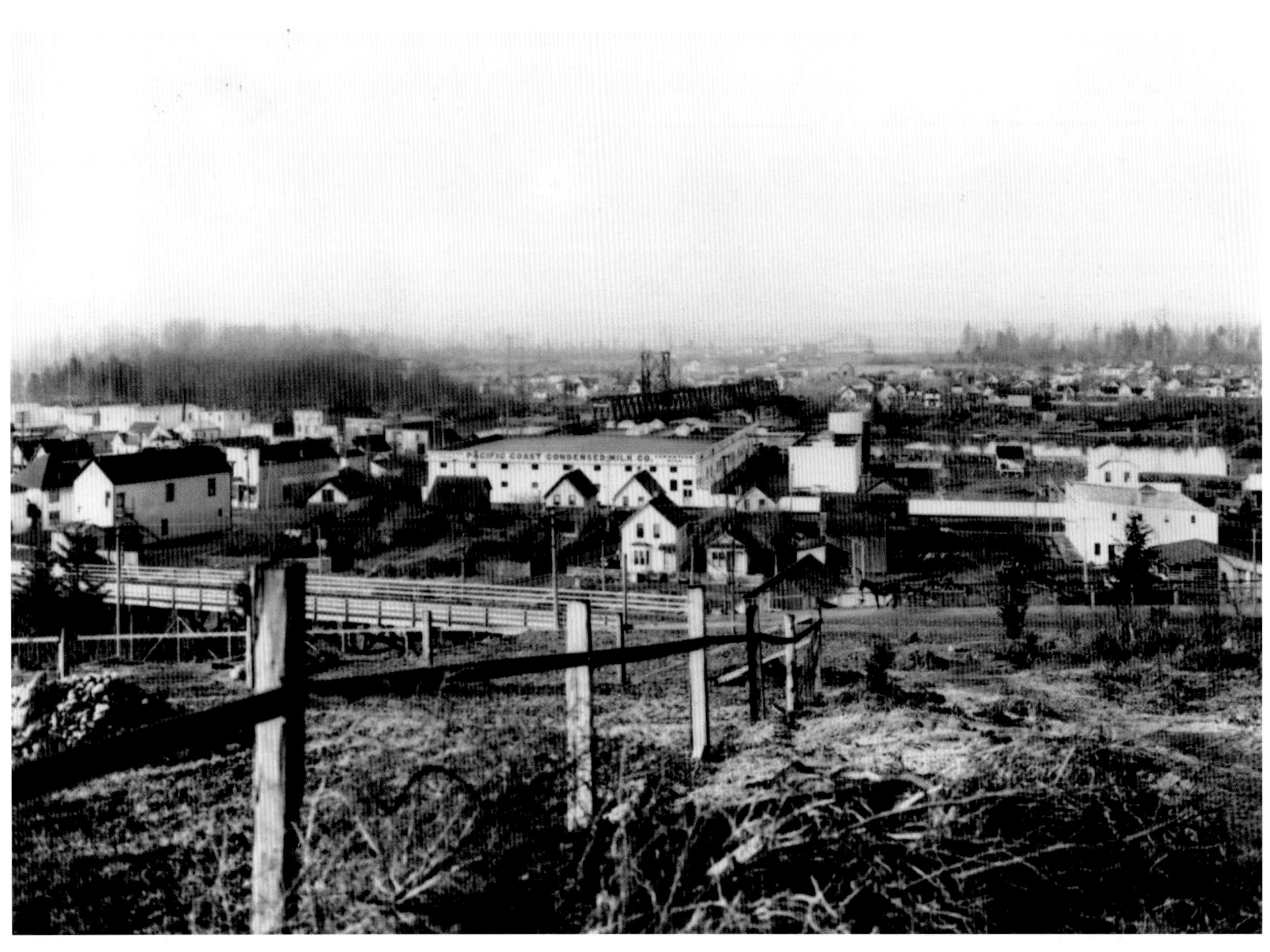

After Joe Wilson and Donald McDonald removed a logjam in the Skagit River in 1876, regular steamer service reached up to Mount Vernon. This allowed the town to grow and eventually become the Skagit County seat. Here in 1908, it is an agricultural center of the Skagit River valley with a Pacific Coast Condensed Milk factory and regular rail service.

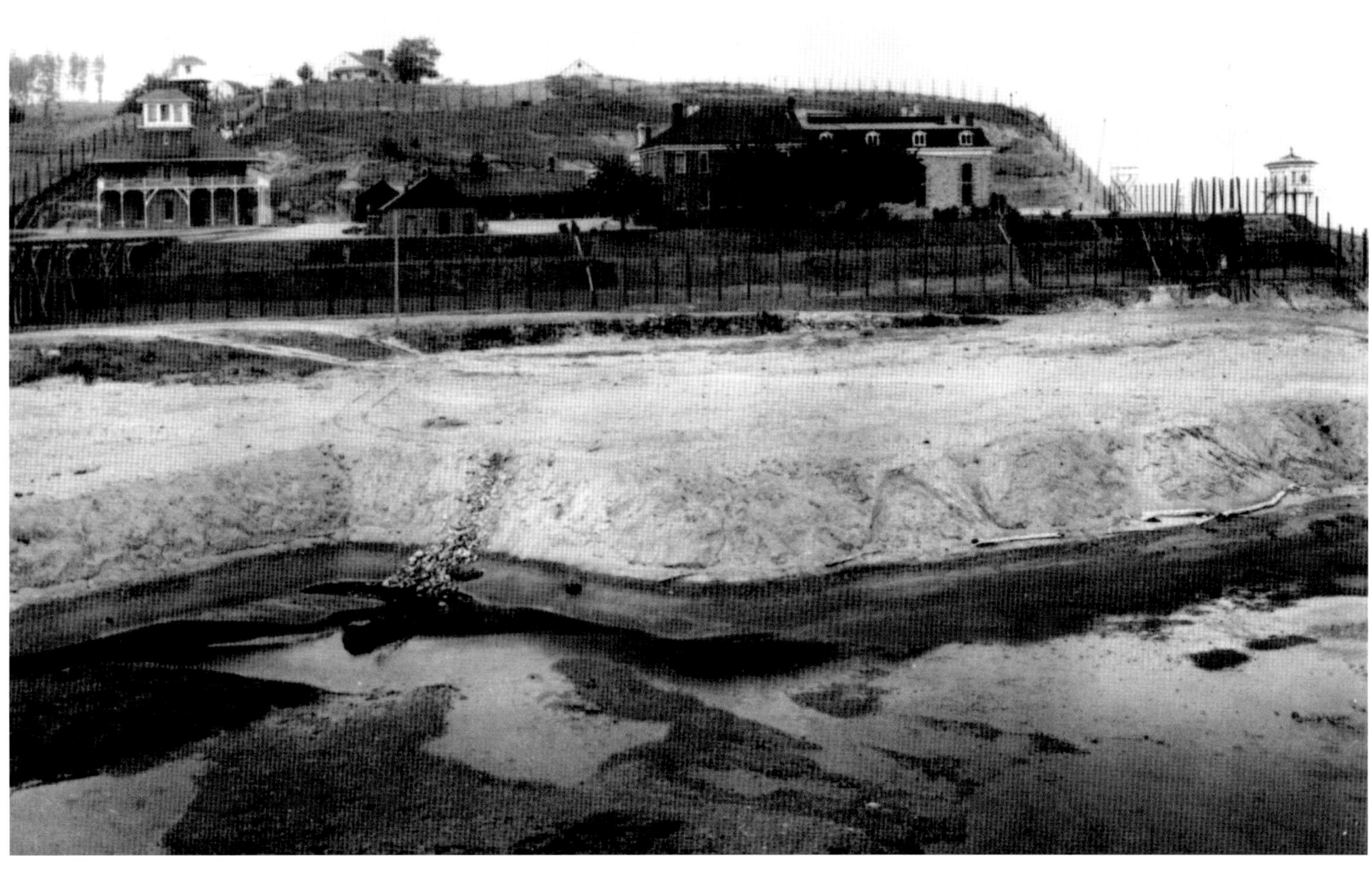

On May 28, 1875, in south Puget Sound, the Washington Territorial Penitentiary on McNeil Island accepted its first prisoners, who had been convicted of robbery and selling whiskey to Indians. In 1889, it became McNeil Island Federal Penitentiary. In this 1908 view by Asahel Curtis, the original Cellhouse No. 1 is visible at right with the officers' quarters just in front. The hospital with its colonnaded veranda sits at left.

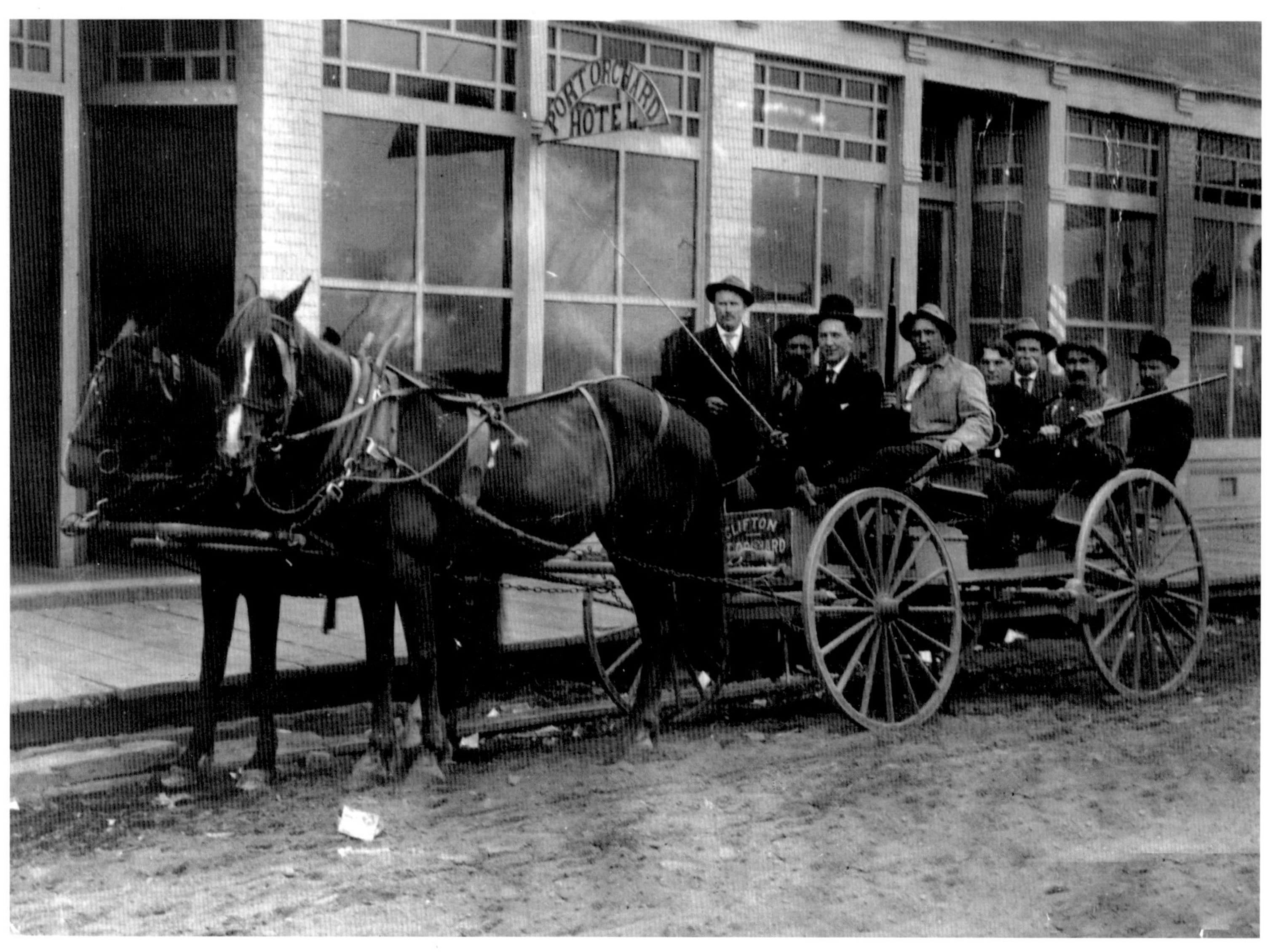

Public transportation took many forms in 1907. Here the *Gamble* stage—with a full load of passengers—prepares to depart the Port Orchard Hotel for Clifton. One man shows off his shotgun.

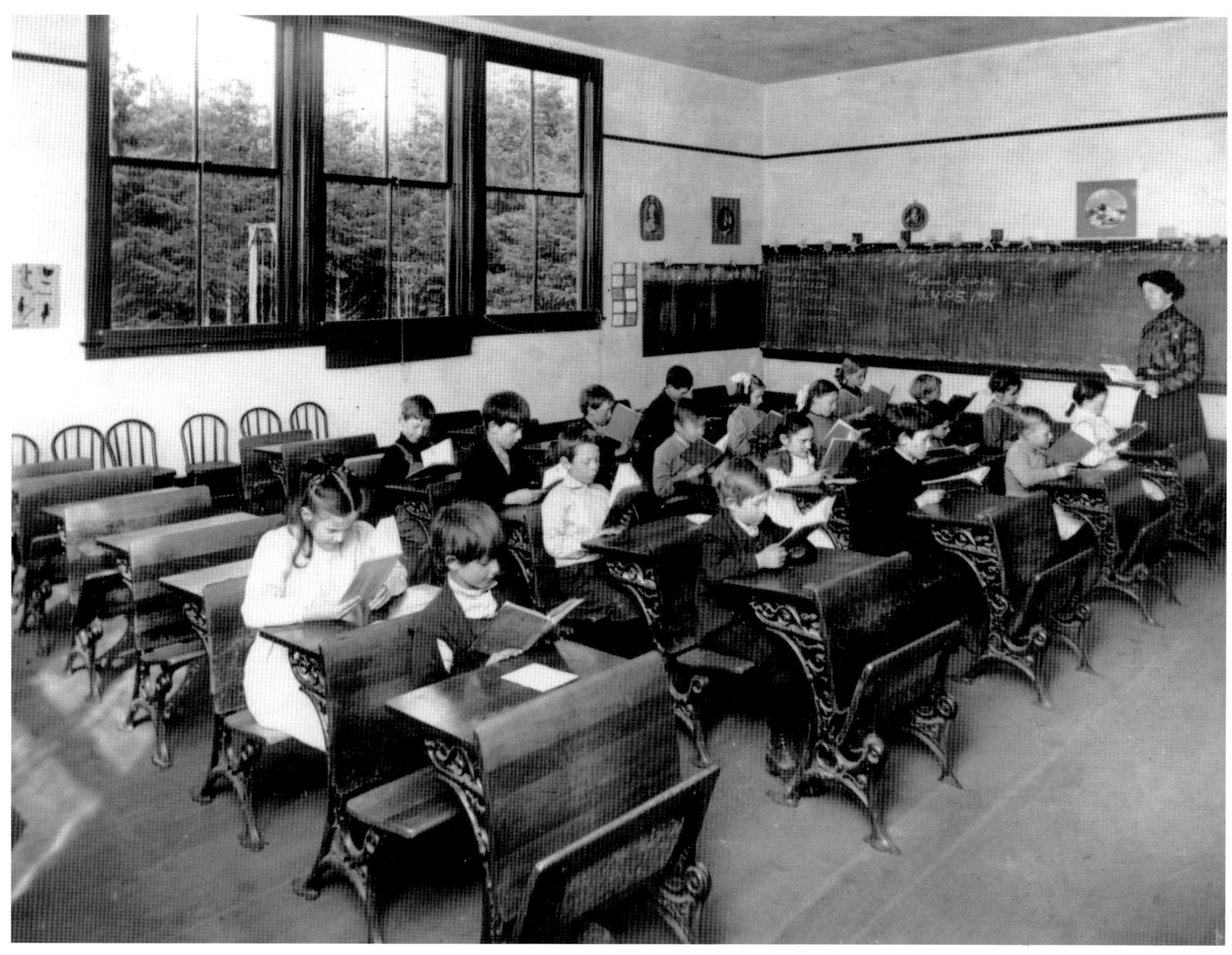

Under the watchful eye of their teacher, Redmond Elementary School students stare intently at their books as they sit for this photo for the 1909 Alaska–Yukon–Pacific Exposition. The A-Y-P, which ran from June to October, celebrated Puget Sound's importance to trade across the Pacific. Three million people attended the fair built on the University of Washington campus.

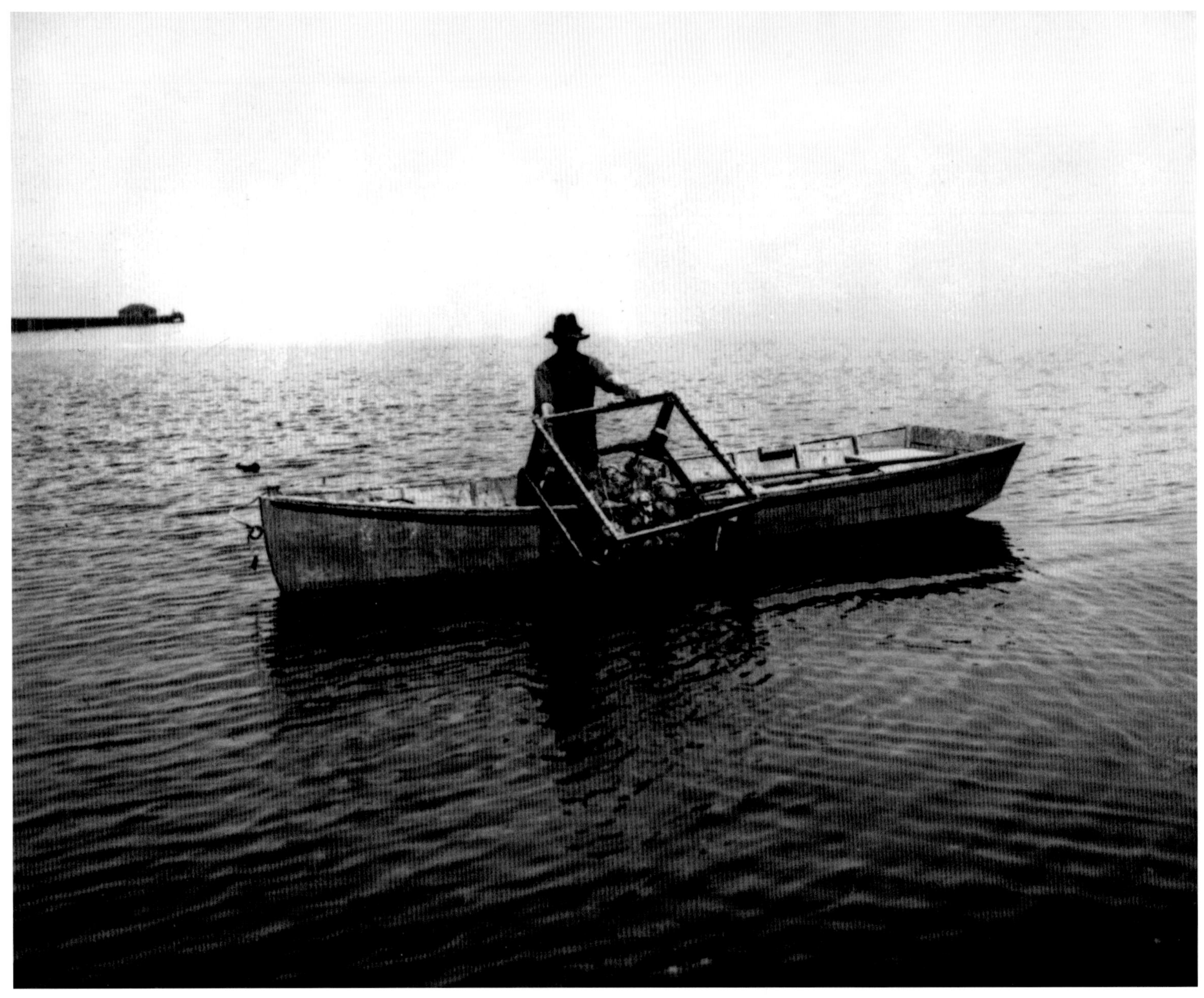

In 1909, this Puget Sound fisherman retrieves his crab pot and what appears to be a fair catch.

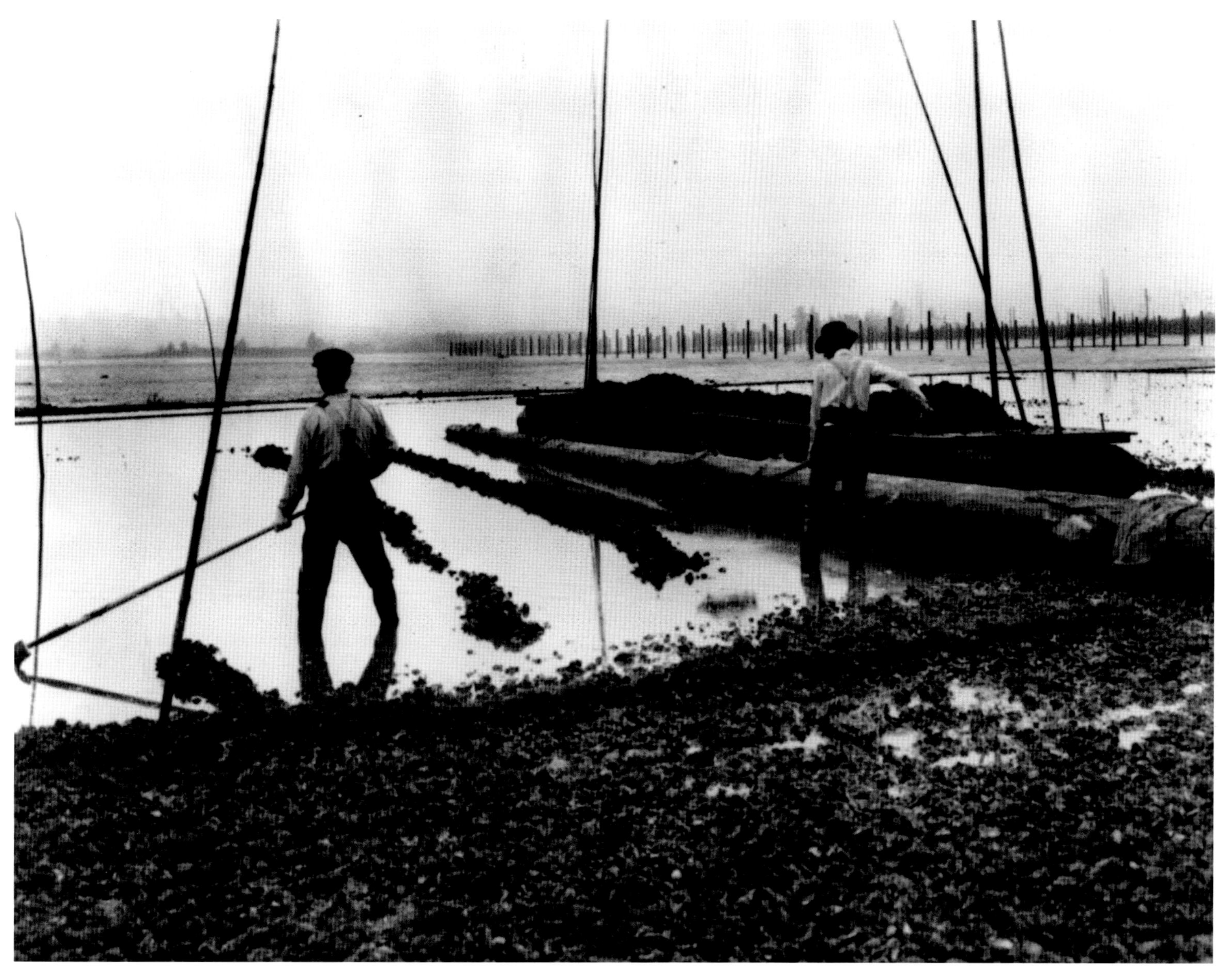

In 1910, oyster farmers rake in their harvest from tidal beds near Olympia. After overharvesting and pollution from lumber and pulp mills depleted native Olympia oysters in the 1890s, commercial growers replaced them with the larger, heartier Japanese oyster *Ostrea gigas*.

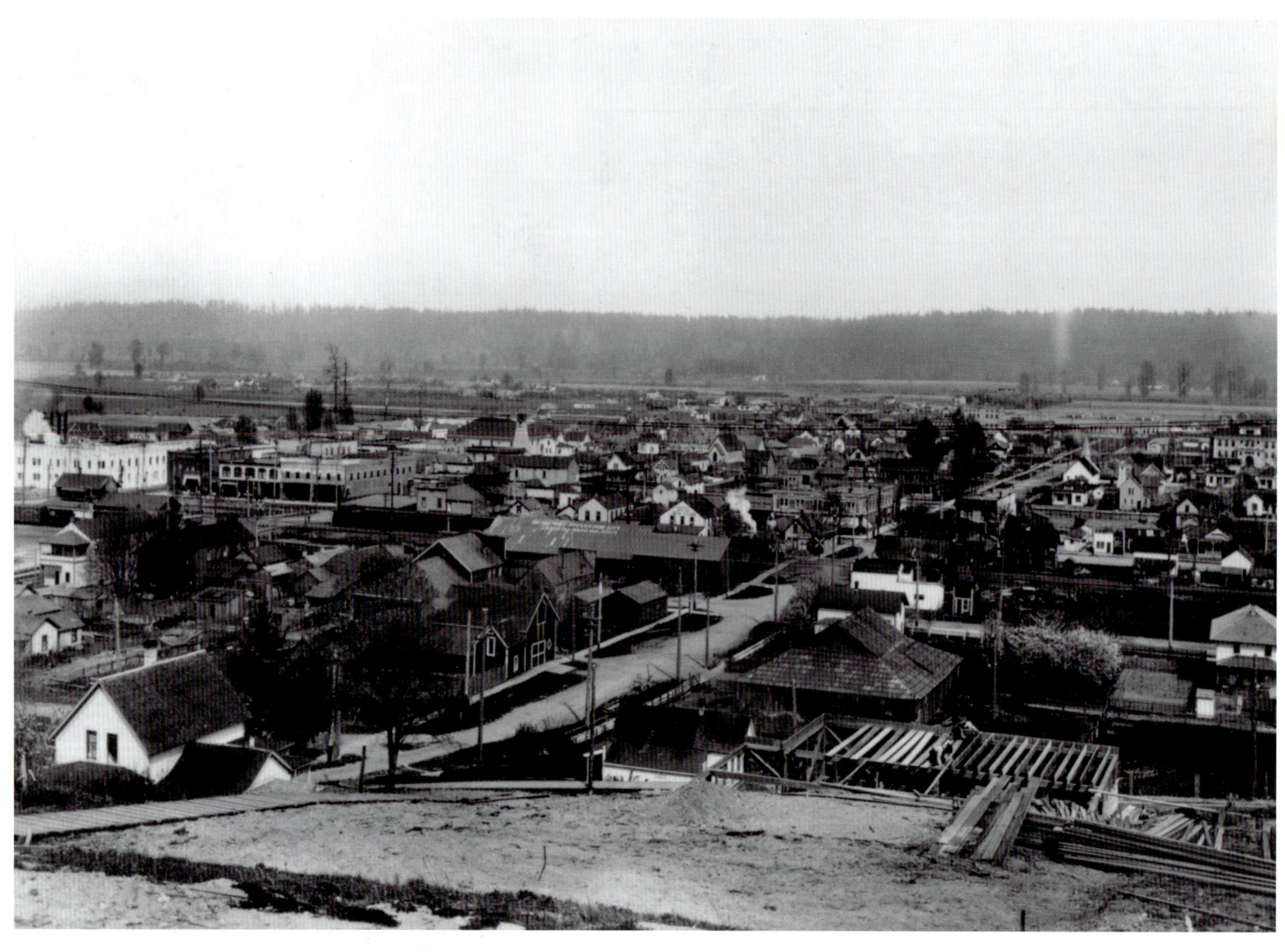

In 1862, John Langston opened a store on the White River 15 miles south of Seattle. The early settlers there called their community Titusville. Twenty-three years later, the Northern Pacific Railroad decided that their station should be called Kent instead. Photographer L. W. Clark catches this bird's-eye view of Kent at the center of a prosperous agricultural region.

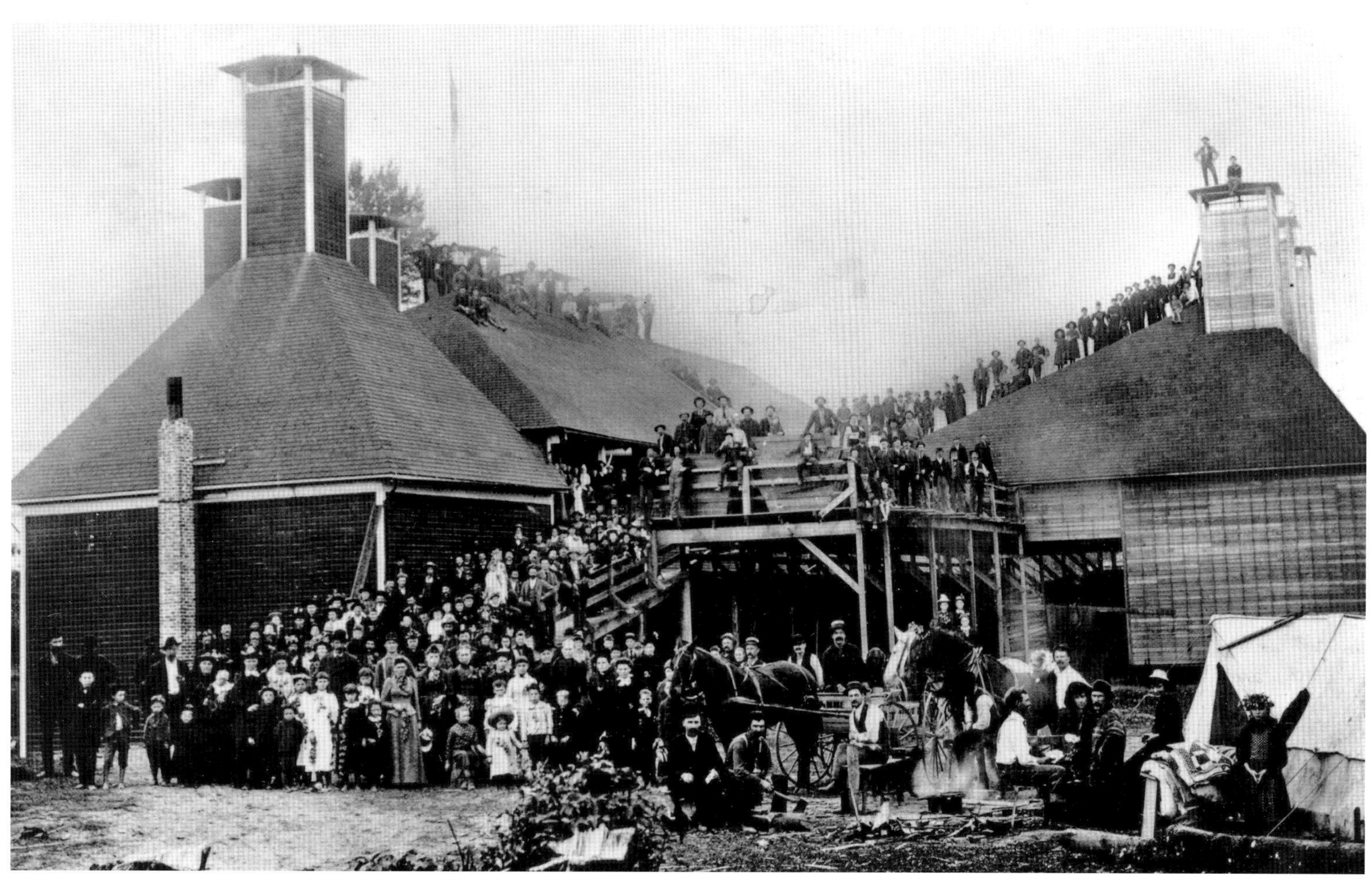

The fertile river valleys that fed Puget Sound proved ideal for growing hops, essential in brewing beer. Growers often hired Native Americans to harvest the plant. In this 1910 view, pickers and residents pose on and in front of kilns where the hops were toasted.

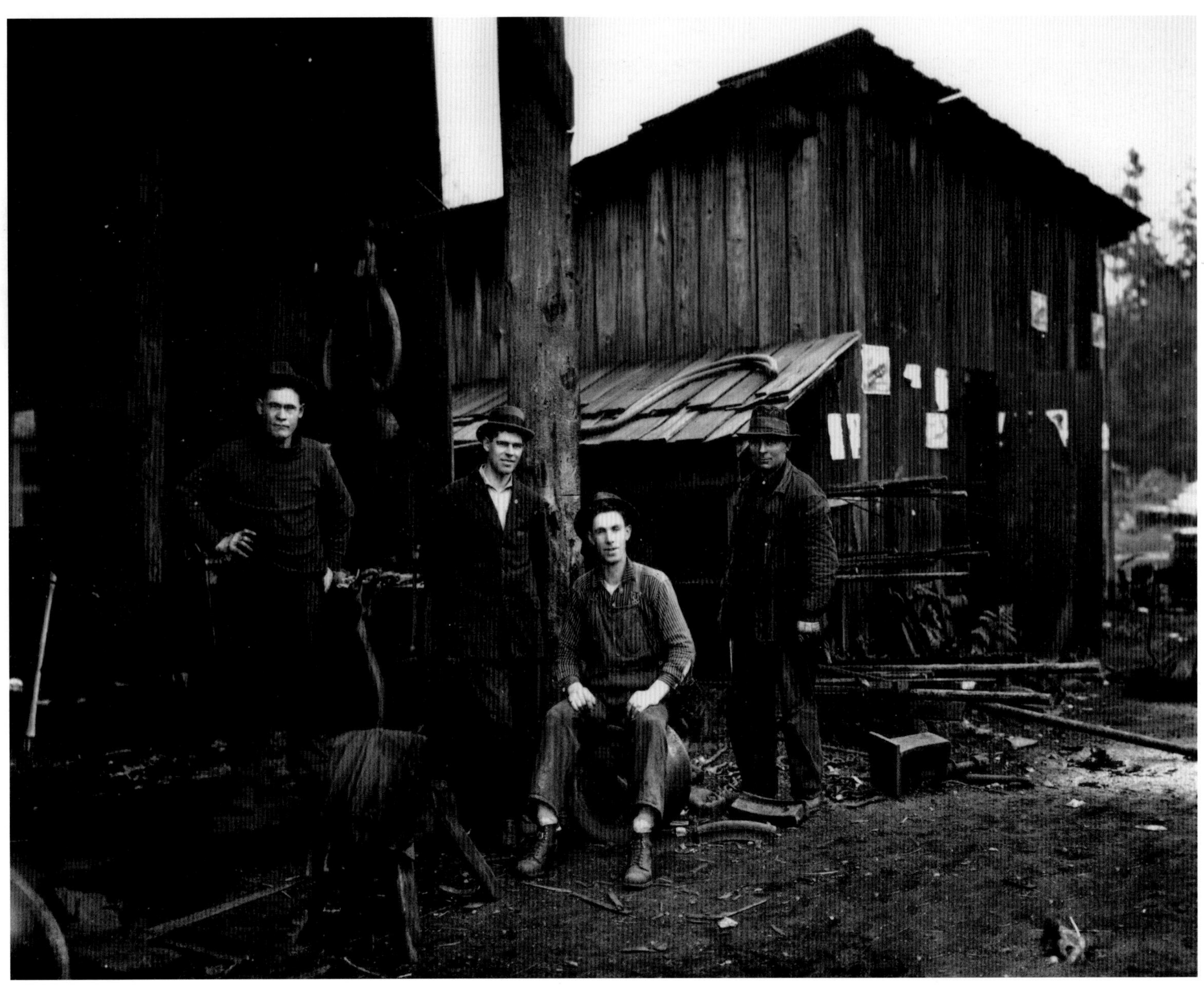

The blacksmith shop staff of the Mud Bay Logging Company takes a break to be photographed by Clark Kinsey. Loggers operated in remote locations, so if a piece of hardware broke, they had to fix it there or wait days or even weeks for a part. Blacksmiths fashioned anything needed to maintain production.

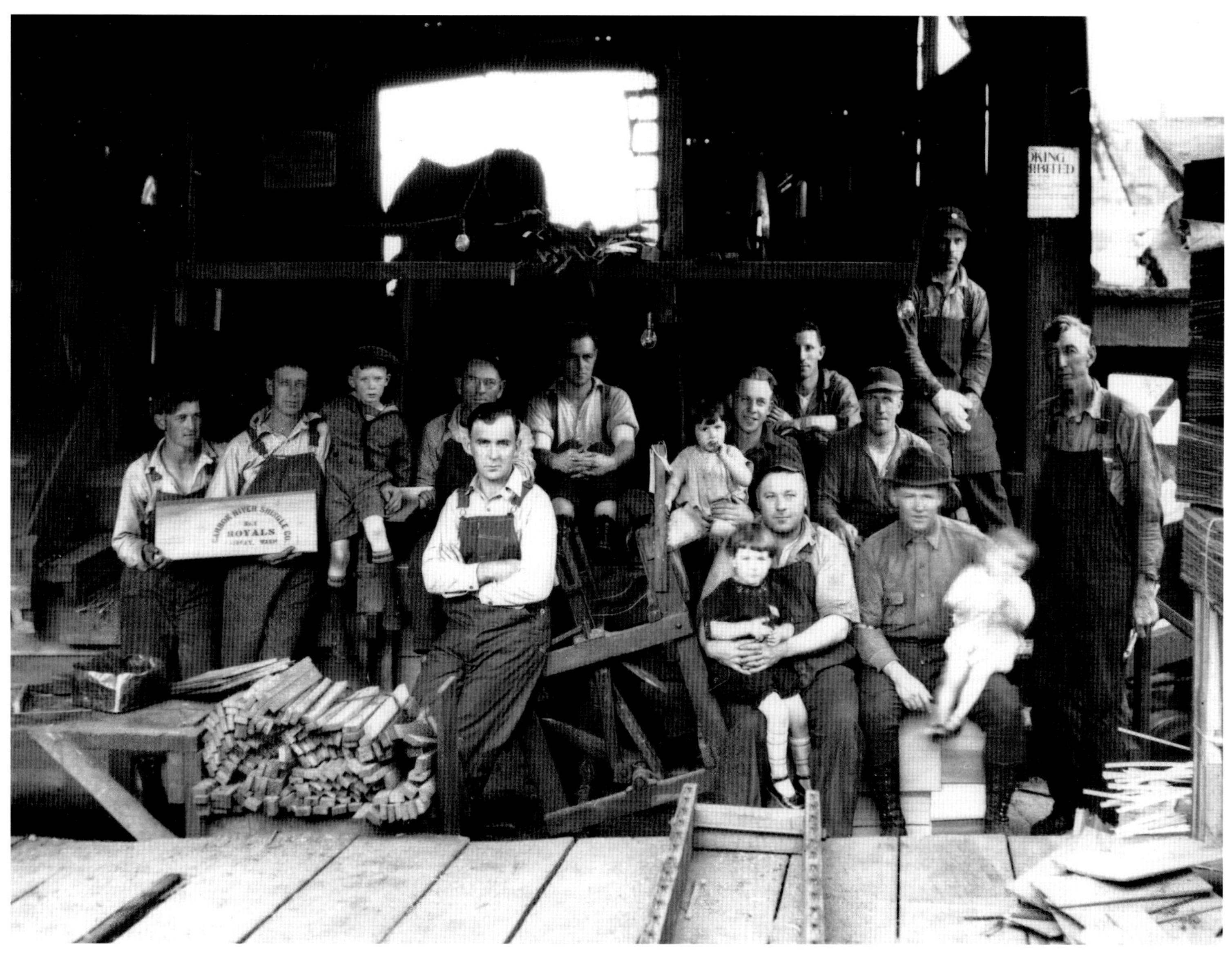

Sitting here with their children in the 1910s, shingle weavers of the Carbon River Shingle Company pause for a photograph at Fairfax, Pierce County. These mill men fed cedar-shingle bolts by hand into the machines' flashing knives, producing up to 30,000 shingles a day. Not a few weavers lost fingers in the process.

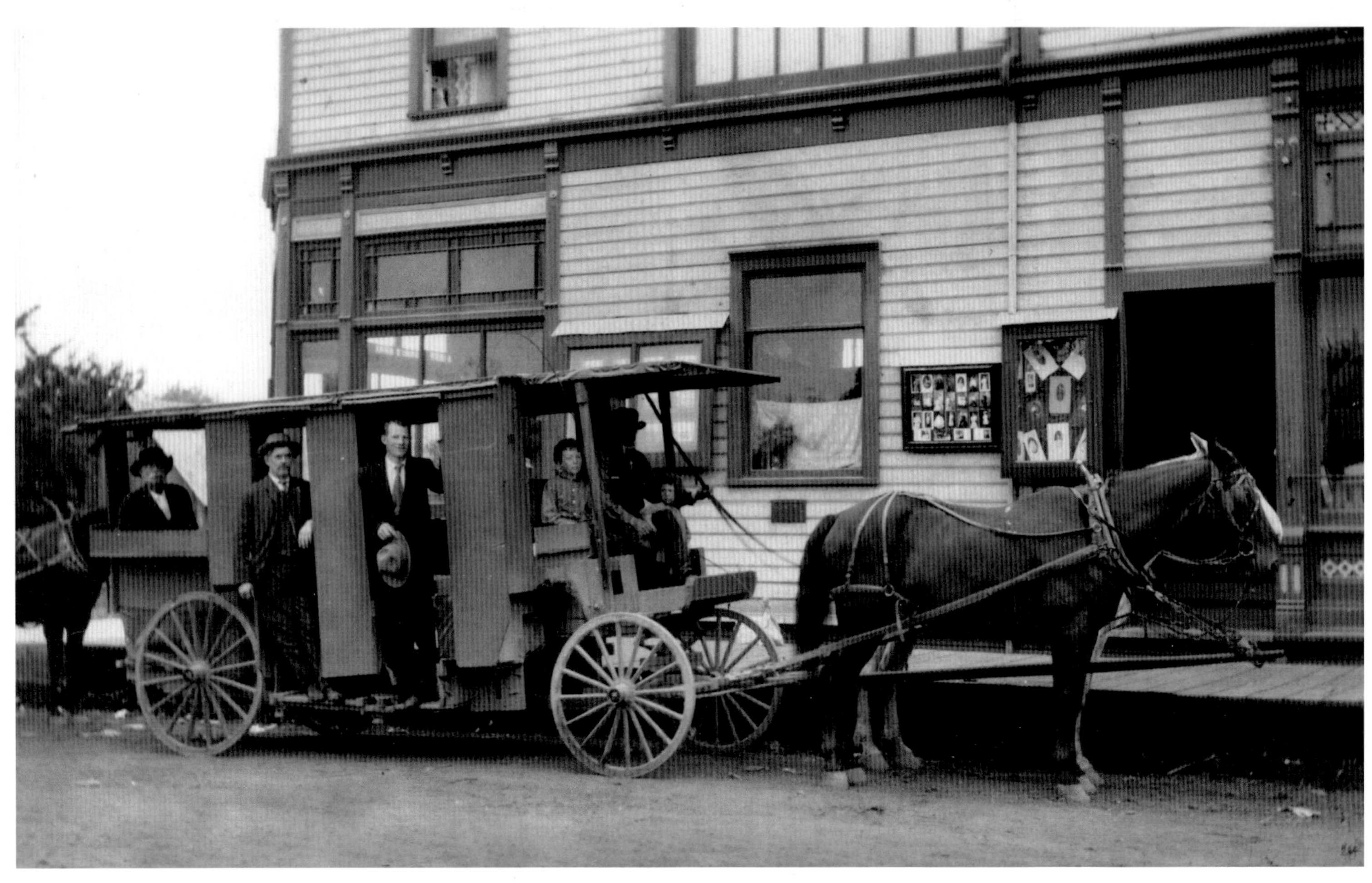

In 1907 and again in 1914, downtown Shelton, in Mason County, burned to the ground. Around that time, these sightseers get ready for a tour of the town in a makeshift stage, probably to size up real estate opportunities. At the beginning of the twentieth century, four of the largest logging companies in the state operated in the county.

INDUSTRY FINDS A HOME

(1911–1939)

Now that railroads reached the Pacific, eastern investors found many opportunities on Puget Sound. Within a few short years of its founding in 1890, Everett's waterfront bustled with lumber and shake mills, shipyards, and a smelter. Salmon canneries popped up on wharves to process the hundreds of millions of fish caught by seiner fleets. Every small Sound community was home port to at least one boat and crew. The opening of the Panama Canal in 1914 also improved maritime traffic with the East Coast and Europe.

Business and civic leaders had recently celebrated Puget Sound's future with the 1909 Alaska–Yukon–Pacific Exposition in Seattle. Its symbol of three women—one from North America holding a locomotive, one from Alaska holding gold nuggets, and one from Asia holding a ship—celebrated trade, prosperity, and the region's strategic position in the world.

Puget Sound's prosperous location proved beneficial to the country during the First World War. Fighting broke out in Europe in 1914, and the conflict spread so far that it became a world war. The Sound provided materiel for the combatants and, after the U.S. entered the conflict, shipyards turned out thousands of ships and craft to expand the fleet. Thousands of soldiers and sailors trained ashore, and many stayed behind after the Armistice.

Travel on Puget Sound continued to rely heavily on the Mosquito Fleet, but advancing technology required that the steamers transport automobiles. Passenger ships emerged from dry docks as car ferries. Lines of trucks and automobiles waiting for the next ferry became a permanent part of the Puget Sound scenery and culture.

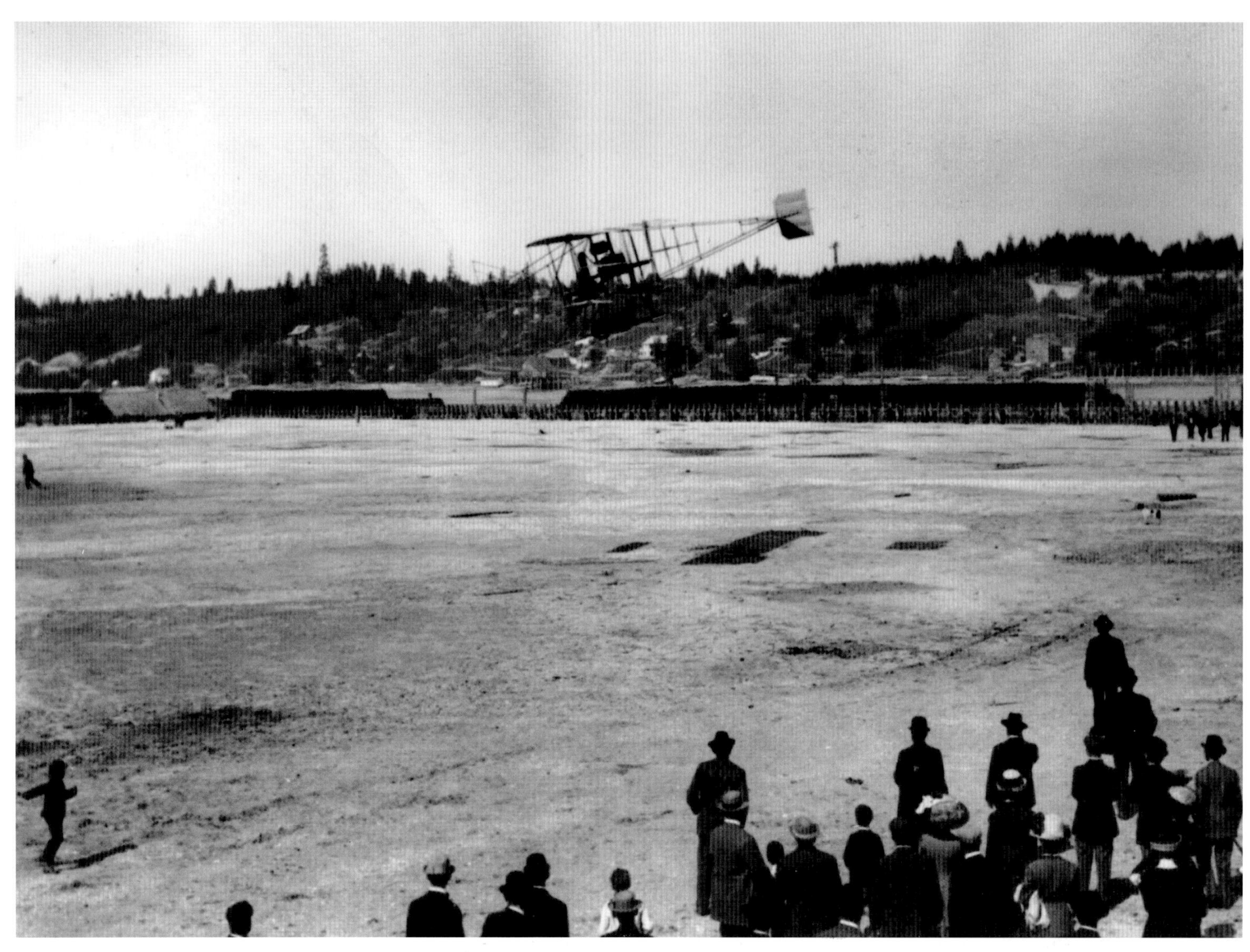

In the spring of 1911, race car driver–turned aviator Fred J. Wiseman toured the Puget Sound region, demonstrating powered flight in a Curtiss–Wright–Farman biplane. Wiseman had to use whatever open ground was available for landings and takeoffs, including this recently filled tide land on Budd Inlet in Olympia. Wiseman went on to become an oil executive. His plane is displayed at the National Postal Museum in Washington, D.C.

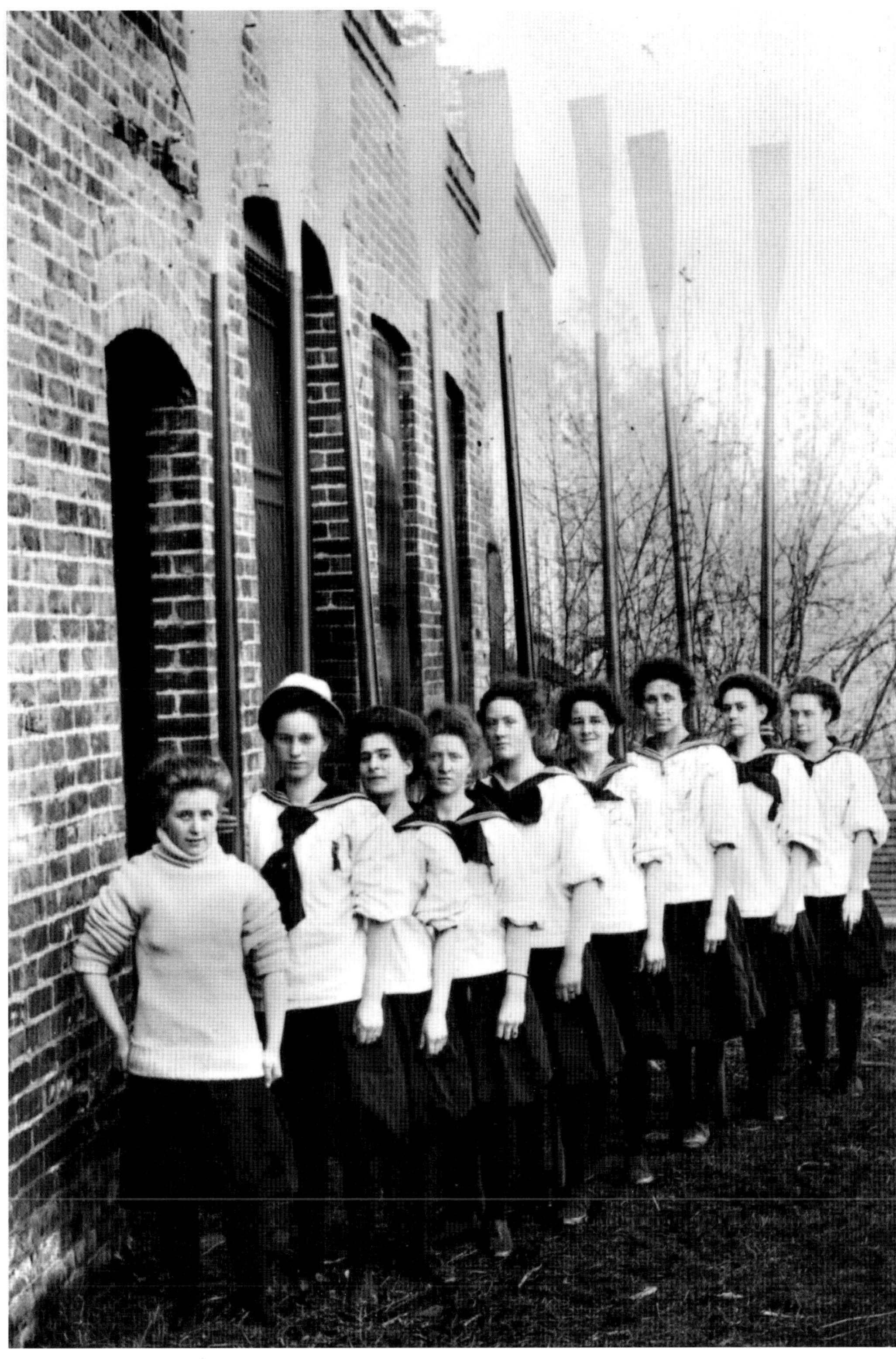

Women at the University of Washington first rowed competitively in 1903, the season that the men beat the University of California. The 1911 women's crew show off their oars and uniforms during a period when they were prohibited from competing because the faculty considered rowing too strenuous for them. Nonetheless, they trained and competed among themselves. They named their teams after prominent leaders in the women's suffrage movement.

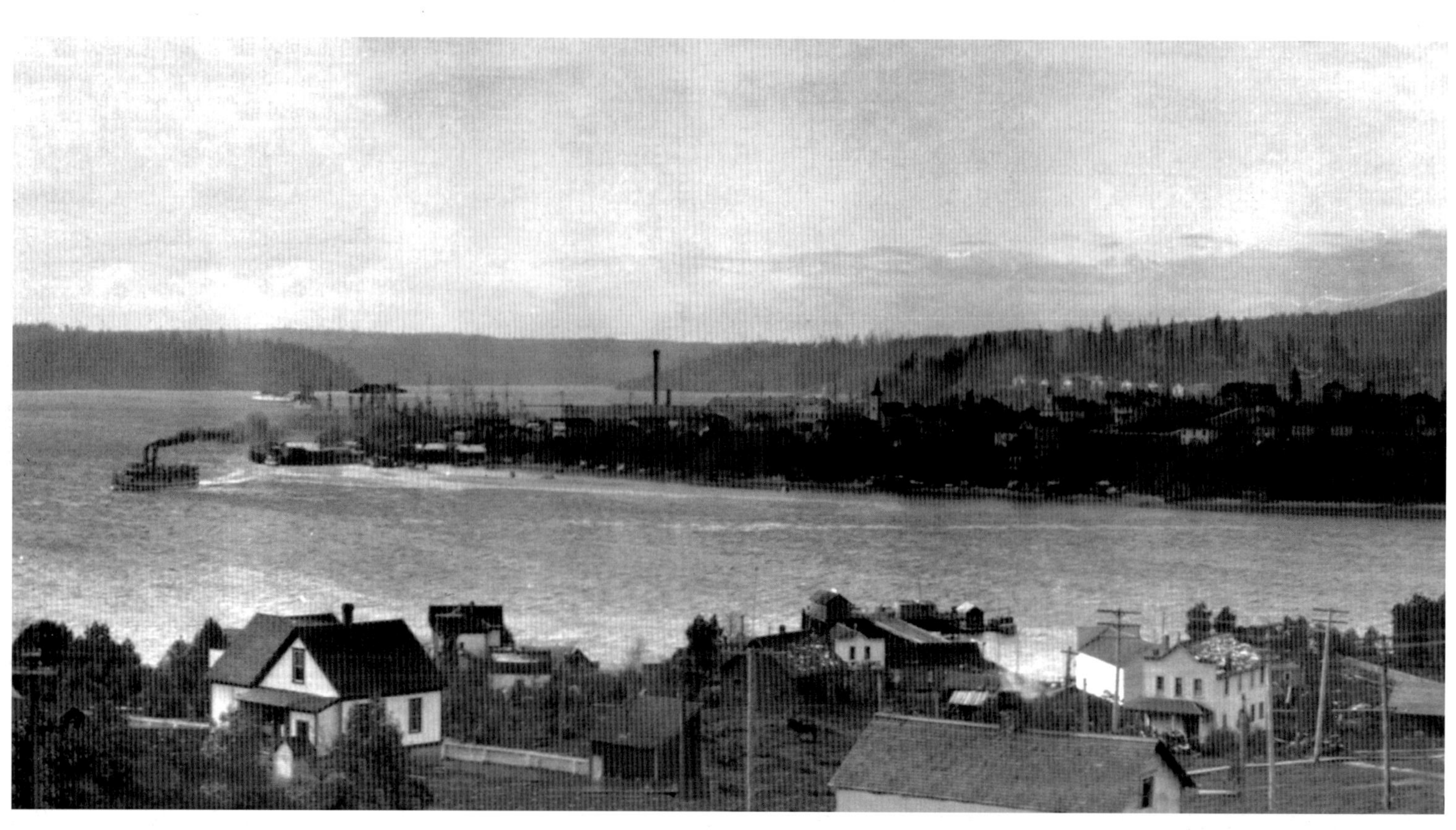

This panorama of Bremerton looks west across Washington Narrows from Point Herron. A Mosquito Fleet steamer departs with passengers, probably for Seattle.

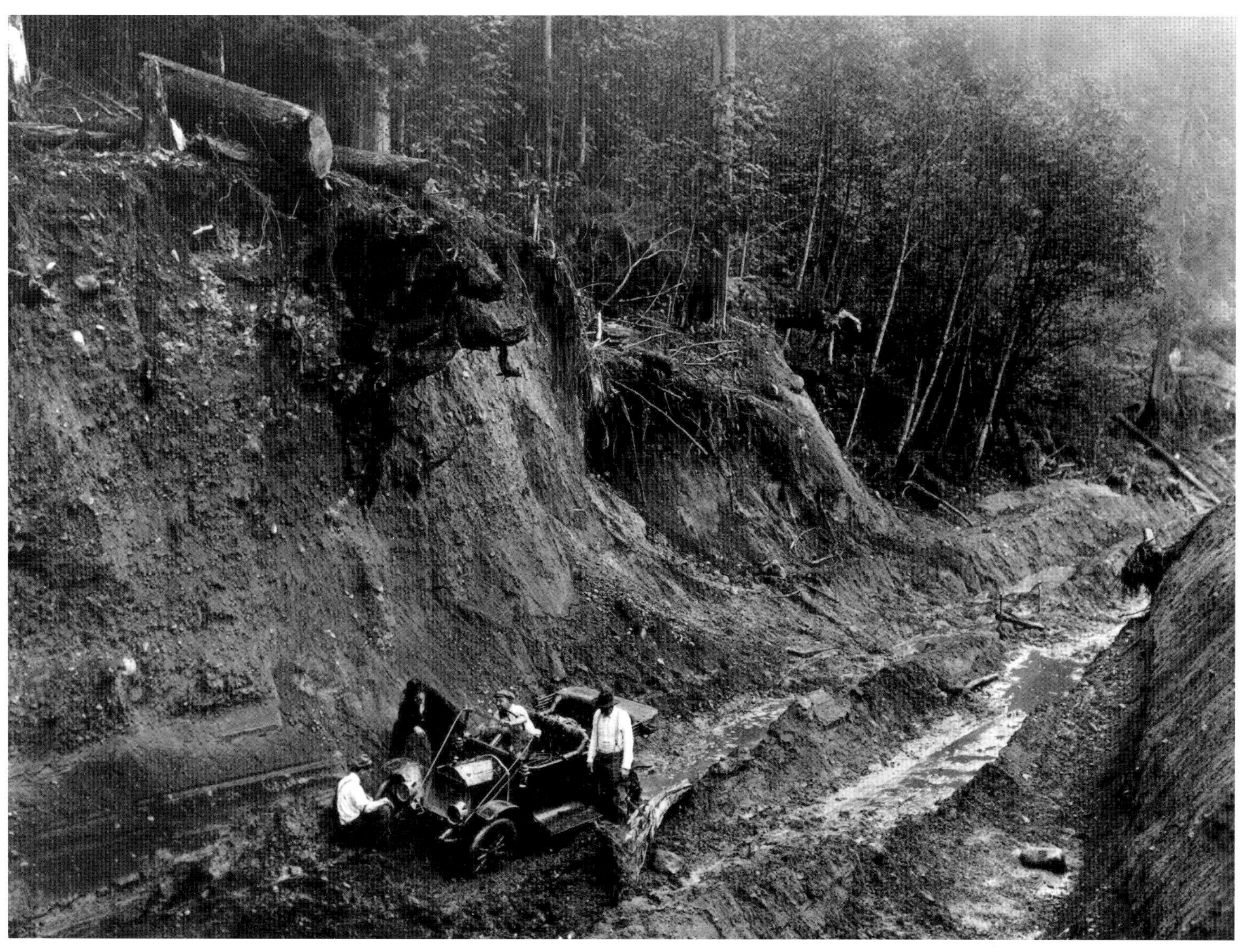

Automobile travel in 1911 presented many challenges. In this case, a Flanders Model 20 and its five passengers—including photographer Lee Pickett—have become mired in the New County Road while returning to Everett from Index. The Flanders car was manufactured by the E-M-F Company from 1909 to 1912. Although the company name stood for its founders, the car owners claimed it stood for Every Morning Fix it and Every Mechanical Fault.

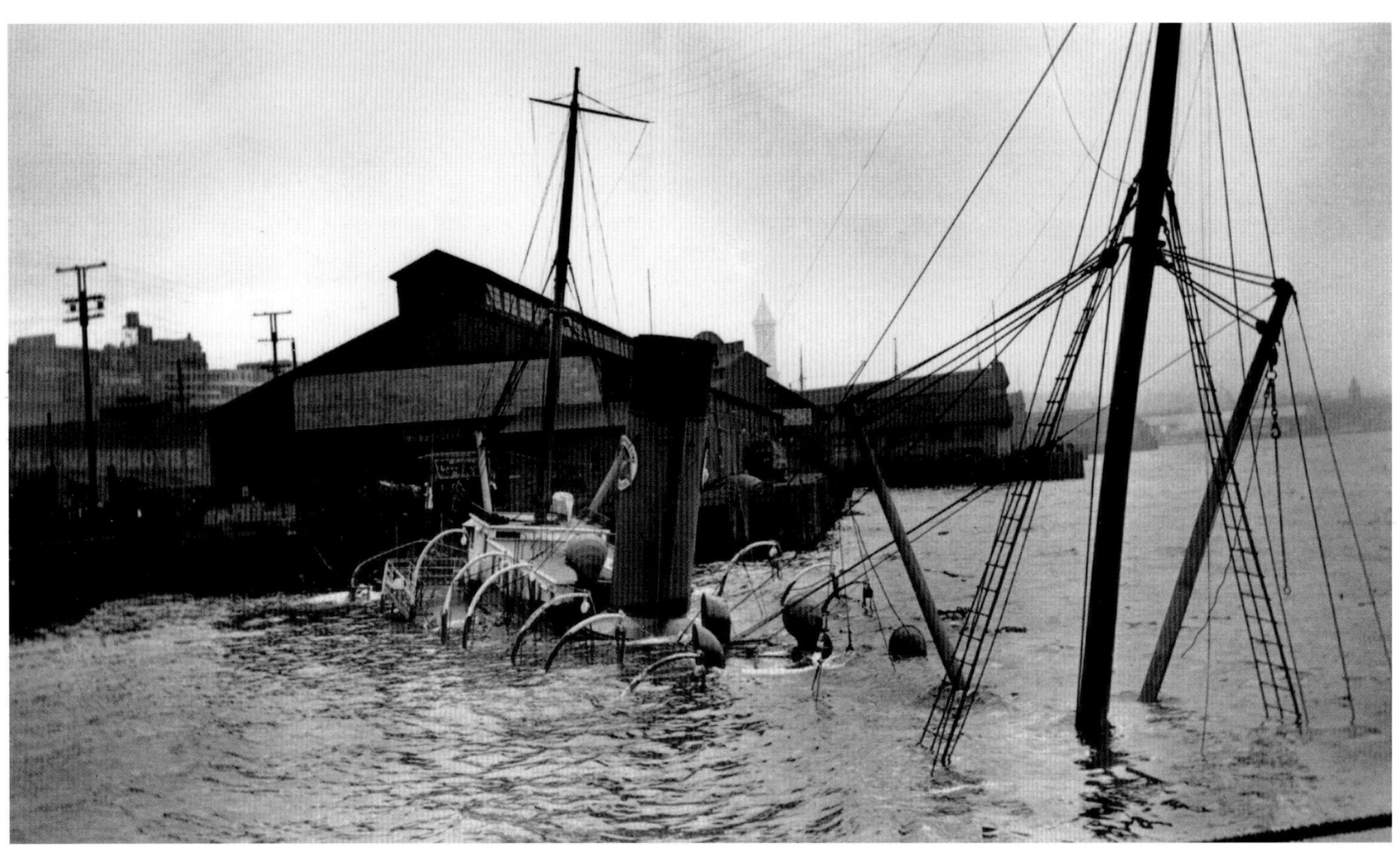

At midnight on May 18, 1911, the steamer *Tampico* experienced hull trouble at the Pacific Coast Coal Company dock on Seattle's waterfront. Despite rescue efforts by her crew and crews of the fireboat *Snoqualmie* and the tug *Lumberman*, the *Tampico* sank. The owners raised the *Tampico* six weeks later.

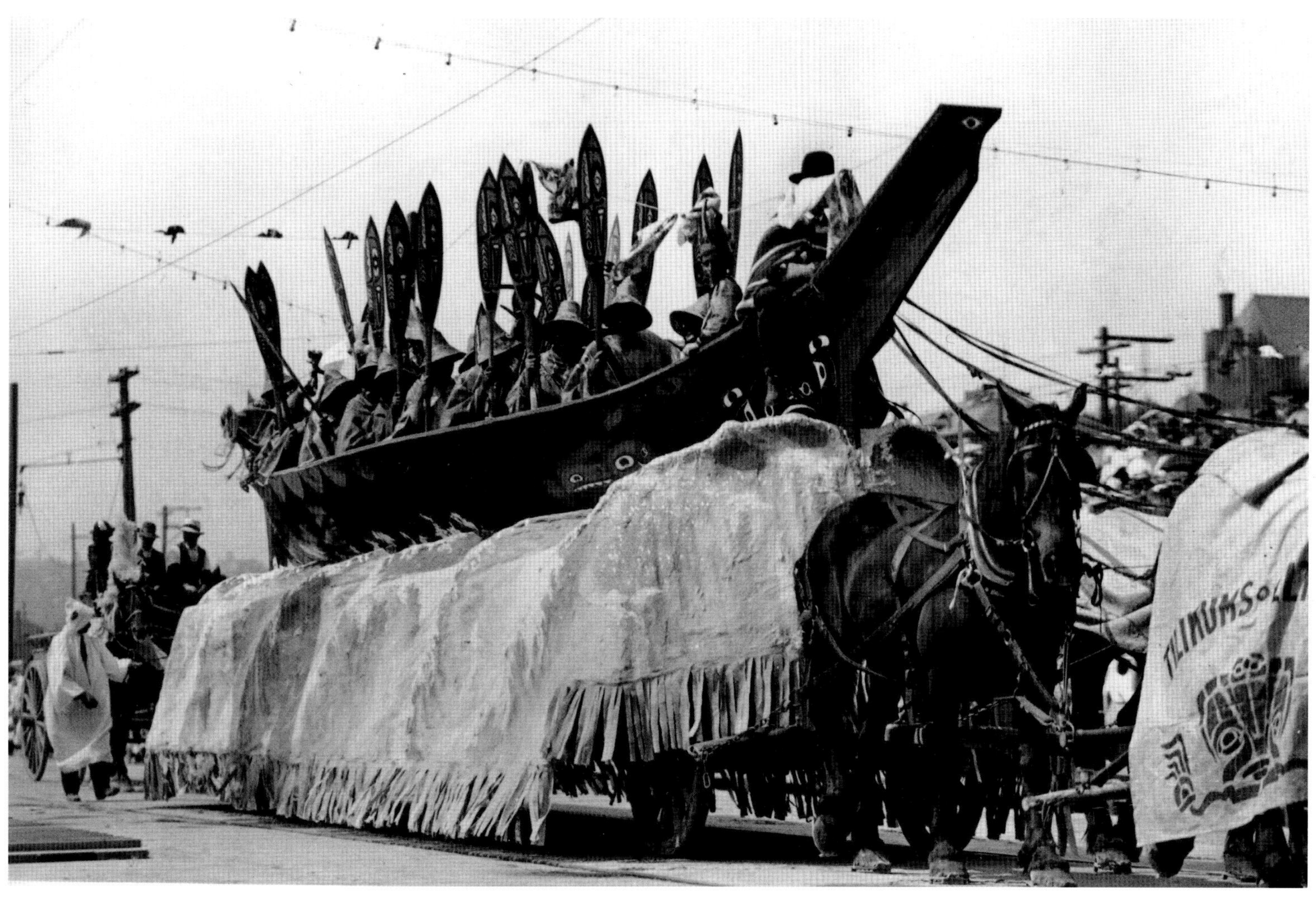

On July 17, 1911, Seattle held its first Golden Potlatch festival to commemorate the 1897 arrival of the steamer *Portland* and its "ton of pure gold" from the Klondike. A potlatch is a Puget Sound Native American celebration. The Klondike Gold Rush jolted Seattle out of a national economic depression into unprecedented prosperity and growth. In 1912, a Potlatch float from a group calling themselves Tillikums parades in an Indian canoe, complete with painted paddles and traditional costume.

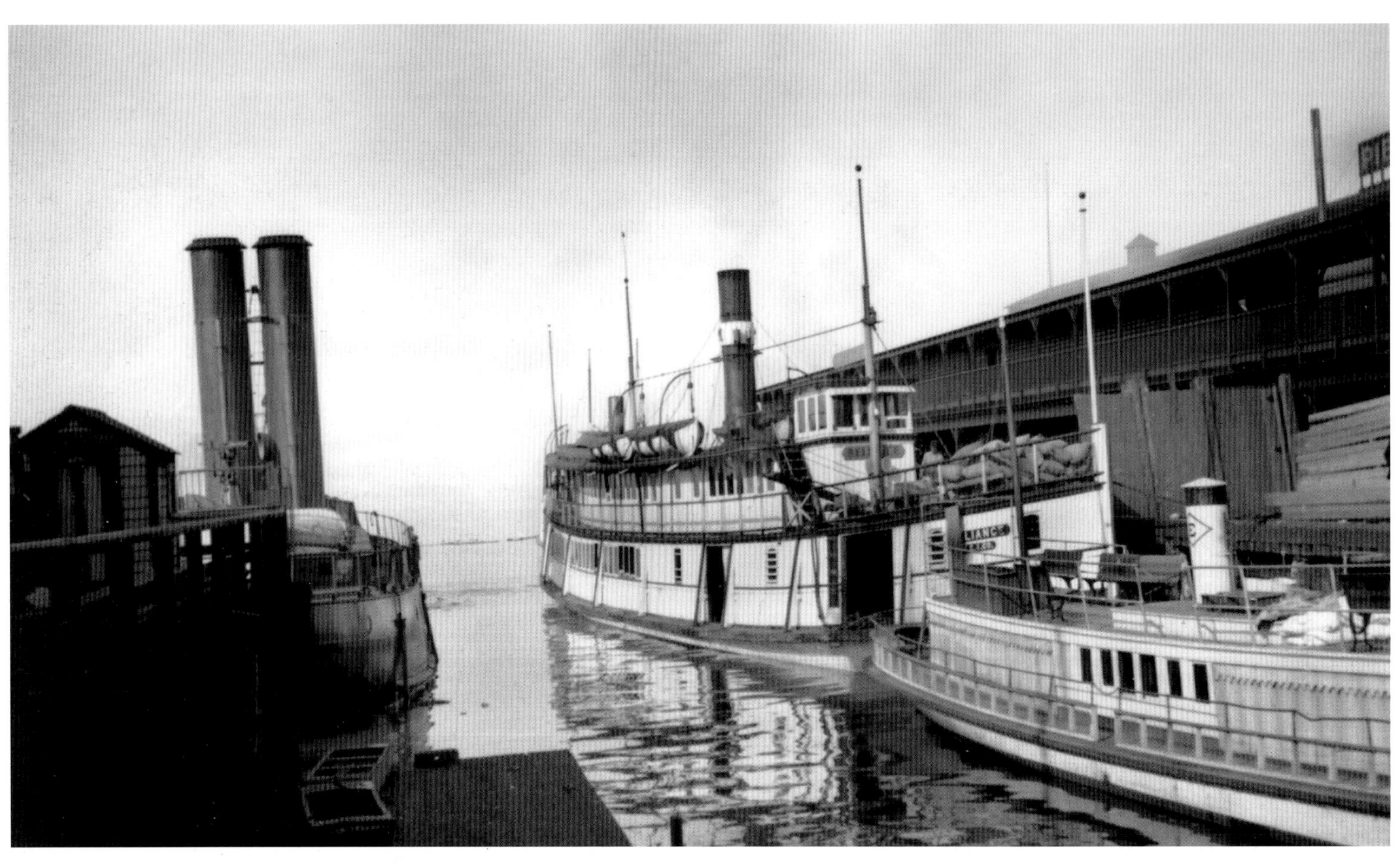

The Kitsap County Transportation Company's steamer *Reliance* served the Poulsbo–Seattle run. The *Reliance* is tied up here in Seattle along with other members of the Puget Sound Mosquito Fleet.

Seattle's first settlers traveled the Oregon Trail to the Columbia River in 1851. They took the schooner *Exact* to Alki Point, where they landed on November 13 of that year. They hoped to build a great city and named their settlement New York Alki, or New York "by and by." A few months later, they moved to Elliott Bay and called it Seattle. By August 1912, when this picture was taken, Alki Beach was a quiet vacation destination for Seattle residents.

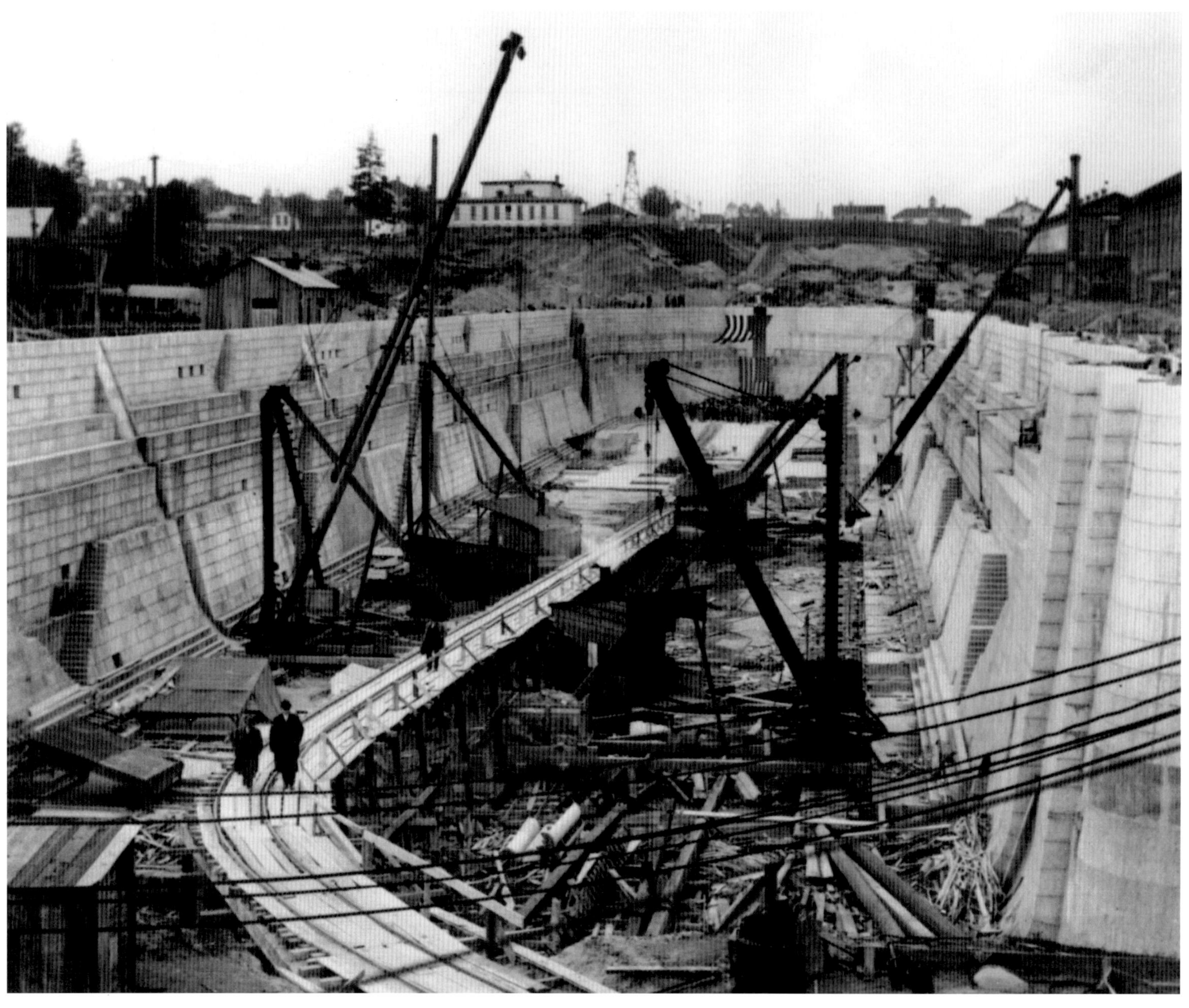

In 1912, two Navy Department officials inspect the Dry Dock No. 2 under construction at the Puget Sound Naval Shipyard in Bremerton. The new facility, made of granite and concrete, would be the Navy's largest dry dock and the only one on the West Coast capable of handling modern battleships.

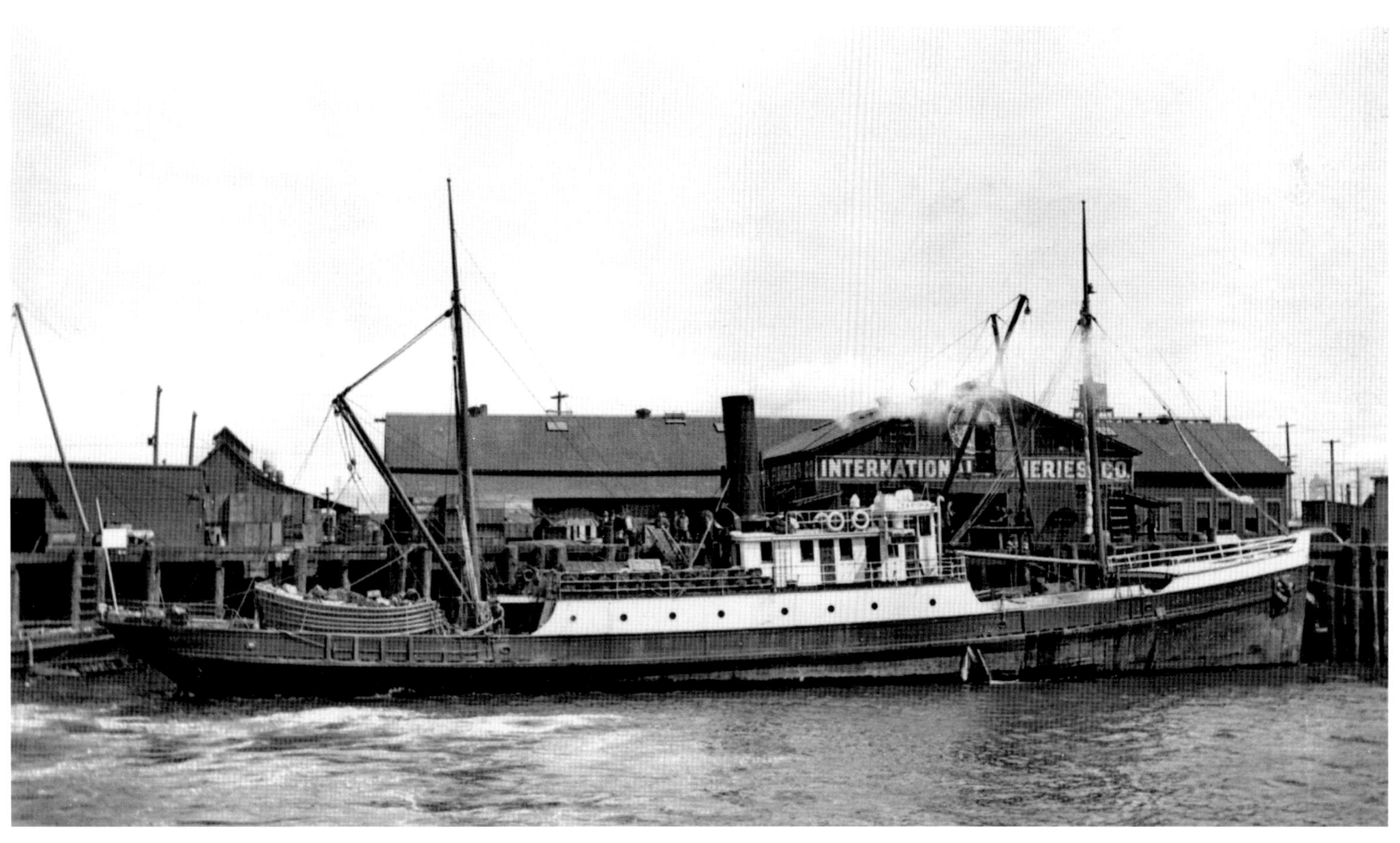

A gill netter unloads its catch at the Tacoma Fish Dock in front of the International Fisheries Company. The small boat on the stern is used to set and then close the net wall before it is hauled in, hopefully full of salmon.

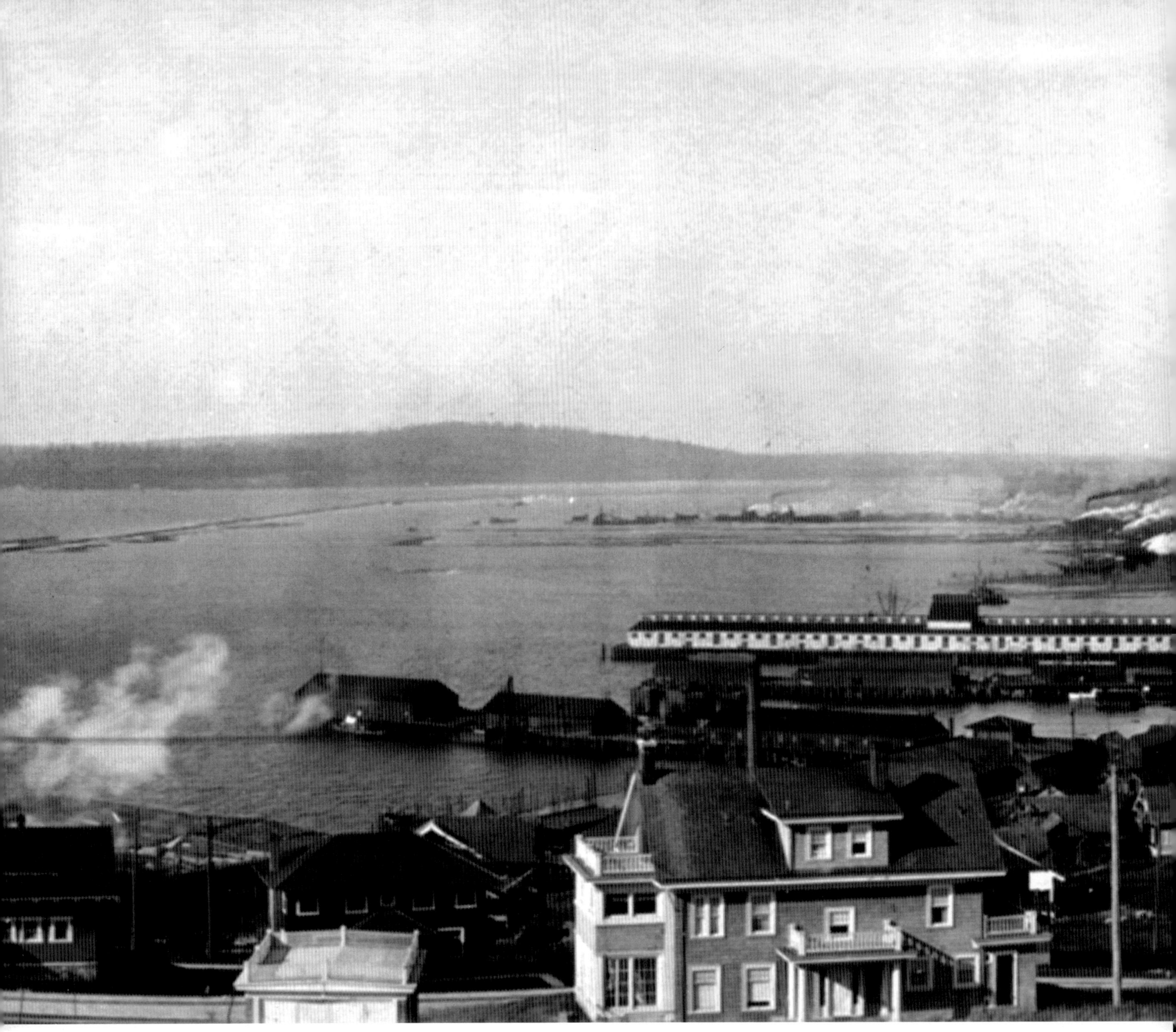

This bird's-eye view of Everett and Port Gardiner Bay was recorded on April 6, 1912.

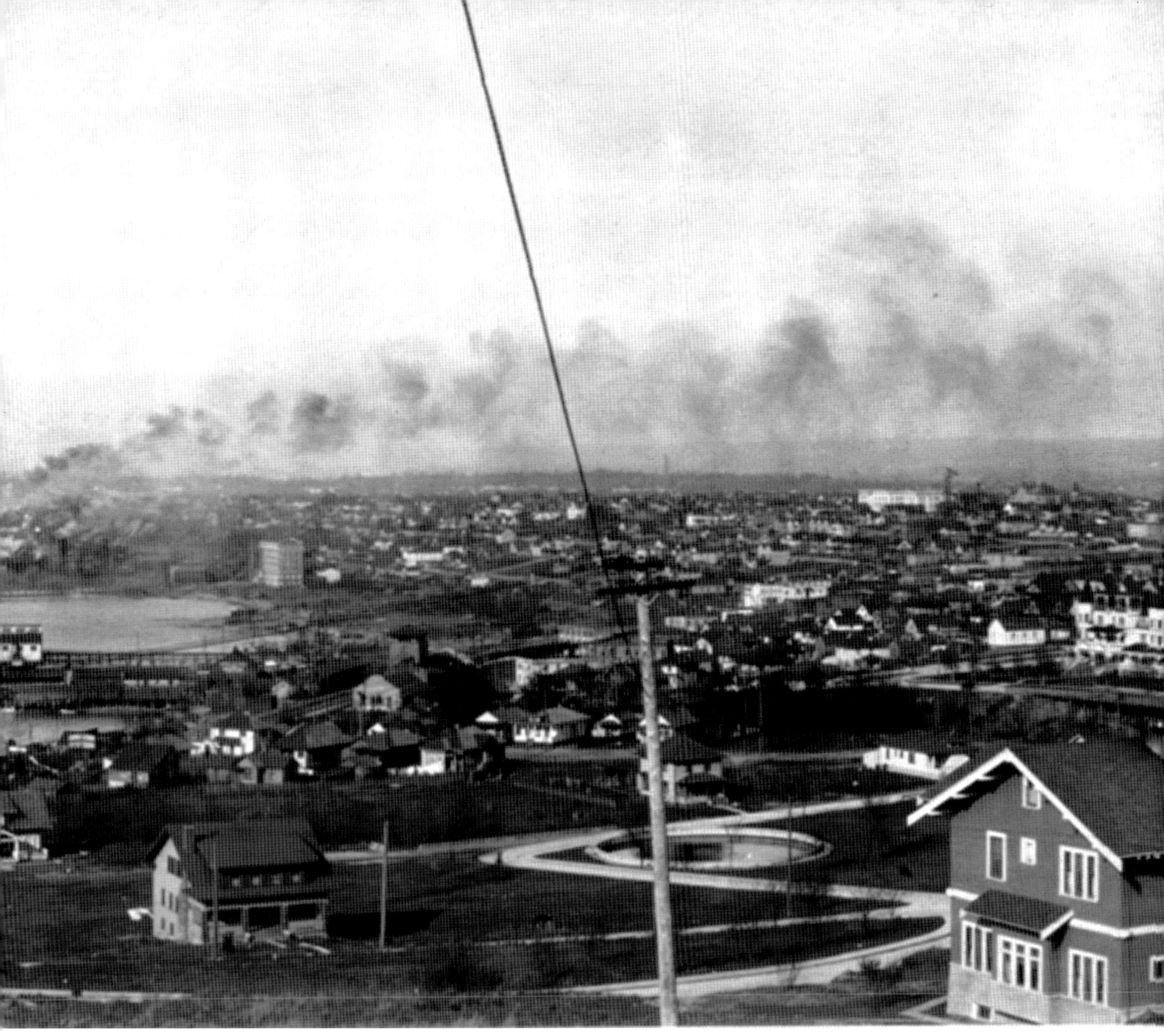

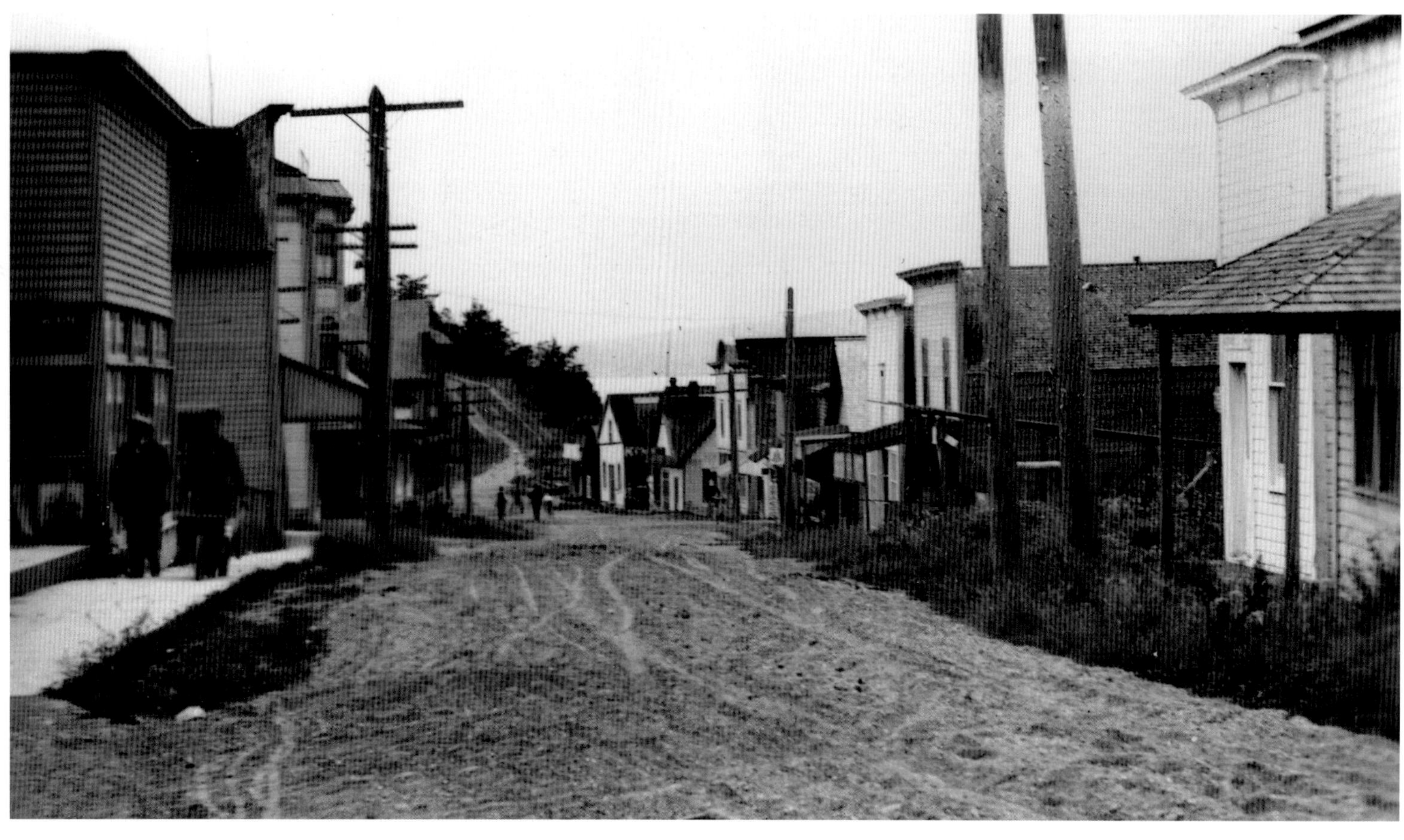

Coupeville on Penn Cove and Whidbey Island, 1912. Tracks from automobile wheels cover the dirt road.

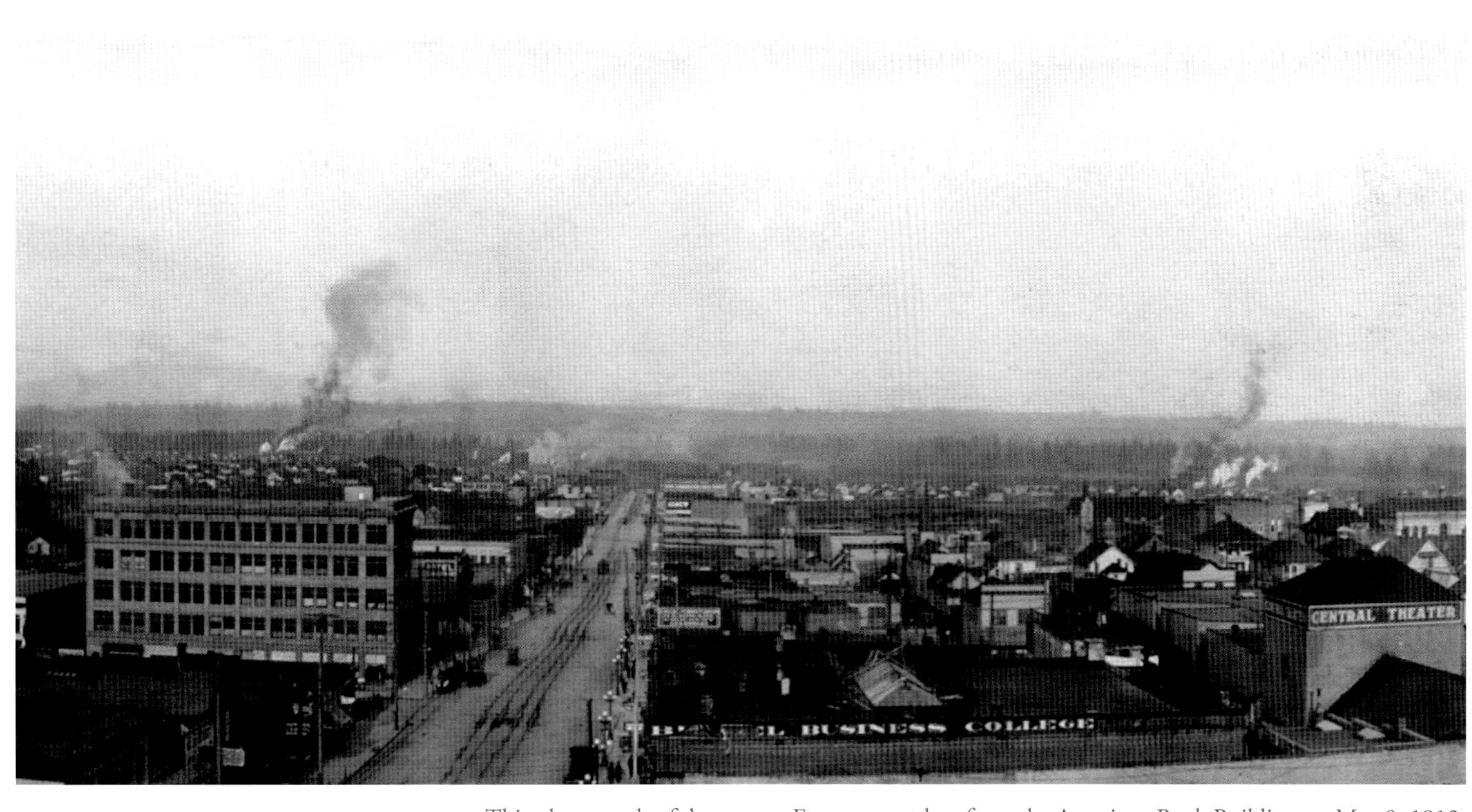

This photograph of downtown Everett was taken from the American Bank Building on May 8, 1912.

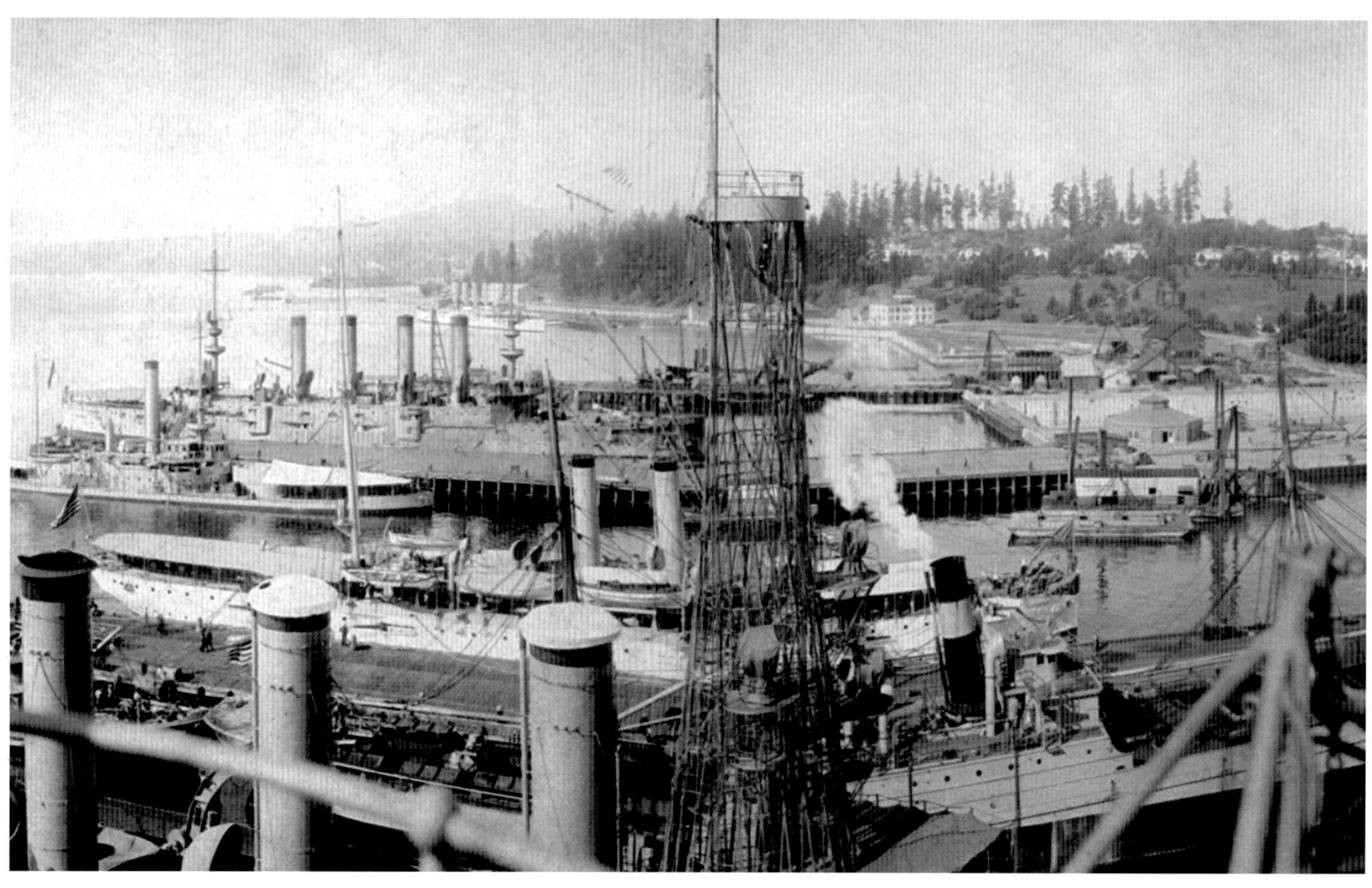

This panorama of the Puget Sound Naval Shipyard, recorded sometime after 1913, captures large warships in both dry docks as well as other ships tied at wharves.

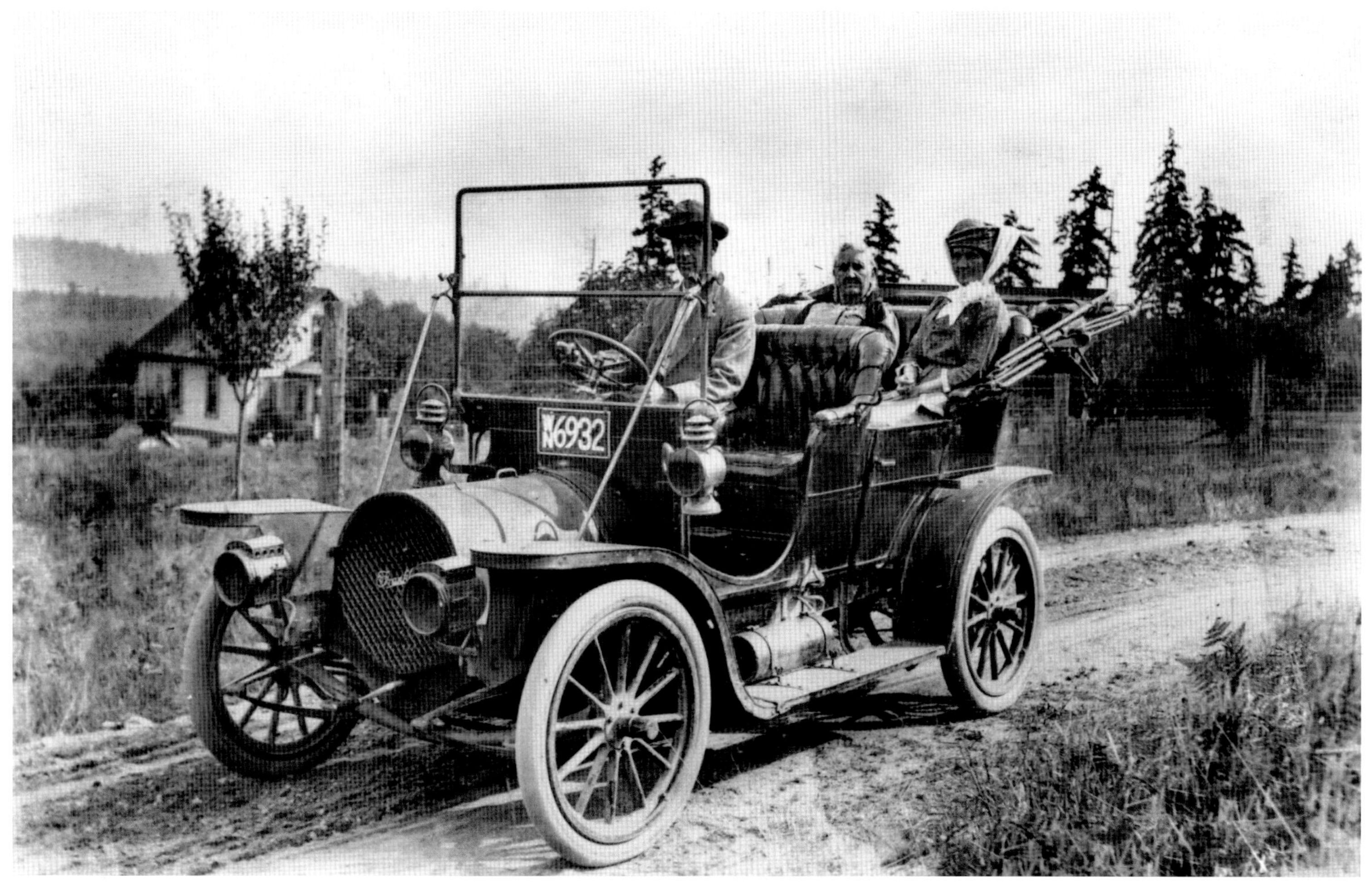

Vashon Islander Oliver S. Van Olinda poses E. W. and Lizzie Lindley and another passenger in Van Olinda's Franklin automobile. The Franklin featured an air-cooled engine, an immense advantage in cold weather when liquid-cooled cars might not start.

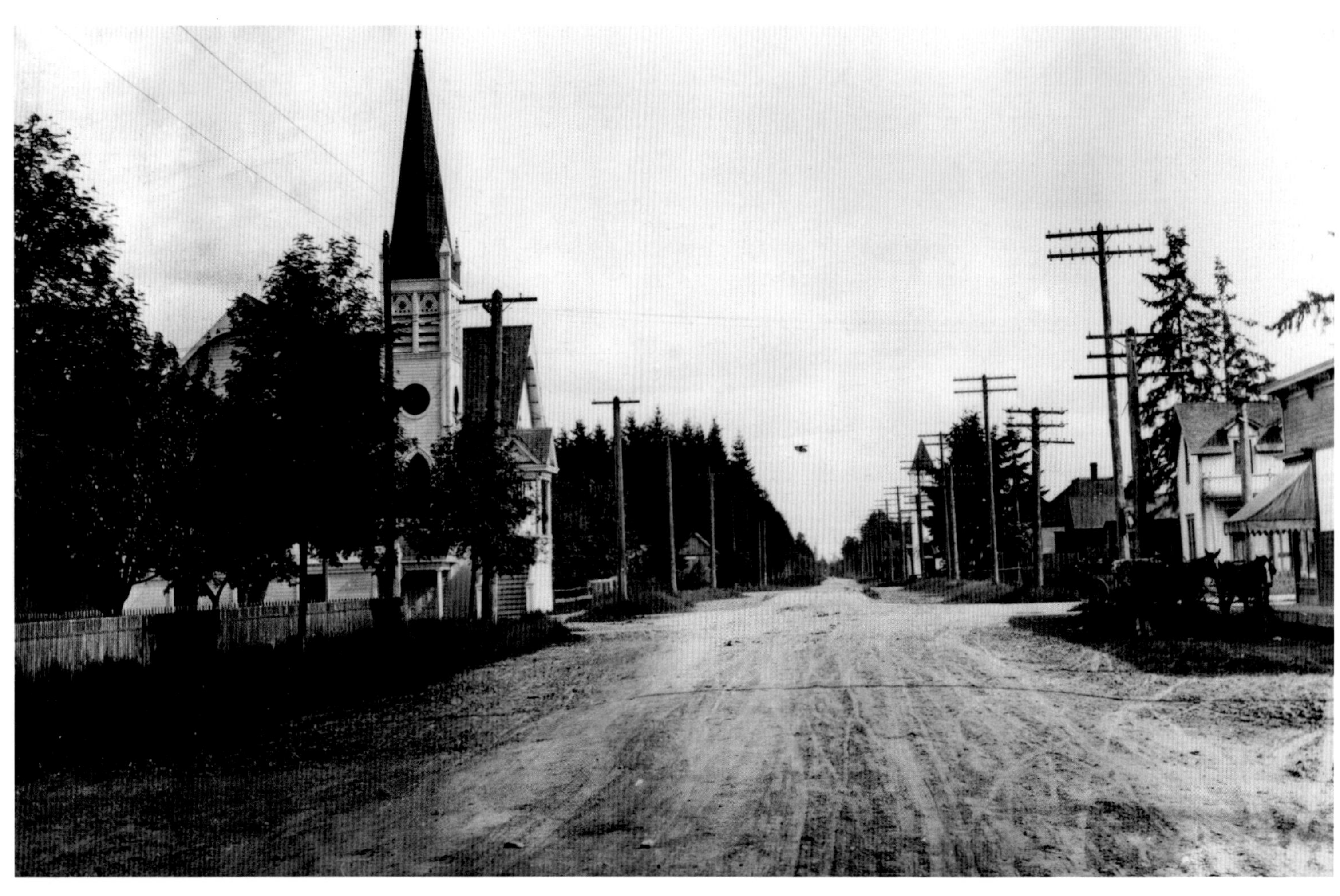

In 1913, Marysville, across the Snohomish River from industrial Everett, is expanding from a lumber and milling center to a center for growing strawberries. Good rail and water connections gave farmers swift access to outside markets.

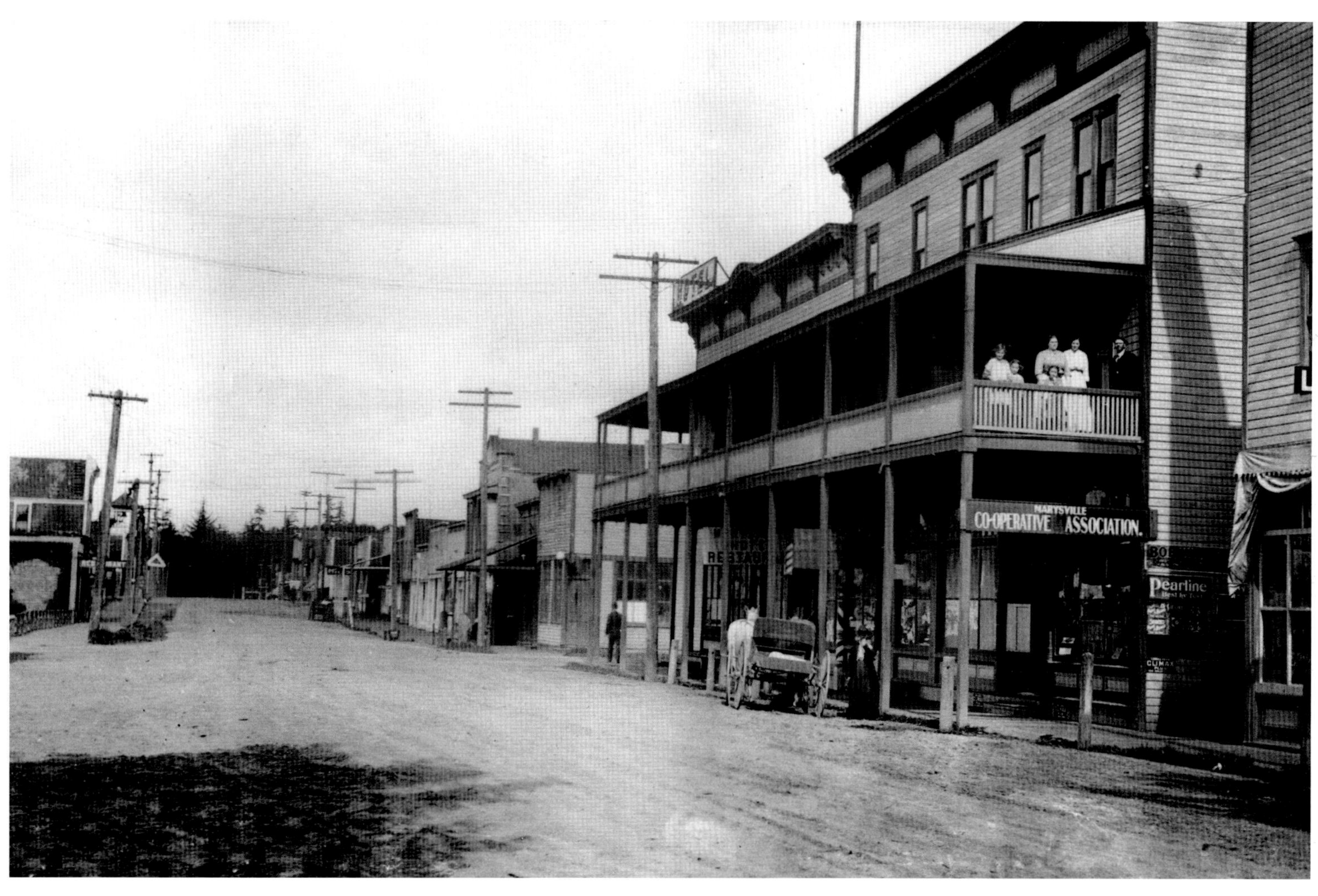

This downtown view of Marysville in 1913 includes the Marysville Hotel and the Farmers Cooperative Association. The city boasts a city hall, a water system, electricity service, a high school, a library, a board of health, and a chamber of commerce.

Following Spread: Around 1914 in Port Madison, the Mosquito Fleet steamer *Reliance* awaits passengers at low tide. Port Madison was a popular destination for excursionists from Seattle and other cities of Puget Sound.

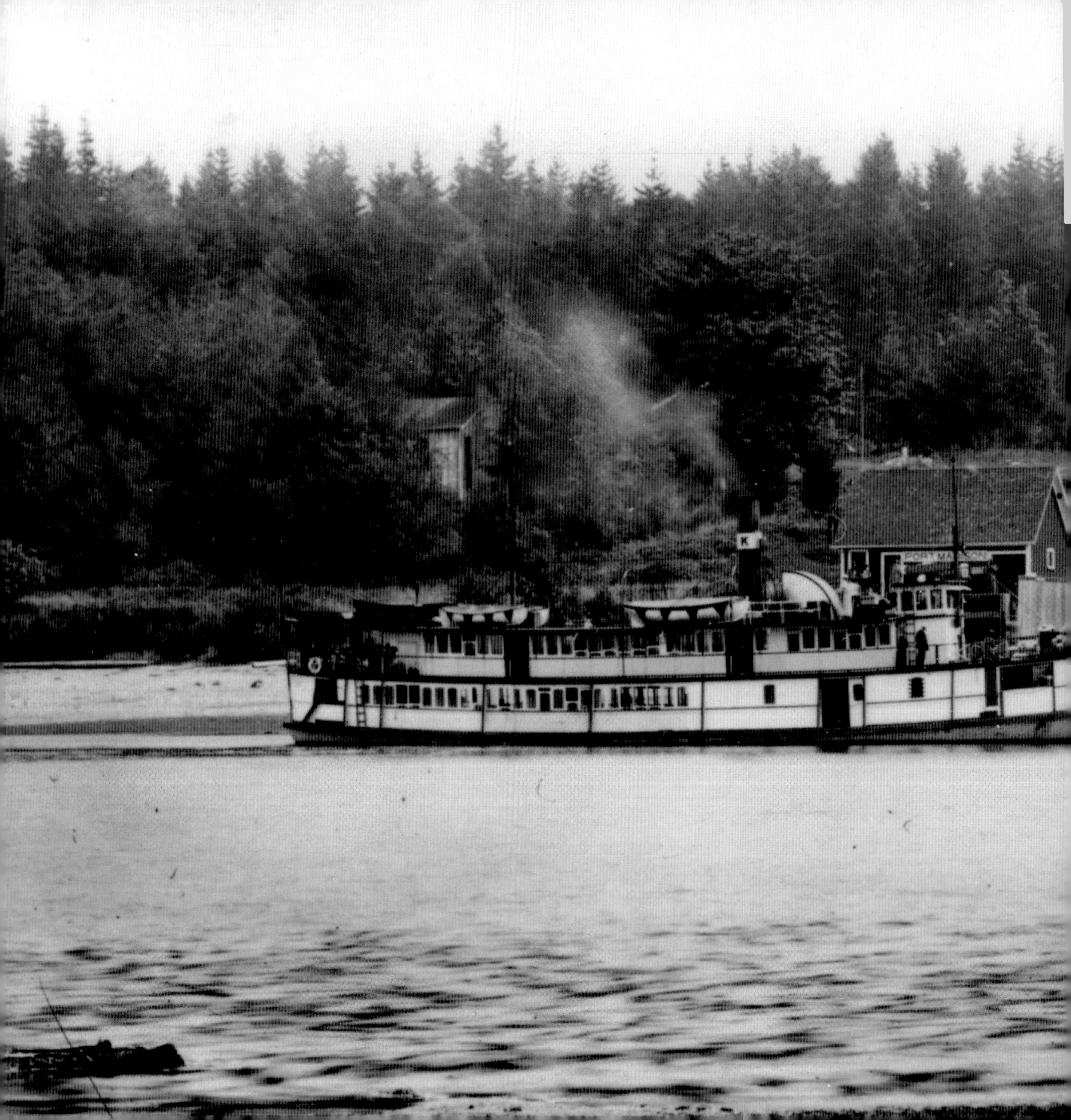
PORT MADISON

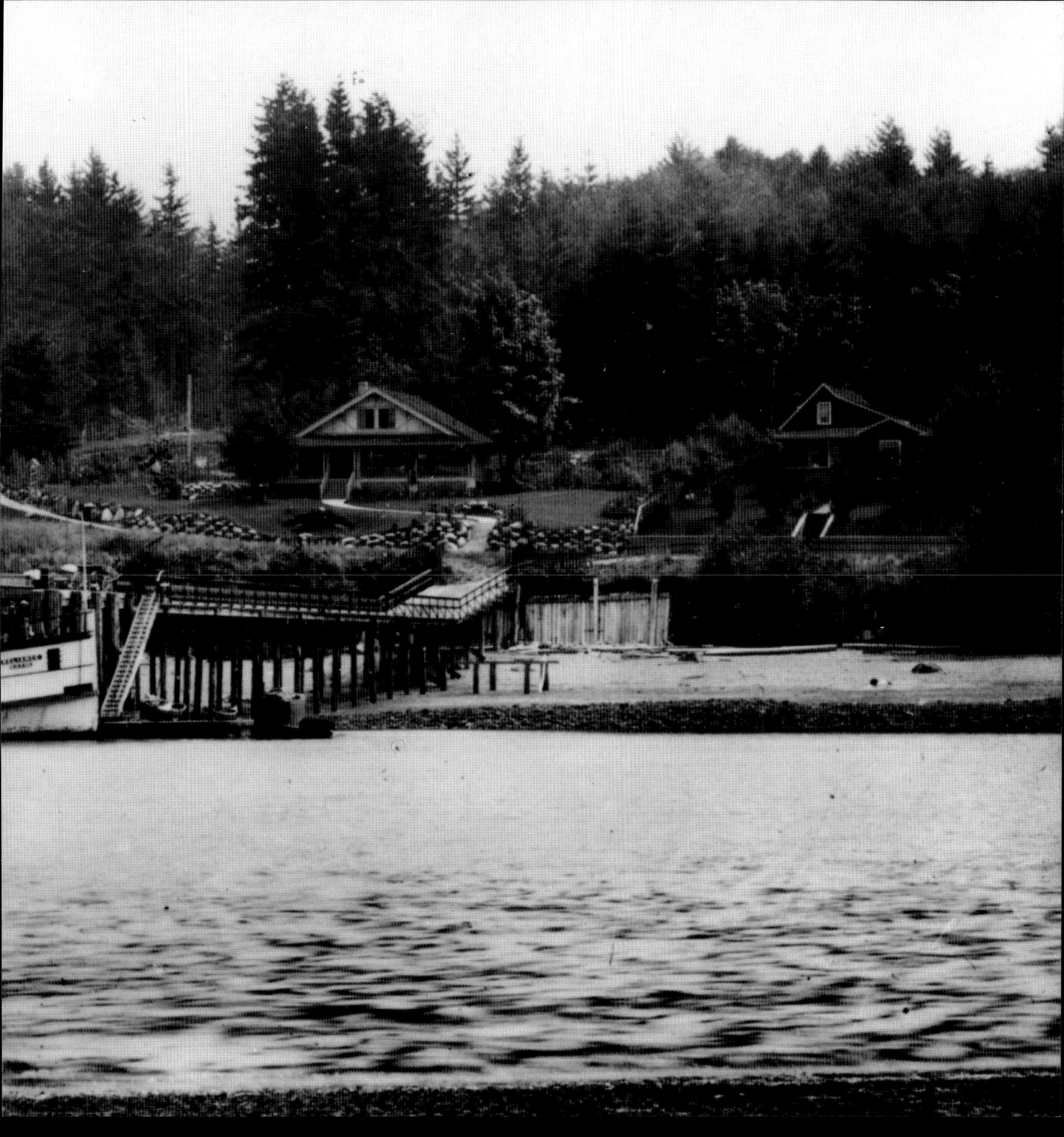

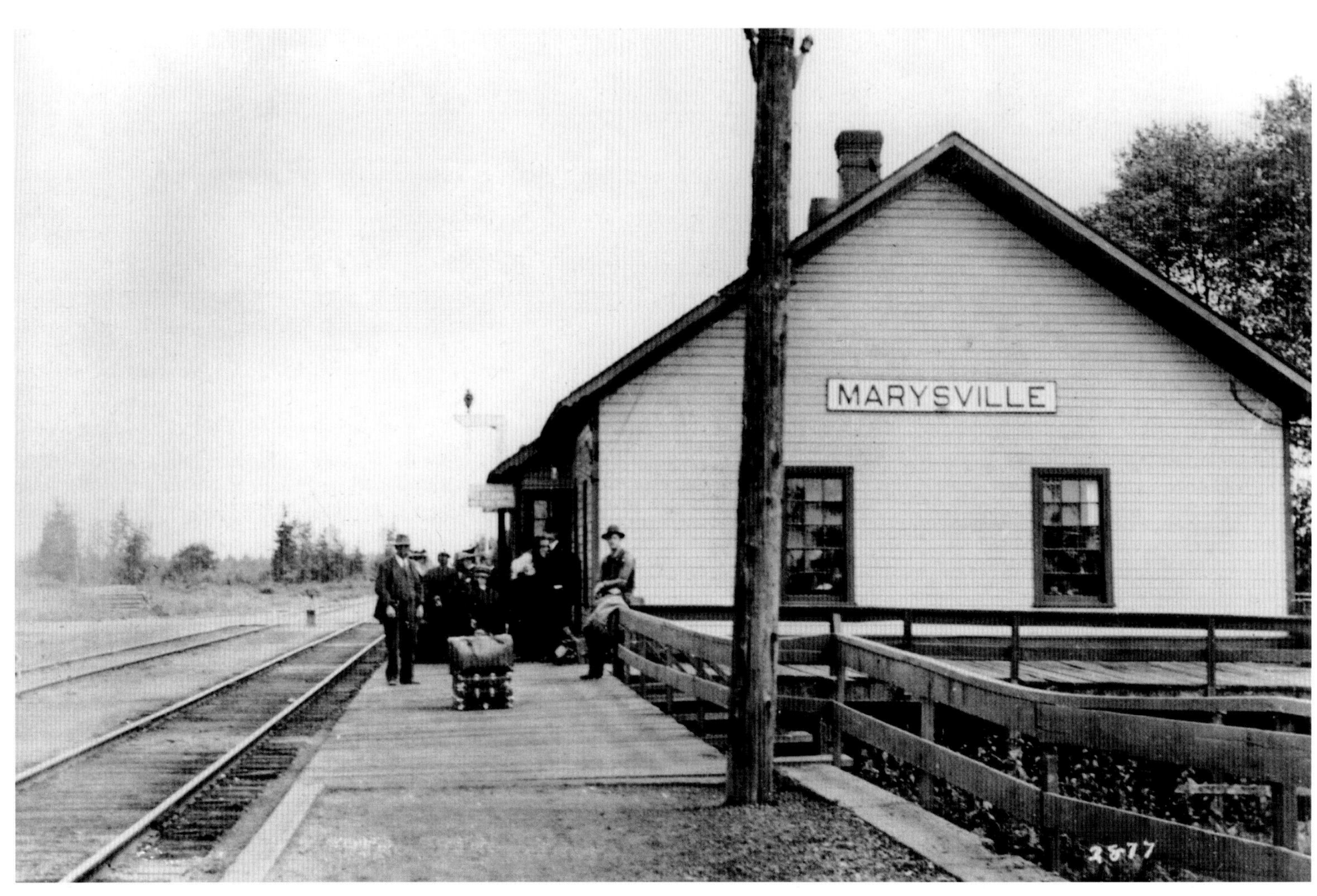

The Great Northern Railway arrived in Marysville in 1891, allowing the small town to blossom into a center for lumber and shake mills. Within a few years, ten mills cut a million board feet of wood a day. Here in 1913, travelers regard the photographer as they wait for the next train.

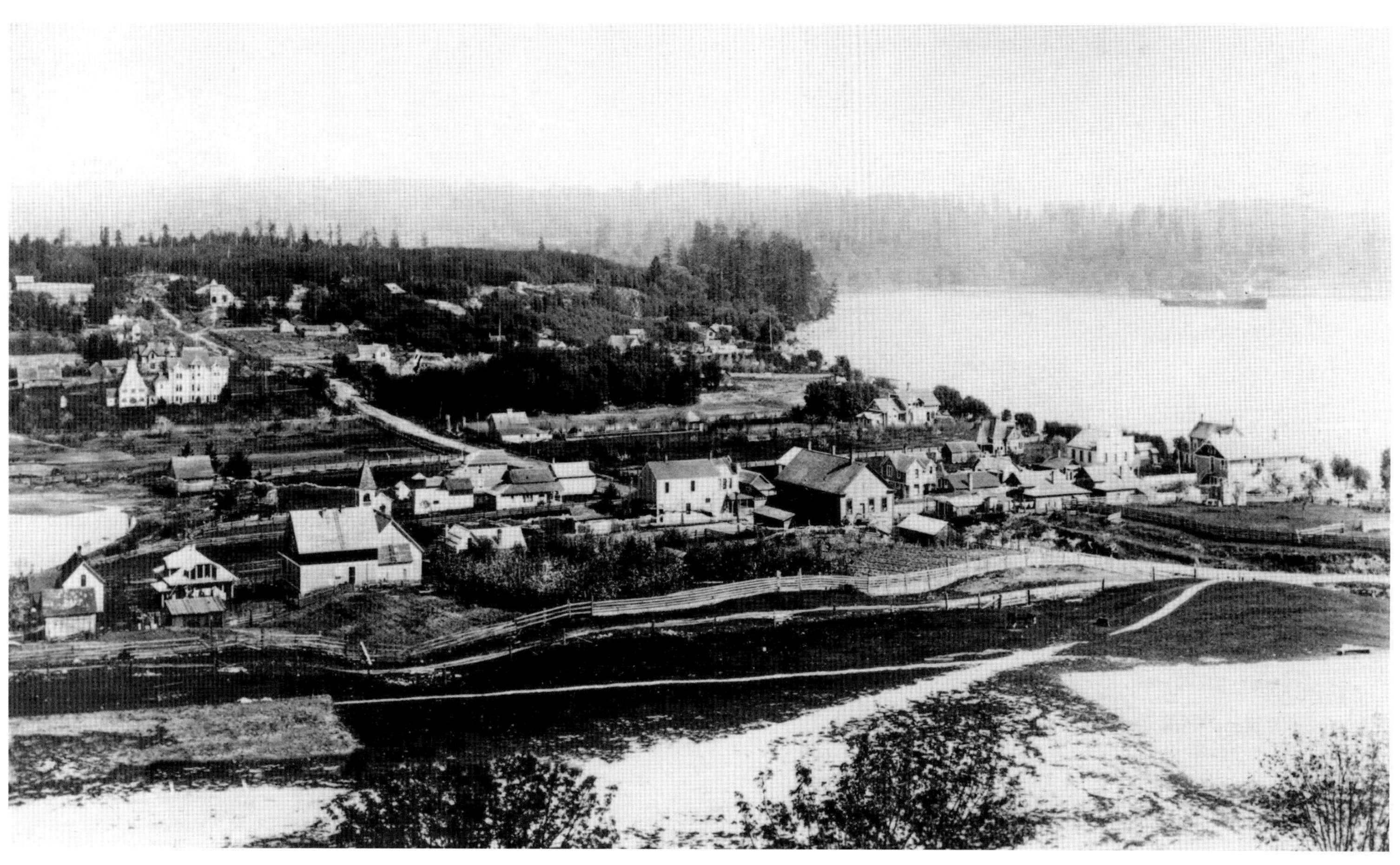

The town of Burton sits on the shore of Quartermaster Harbor, which separates Vashon from Maury Island as seen in this 1914 view. Mrs. Miles F. Hatch, wife of the community's first store owner, named it after her birthplace, Burton-in-Kendall, England.

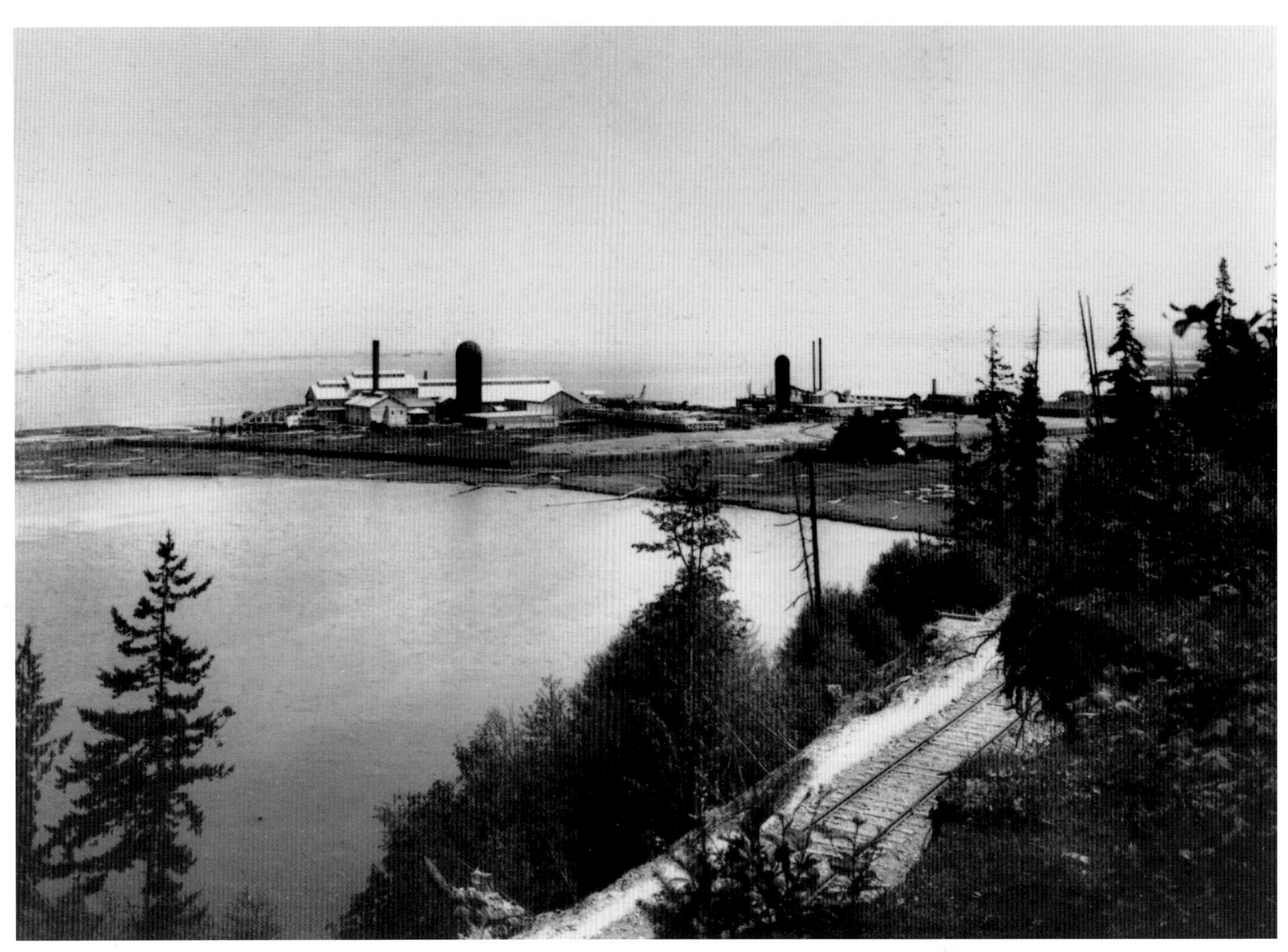

As mariners left the storms of the Pacific en route to Puget Sound, the first safe haven was Ediz Hook in Port Angeles, located on the Strait of Juan de Fuca. The Puget Sound Mills and Timber Company cut lumber outside the town to process the forest wealth of the Olympic Peninsula.

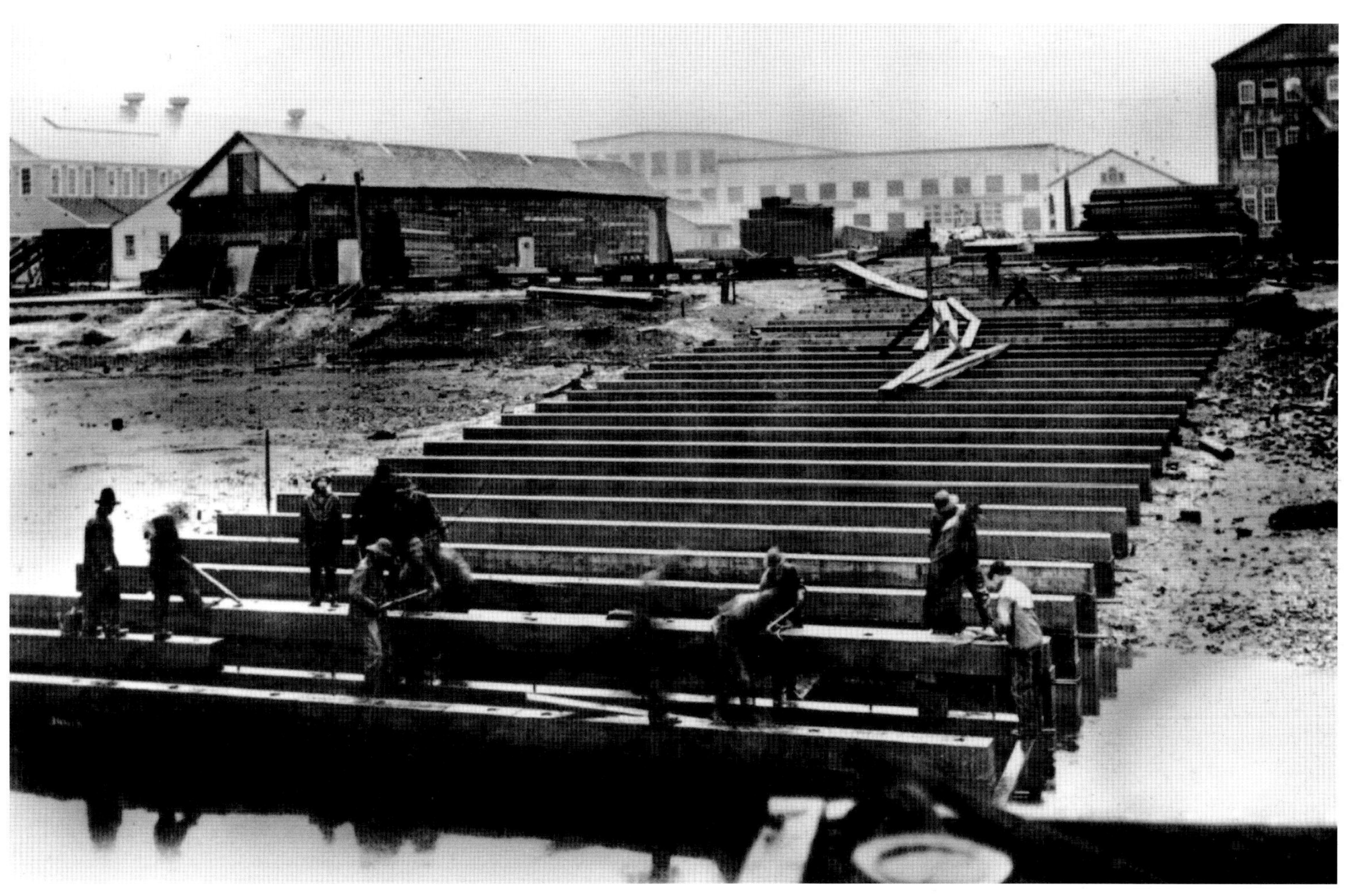

In 1915, construction workers complete ways for a marine railway at the Puget Sound Naval Shipyard in Bremerton.

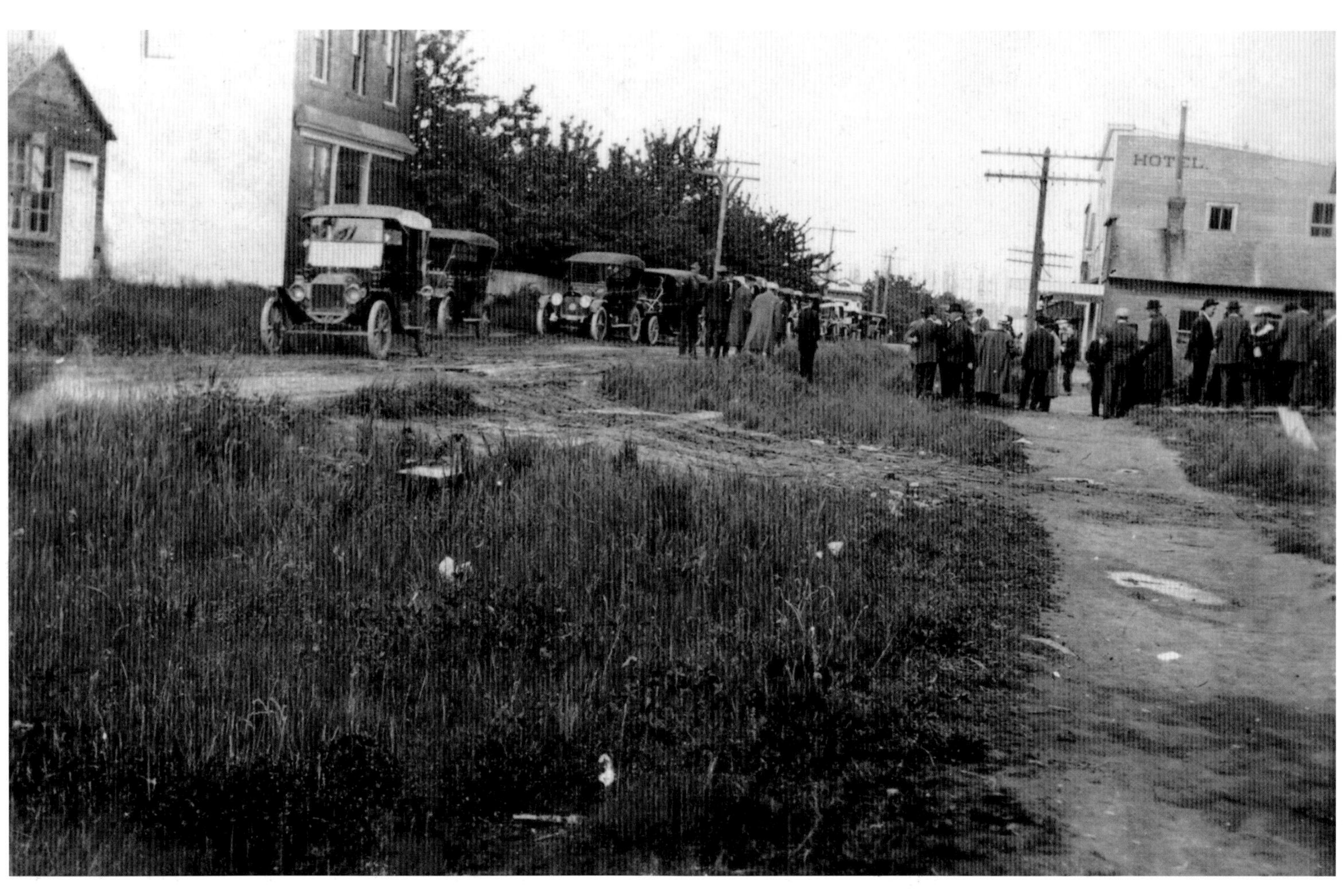

Residents gather on Vashon Island in 1915 after a fire in the Martin Building at extreme right. On the left is the Mason Building, which housed the bank. Behind the crowd is the Hotel.

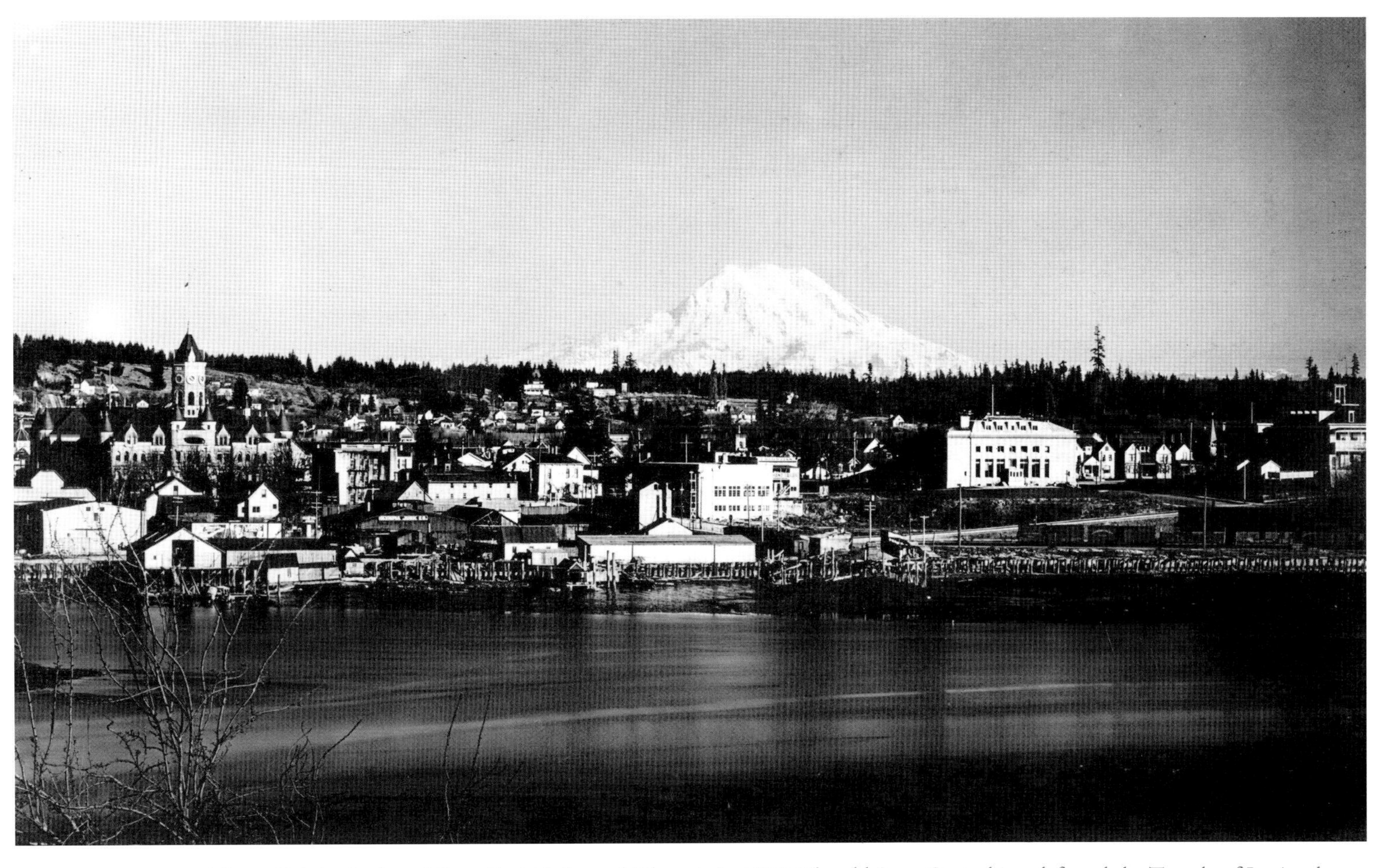

Mount Rainier is viewed from Budd Inlet and Olympia in 1916. The old State Capitol is at left and the Temple of Justice, home to the Supreme Court, sits at right.

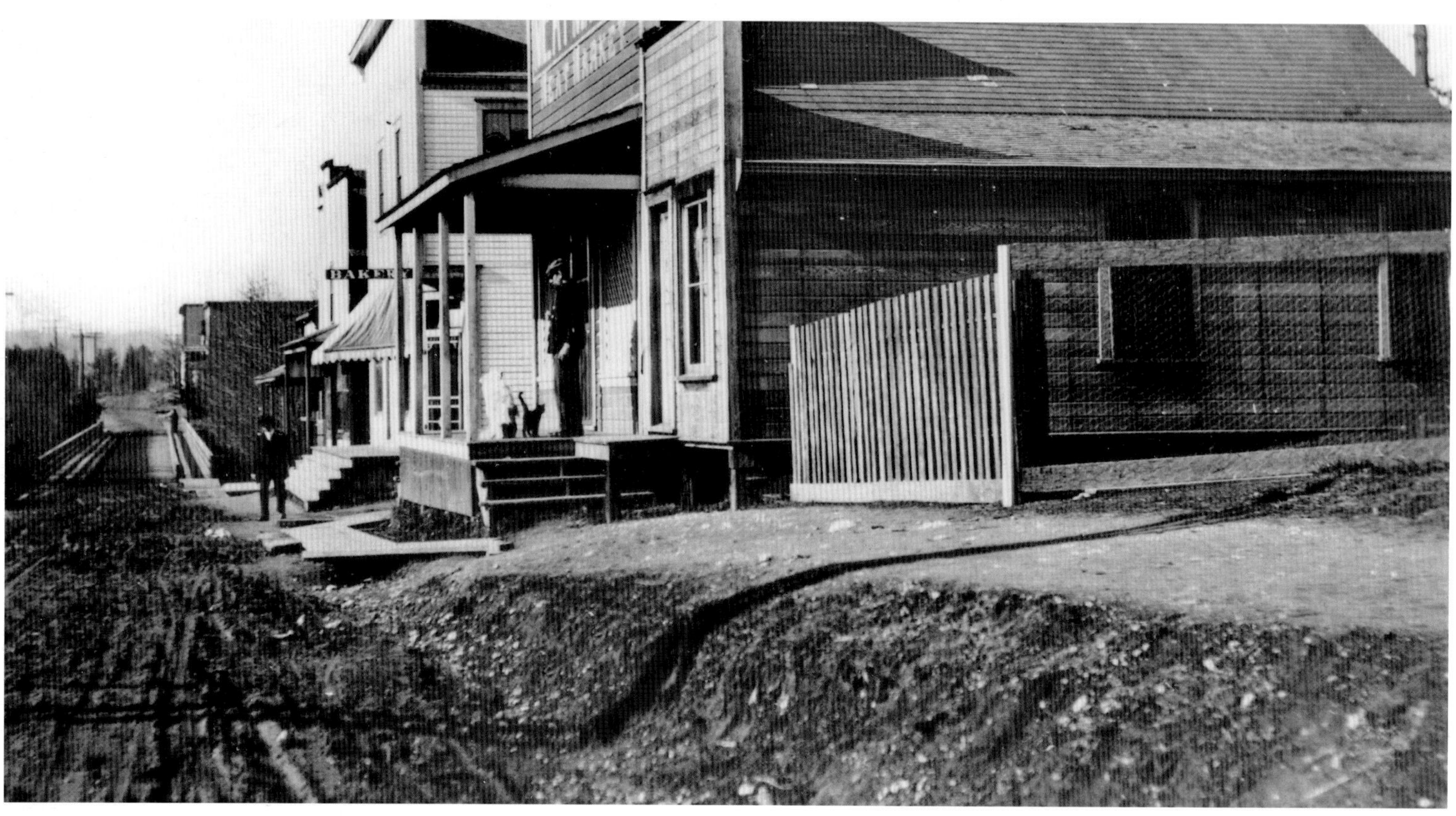

The first white settlers on Eagle Harbor in the 1870s called their community Madrone. With the 1902 arrival of the Hall Brothers Shipyard, the name changed to Winslow (after Winslow Hall). The town grew up on two sides of a ravine crossed by a bridge and Winslow Way, shown here with a meat market in 1916.

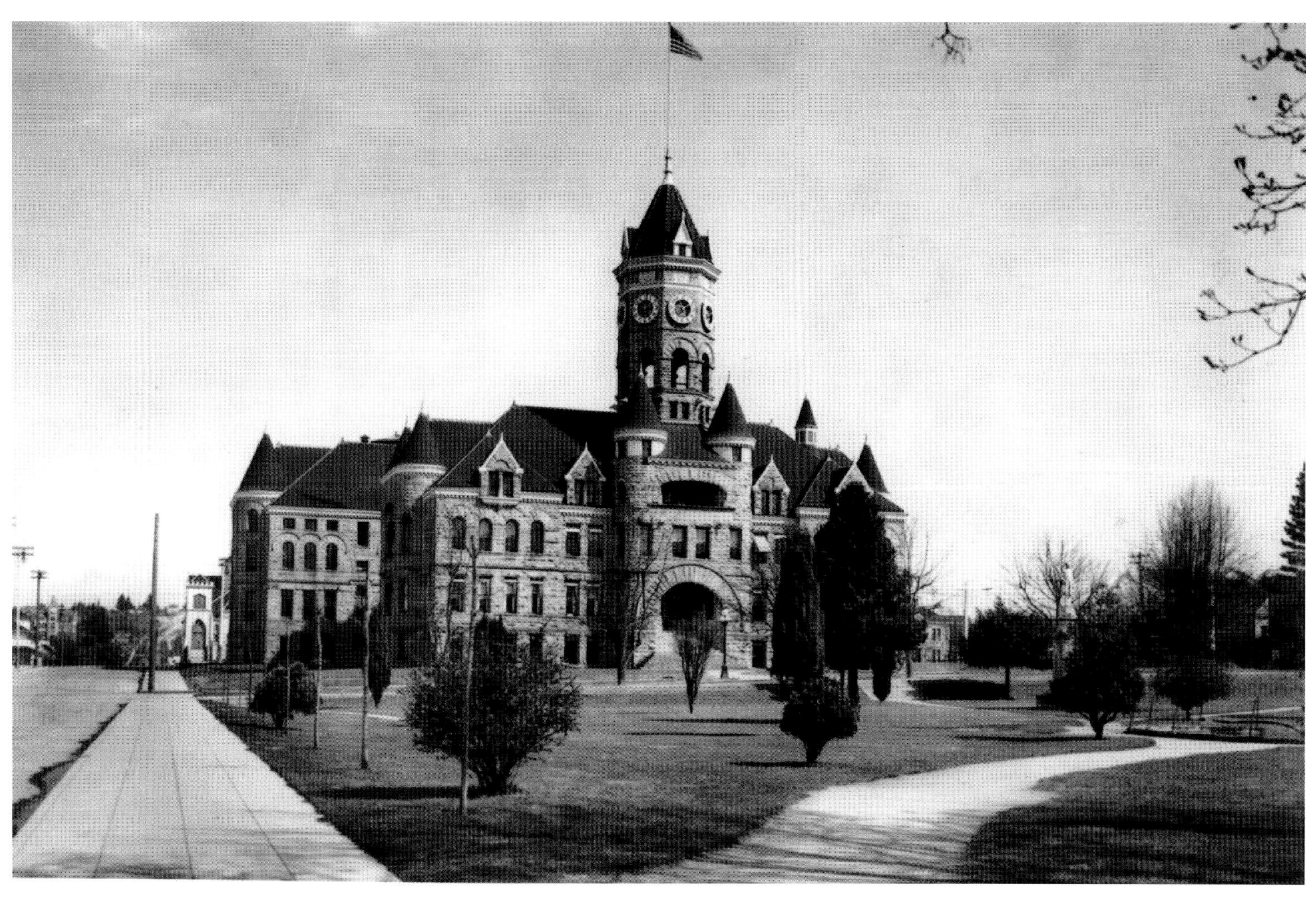

Architect W. A. Ritchie crowned the 150-foot, 1892 Thurston County Courthouse with an octagonal clock tower. Each face had an illuminated dial. From 1905 to 1928, the building housed the state legislature, the Supreme Court, the state library, and most of the executive branch. This 1916 view shows the west face of the building.

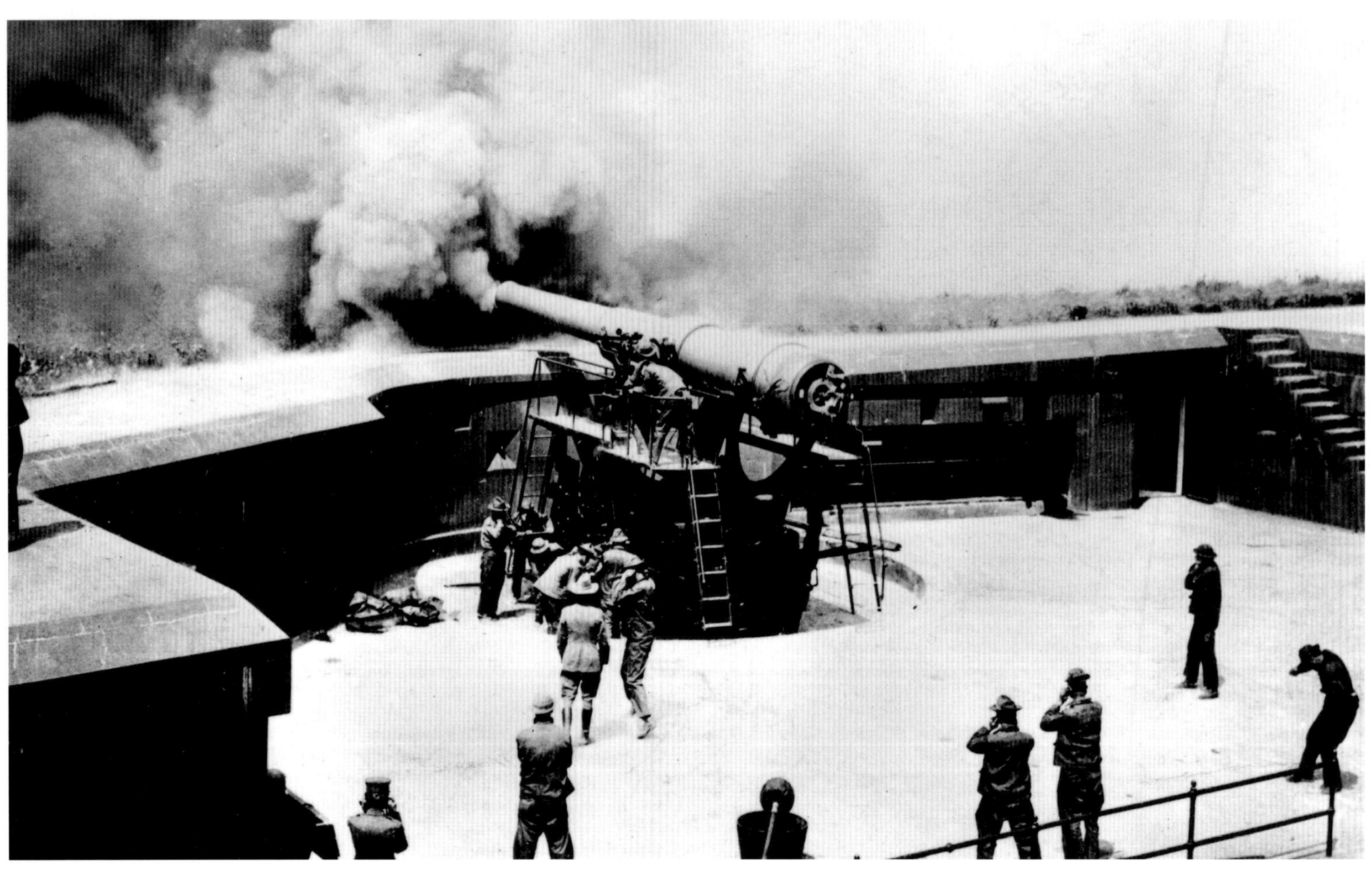

Located near Port Townsend, Fort Worden, along with Fort Casey on Whidbey Island and Fort Flagler on Marrowstone Island, guarded the entrance of Puget Sound. The three bastions created a "triangle of fire" against invaders. Here in 1916, gunners cover their ears as they fire a 12-inch disappearing rifle.

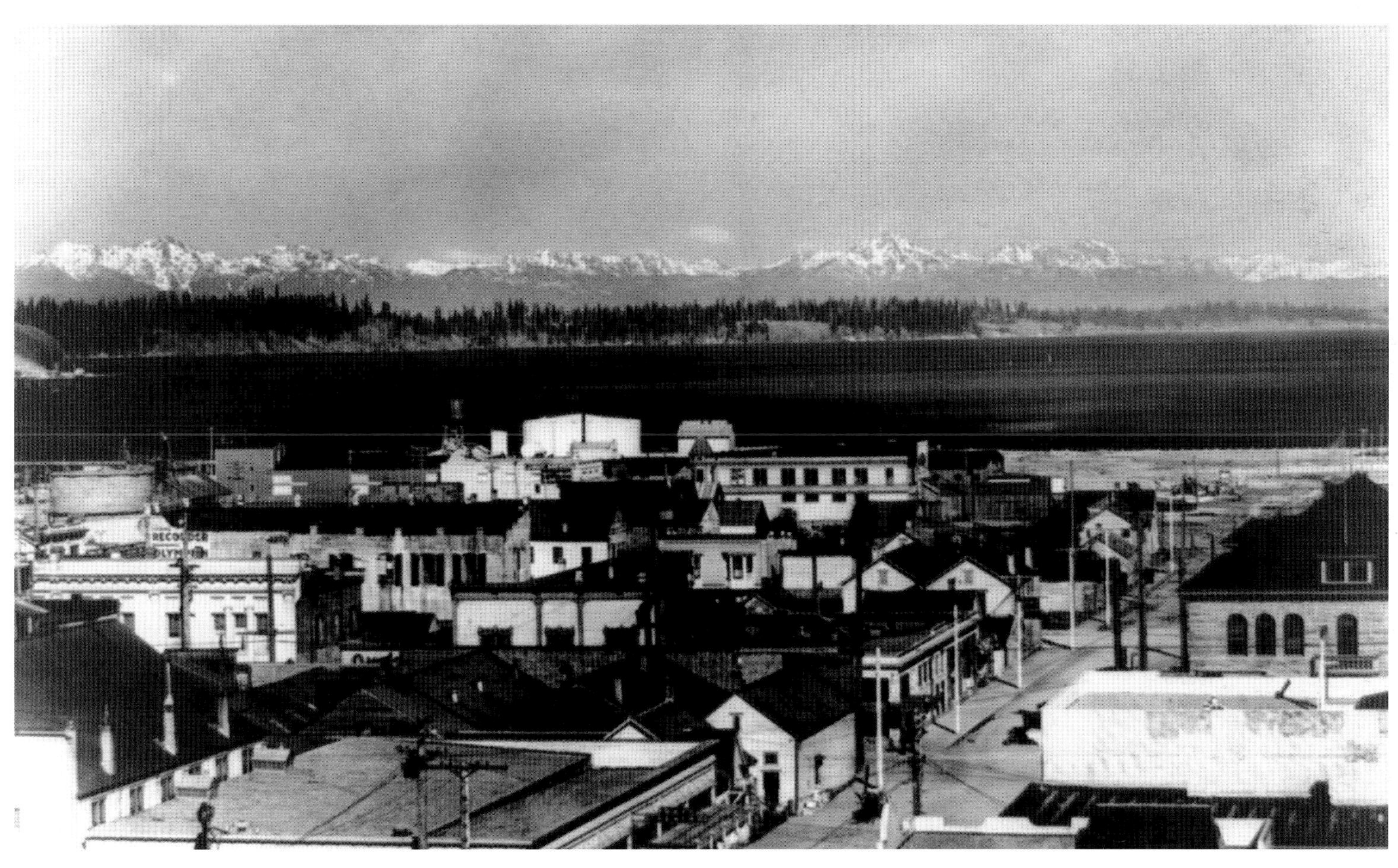

Looking west in 1916, probably from the clock tower of the State Capitol, this view captures Budd Inlet and the snow-capped Olympic Range.

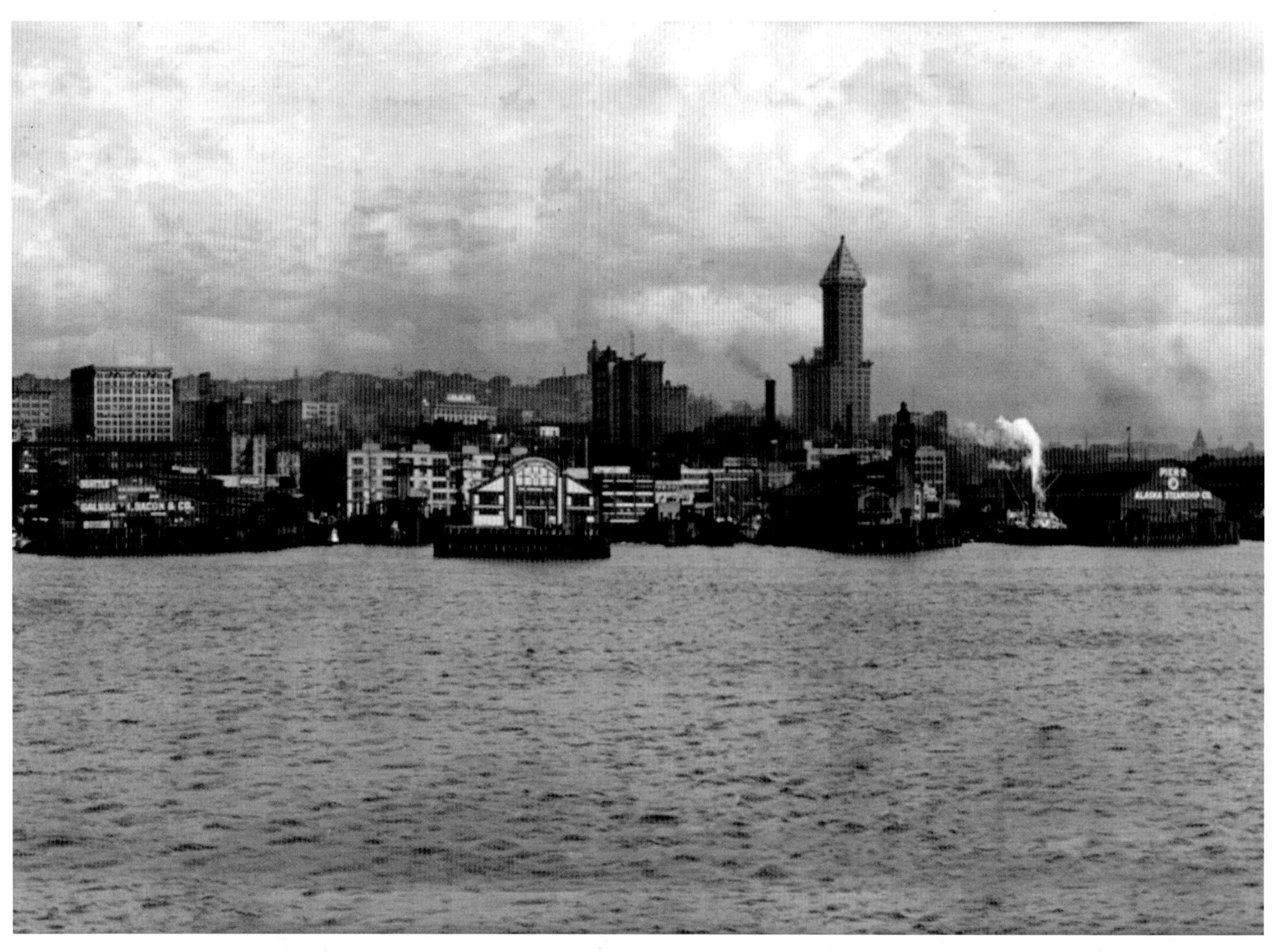

This 1917 panorama takes in the Seattle waterfront and the skyline's predominant feature for many years, the Smith Tower at right. Industrialist Lyman C. Smith financed the 462-foot steel skyscraper but died before the doors opened in 1914. When this photograph was taken, Smith Tower was the tallest structure west of Chicago.

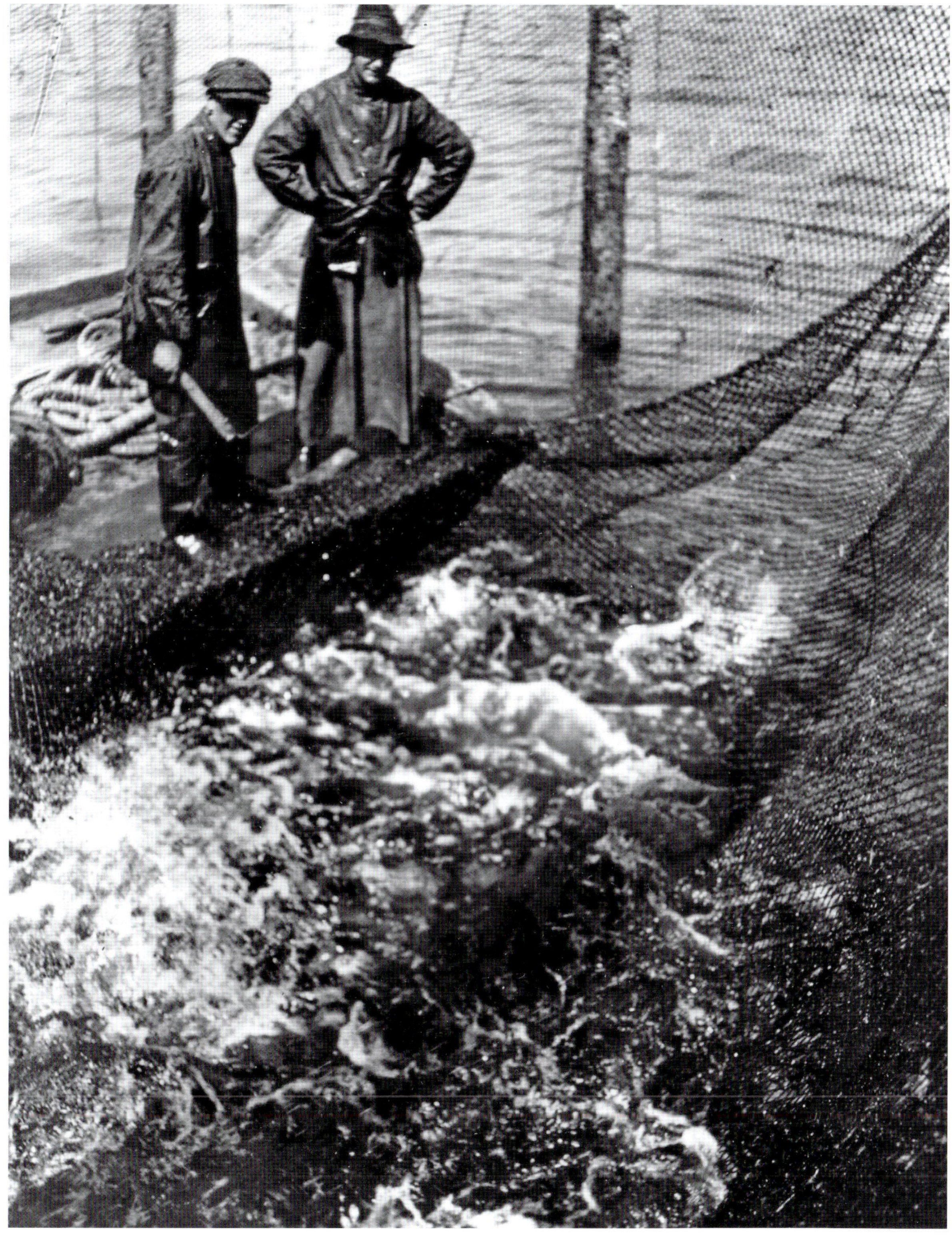

In 1917, the salmon ran so plentifully that commercial operations did not even need boats. Nets stretched across rivers were enough to turn a profit. Two workers wait here for the photographer to record their catch in a river before they haul it in and ship it to a cannery.

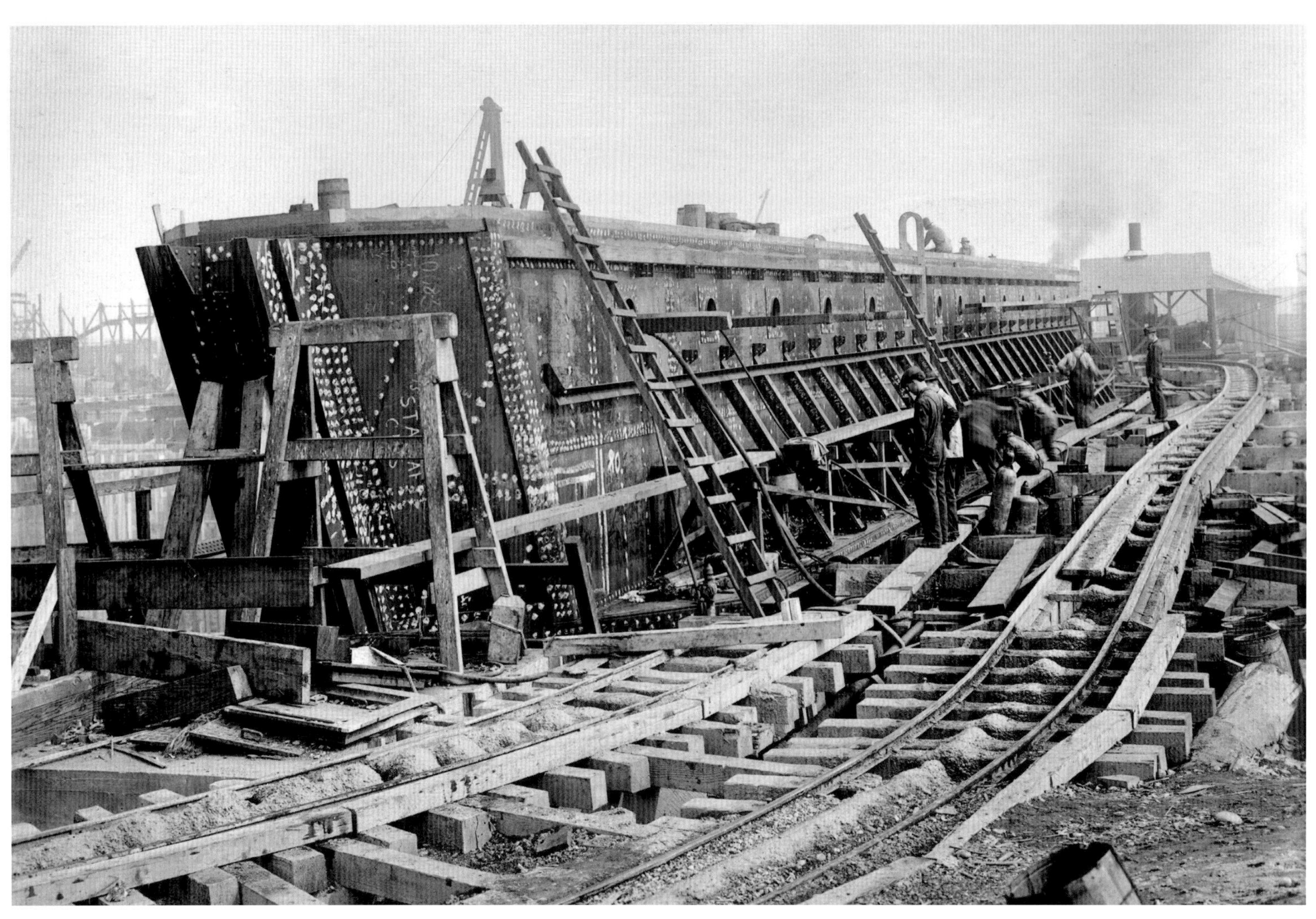

In March 1917, the U.S. Navy authorized construction of a new shallow-draft dry dock at the Puget Sound Naval Shipyard. This dock marked a shift in the yard's mission from just maintenance and repair to construction. Here on October 2, 1918, six weeks before the Armistice that would end the First World War, Dry Dock No. 3 is still under construction.

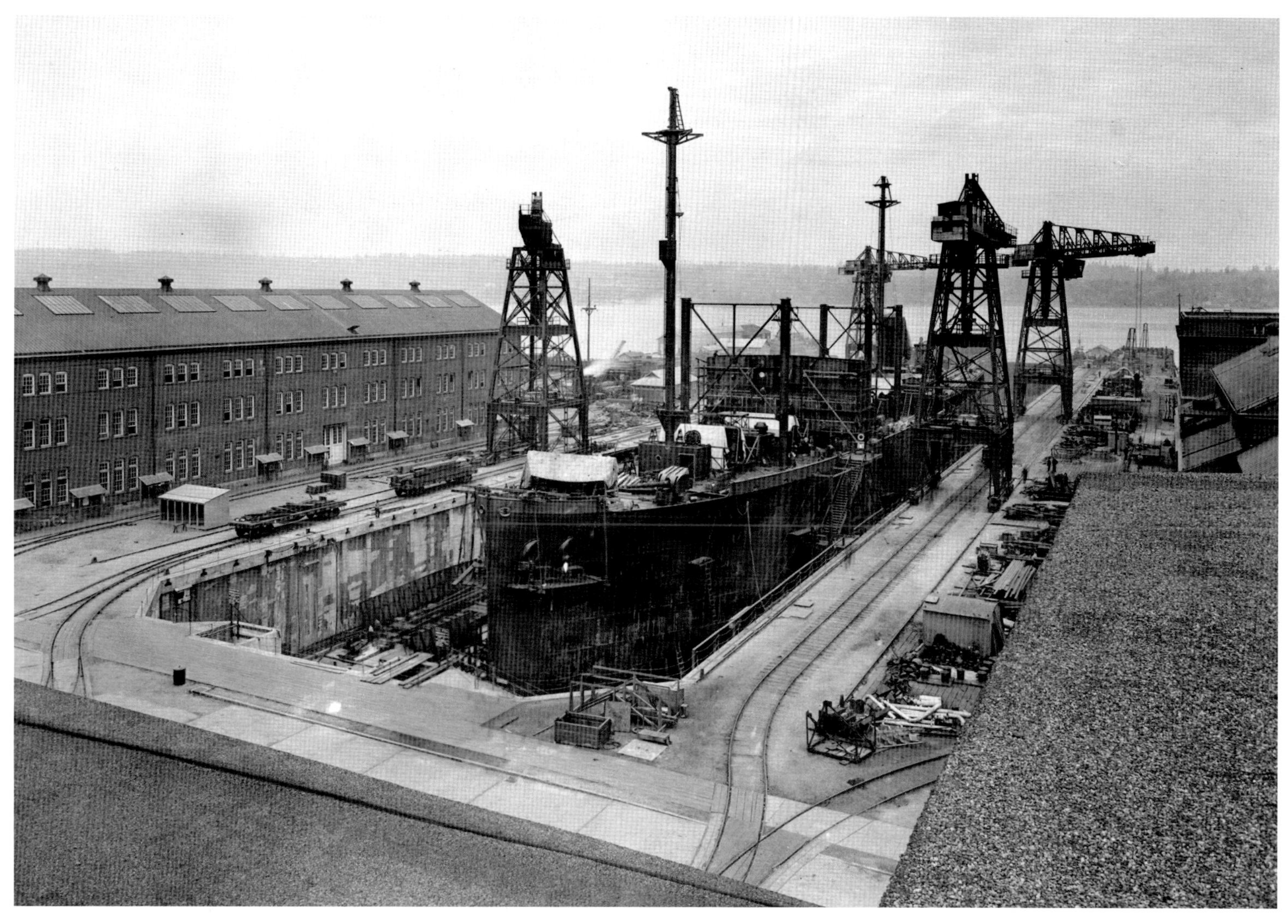

On August 19, 1919, the Puget Sound Naval Shipyard completes construction of an ammunition ship in Dry Dock No. 3. During and after the First World War, the shipyard built 25 submarine chasers, 6 submarines, 2 mine sweepers, 7 seagoing tugboats, and 2 ammunition ships, as well as 1,700 small boats.

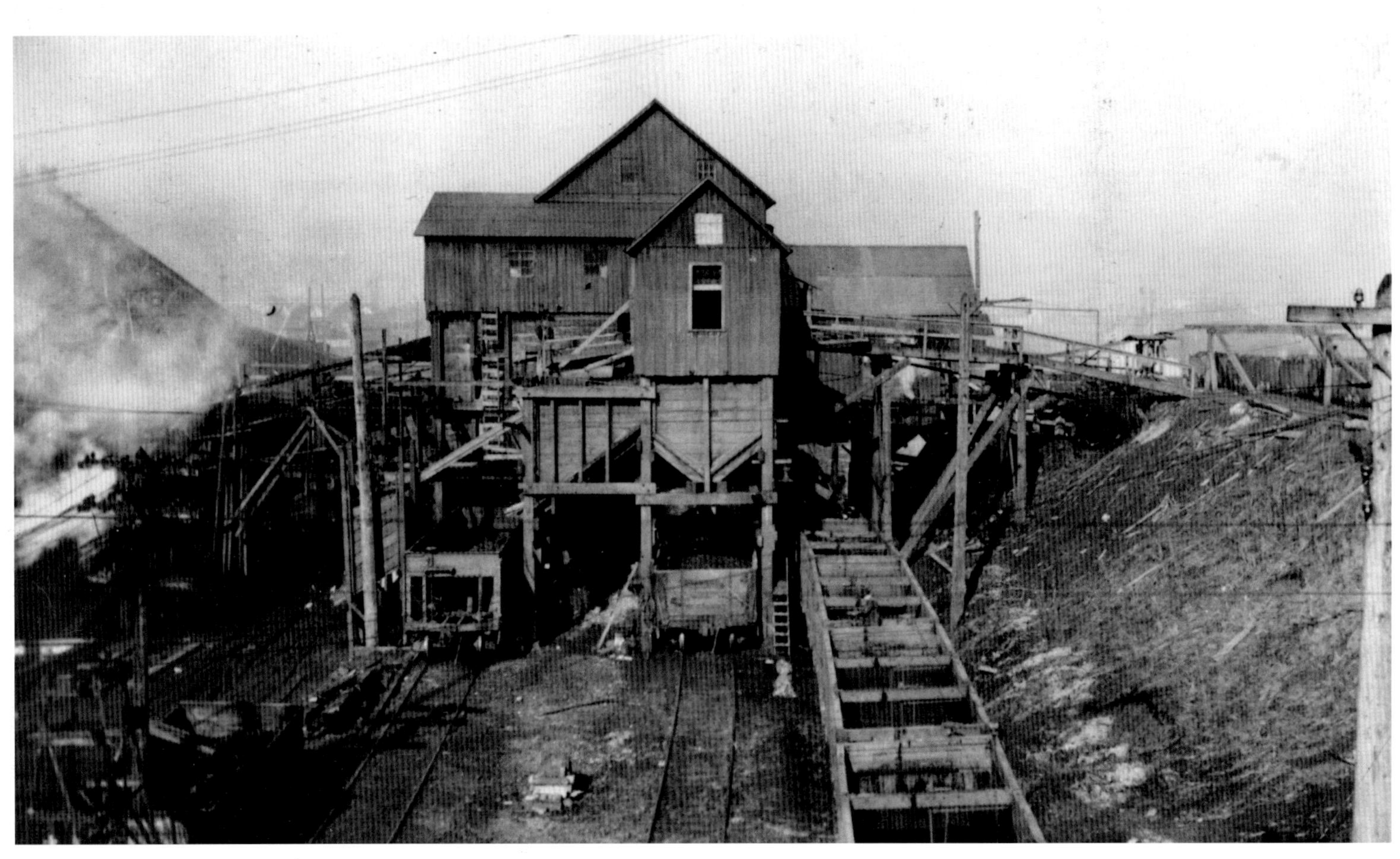

In 1853, Dr. R. M. Bigelow discovered coal near what would become Renton. He formed the Duwamish Coal Company, the first of many that produced one of Puget Sound's most important exports for over 50 years. Most of the coal was shipped through Seattle to fuel stoves and furnaces in San Francisco and the Hawaiian Islands. Here in 1919, the tipple and washery of the Renton Mine continues to process ore.

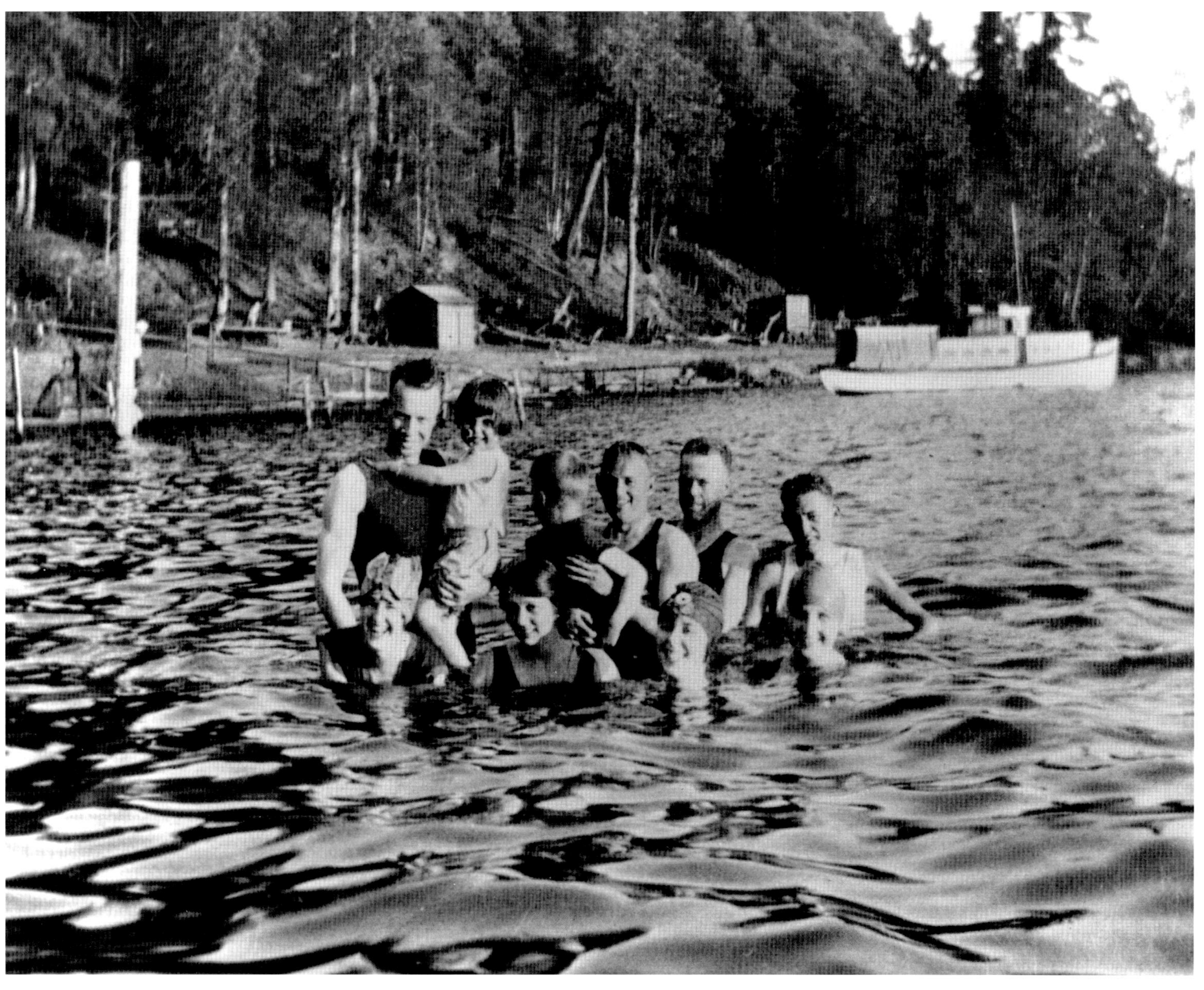

In 1919, the future Bellevue and the eastern shore of Lake Washington was rural and almost remote, accessible from Seattle only by ferry. Seattle residents found the quiet shores appealing. In 1919, the Albert Burrows family enjoys a swim at their property they call Burrows Landing.

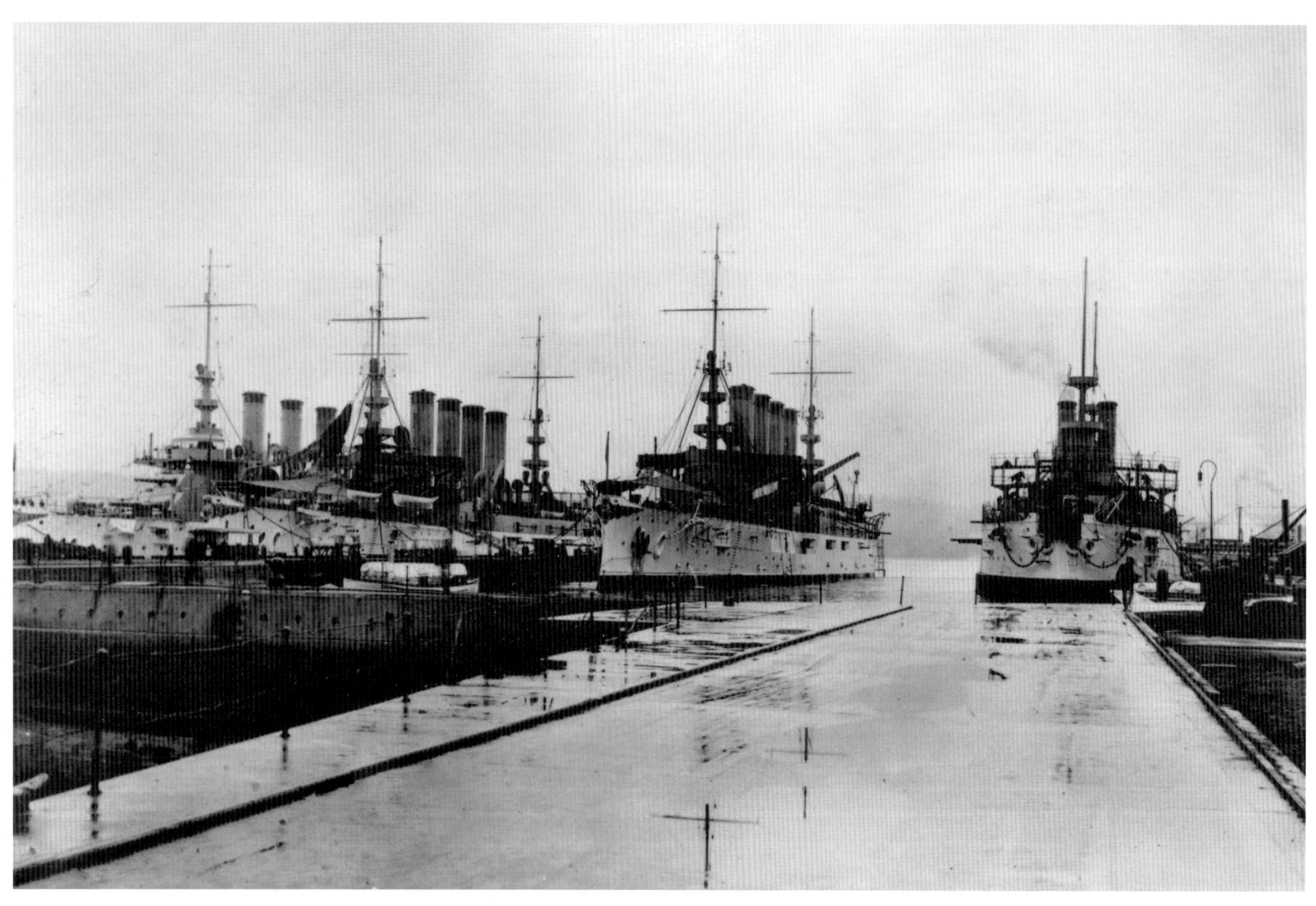

The big guns of the U.S. Navy's Pacific Fleet refit at the Puget Sound Naval Shipyard in 1919. From left to right are the battleship *Nebraska,* the armored cruisers *Colorado* and *Pennsylvania,* and the battleship *Wisconsin.*

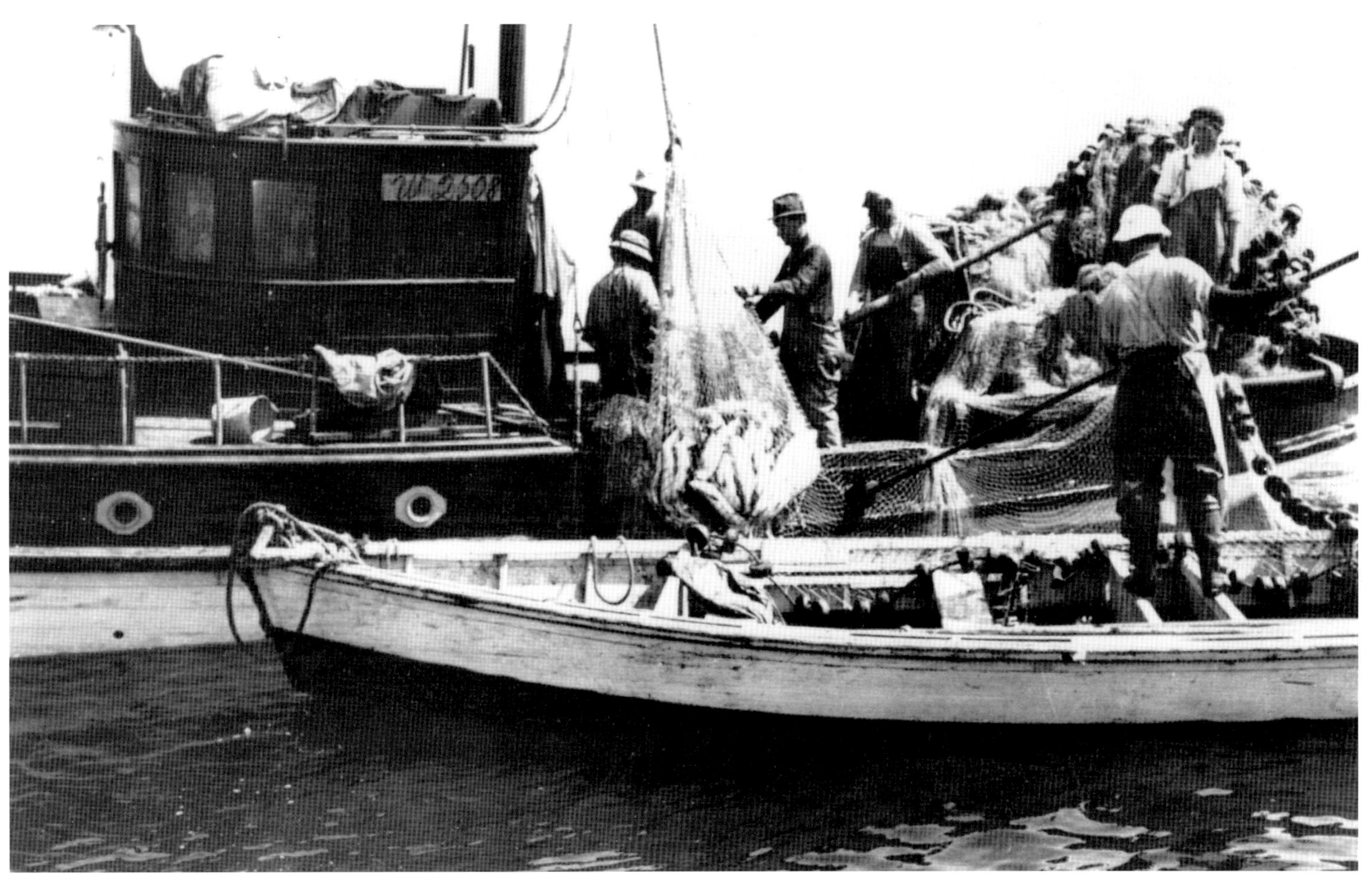

Puget Sound fishermen haul in a seine of salmon. Photographer John N. Cobb took this action shot in the 1920s.

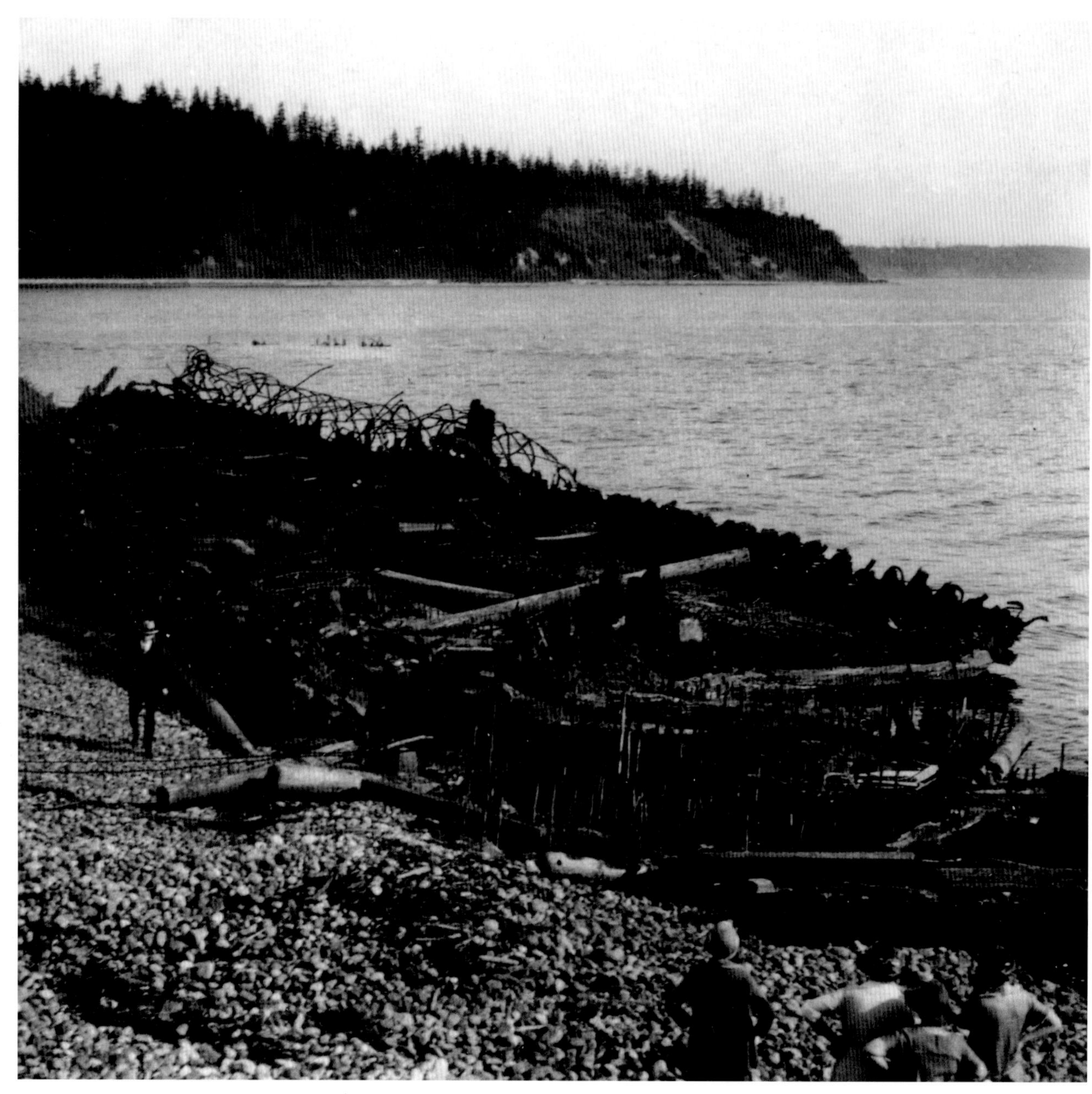

This nameless ship, apparently lost to fire, rests at Richmond Beach north of Seattle. The shipwreck was photographed around 1920.

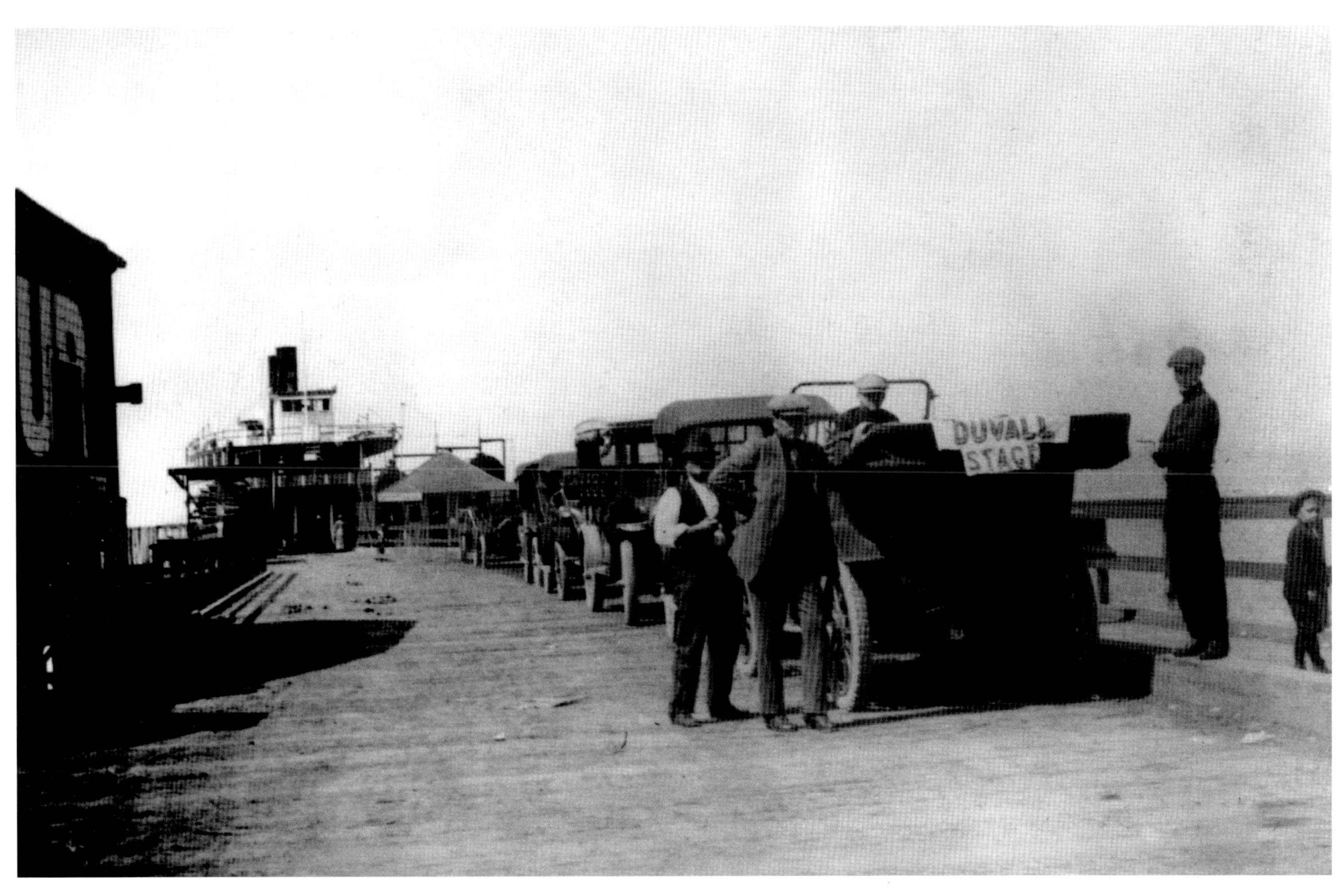

In this enduring image of life on Puget Sound, a group of motorists waits to board the side-wheel steam ferry *Leschi* at Moss Bay in Kirkland (ca. 1920). In 1913, *Leschi* began serving runs from Madison Park in Seattle to communities at Lake Washington's eastern shore. She was the first ferry built in western Washington to accommodate automobiles.

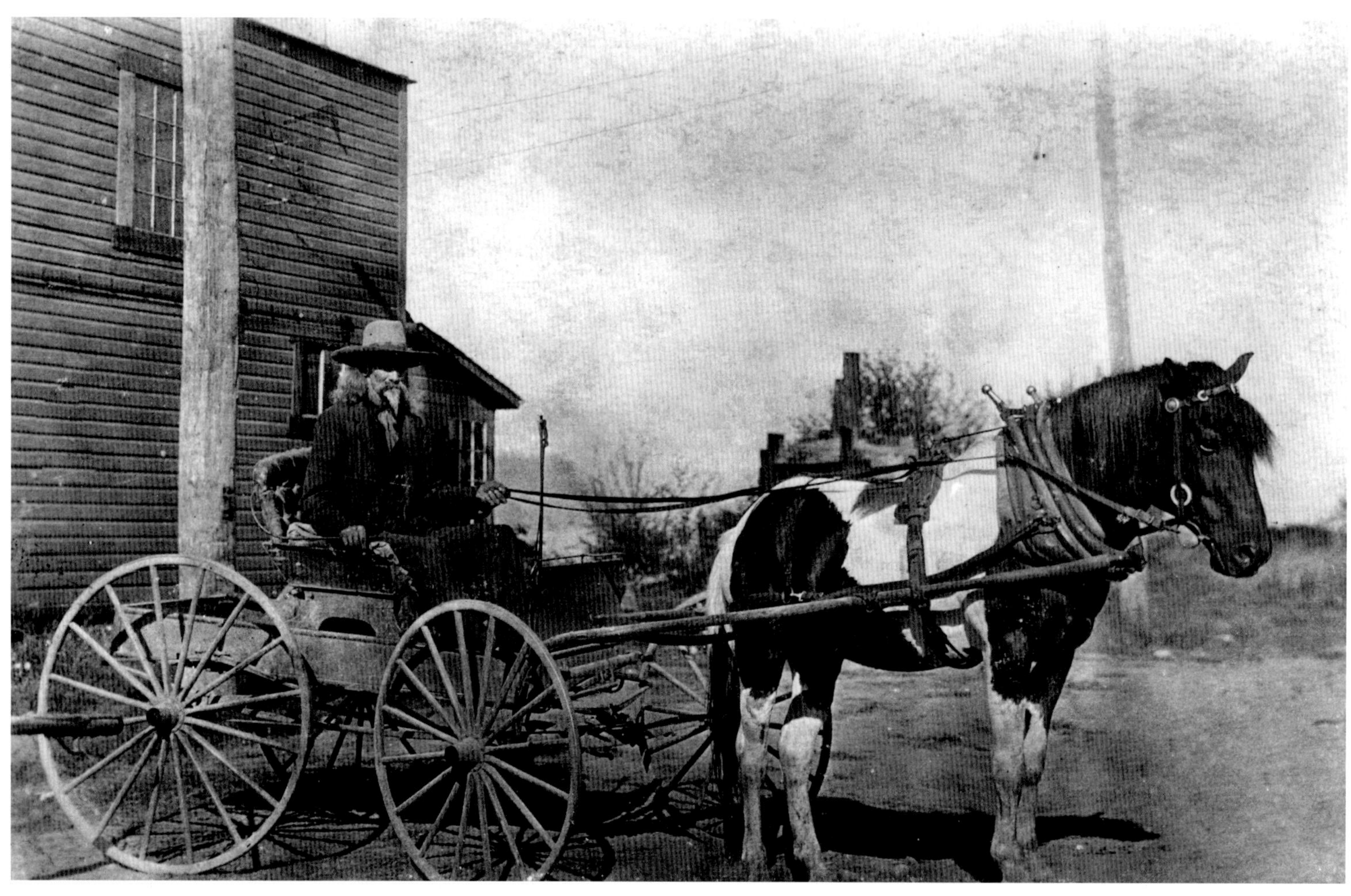

Paul Cunningham was born in Ontario in 1846, went west at the age of 18, homesteaded in the Dakotas, scouted for General Custer, guided wagon trains across the Rockies, and performed with Annie Oakley in Buffalo Bill Cody's Wild West Show. He also served as Colonel Cody's stand-in. Cunningham retired near Langley on Whidbey Island to write poetry. Here in 1921, he poses in a buckboard with his horse Peanut.

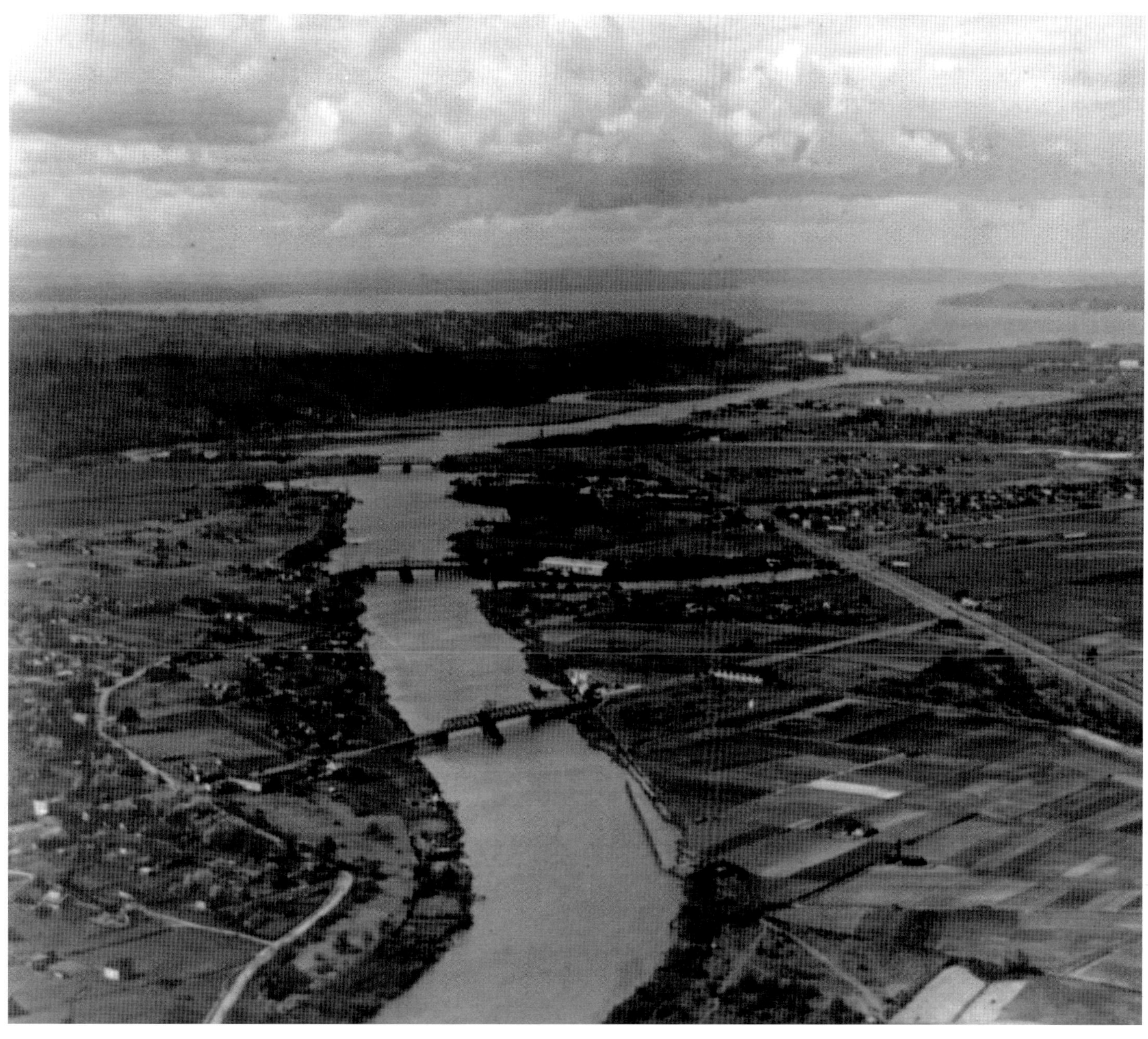

This 1920 aerial view of the Duwamish Waterway in Seattle captures Elliott Bay and Puget Sound beyond. Originally, the Duwamish River meandered through a fertile valley to its mouth at Seattle. Beginning in 1913, dredgers moved 20 million cubic yards of spoil to straighten the river, better accommodating oceangoing ships. The spoils helped fill in the meanders, some of which became city streets.

By the early 1920s, Shelton had rebuilt from two disastrous fires, the second time using brick. Transit service is still by motor stage in this undated photo. In 1926, the Northern Pacific completed a branch line, giving Shelton regular rail service to the new lumber and pulp mills.

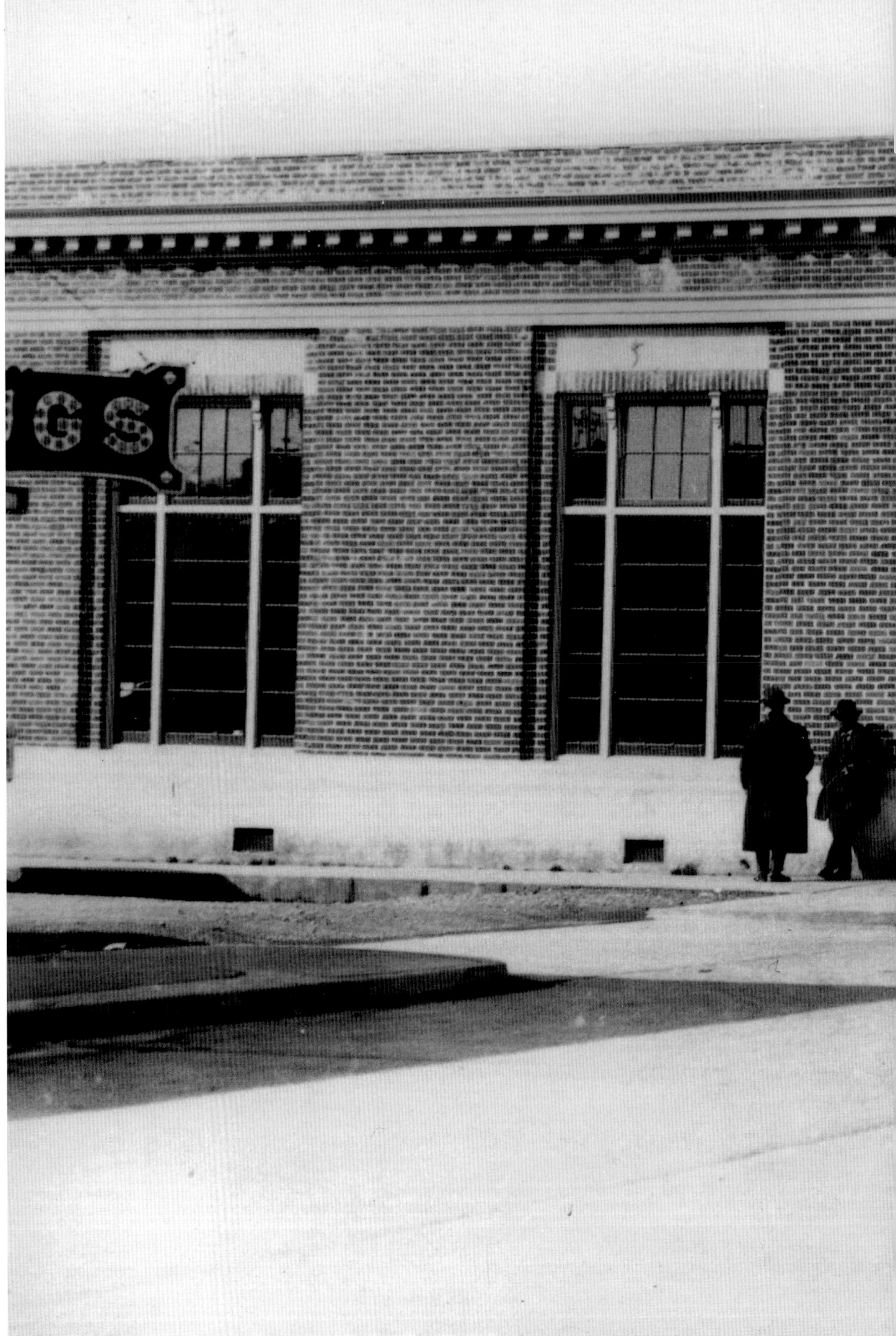

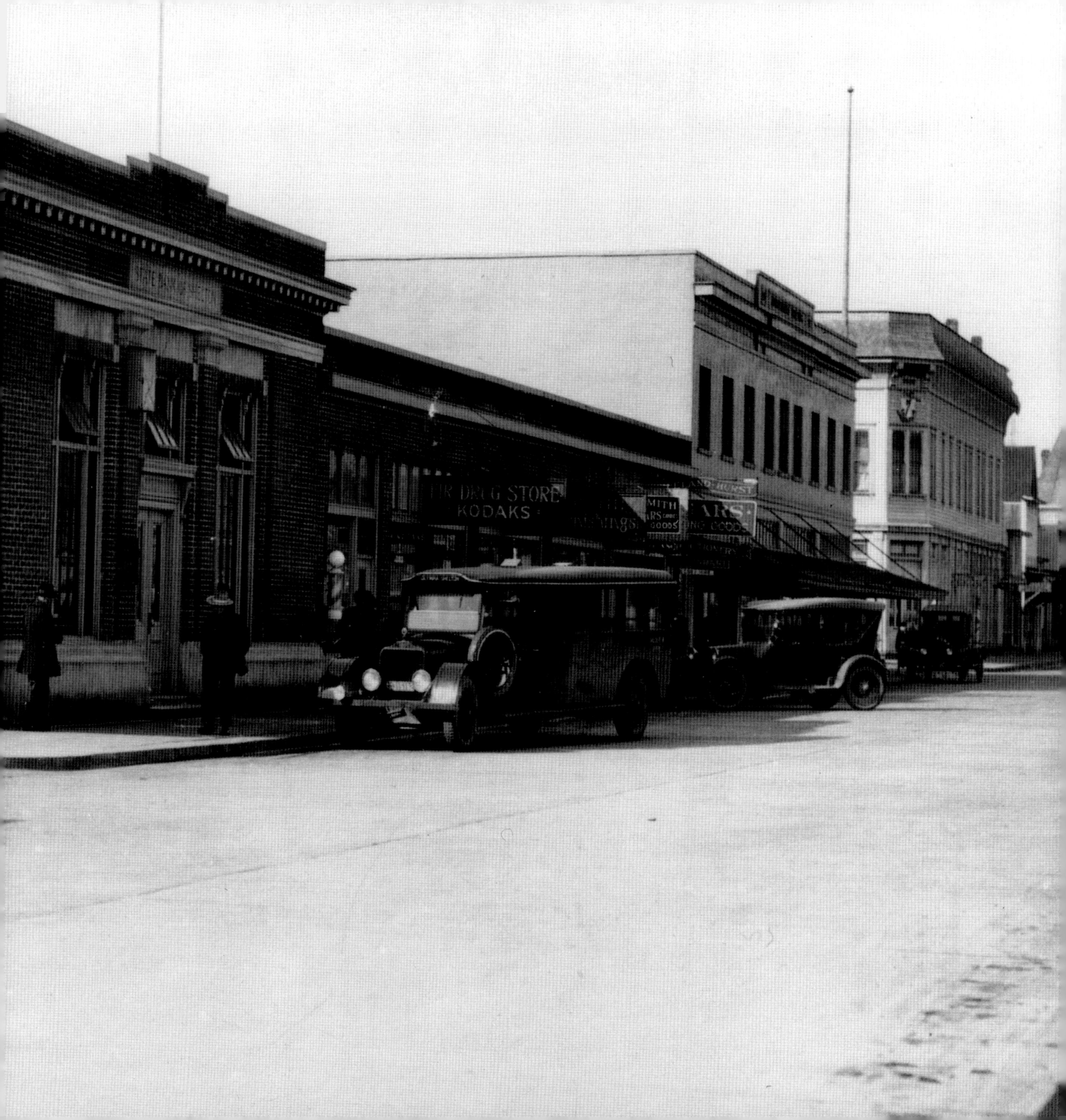
STATE BANK
FIR DRUG STORE
KODAKS
SMITH
ARS
GOODS
NG GOODS

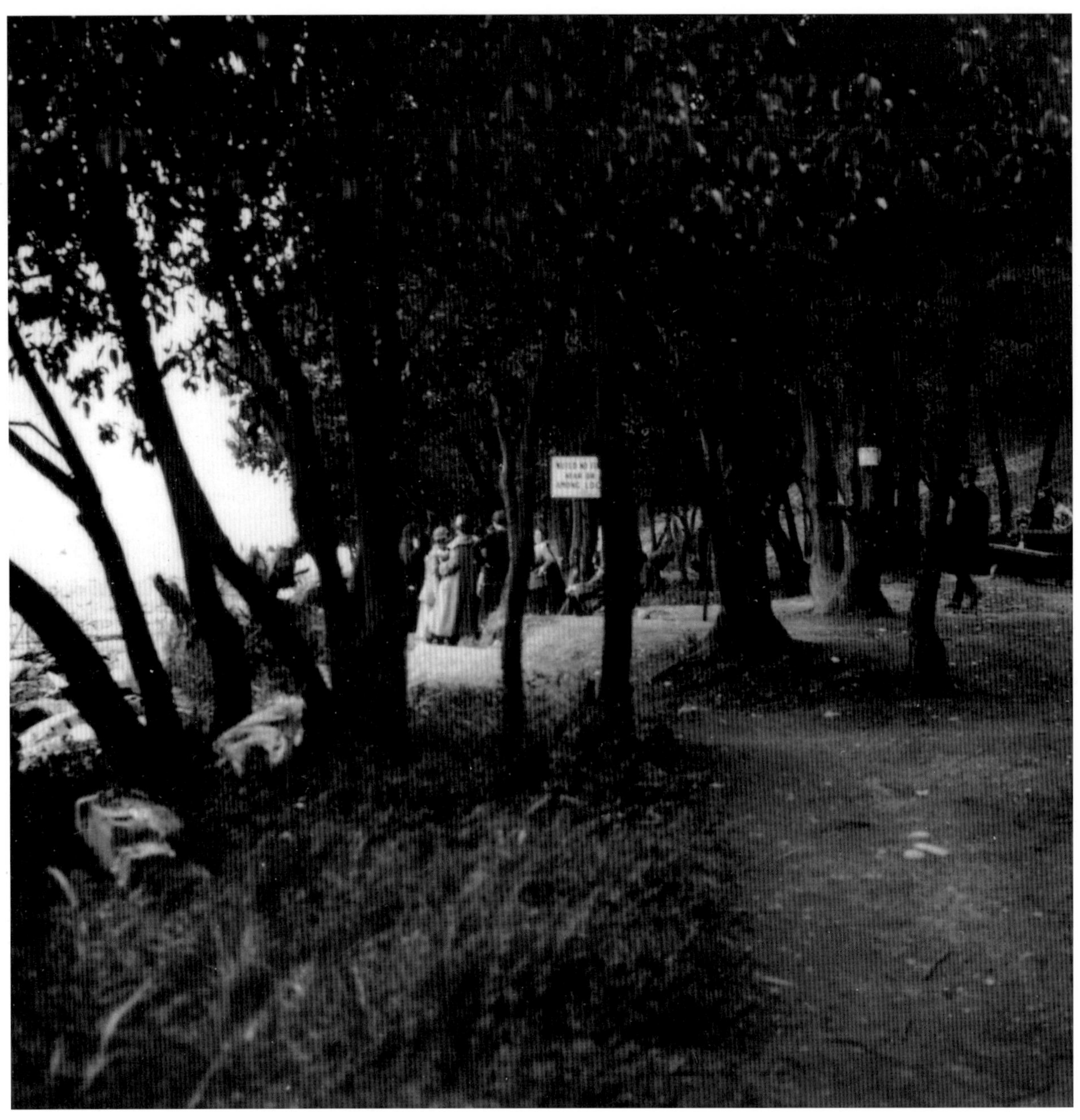

In 1909, the Yesler Logging Company deeded 300 feet of West Seattle's waterfront acreage to Seattle as a park. Sixteen years later, the city changed the name from Lincoln Beach Park to Lowman Beach Park to avoid confusion with the larger park just to the south. In this stereopticon view from the early 1920s, visitors stroll through trees near the shore.

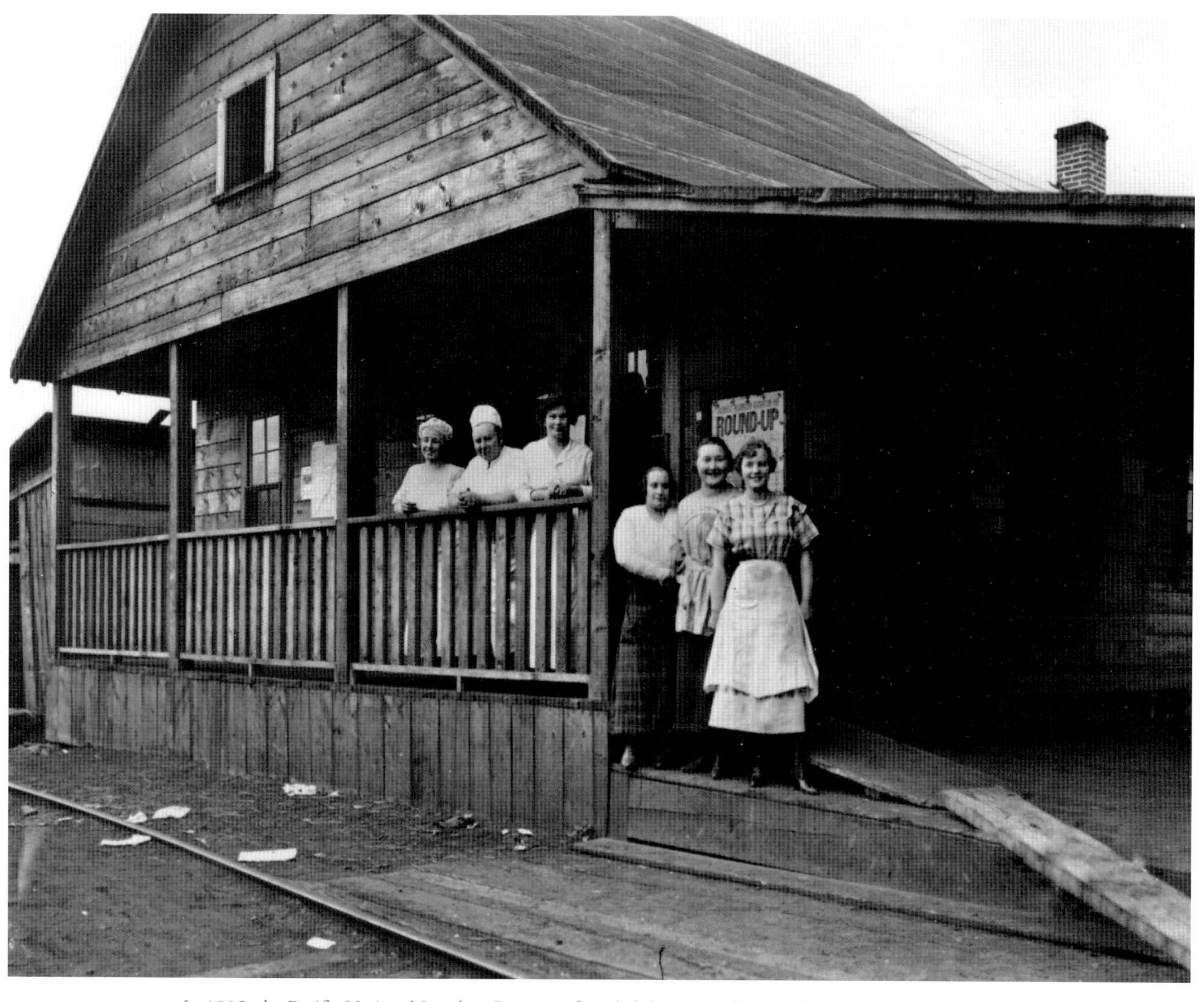

In 1905, the Pacific National Lumber Company founded the town of National seven miles west of the Mount Rainier National Park entrance. Small, red, boxlike cottages crowded onto crooked, planked streets and were dominated by the large red sawmill. The smiles on this group of mess hall workers suggests that life in National was not entirely dreary.

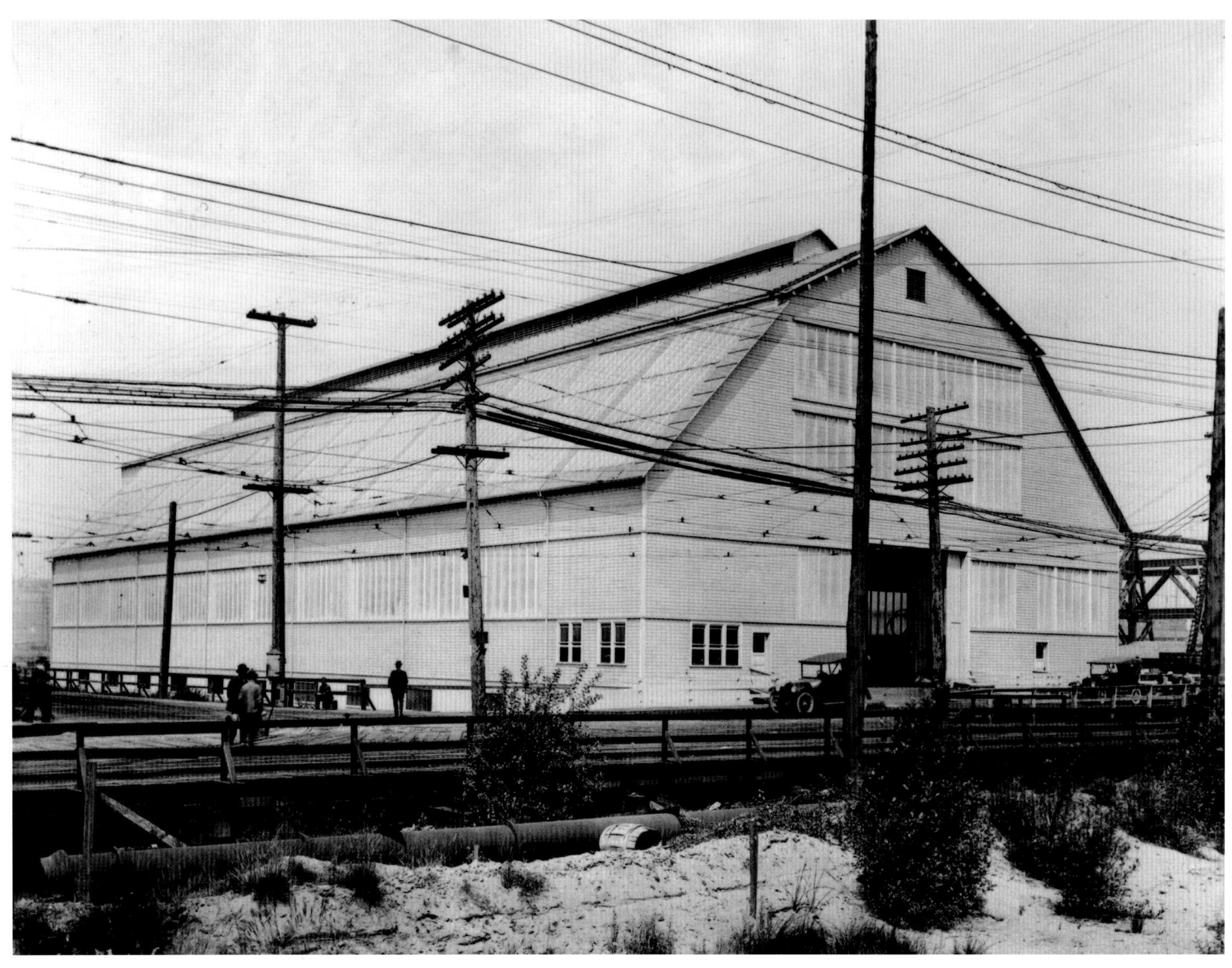

Boiler Shop Building, Puget Sound Machinery Depot, Seattle, 1922. In this sizable wood structure at First Avenue and Massachusetts Street, workers repaired and refurbished Great Northern and Northern Pacific locomotives as well as marine engines.

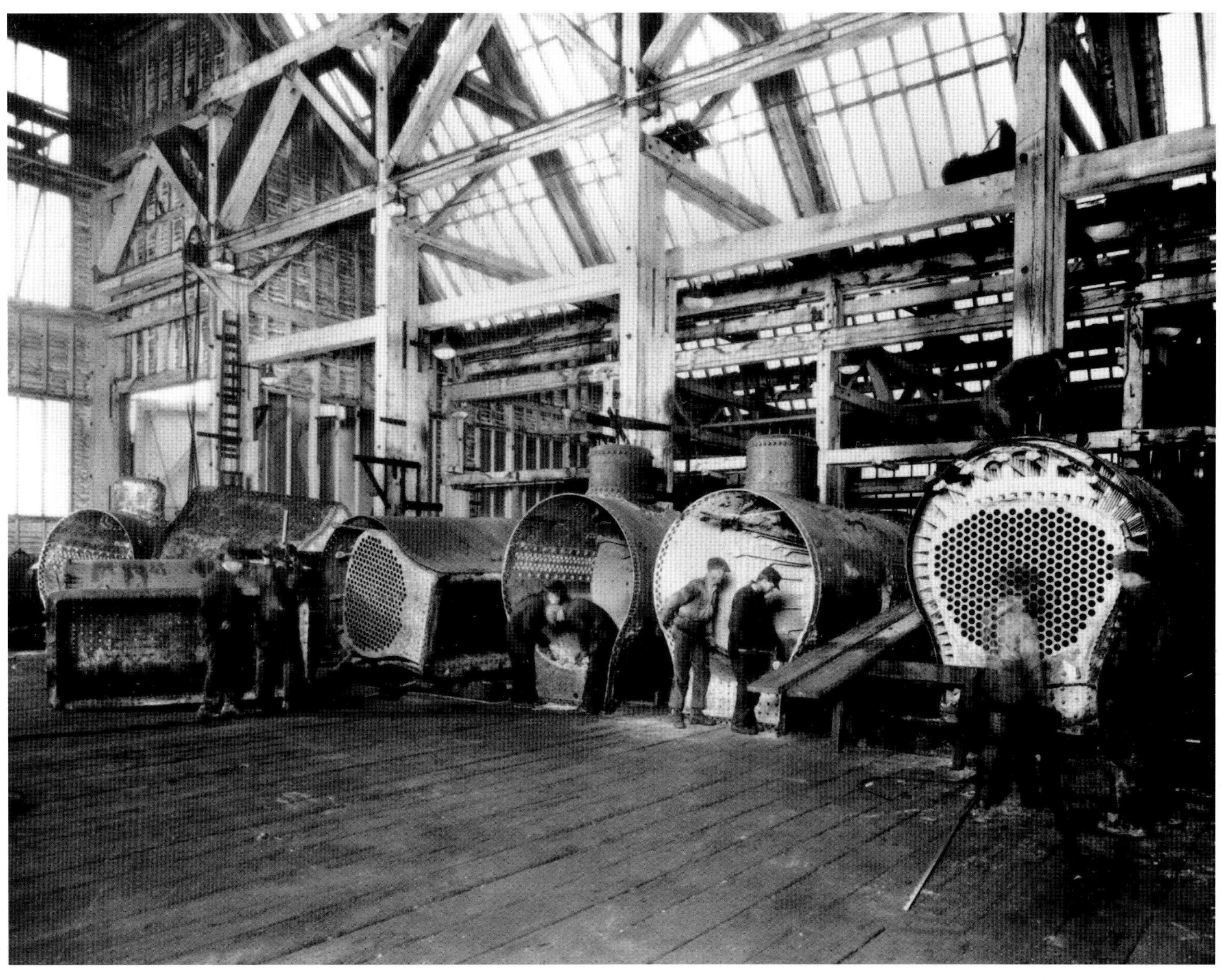

The Puget Sound Machinery Depot, located at First Avenue and Massachusetts Street in Seattle, repaired steam locomotives and ship engines. In 1922, workers here repair the fireboxes of three locomotives.

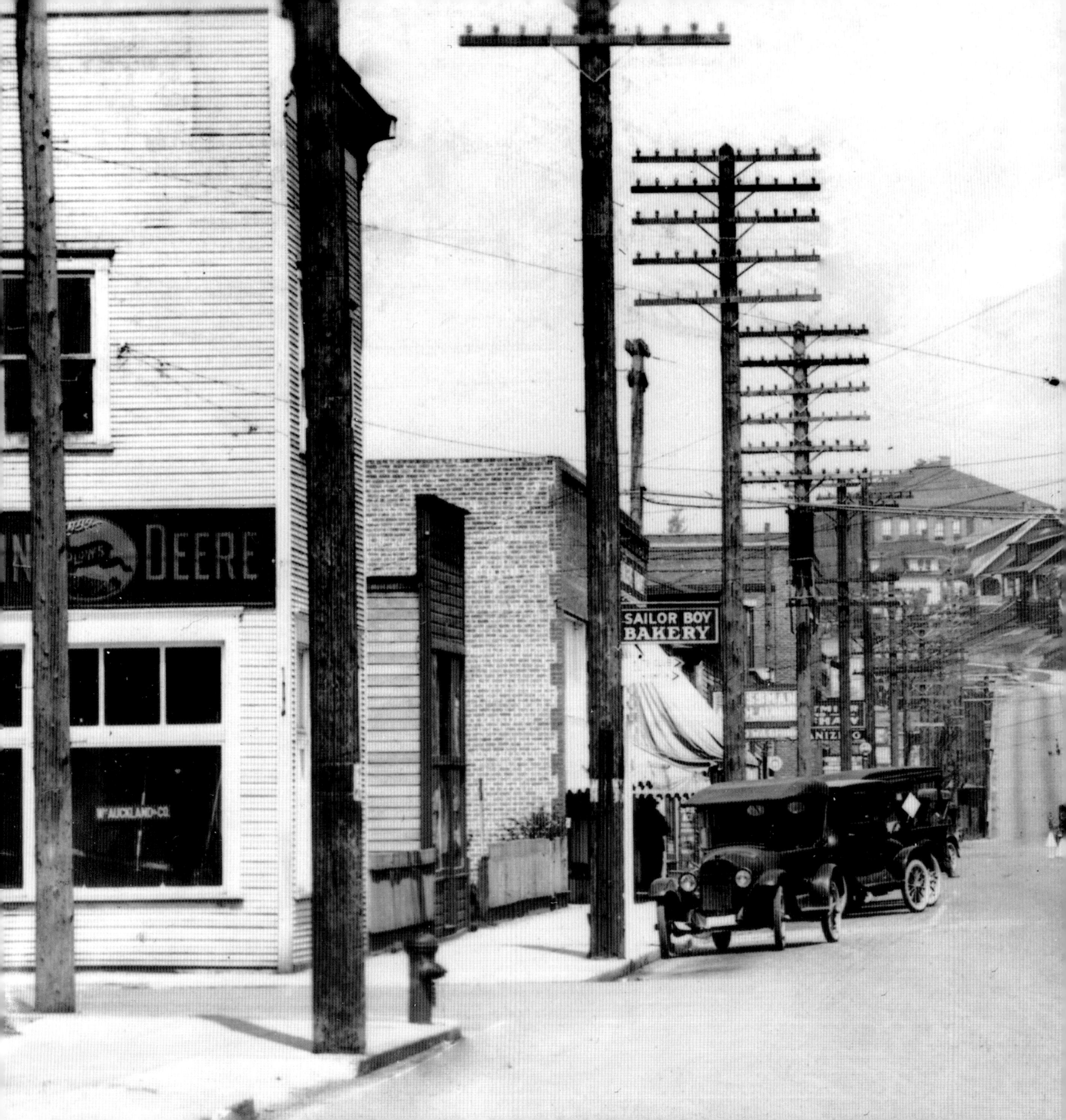
DEERE
Wᴹ AUCKLAND CO
SAILOR BOY
BAKERY

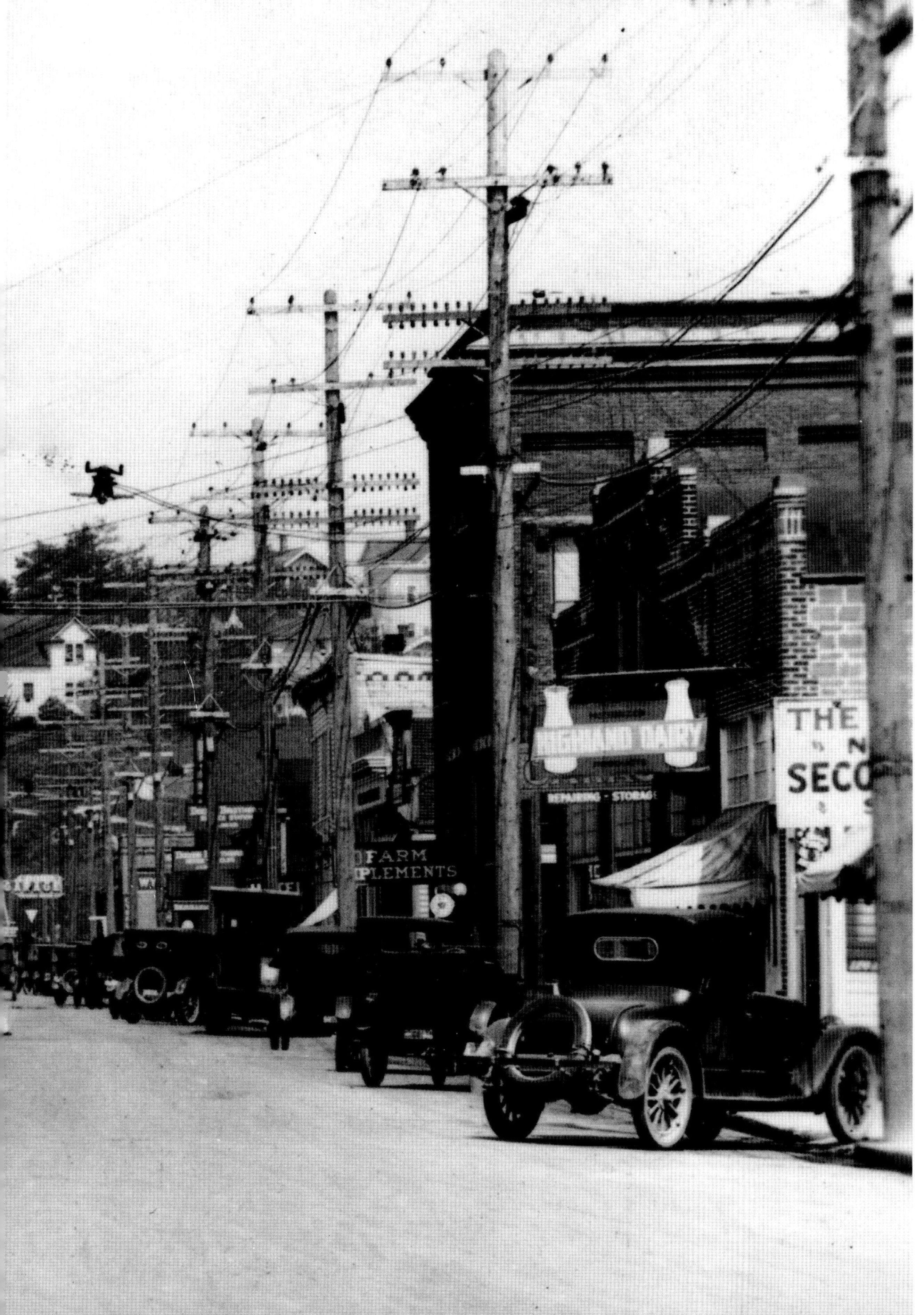

Around 1924, photographer J. A. Juleen recorded this Second Street view in Mount Vernon on the Skagit River. The dramatic growth of automobile use over 20 years is evidenced in the cars parked on the street, some rather casually.

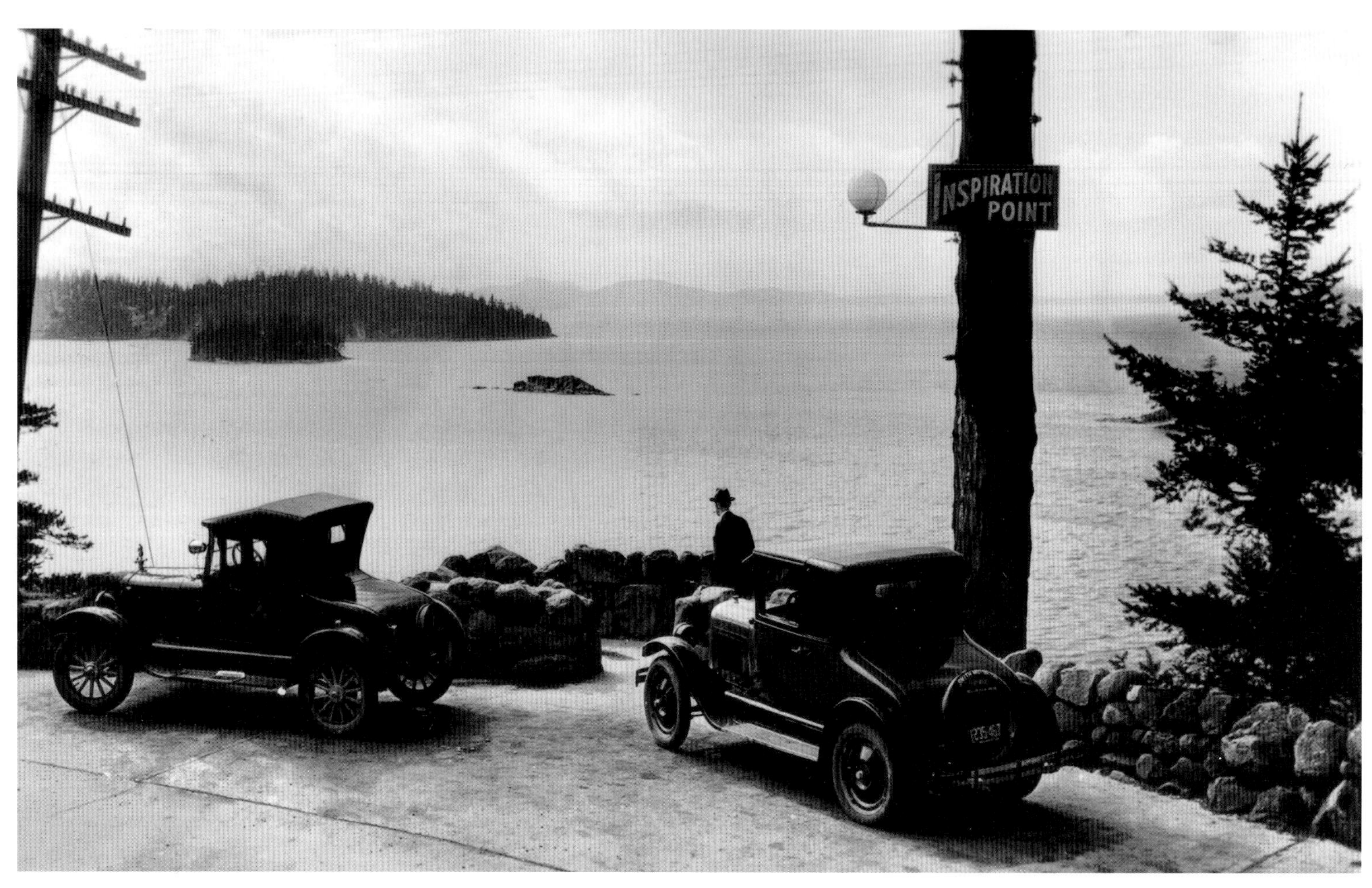

Motorists in 1926 marvel at the view from Inspiration Point, located on Chuckanut Drive near Bellingham. In the far distance is Lummi Island.

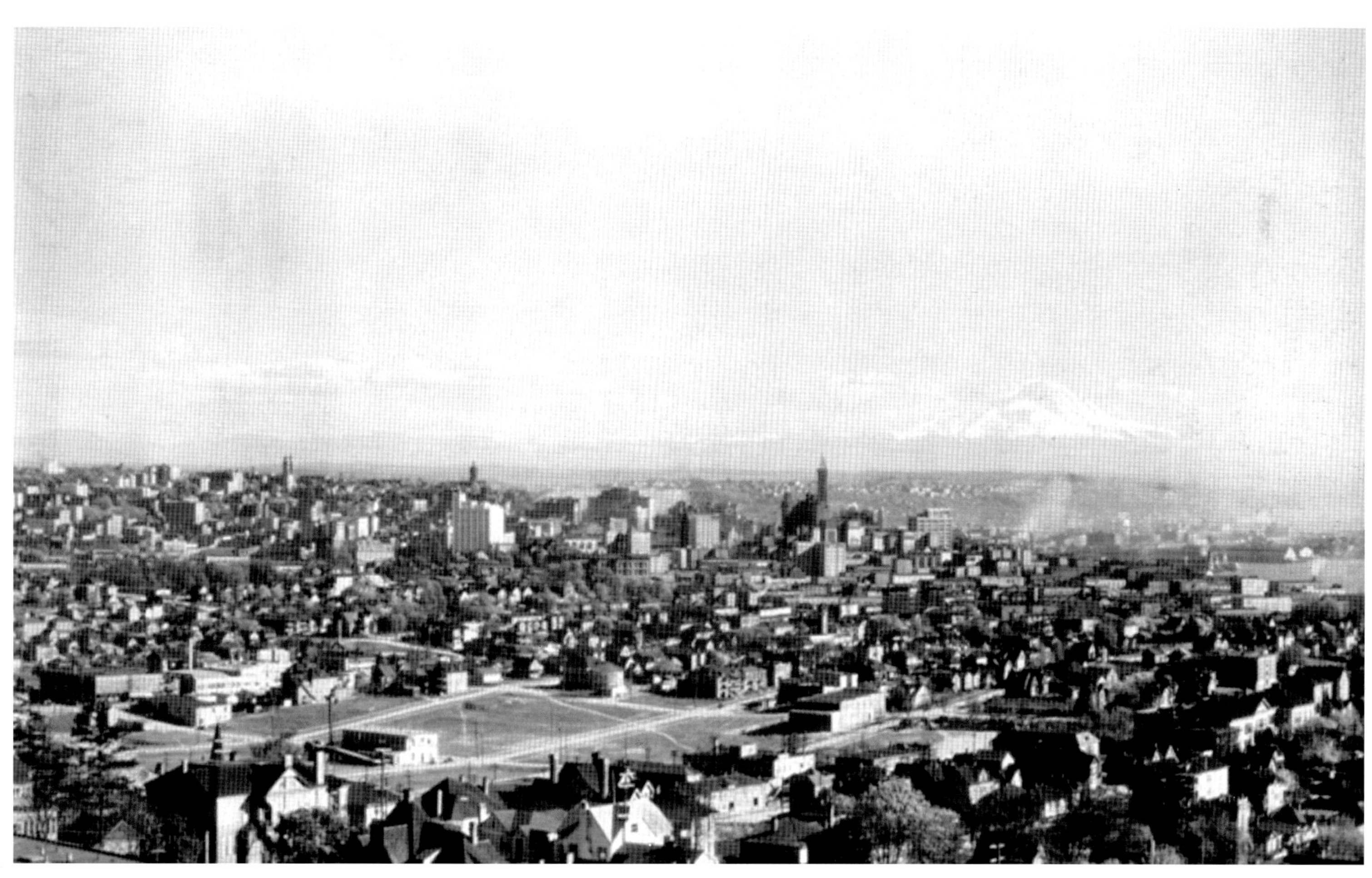

This 1926 panorama of Seattle from Queen Anne Hill captures the city before the 1920s building boom would give the skyline its form for 40 years. Prominent in the distance is the Smith Tower, completed in 1914. In the 1960s, new skyscrapers would rise, foreshadowing more dramatic structures in the decades to come.

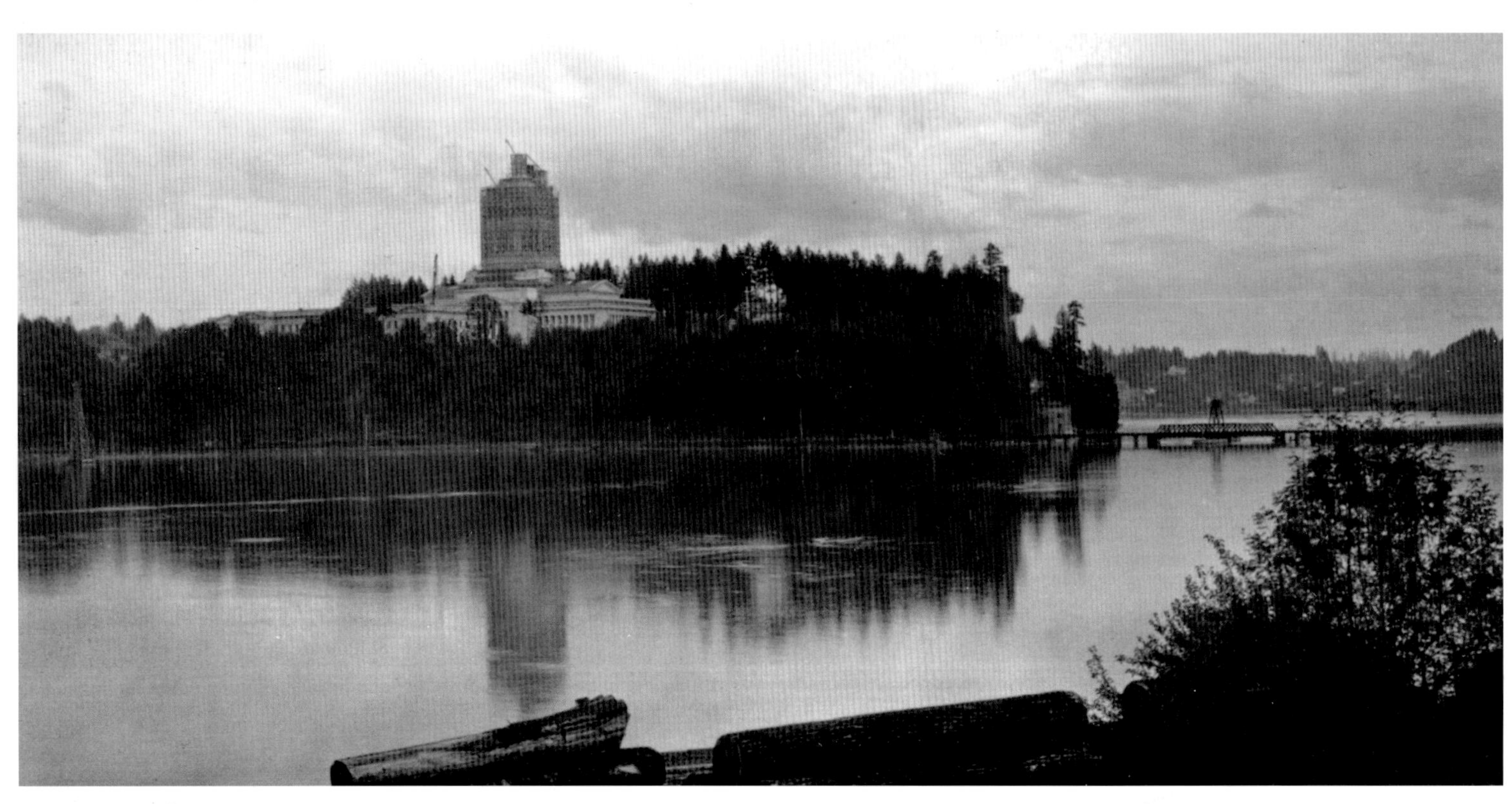

On October 10, 1926, the new State Capitol rises above Budd Inlet in Olympia. Construction derricks still surround the dome, which would rise to 278 feet. The building would not receive legislators until 1928, and only then with harsh criticism for its expense from budget-cutting Republican governor Roland E. Hartley.

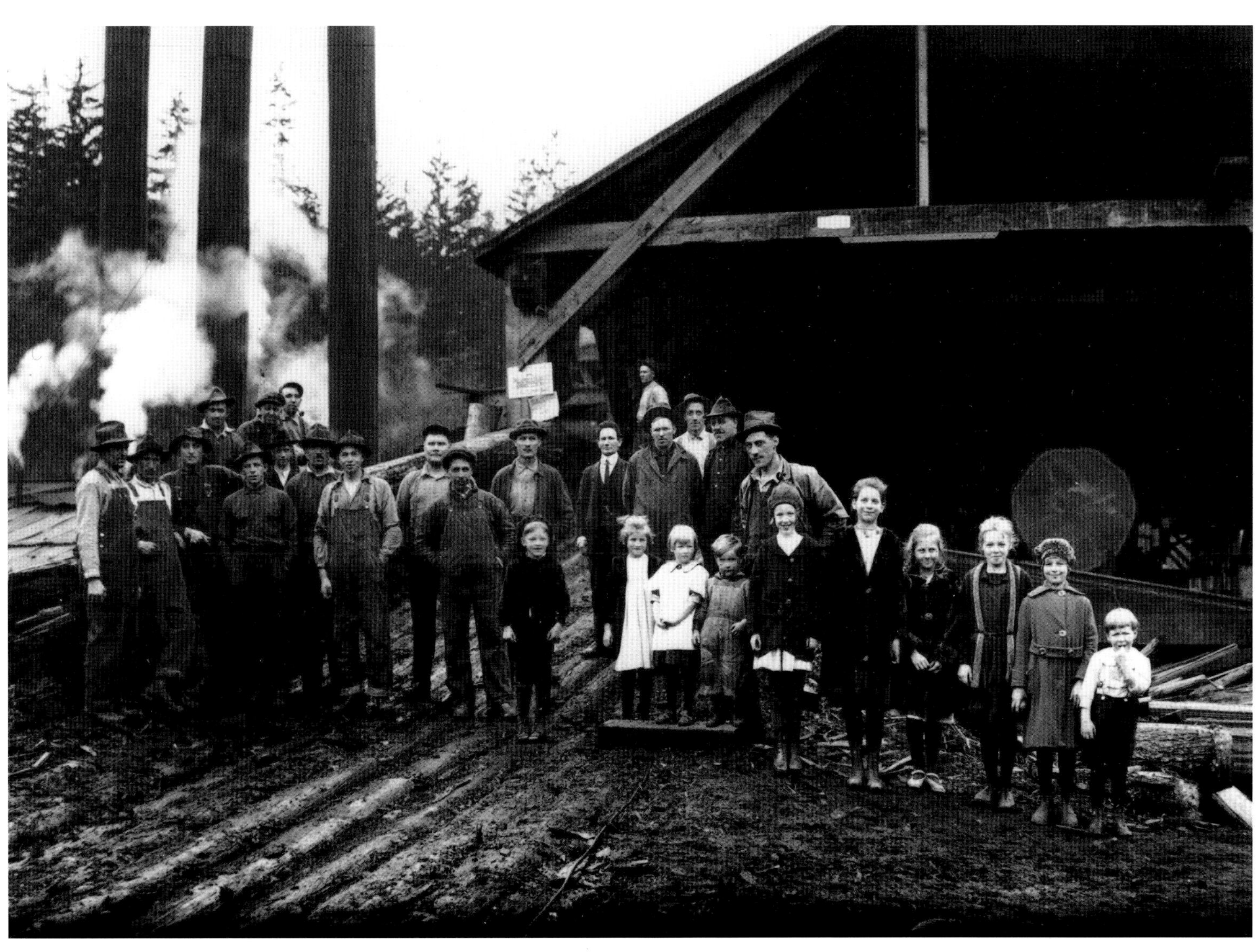

In the 1890s, Swedish immigrant August Lovgren founded the Preston Mill Company, located on the Raging River in eastern King County. He lured many other Swedes to Preston, where they built a classic immigrant community. In this 1920s image by Darius Kinsey, workers and their families pose in front of a mill building with a sawn log in the background.

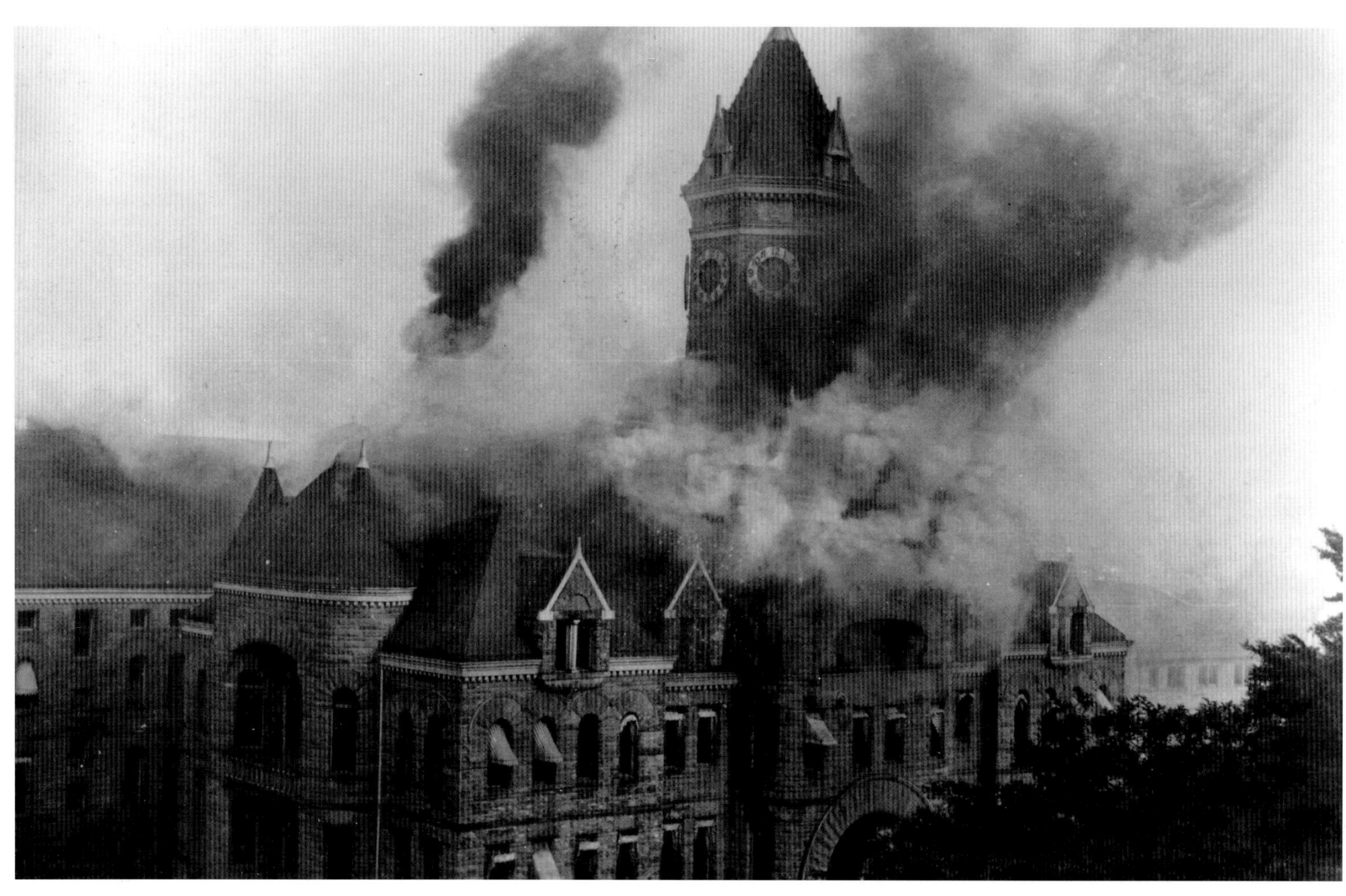

On Saturday afternoon, September 28, 1928, fire guts the third floor and clock tower of the old Capitol in Olympia. Fire fighters from Tacoma, 32 miles away, helped battle the blaze. Citizens and Boy Scouts ran into the building and rescued historical artifacts, important state records, and even stuffed animals. Repairs took just three months to complete, but the state never restored the clock tower.

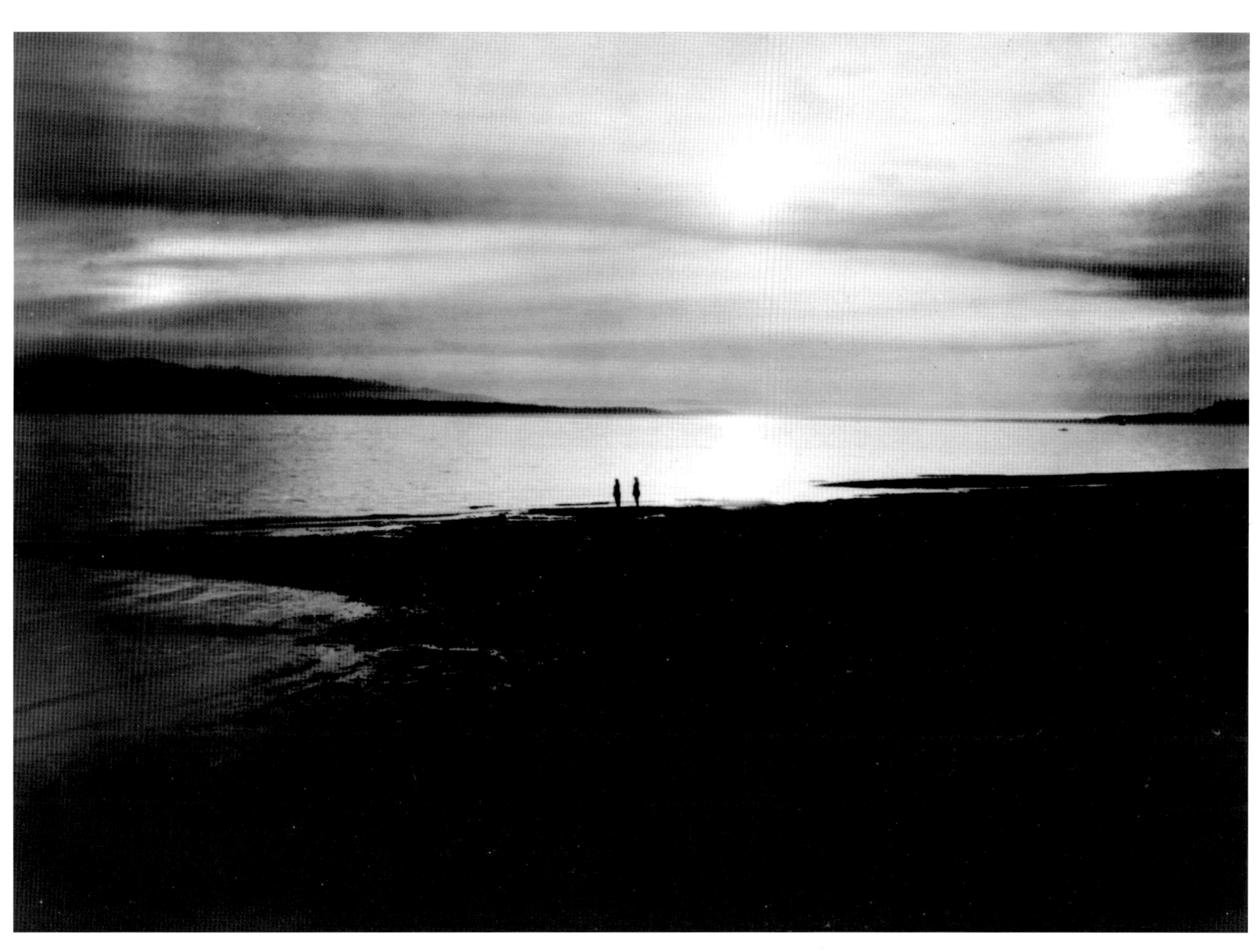

Photographer Lee Pickett caught two strollers on a Puget Sound beach around 1930.

Traveling along Puget Sound, a Great Northern freight train heads from Everett into Seattle. In addition to the GN, three other railroads—the Northern Pacific, the Union Pacific, and the Chicago, Milwaukee, St. Paul and Pacific (the Milwaukee Road)—provided transcontinental connections to the Sound.

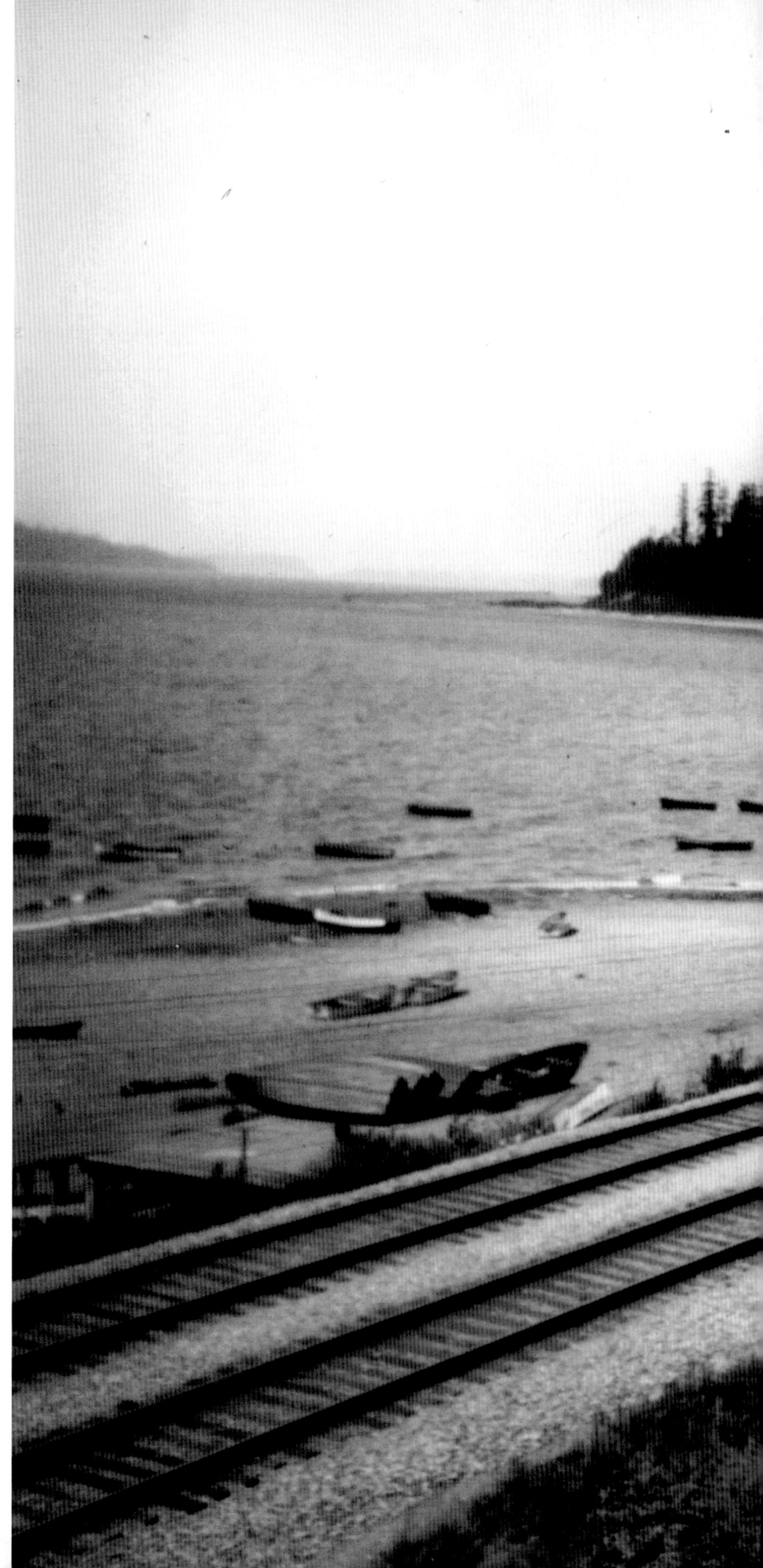

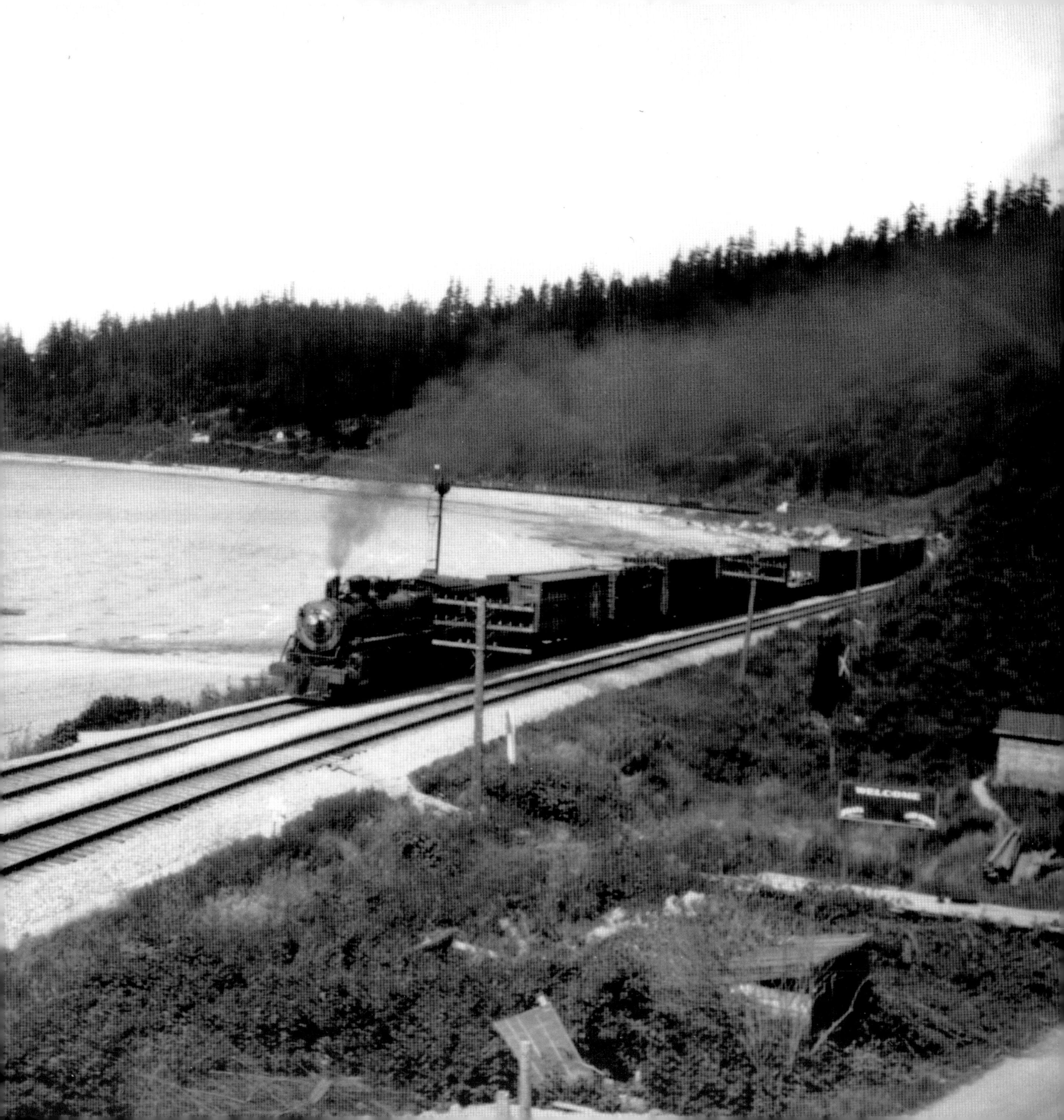

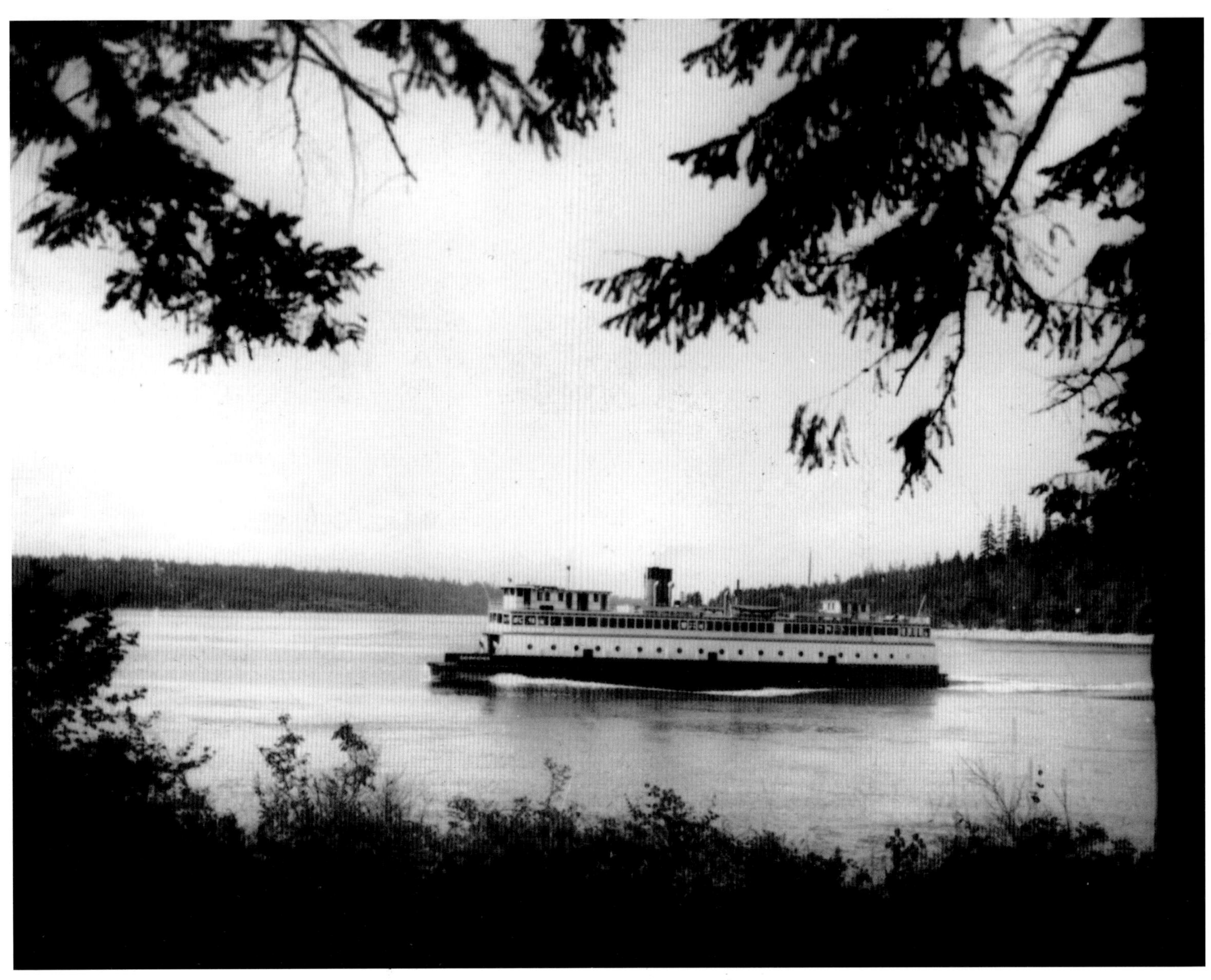

The Puget Sound Navigation Company—the Black Ball Line—bought the Great Lakes passenger ferry *Chippewa* in 1907, towed her 16,000 miles around South America, and put her into service on Puget Sound. In 1926, the line converted her to carry 90 automobiles and 2,000 passengers. Here in 1930, she handles the Seattle-Bremerton run. The *Chippewa* served Puget Sound travelers for more than 50 years.

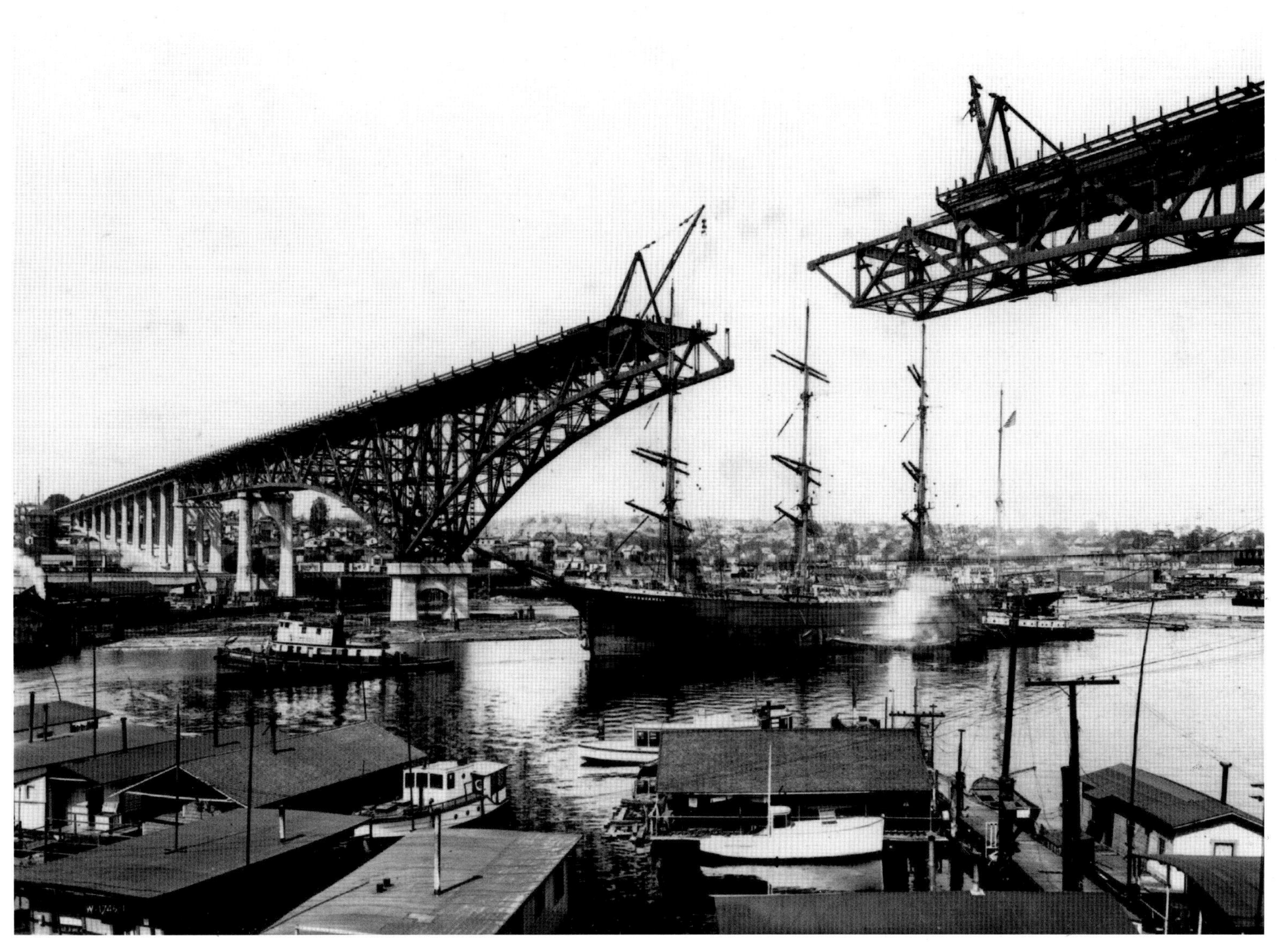

In 1931, the George Washington Memorial Bridge, or the Aurora Bridge, is nearing completion in Seattle. Before the last girders are riveted into place, the three-masted *Monongahela* is towed out of Lake Union into the Lake Washington Ship Canal. The height of the *Monongahela*'s masts exceeds 150 feet, the minimum allowed by the War Department for a bridge over a federal waterway.

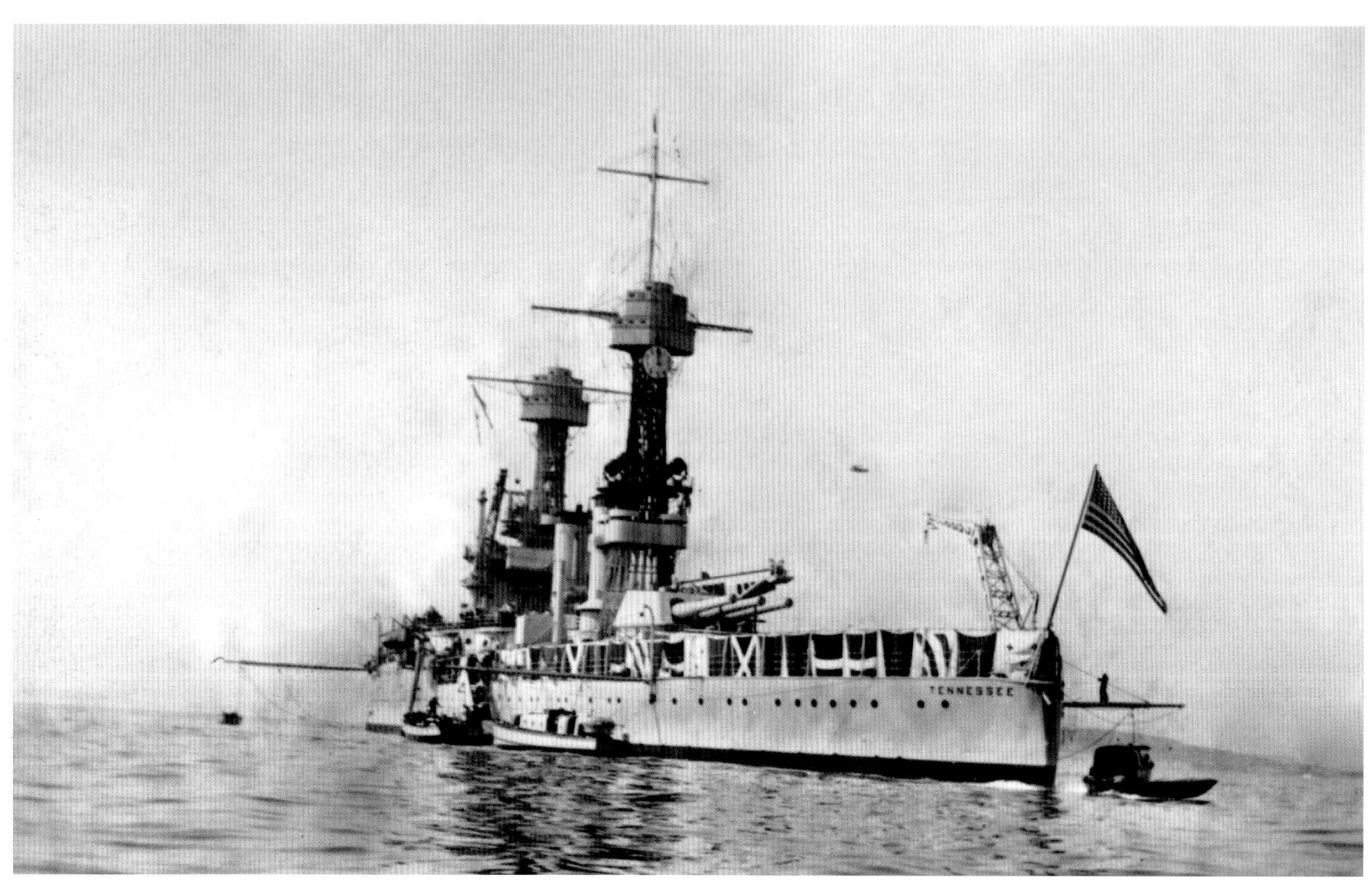

The Pacific Fleet battleship USS *Tennessee* visits Puget Sound in 1932. The *Tennessee* would be sunk on December 7, 1941, at Pearl Harbor; however, she would be raised and repaired at the Puget Sound Naval Shipyard and fight on during World War II. She carried twelve 14-inch guns in her main batteries.

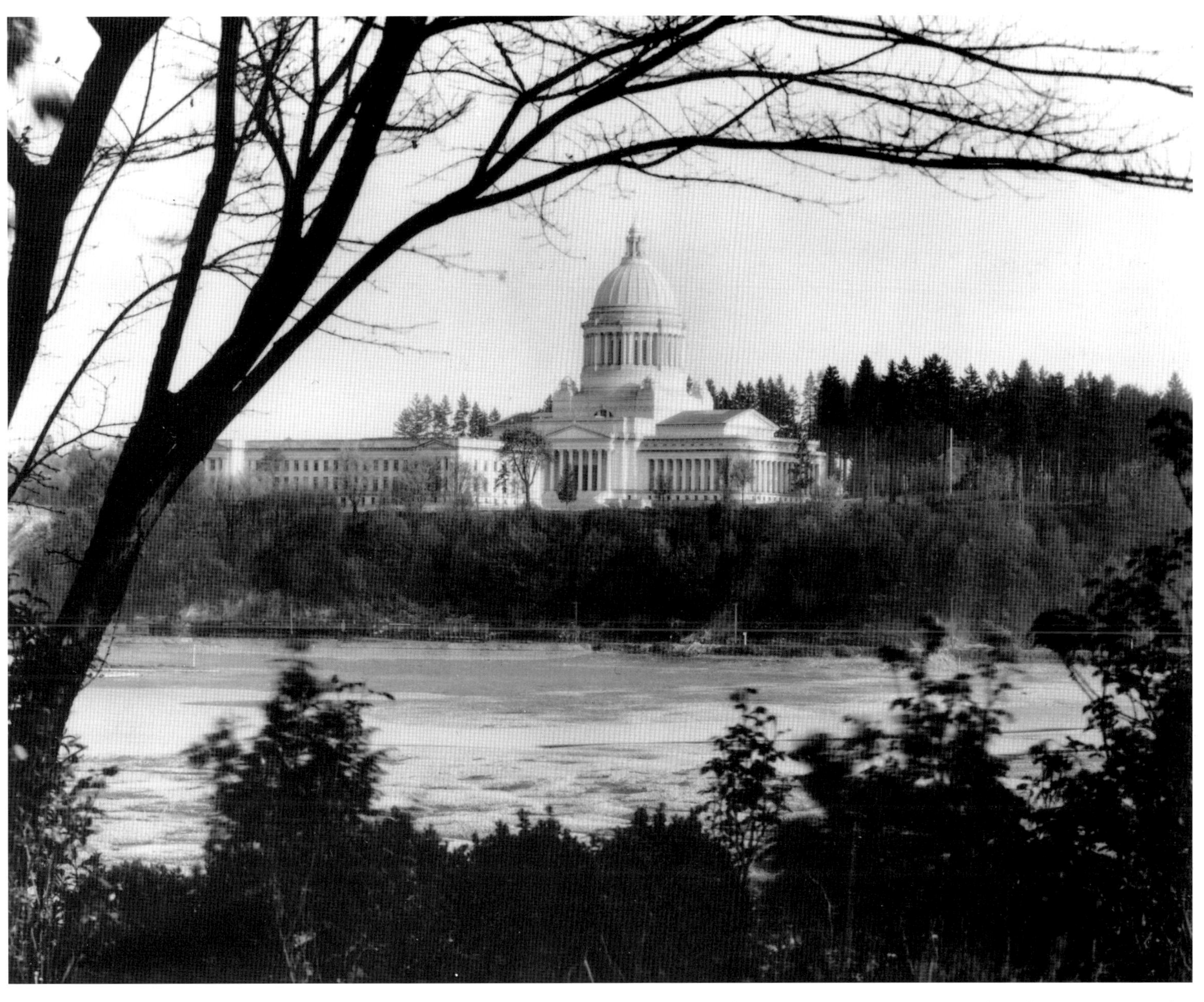

Around 1934 in Olympia, Asahel Curtis framed this portrait of the State Capitol with trees and shrubs across Budd Inlet.

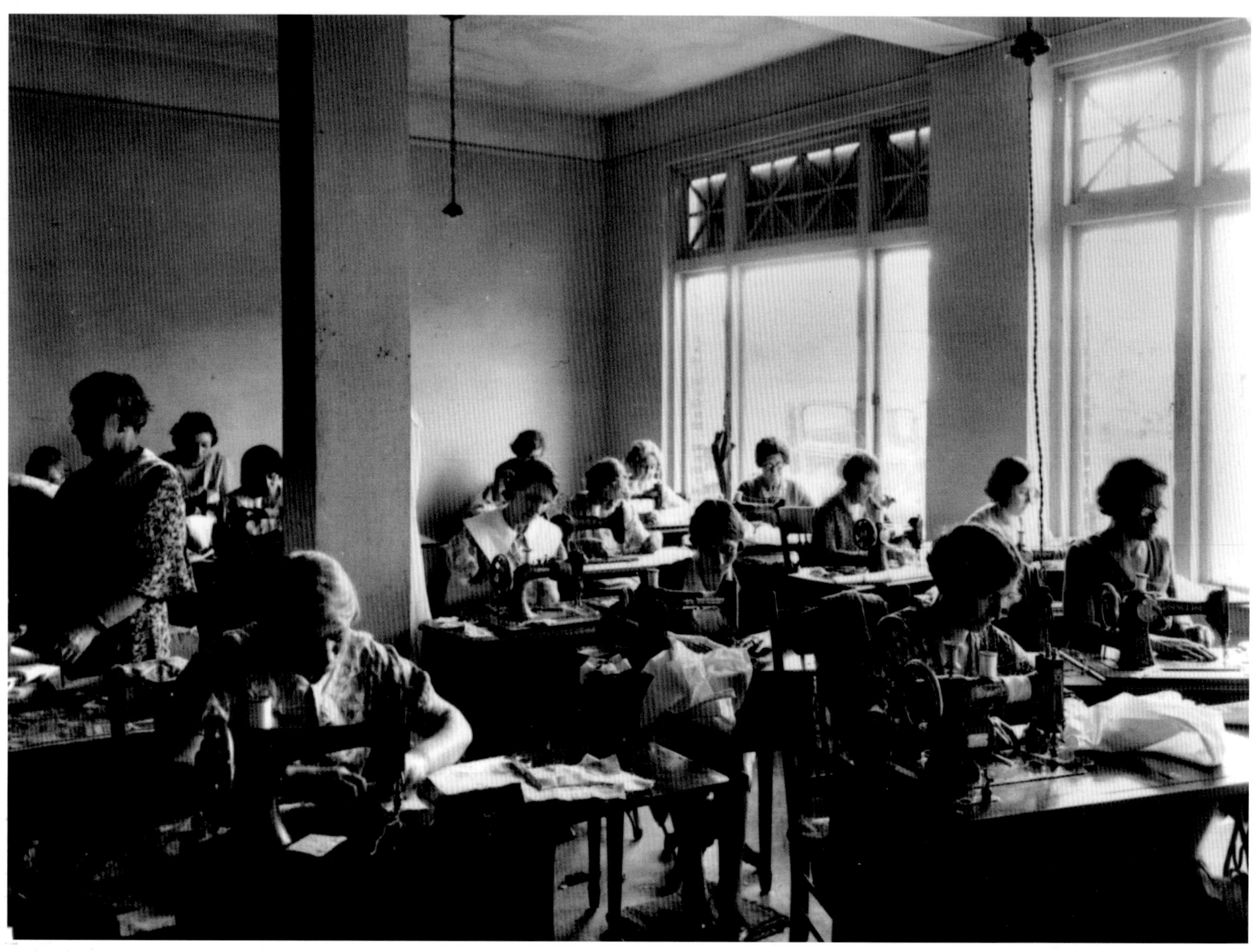

When hard times hit Washington in the 1930s, the U.S. government launched programs such as the Federal Civil Works Service to put the unemployed back to work. Pictured here on February 27, 1934, women of the Auburn Sewing Center work at their machines under the tall second-floor windows of the old Angora Woolen Mill.

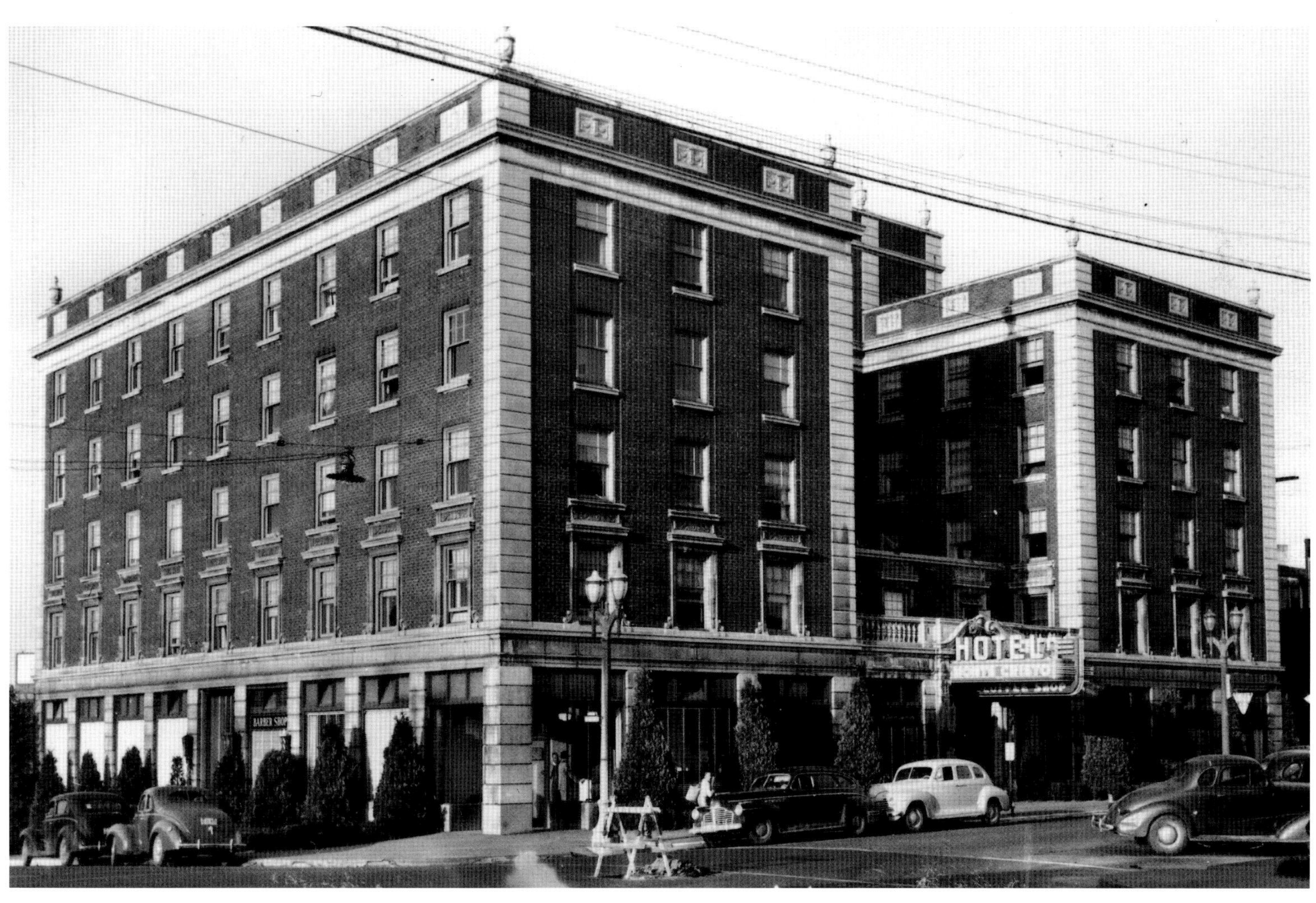

The Hotel Monte Cristo, at 1507 Wall Street, Everett, opened in May 1925 at a cost of half a million dollars. In 1932, when this image was captured by Clifford Ellis, it was still the premier hostelry on Port Gardiner Bay. The hotel would decline and sit vacant for 20 years before reemerging in 1995 as an arts center, restaurant, and affordable housing.

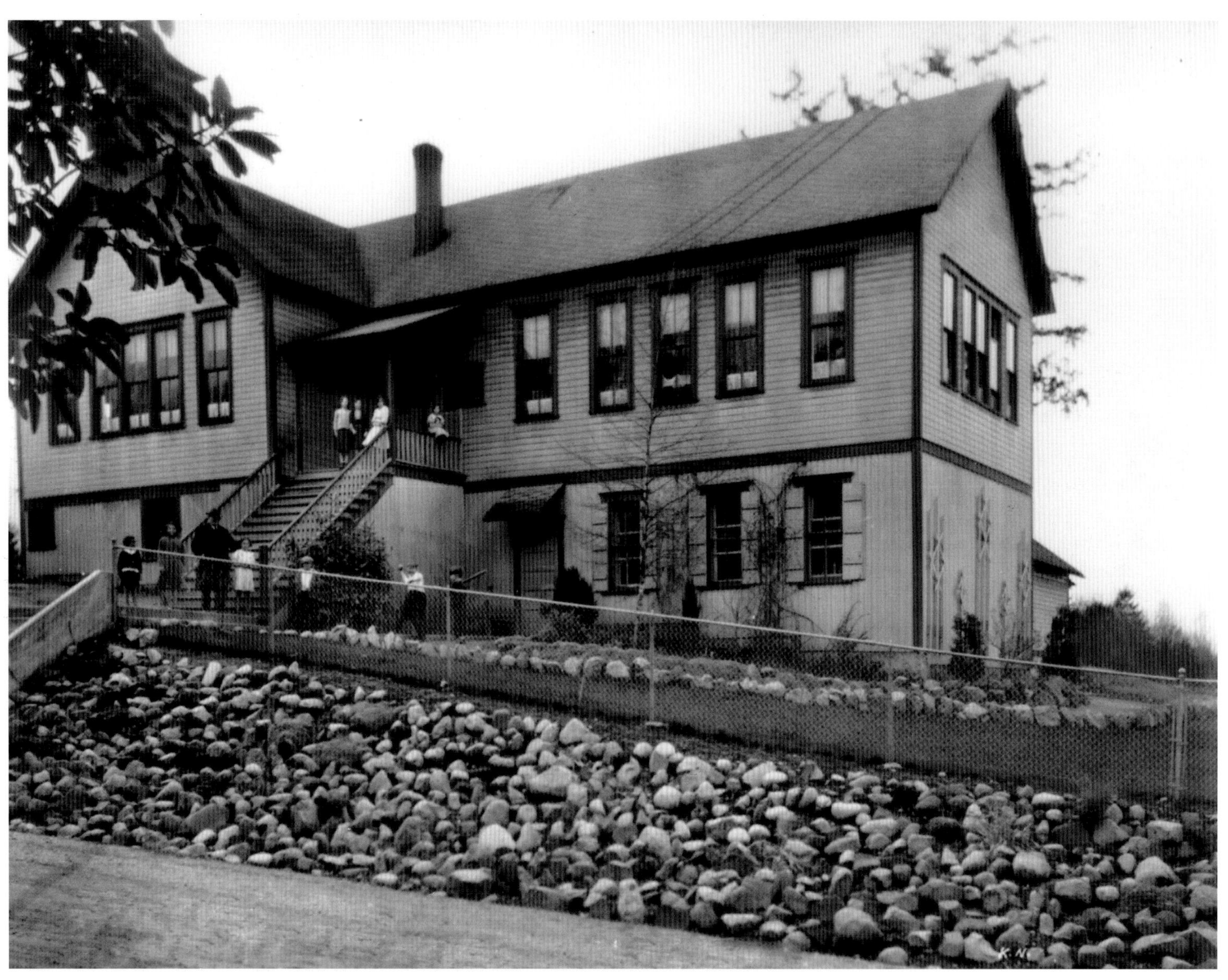

Funds from the state of Washington and the Federal Emergency Relief Administration allowed Angle Lake School near Des Moines to undertake exterior improvements, which were completed in 1935. Within seven years, the Port of Seattle would select the Angle Lake area as the site of Seattle Tacoma Airport, later Sea-Tac International Airport.

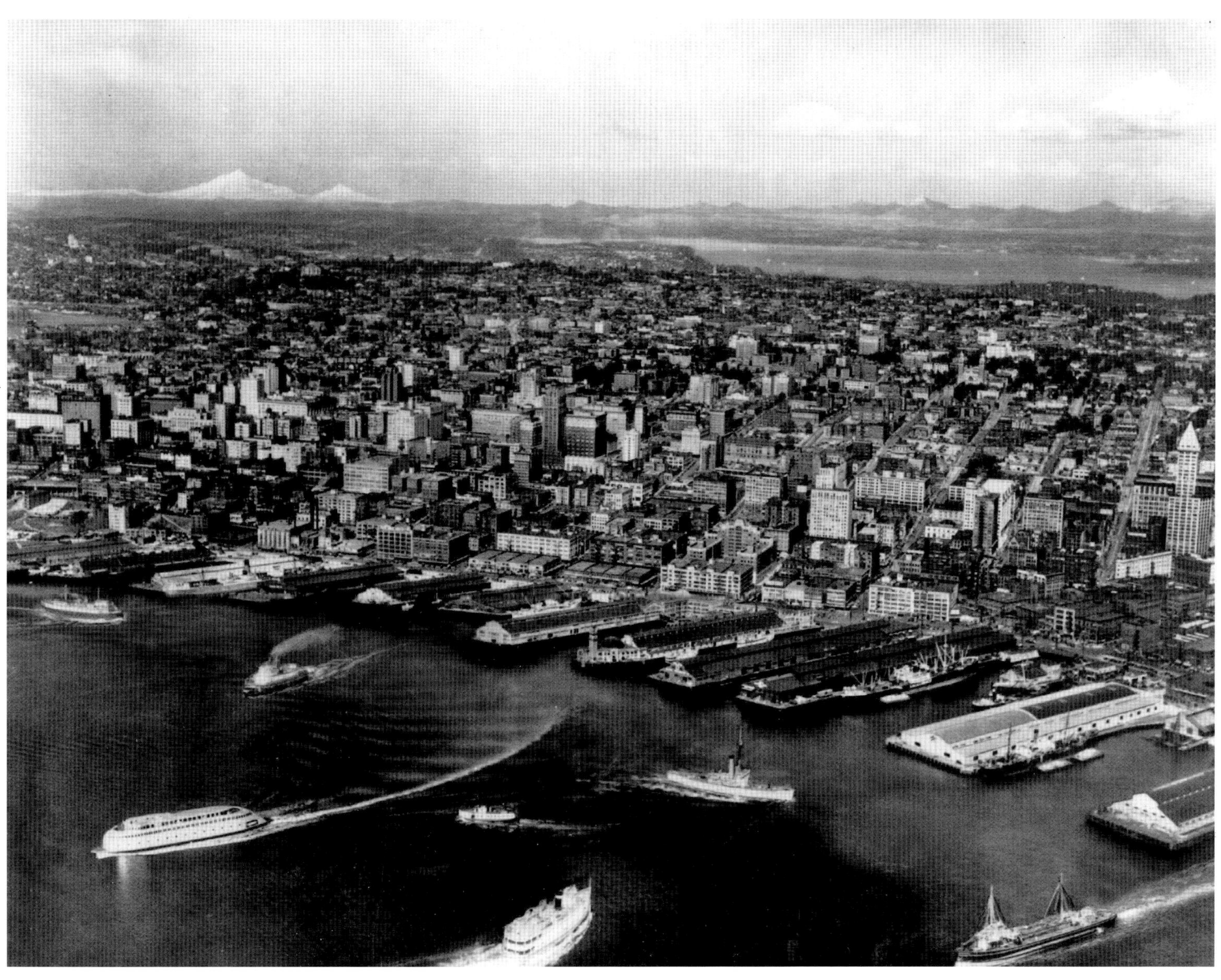

This 1936 view of the Seattle waterfront and harbor traffic has been retouched to include the Black Ball Line ferry *Kalakala*. The *Kalakala* began life nine years earlier as the *Peralta* for the San Francisco Bay's Key Transit System. After a fire in 1933, the Puget Sound Navigation Company rebuilt her with a distinctive Art-Deco superstructure to handle the Seattle-Bremerton run.

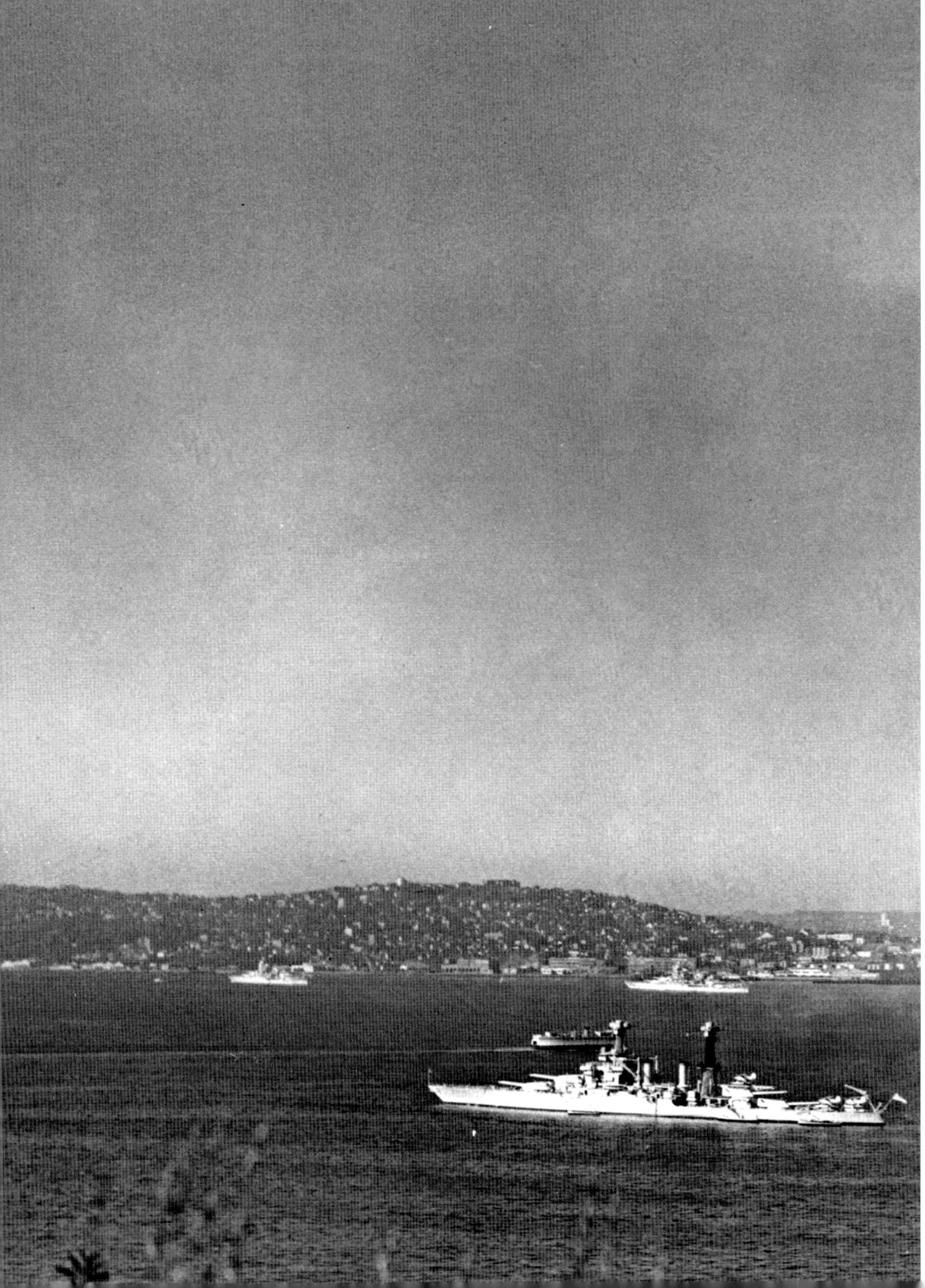

In this view from West Seattle in 1939, U.S. Navy battleships swing at anchor in Elliott Bay. A Seattle City Light photographer caught this view toward Queen Anne Hill, Interbay, and Magnolia Bluff.

179

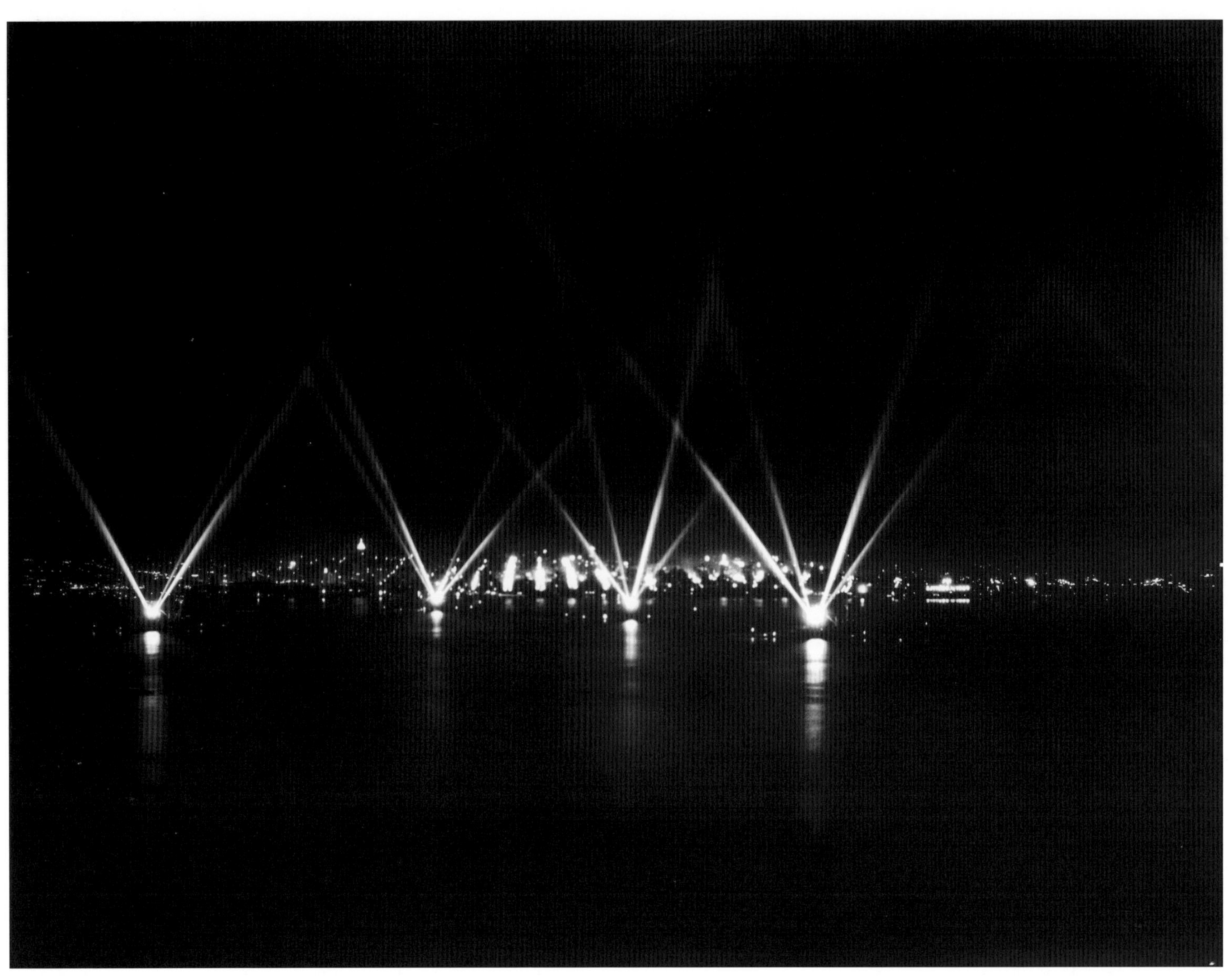

When the Pacific Fleet visited Elliott Bay for Fleet Week in the 1930s, the warships treated Seattle to a light show using their search lights. This time exposure was made from the vantage point of West Seattle.

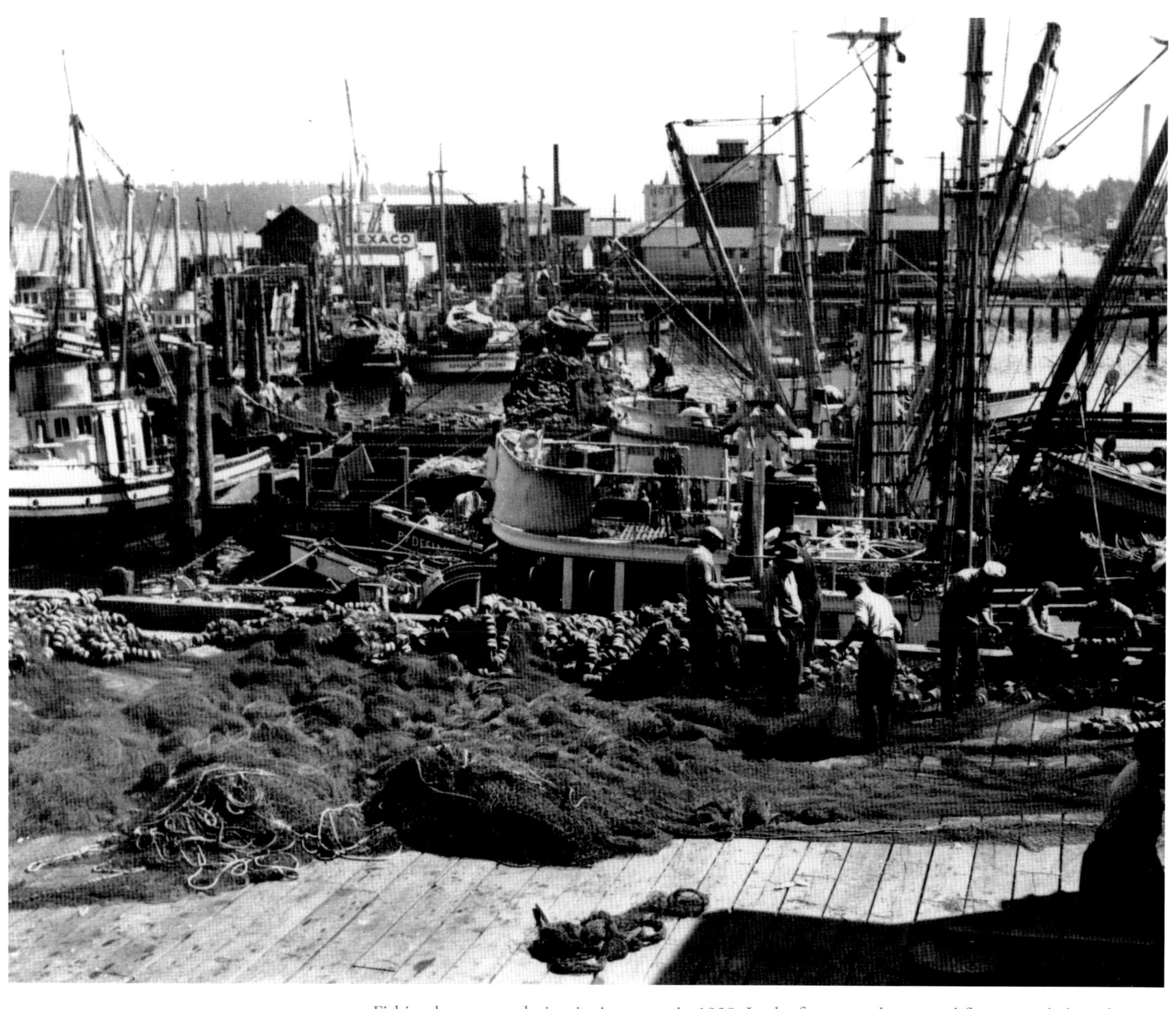

Fishing boats crowd piers in Anacortes in 1939. In the foreground, nets and floats sit piled on the pier.

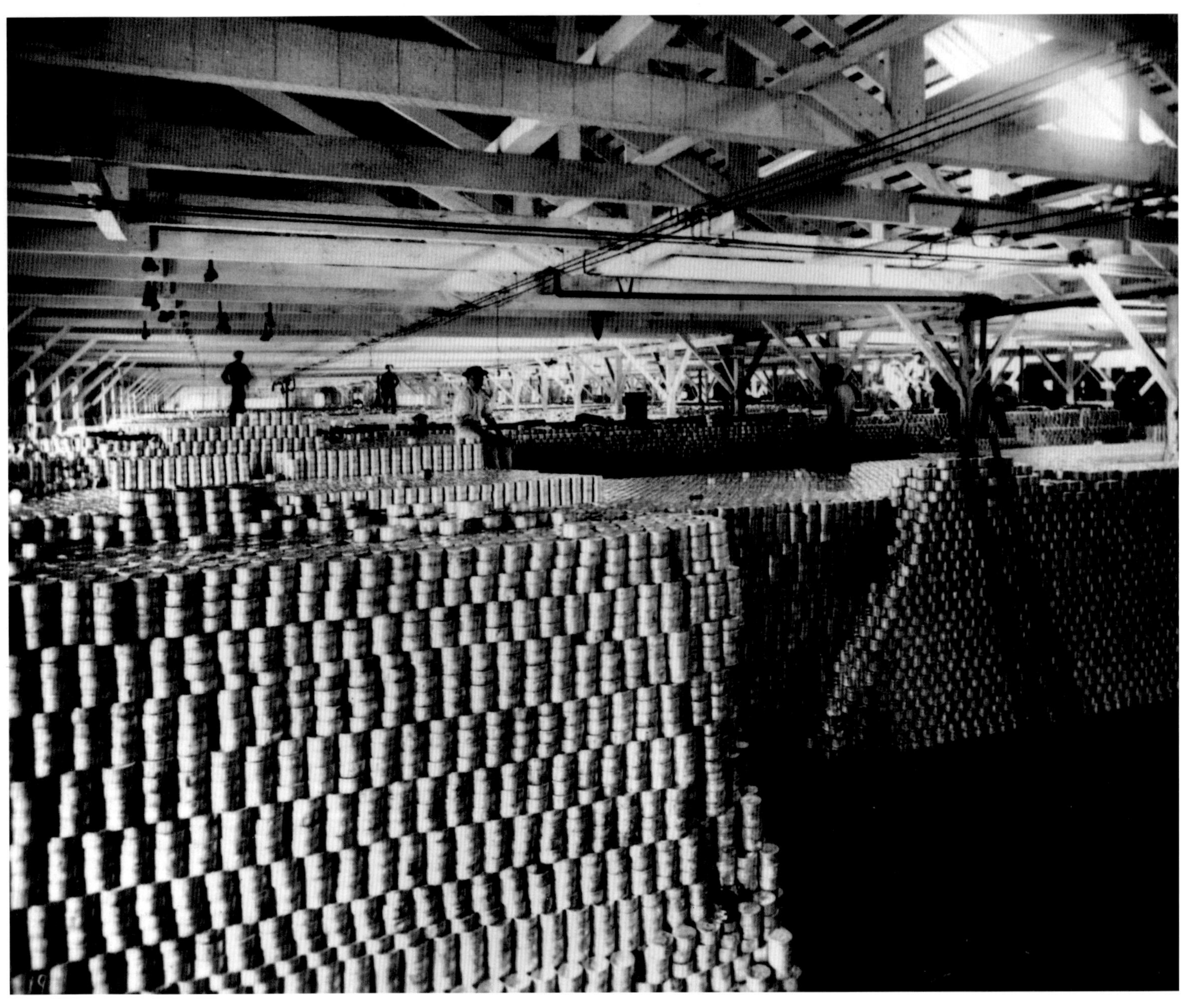

At this Anacortes cannery, 200,000 cases of canned salmon await shipping to customers around the world.

PROSPERITY AND CHANGE

(1940–1979)

After World War I, the people and economy of Puget Sound shifted into cruise, and the region prospered. The automobile transformed society, business, and even geography of the Sound. Modern engineering wonders of steel and concrete bridged Lake Washington, the Tacoma Narrows, Agate Pass, Deception Pass, and Hood Canal. The Mosquito Fleet shrank to a system of automobile ferry runs, and the great distances to be spanned by road challenged even the most ambitious highway engineers.

The Second World War pulled the region into another great conflict. Shipyards sprang to life in Tacoma, Everett, and Seattle. Even tiny Kirkland on Lake Washington built warships. The airplane burst into prominence in modern warfare, and the Boeing Airplane Company built powerful bombers in Seattle and Renton. Army and Navy bases transformed citizens into warriors. A new wave of immigrants—including tens of thousands of African-Americans—stepped off trains and out of battered cars to staff assembly lines. Many of these wartime visitors became postwar residents. Residents of Japanese descent, in contrast, spent the war in internment camps as a result of the government's effort to grapple with the threat of espionage. In recent times, this action has been criticized.

Despite a sincere desire for stability after the hectic war years, the people of Puget Sound expanded their grasp of the region and built suburbs and the bridges and highways to reach them. The economy shifted away from the extraction of resources—coal, lumber, and fish—and toward producing airliners, computers, educated citizens, and new ideas. The 1962 Century 21 World's Fair in Seattle threw a spotlight on the region—a spotlight that remained on even after the fair closed.

Soon, Puget Sound residents woke up to realize that the unrestricted exploitation of resources had come at a price. The once unlimited salmon runs shrank to threatened levels. Logging—now the forest products industry—exhausted most of the old-growth timber. Company towns built around lumber mills drifted into memory. Appreciation of the matchless scenery generated concern for the environment, so new industry was evaluated more for its impact than its potential profits. This environmental consciousness will allow Puget Sound to maintain its idyllic setting for years to come.

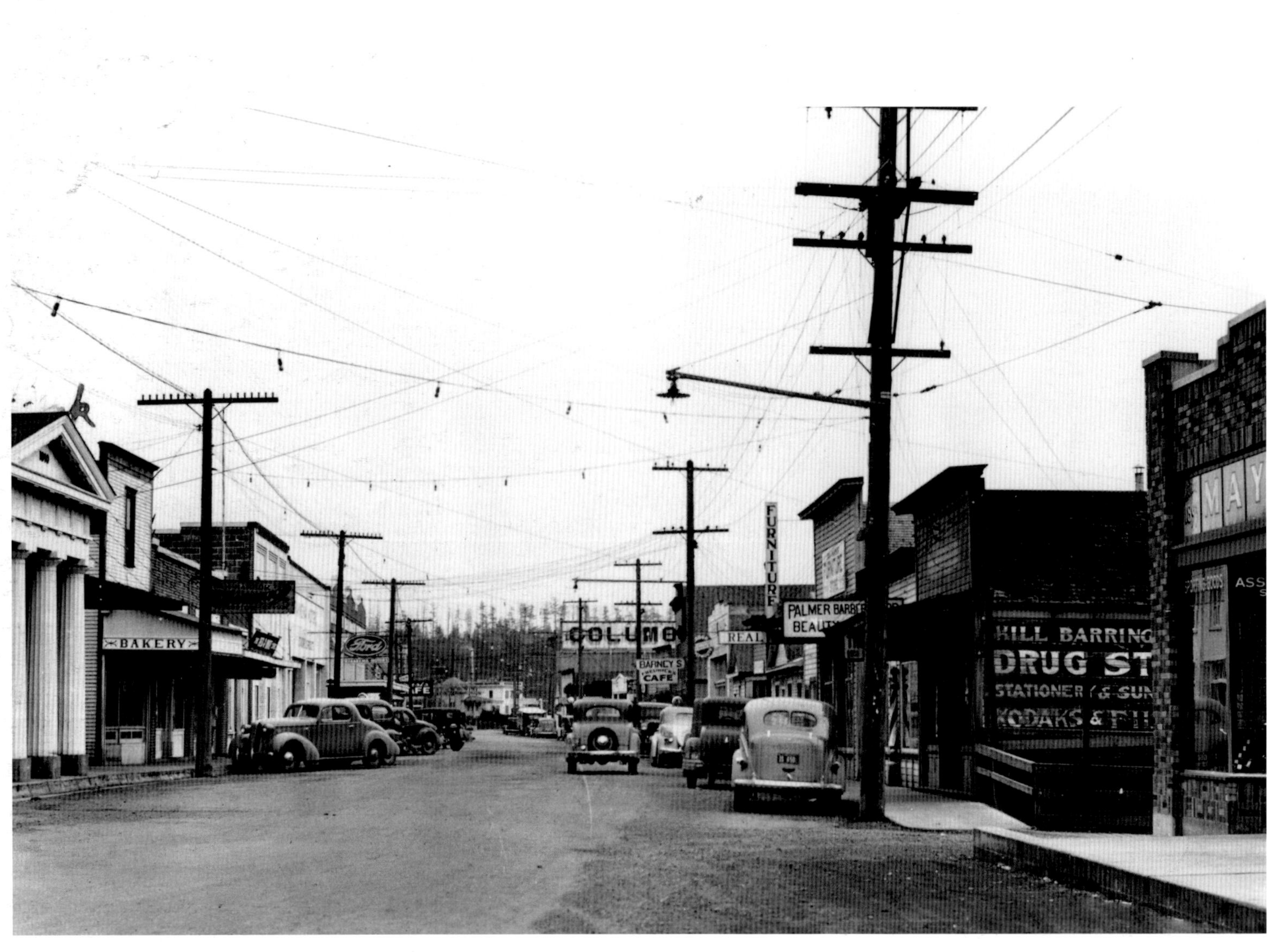

Oak Harbor dozes on the verge of dramatic growth when this Barrington Avenue view was captured in 1940. On December 8, 1941, U.S. Navy surveyors began to lay out what would become Naval Air Station Whidbey Island. Tens of thousands of naval aviators and their families would transform the community and give it long-lasting character.

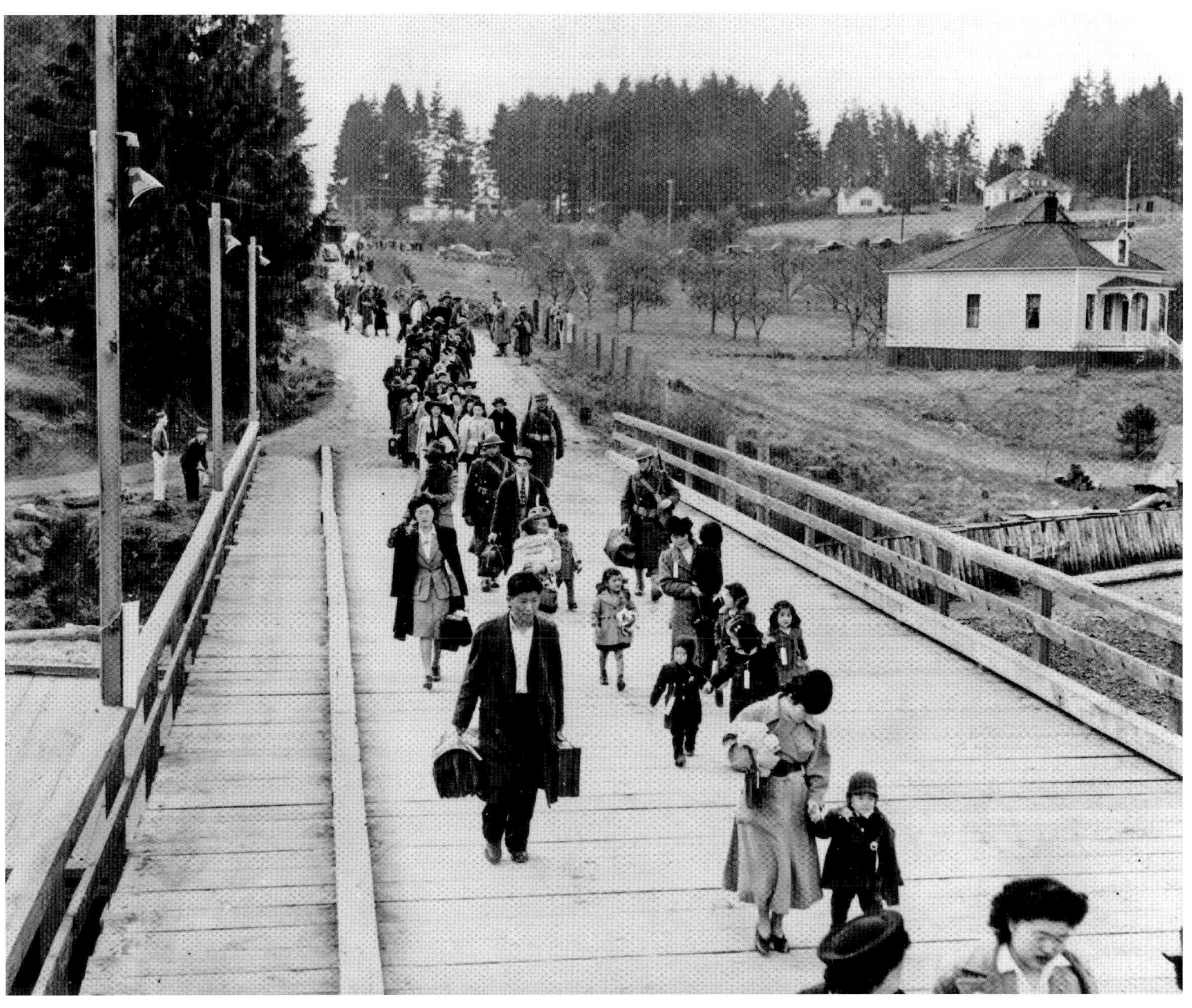

In one of World War II's most dramatic episodes on the home front, some 275 Japanese Americans from Bainbridge Island leave their homes and farms on March 30, 1942. Pursuant to Executive Order 9066, all persons of Japanese descent had to leave the West Coast defense area. The evacuees pictured here were given eight days to dispose of their homes and property before being removed to internment camps in Idaho.

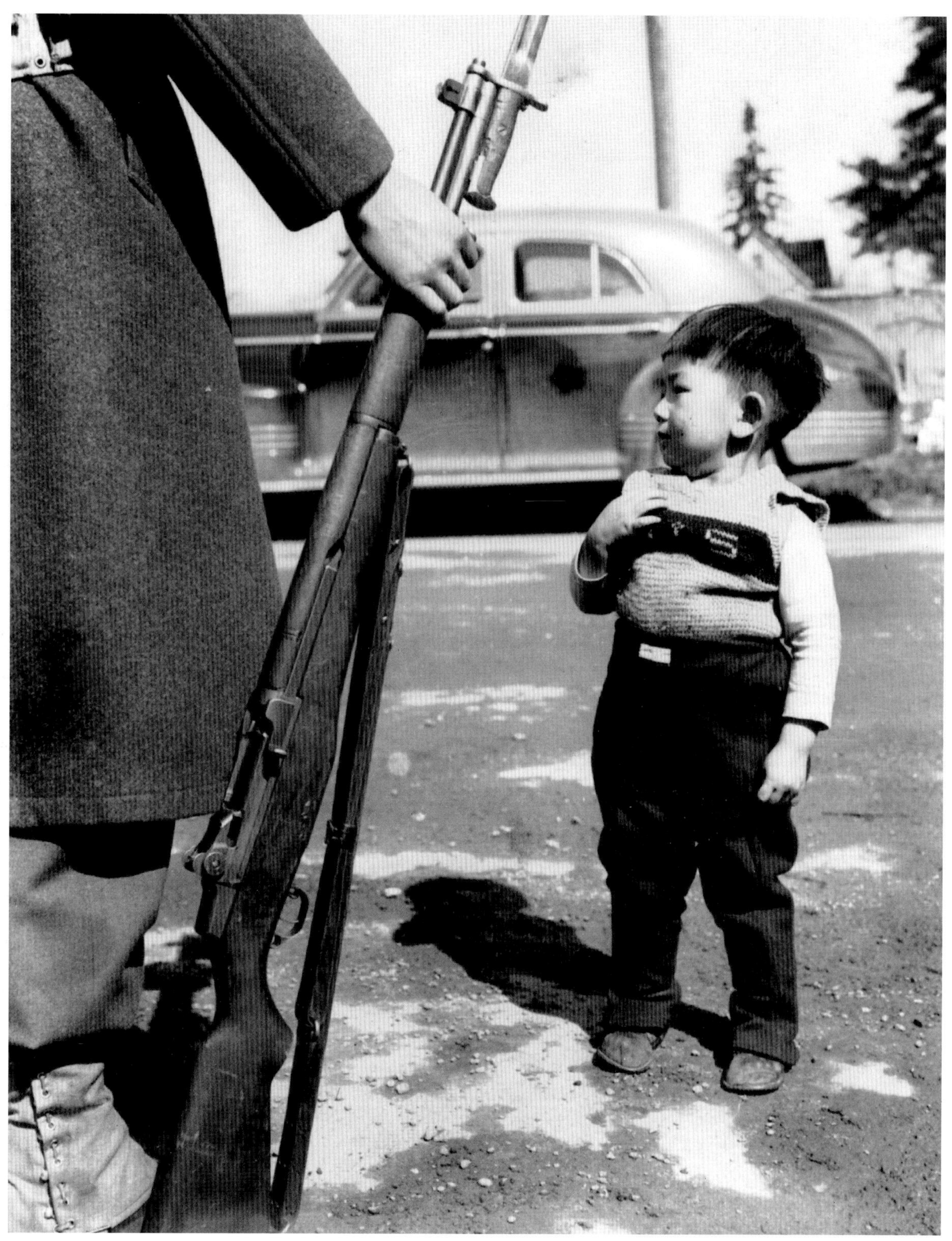

This boy appears unimpressed with the rifled soldier assigned to escort him, his family, and their neighbors to an internment camp. Their final destination is a War Relocation Authority camp near Minidoka, Idaho.

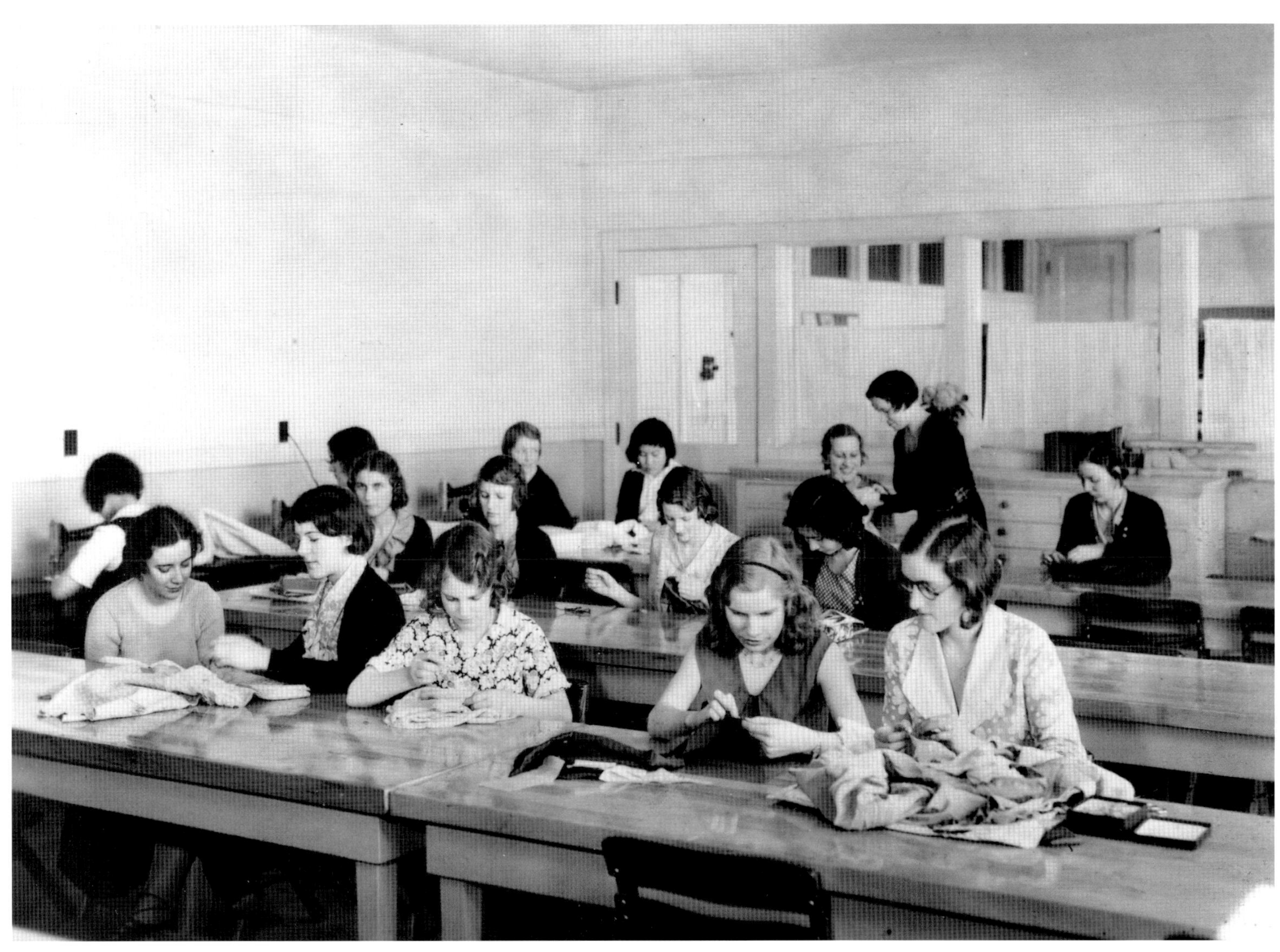

Eleventh-grade girls at Bainbridge High School learn sewing in a home economics class.

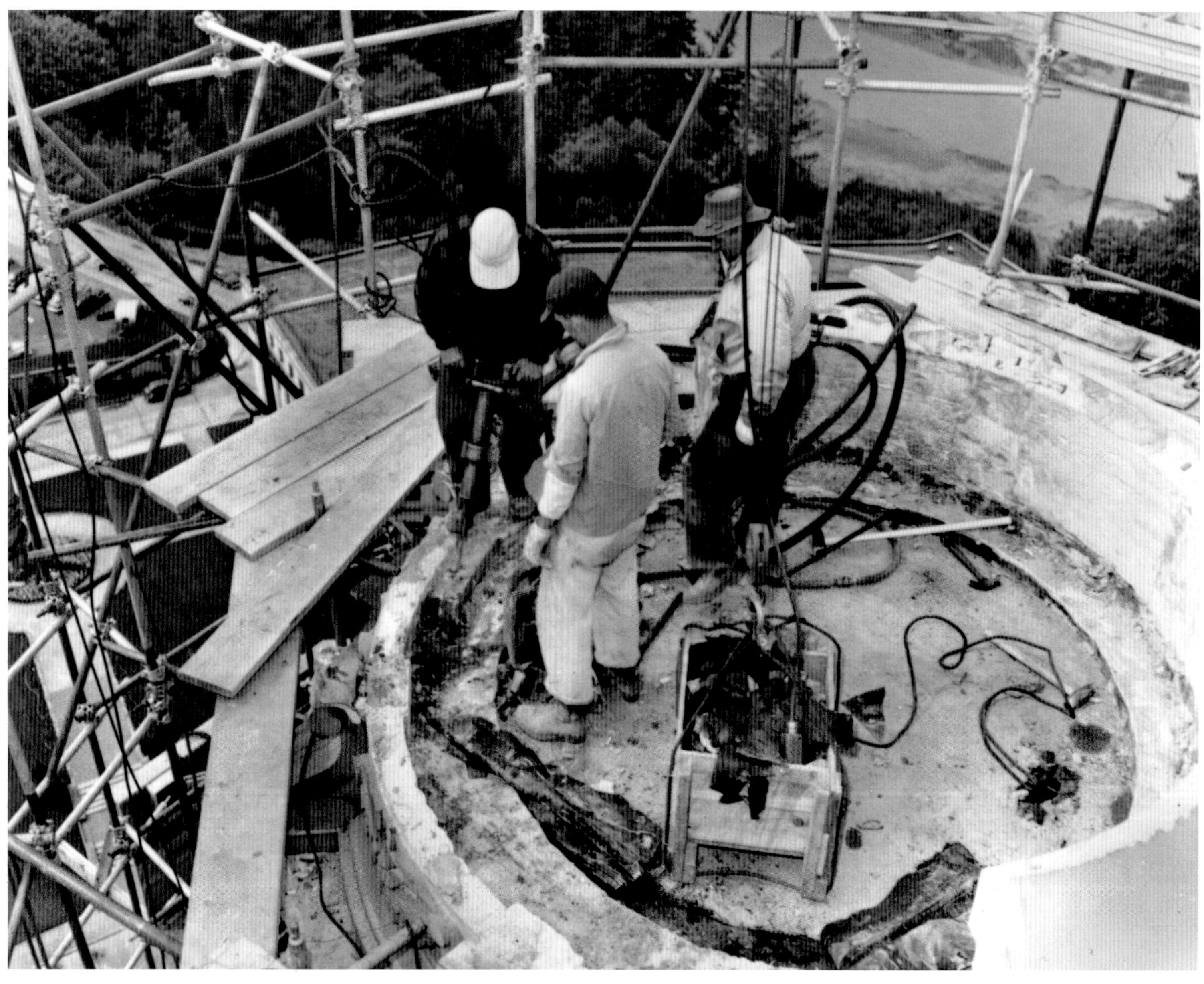

On April 13, 1949, a 7.1-magnitude earthquake centered between Olympia and Tacoma struck Puget Sound. Although the quake lasted only 30 seconds, eight people died, and dozens received serious injuries. Among thousands of heavily damaged buildings was the Legislative Building and its dome at the State Capitol. Here workmen use a jackhammer to ready the dome for repair.

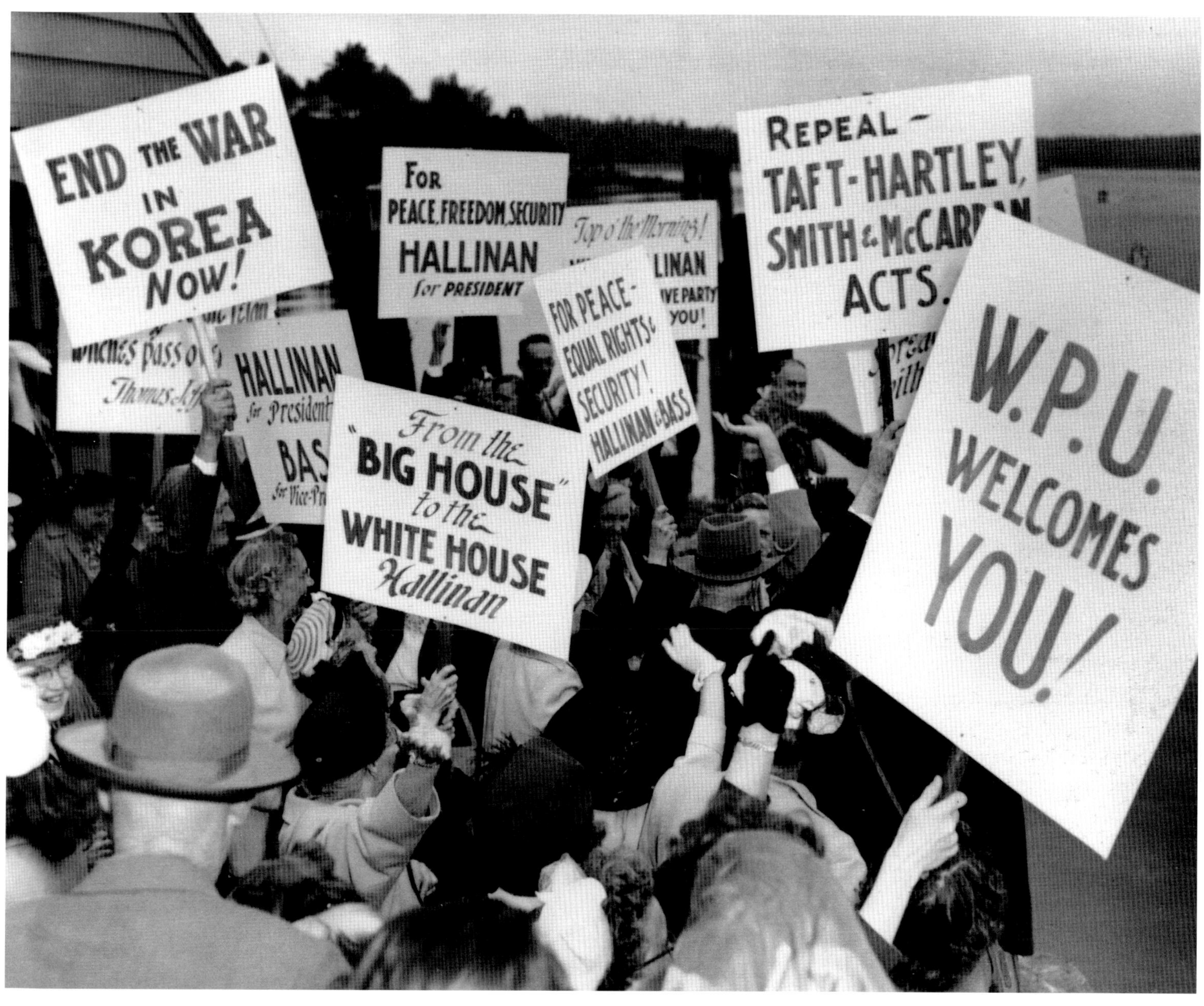

In 1952, San Francisco labor lawyer and union leader Vincent Hallinan served a six-month prison sentence at McNeil Island Federal Penitentiary for contempt of court. These protesters and supporters greet Hallinan at the Steilacoom ferry dock upon his release. That same year, Hallinan ran for president on the Progressive Party ticket.

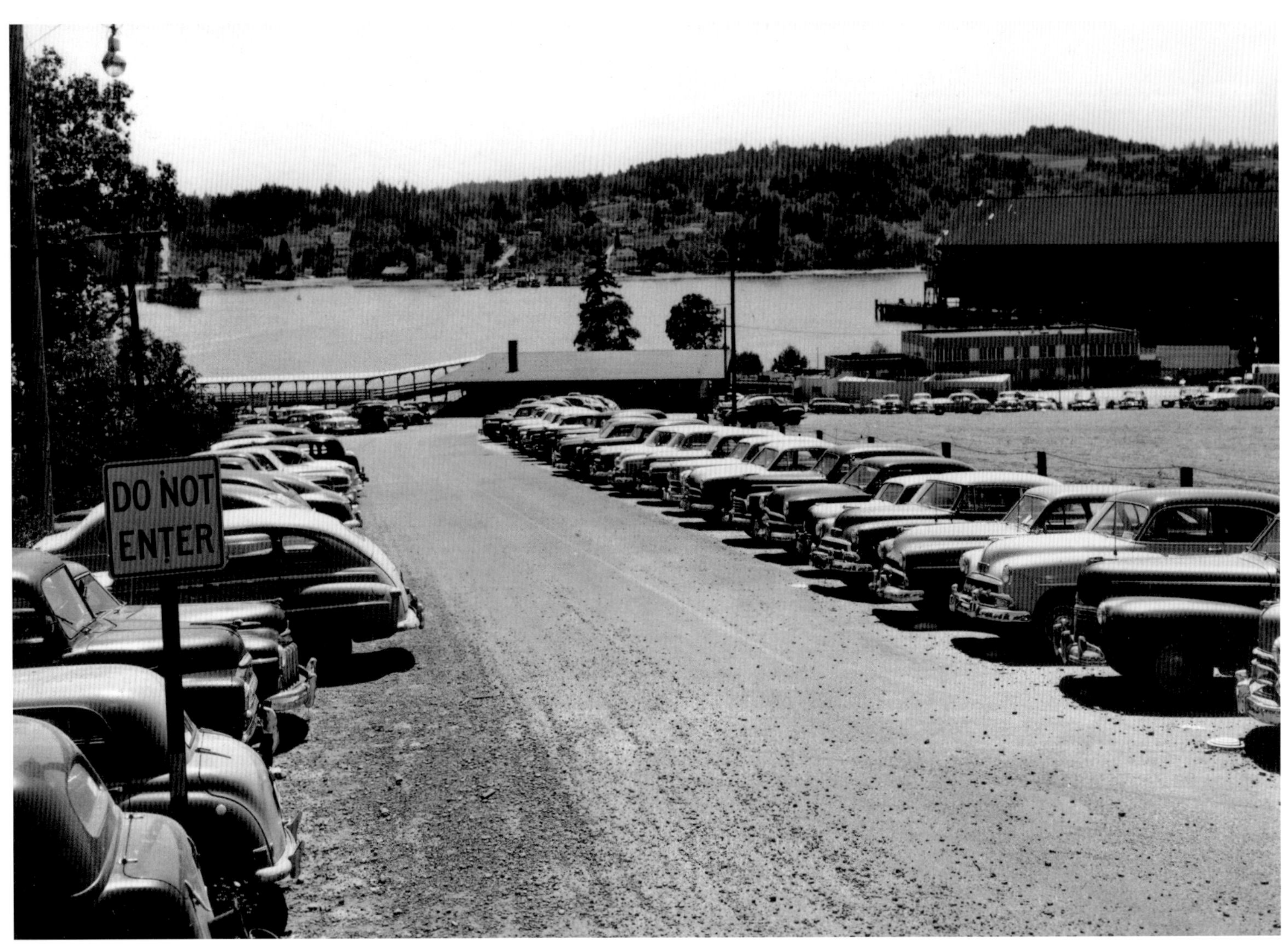

When workers in Seattle discovered they could live quiet lives on Bainbridge Island and still work downtown, a ferry culture evolved. They drove their cars a short distance from their rural homes, parked at the Winslow ferry terminal, and, after a peaceful, picturesque, 45-minute ride, walked to their jobs in the city. Here on July 3, 1953, commuters' cars crowd the lot.

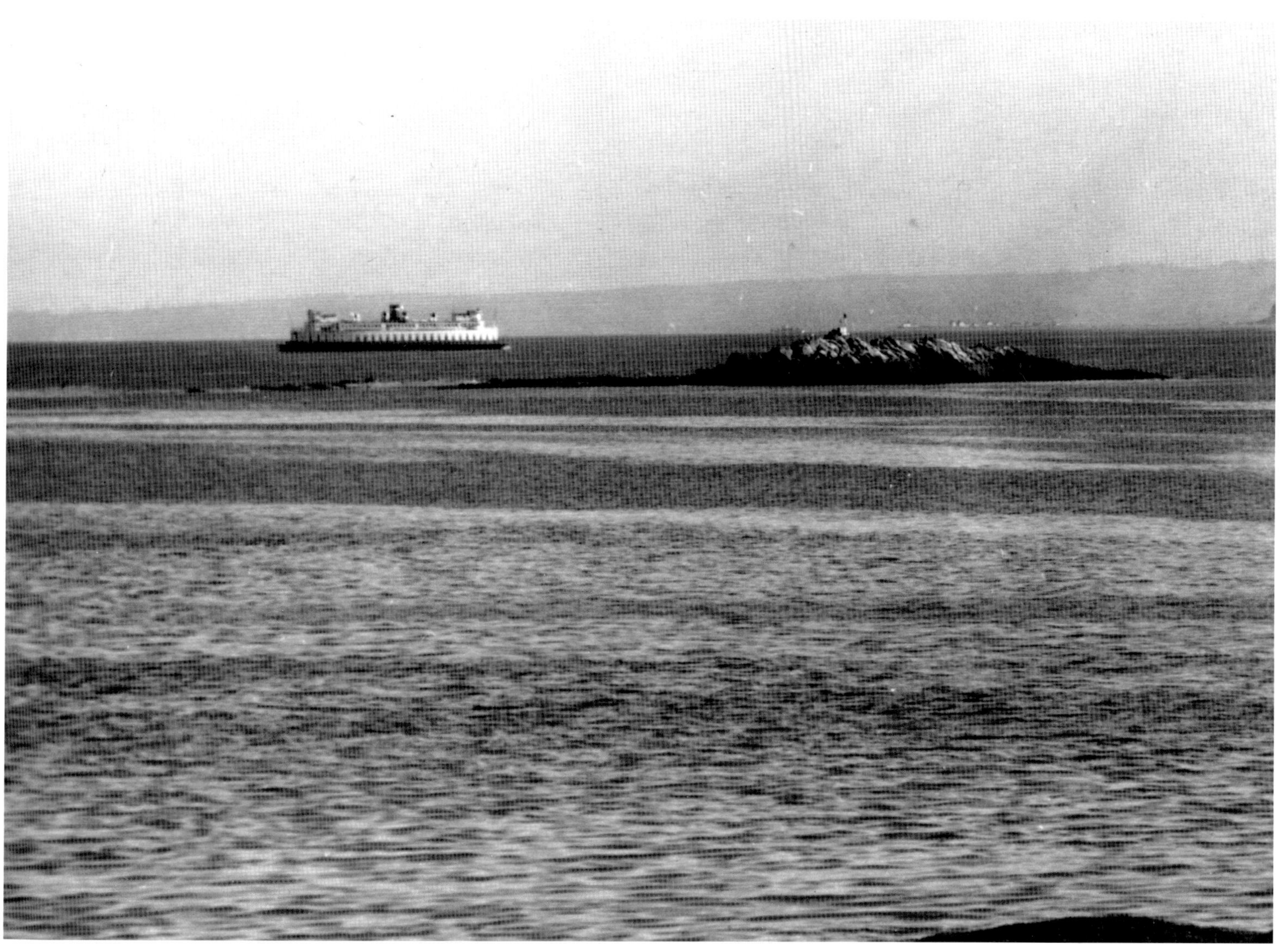

Heading from Bremerton to Seattle on April 24, 1953, a member of the new Washington State Ferries passes Blakely Rock at the entrance to Eagle Harbor. Washington entered the ferry business in 1951 after forcing the Puget Sound Navigation Company, or the Black Ball Line, to sell their company.

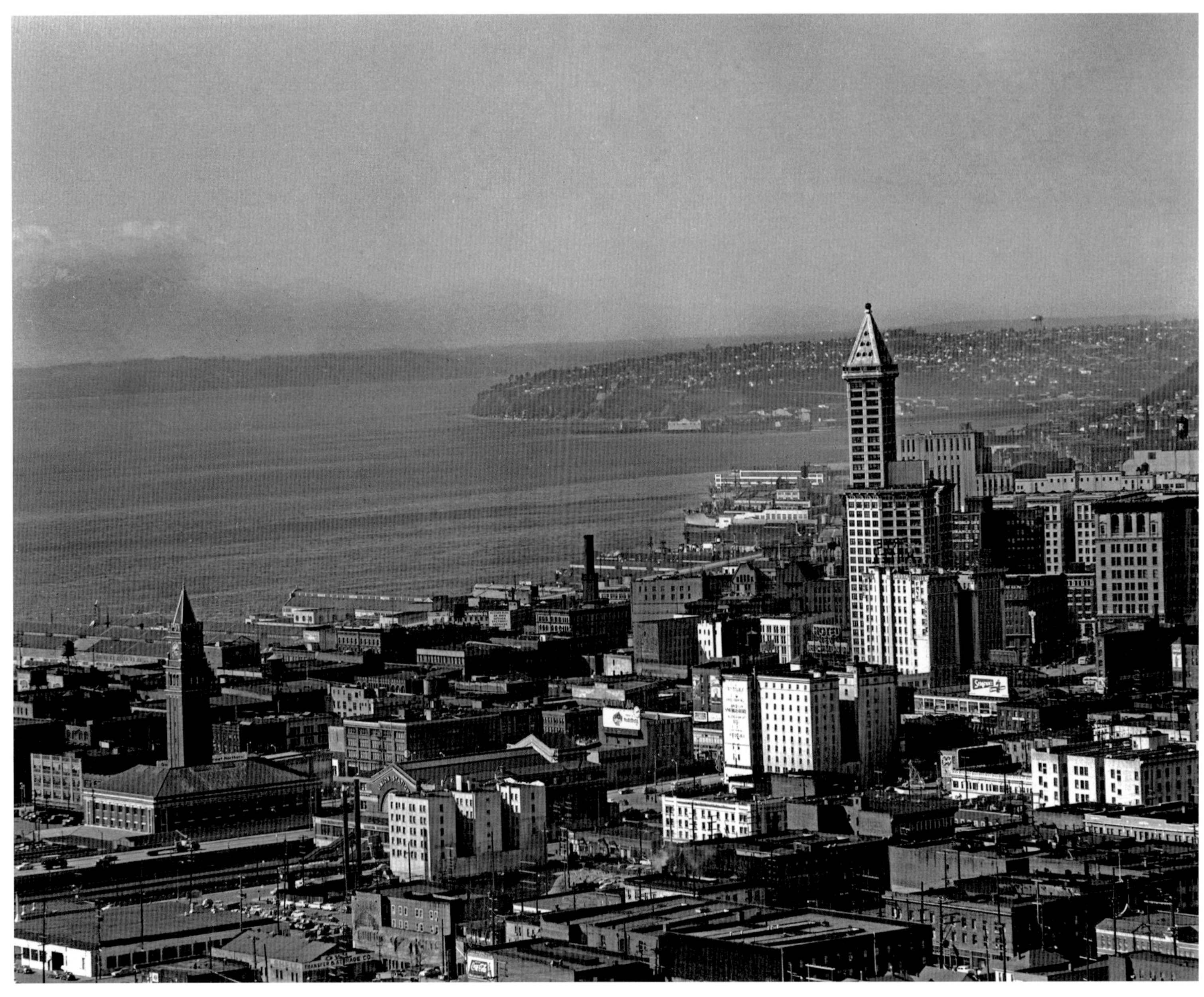

On March 24, 1954, a Seattle Engineering Department photographer climbed to the top of the Marine Hospital (later the headquarters of Amazon.com) to snap this view of the Smith Tower, Elliott Bay, and Magnolia Bluff. At left is the clock tower of the Great Northern's King Street Station.

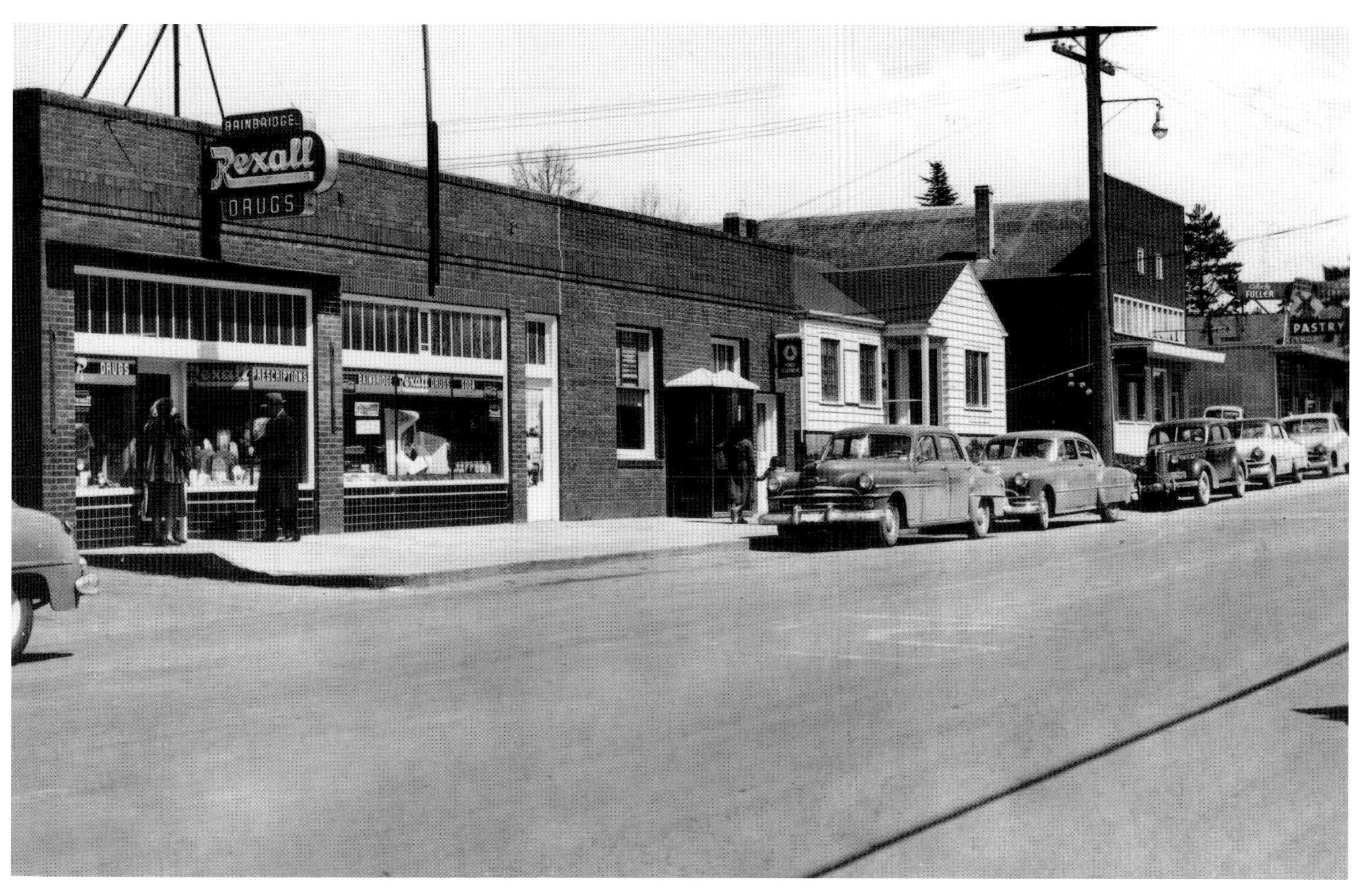

Anyone needing a prescription filled at this Winslow pharmacy in 1953 does not have to look far to park. Winslow would become part of the city of Bainbridge Island in 1991.

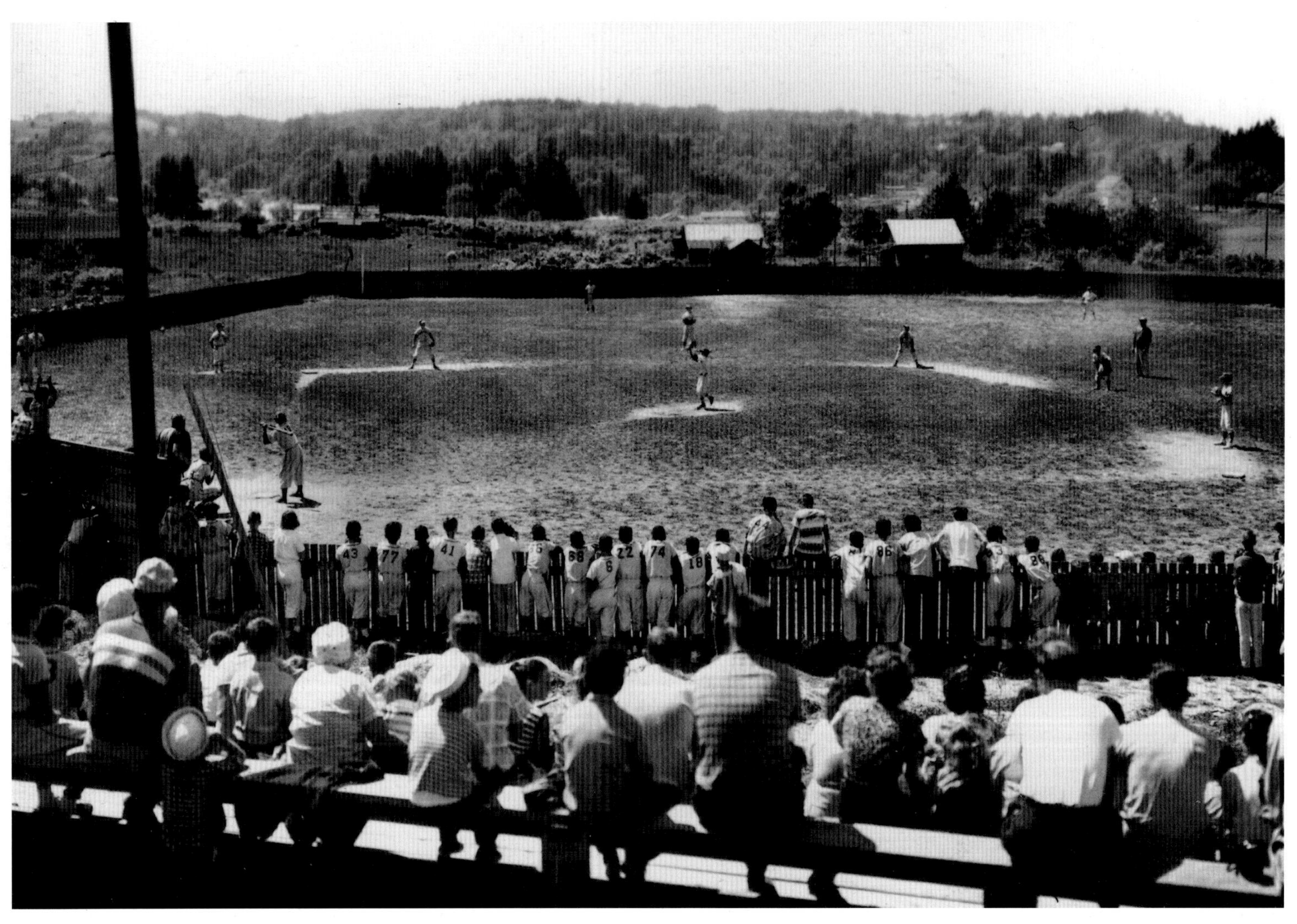

Fans on Bainbridge Island, including several boys, enjoy a game of baseball on May 17, 1958.

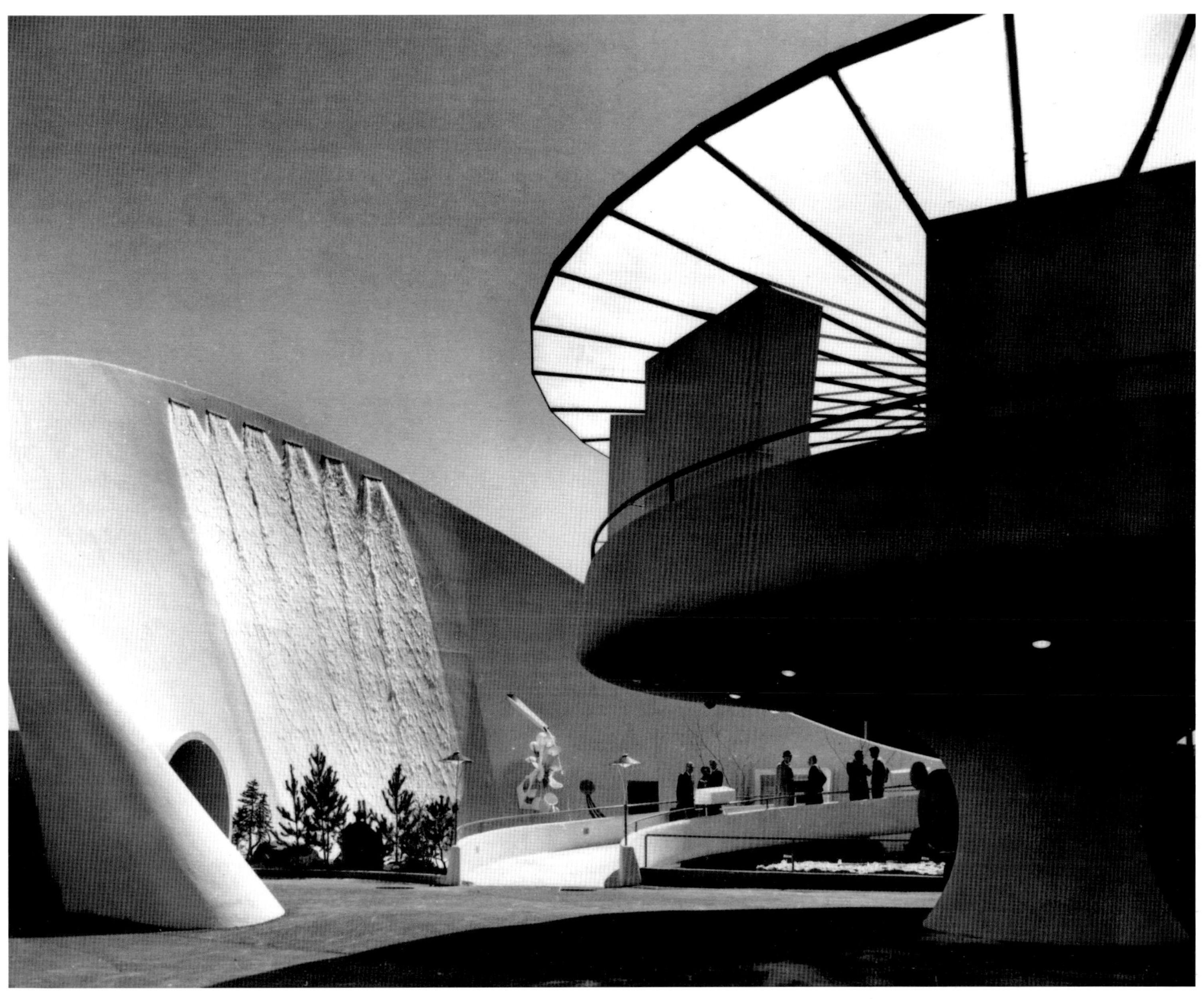

At the 1962 Century 21 Exposition in Seattle, the Pavilion of Electric Power celebrates hydroelectric power with a 40-foot-tall replica of a dam through which visitors entered the exhibit. The swift running rivers and steep mountainsides of Puget Sound allowed construction of dams that produce some of the most inexpensive and environmentally friendly power in the nation.

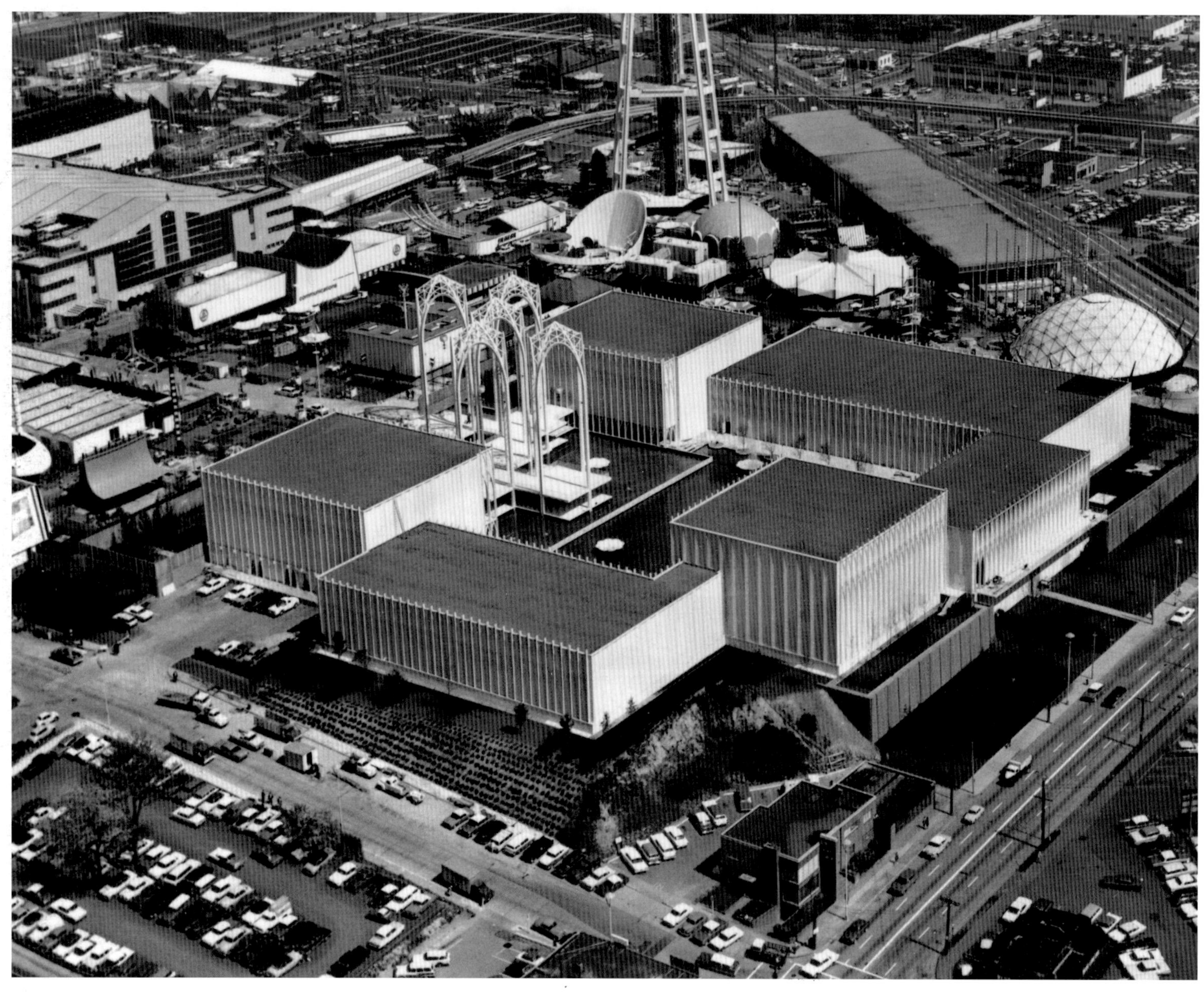

The United States Science Pavilion of the 1962 Century 21 World's Fair surrounds the Space Gothic sculpture. The exhibits included a simulated ten-minute space excursion to outer galaxies. After the fair, the building would become the Pacific Science Center.

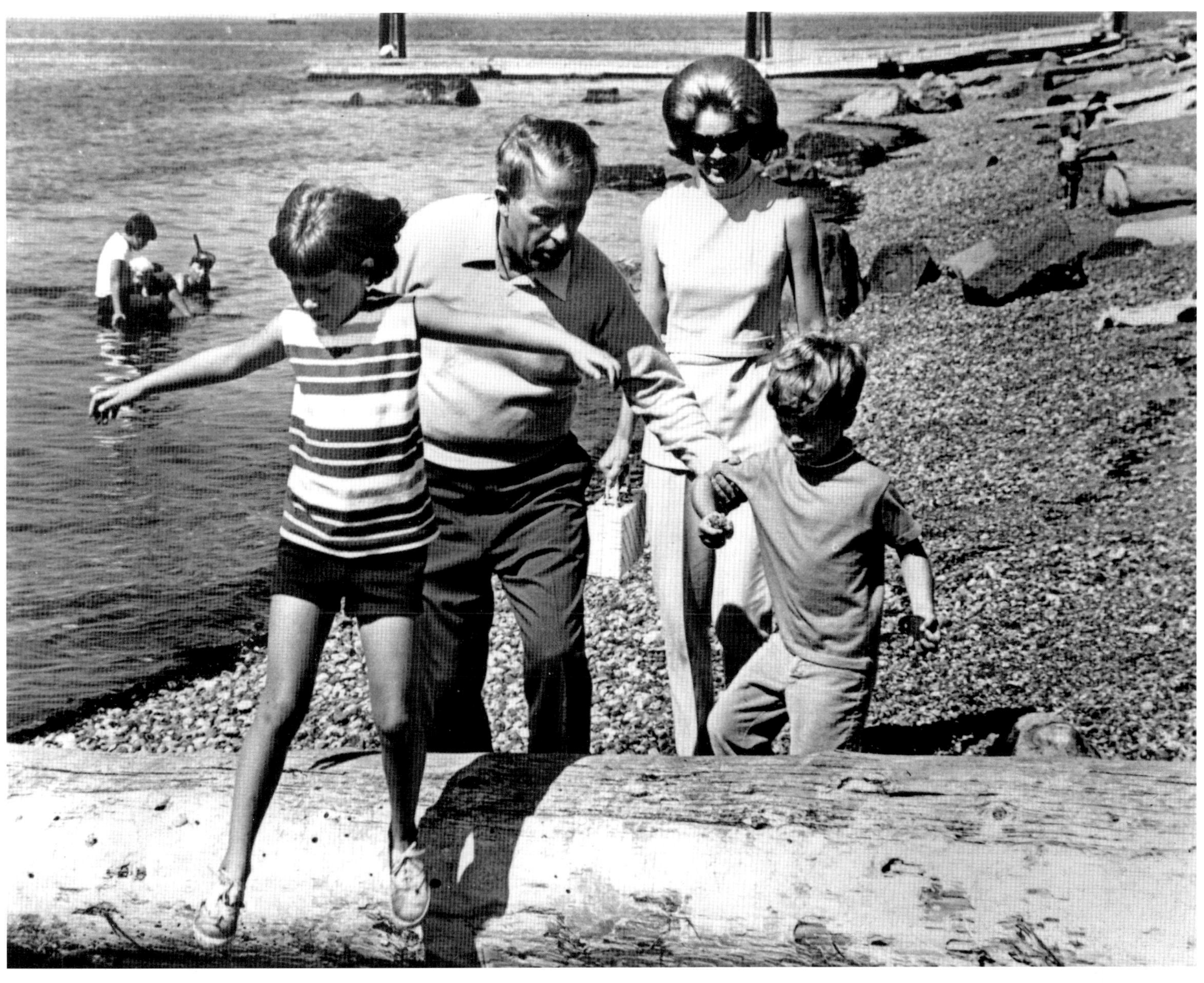

U.S. Senator Henry M. "Scoop" Jackson and his family enjoy a walk along a Puget Sound beach in 1972. At left is Anna Marie, at right is Peter, and following is Helen Hardin Jackson. Senator Jackson served six terms as a Washington congressman and six as a senator. One version of his nickname's origin holds that early in life, he delivered 74,880 copies of the *Everett Herald* without a single complaint.

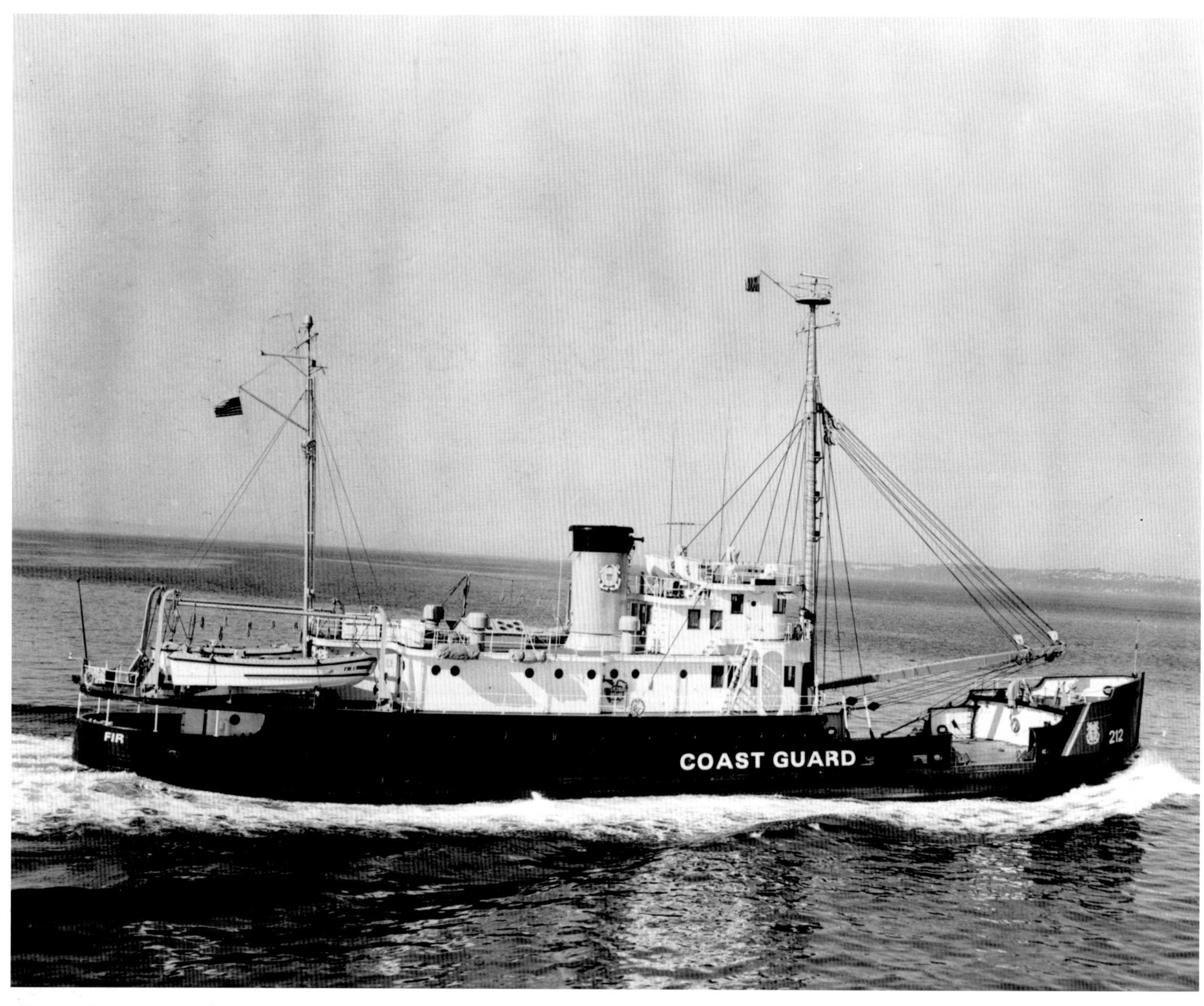

The U.S. Coast Guard can trace its service on Puget Sound to the 1850s with the lighthouse service and revenue cutters. For 51 years beginning in 1939, the Coast Guard cutter *Fir* was a familiar and comforting sight on Puget Sound and maintained beacons, buoys, and other navigational aids. The *Fir* is shown here in 1974 with a red hull and a white superstructure. In 1992, the *Fir* was declared a National Historic Landmark.

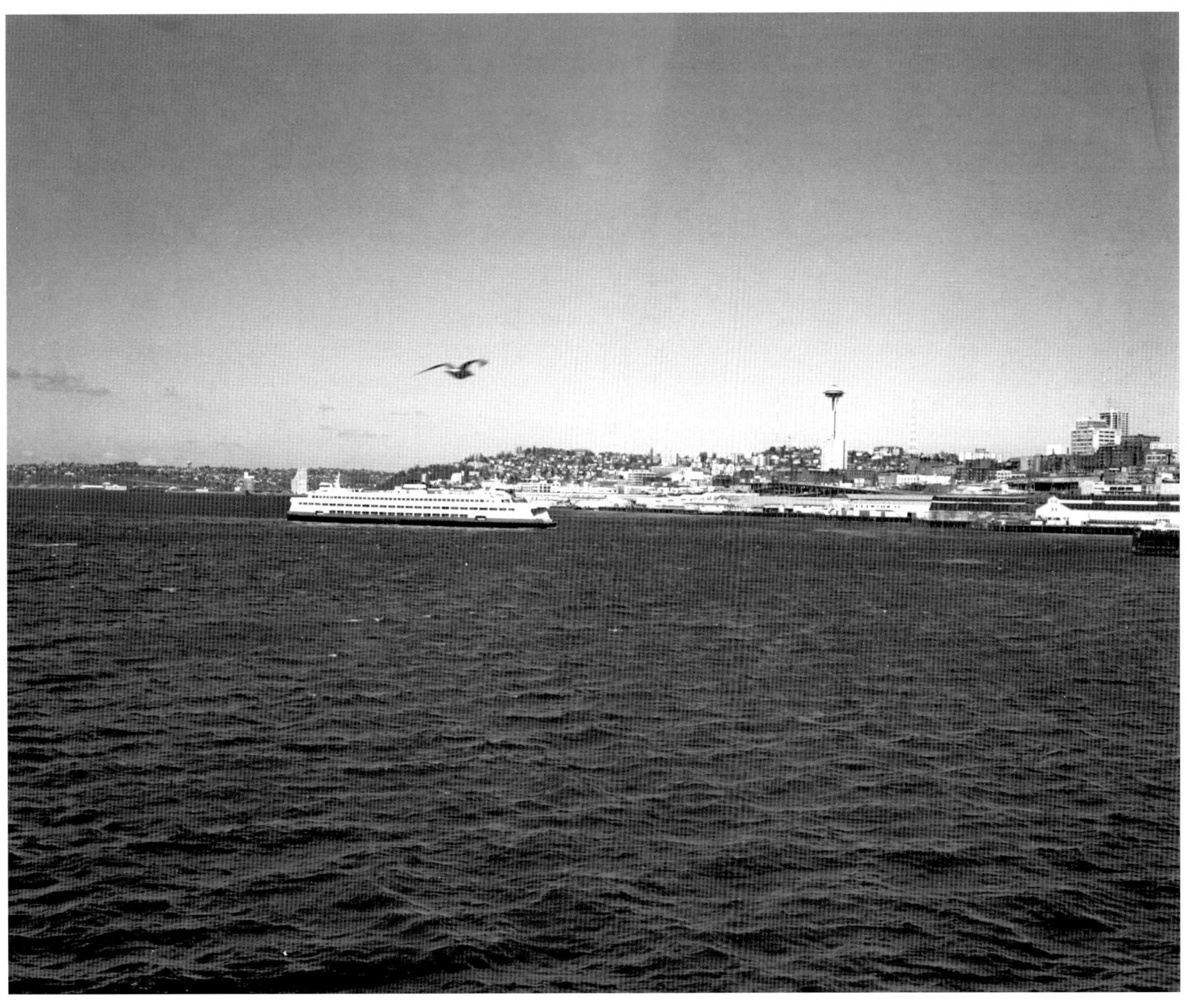

On March 5, 1975, a ferry glides across Elliott Bay with the Space Needle in the background. The 605-foot Space Needle was designed to be the symbol of the 1962 Century 21 World's Fair. It became an icon for Seattle and the Pacific Northwest.

Following Spread: The Puget Sound Naval Shipyard served as a home to mothballed warships, including the aircraft carriers USS *Hornet* on the left and the USS *Oriskany* on the right. The battleship USS *New Jersey* is moored at the center. Shown here in the 1990s, the ships were sealed and pumped full of low-humidity air to preserve them. The *Hornet* and the *New Jersey* eventually became floating museums. The *Oriskany* became an artificial reef off Florida.

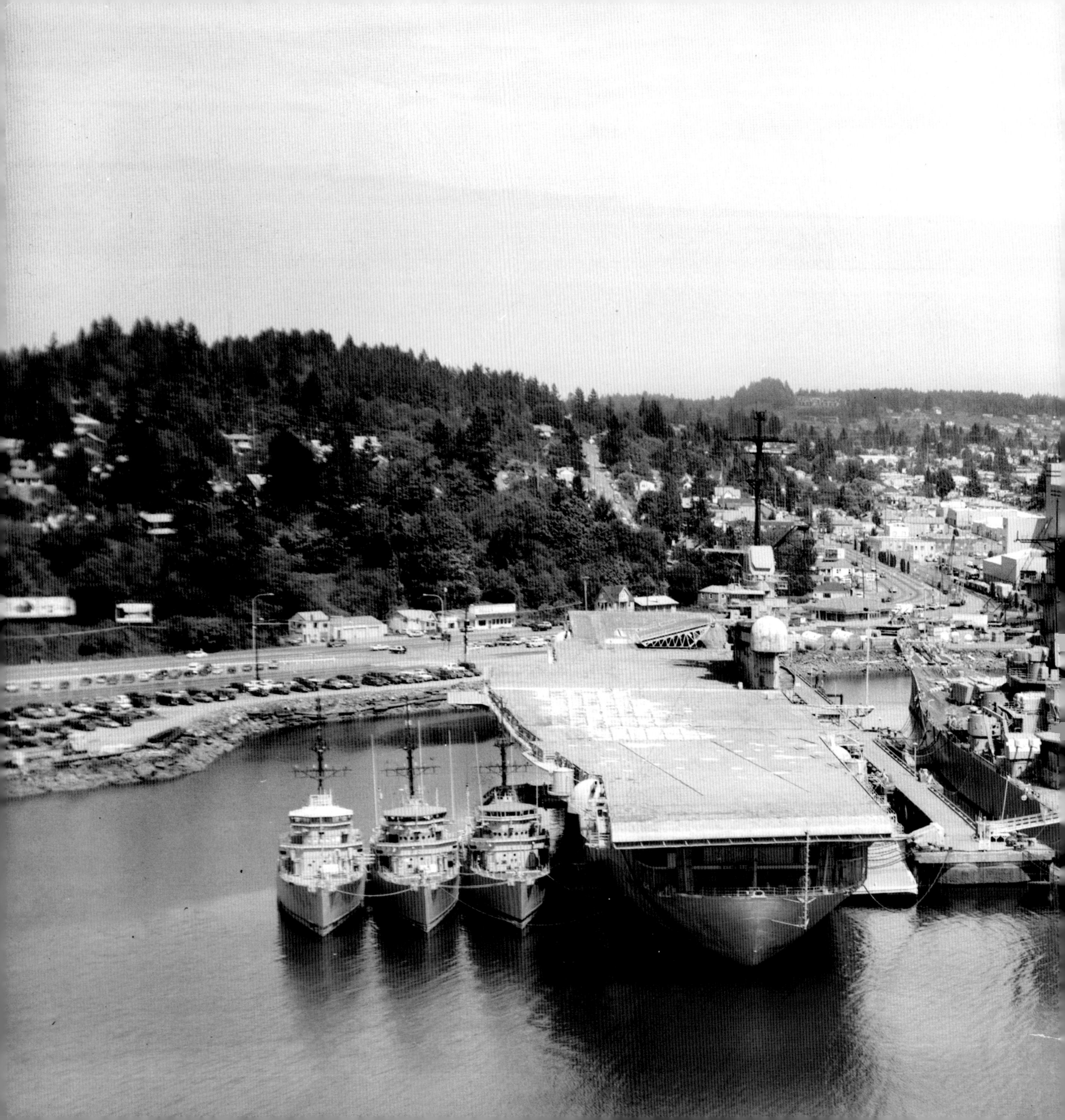

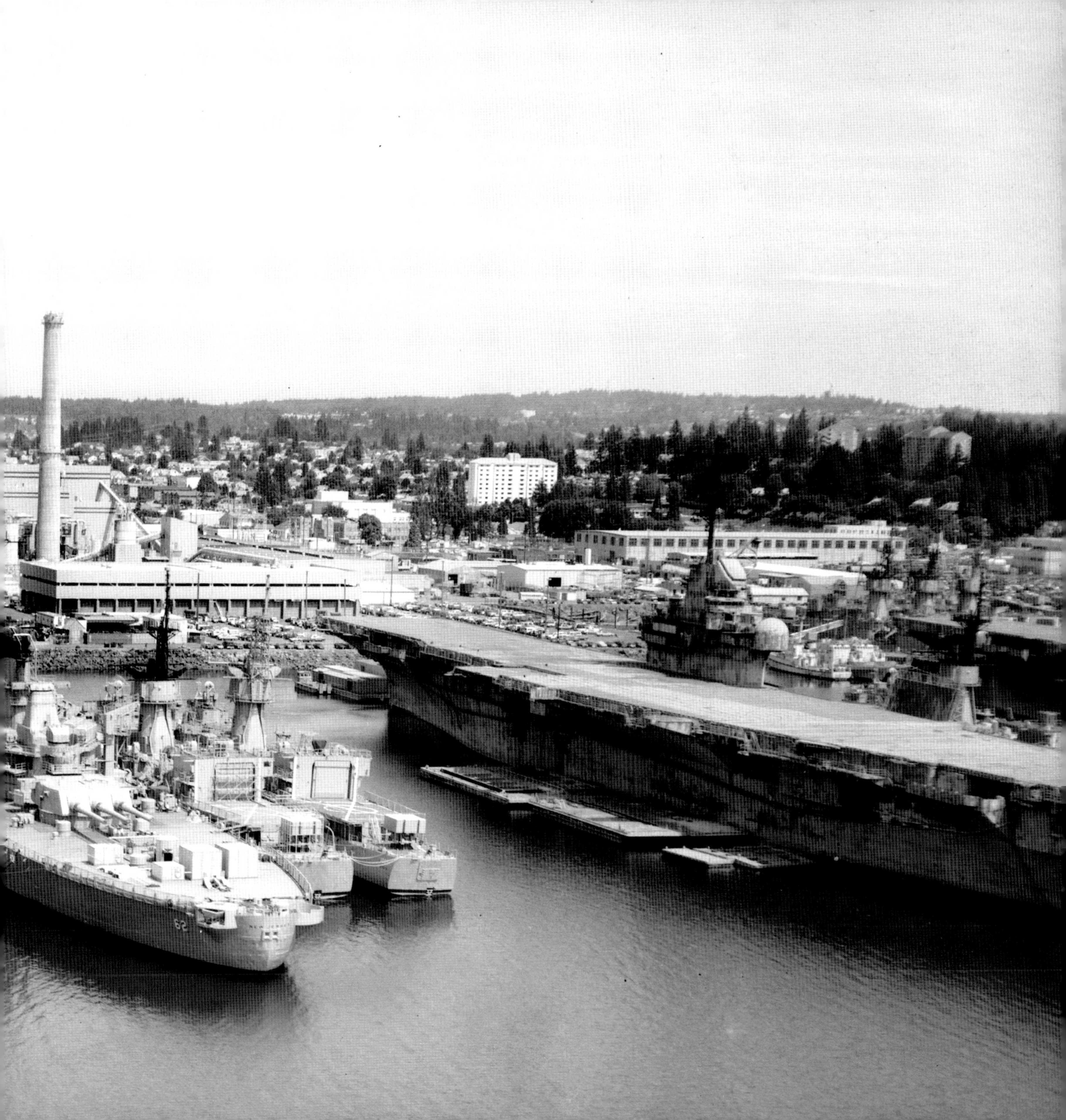

NOTES ON THE PHOTOGRAPHS

These notes, listed by page number, attempt to include all aspects known of the photographs. Each of the photographs is identified by the page number, photograph's title or description, photographer and collection, archive, and call or box number when applicable. Although every attempt was made to collect all data, in some cases complete data was unavailable due to the age and condition of some of the photographs and records.

II KIRKLAND: PITTSBURGH OF THE WEST
University of Washington
UW_1871

VI UNIVERSITY OF WASHINGTON, 1880s
Seattle Municipal Archives
2873

X STATE OF WASHINGTON STEAMER
University of Washington
UW_26961 - PH Coll 291.33

2 SNOHOMISH, 1850s
University of Washington
UW_28491 - PH Coll 334

3 FIDALGO
University of Washington
UW_4344

4 PORT MADISON, 1880
University of Washington
UW_5965

5 COLUMBIA AND PUGET SOUND RAILWAY TRESTLE, 1880s
University of Washington
UW_2297 - PH Coll 482

6 HALL BROTHERS MARINE RAILWAY AND SHIPBUILDING COMPANY
University of Washington
UW_26571 - PH Coll 268.11

7 STETSON AND POST COMPANY BEFORE 1885
University of Washington
UW_2256 - PH Coll 286.2

8 SHIPS ON PORT BLAKELY
University of Washington
UW_26574 - PH Coll 286.8

9 THE WILLIAM RENTON AND THE HESPER
University of Washington
UW_26580 - PH Coll 286.15

10 1884 RAILROAD JUBILEE
University of Washington
NA_1390 - PH Coll 28

11 PUGET MILL COMPANY
University of Washington
UW_5422

12 ELIZA ANDERSON AT COLMAN FERRY DOCK
University of Washington
UW_5931 - PH Coll 27

13 OX TEAM HAULING LOGS AT UTSALADY
University of Washington
UW_12331 - PH Coll 279

14 1880s DONKEY ENGINE
University of Washington
PH Coll 516 - Kinsey 3976

16 STEAMER IDAHO
University of Washington
UW_5928

18 PUGET SOUND SAWMILLS
University of Washington
UW_5967 - PH Coll 27

19 MASON COUNTY CENTRAL RAILROAD LOCOMOTIVE CREW
University of Washington
UW_15597

20 MIGRANT FARM WORKERS AT TENTS
University of Washington
NA_4181 - PH Coll 34

21 ONLY SURVIVING DOCK
University of Washington
UW_28492 - PH Coll 26.21

22 UMATILLA AND CITY OF PUEBLA
University of Washington
UW_12230 - PH Coll 277

23 GREAT FIRE REMAINS
University of Washington
UW_6992 - PH Coll 684.33

24 CALKINS HOTEL, MERCER ISLAND
University of Washington
UW_28462 - PH Coll 141.22

25 COUPEVILLE, 1890s
University of Washington
UW_19155 - PH Coll 376.72

26 HYNER RESIDENCE, POINT EDMONDS
University of Washington
UW_4322